University of Glamorgan
Learning Resources Centre -
Treforest
Self Issue Receipt (TR2)

Customer name: MR YANNICK
KEREYN CHARLES
Customer ID: **********301

Title: Tort
ID: 7311265604
Due: 19/04/2010 23:59

Title: analysis of the economic torts

ID: 7312082473
Due: 19/04/2010 23:59

Total items: 2
24/03/2010 18:08

Thank you for using the Self-
Service system
Diolch yn fawr

AN ANALYSIS OF THE ECONOMIC TORTS

An Analysis of the Economic Torts

HAZEL CARTY

OXFORD
UNIVERSITY PRESS

OXFORD

UNIVERSITY PRESS

Great Clarendon Street, Oxford OX2 6DP

Oxford University Press is a department of the University of Oxford.
It furthers the University's objective of excellence in research, scholarship,
and education by publishing worldwide in

Oxford New York

Athens Auckland Bangkok Bogotá Buenos Aires
Cape Town Chennai Dar es Salaam Delhi Florence Hong Kong Istanbul
Karachi Kolkata Kuala Lumpur Madrid Melbourne Mexico City Mumbai
Nairobi Paris São Paulo Singapore Taipei Tokyo Toronto Warsaw

and associated companies in Berlin Ibadan

Oxford is a registered trade mark of Oxford University Press
in the UK and in certain other countries

Published in the United States
by Oxford University Press Inc., New York

© Hazel Carty 2001

The moral rights of the author have been asserted
Database right Oxford University Press (maker)

First published 2001

All rights reserved. No part of this publication may be reproduced,
stored in a retrieval system, or transmitted, in any form or by any means,
without the prior permission in writing of Oxford University Press,
or as expressly permitted by law, or under terms agreed with the appropriate
reprographics rights organization. Enquiries concerning reproduction
outside the scope of the above should be sent to the Rights Department,
Oxford University Press, at the address above

You must not circulate this book in any other binding or cover
and you must impose this same condition on any acquirer

British Library Cataloguing in Publication Data

Data available

Library of Congress Cataloging in Publication Data

Carty, Hazel.
An analysis of the economic torts/Hazel Carty.
p. cm.
Includes bibliographical references and index.
1. Torts—Economic aspects—Great Britain. 2. Competition, Unfair—Great Britain.
I. Title.
KD1949.C37 2001
343.41'072—dc21   00–067834
ISBN 0–19–825743–0

1 3 5 7 9 10 8 6 4 2

Typeset in Times by
Cambrian Typesetters, Frimley, Surrey
Printed in Great Britain by
T.J. International Ltd, Padstow, Cornwall

Preface

I became fascinated by the economic torts as a student. Though a topic largely sidelined by textbook writer and commentator alike, this fascination was fuelled by the splendid writings of Tony Weir, Bill Wedderburn, and, of course, J. D. Heydon and by the equally splendid teaching of Anthony Ogus.

There are a number of reasons for this fascination. First, these torts present an obvious challenge to create order out of their chaos. To achieve some sort of framework for their development appears a worthwhile ambition. Second, their application to the competitive process (in which I include the competition between employers and their workers) attracts: how does the common law balance the need to protect claimants against those who inflict economic harm with the wider need to allow effective, even aggressive, competition? How, in short, does the common law identify 'excessive' competitive practice? Liability based on intended economic harm is not the answer to the riddle presented by the economic torts because all competition is based on intended economic harm to rivals while the tort of passing off—arguably the most important economic tort—is one of strict liability. Finally, any assessment of these torts, protecting against harm to wealth and economic expectations, requires a consideration of their relationship to the tort of negligence and an answer to the question whether that tort should be identified as an economic tort.

It is the aim of this book to bring some order to the common law rules on liability for the infliction of pure economic loss. At present this area of tort law is confused and confusing, with the limits of liability imprecise. Yet the torts themselves are under pressure to expand. This is most notable in the case of the tort of passing off, but even the obscure tort of malicious falsehood has been the subject of expansion in recent years. In an attempt to provide 'practical legal scholarship' these torts will be fully analysed and a framework for the liability they impose (and, therefore, guidance for their development) will be offered. For this purpose, the traditional separation of these torts into general (industrial action) economic torts and misrepresentation (trade competition) economic torts is abandoned. Such a separation compounds the mess of these torts and obscures the categories of liability that lie within them.

It will be seen that the basis for this framework—at odds with Heydon's conclusion—is the view that the economic torts should remain limited in application. The analysis reveals these torts as a failsafe device created by the common law to prevent extreme competitive or economic behaviour. This means that the major role in the regulation of economic behaviour is left to the State. It is hoped that the end result is both intellectually satisfying and of practical importance, providing a guide to the modern application of the economic torts and a rationale or blueprint for their development.

In this attempt to produce a comprehensible account of the economic torts many debts of gratitude are owed. As well as those mentioned above who inspired my interest, my colleagues in Manchester University Law Faculty have proved invaluable sources of help, inspiration, and information during the gestation of this book. Particular thanks are owed to Andrew Bell, Margot Brazier, Diana Kloss, Angus McCulloch, and John Murphy. The more recent writings of Roderick Bagshaw and Philip Sales have also proved fruitful for the analysis in this book. And of course I must thank (and apologize to) Graham, Katherine, and Alexander.

Hazel Carty

Manchester
August 2000

Contents

Table of Cases

Table of Statutes

1

Introduction

THE ECONOMIC TORTS

Unlike other torts,[1] the economic torts, as their name suggests, have as their primary function[2] the protection of claimants' economic interests.[3] They include the torts of simple conspiracy, unlawful conspiracy, inducing breach of contract (and its so-called varieties),[4] intimidation, unlawful interference with trade, deceit, and malicious falsehood. All of these are torts of intention. They also include passing off, one of the most useful of the economic torts, which though in practice normally involving deliberate harm, is in fact a tort of strict liability. Why this should be so will be explored later. Finally, the economic torts also include the tort of negligence,[5] though applied in a narrow way.

The common law having no general tort of unfair competition, these torts represent its chosen method to attack excessive competition or economic endeavour, whether through diversion of custom or attacks on commercial links. Although most commentators concentrate on the tort of passing off to assess the potential for a development of a tort of unfair

---

[1] Most torts have the indirect effect of protecting economic interests.

[2] So, e.g., the tort of intimidation can also involve physical harm (and be two-party) as in *Godwin v Uzoigwe* [1992] TLR 300 CA (physical intimidation of foreign teenage girl by defendants to force her to work as their servant). However, the protection of economic interests is the prime reason for the existence and development of these torts. Compensation for injury to feelings may be recoverable in the torts of inducing breach of contract (*Pratt v BMA* [1919] 1 KB 244, pp. 281–2 McCardie J took humiliation and menace into account when assessing the damages); deceit (*East v Maurer* [1991] 1 WLR 461), malicious falsehood (*Khodaparast v Shad* [2000] 1 All ER 545) and probably also in intimidation and unlawful interference with trade (see McGregor, H., *McGregor on Damages*, 16th edn. (London: Sweet & Maxwell, 1997), para 1941). However it is (surprisingly) not available in the tort of conspiracy (*Lonrho v Fayed (no. 5)* [1993] 1 WLR 1489, CA: critized by McGregor, paras 1938–9).

[3] In the sense of existing wealth or financial expectations. See discussion of 'economic interests' by Cane, P., *Tort Law and Economic Interests*, 2nd edn. (Oxford: Clarendon Press, 1996), ch. 1. He notes (p. 5) 'when the remedy awarded for interference with a non-economic interest is money damages it is, at best, only a poor sort of recompense; in many cases the injured party would still feel a sense of loss no matter how generous the damages awarded. On the other hand, a remedy of money damages is a wholly adequate one for interference with an economic interest.' Thus the use of the word 'trade' in the tort of unlawful interference with trade may be too narrow to cover the actual interests protected: see Ch. 5.

[4] Direct and indirect interference with contract which, as will be seen in Ch. 3, are not varieties of this tort but of another economic tort, unlawful interference with trade.

[5] See Ch. 9, where it is argued that to label the tort of negligence as an economic tort is somewhat misleading. Rather, in exceptional circumstances it performs the functions of an economic tort.

competition, all the economic torts merit analysis as part of this assessment.[6]

The prime importance of these torts is to provide protection and
redress in a three-party setting for, as Weir notes 'while you can take
direct action against a person's body or property . . . to ruin a person
financially the action you take must be indirect, through another person,
the source of his earnings or profits'.[7] For this reason, the tort of deceit (in
its classic version)[8] and the tort of negligence (insofar as it protects against
'pure economic loss') can play little direct part in setting the limits
between aggressive and excessive competitive practice.[9] Both are essentially two-party torts often arising between parties in a contractual or
near-contractual setting.

It is usual to separate the economic torts into two categories: the
general torts and the misrepresentation torts.[10] The general economic
torts comprise conspiracy, inducing breach of contract, intimidation, and
unlawful interference with trade.[11] The misrepresentation economic torts
are deceit, malicious falsehood, and passing off. However, it is a mistake
to make such a rigid division when attempting a proper analysis. Such a
distinction fails to highlight the interconnections between the two

---

[6] Involving both protection against excessive competition and in the case of simple
conspiracy (very limited) protection against attempts to curb competition through cartels
and abuse of a dominant position. This latter role will of course be overtaken by both EC law
(the competition rules in Articles 81 and 82) and domestic statutory law (Competition Act
1998). This is fully discussed in Ch. 2. Apart from these torts, the action for breach of confidence, preventing as it does the unacceptable use of the claimant's confidential commercial
information, can certainly be regarded as a form of protection against unfair competition. As
yet, however, it has not achieved the status of a tort. See discussion in Ch. 10.

[7] Weir, T., *A Casebook on Tort*, 9th edn. (London: Sweet & Maxwell (2000)), 568. Weir notes
in *Economic Torts* (Oxford: Clarendon Press, 1997) that 'pure economic harm and contracts
are intimately connected for the simple reason that unless you steal it, inherit it or get it as a
social security handout, any money you get comes to you via contract . . . economic harm,
therefore, has to do with a person's existing and expected contracts'.

[8] Only the representee can complain about the dishonesty. However, deceit might prove
useful as providing the unlawful means in a wider allegation of unlawful interference with
trade. See discussion in Ch. 6.

[9] Though deceit can cover physical and mental harm as well as economic loss (as in
Langridge v Levy (1837) 2 M&W 519; *Burrows v Rhodes* [1899] 1 QB 816; *Nicholls v Taylor* [1939]
VLR 119), such instances are rare.

[10] It is also argued by some commentators that this categorization into general and
misrepresentation economic torts mirrors the fact that in the general torts the defendant
seeks to attack the plaintiff, whereas in the misrepresentation torts the defendant seeks to
make a gain which properly belongs to the plaintiff (see e.g. Heydon, J. D., 'The Future of
the Economic Torts' 12 WAL Rev (1975) 1 and Elias, P., and Ewing, K.,'Economic Torts and
Labour Law: Old Principles and New Liabilities' 41 CLJ (1982) 321, p. 327). However, this is
an unnecessary gloss on an analysis of these torts and does not always prove to be correct
e.g. misrepresentation cases can involve attacks as well as theft: see *Joyce v Motor Surveys Ltd*
[1948] Ch 252.

[11] Sometimes referred to as the 'genus' economic tort. However this description is incorrect: see Ch. 5.

categories on the one hand and the dissimilarities between individual torts within each category on the other.[12]

Further, those who separate the economic torts in this way are often tempted to refer to the general economic torts as the 'industrial torts'. This is because they commonly arise in the course of industrial action. This categorization is in itself dangerous. It compounds the uncertainty and imprecision that has affected judicial application of these torts *when they occur as part of industrial action*. Judicial hostility to trade unions or inability to appreciate the legitimacy of collective pressure has muddled these torts.[13] New economic torts have emerged from this approach, while the tort of inducing breach of contract has, in particular, been denied a consistent application. So case law resulting from industrial disputes has led to decisions which undermine the strict intention required in that tort,[14] the need for knowledge of the contract in issue,[15] and even the need to prove an actual breach of contract.[16] Such an approach is hardly legitimate in view of the fact that it may deny trade unions the immunities from liability that Parliament intended they should have.[17] This process is also to be regretted for unsettling the application of these torts when they are pleaded in other contexts. So the uncertainty generated by the application of these torts within the context of an industrial dispute is transferred to subsequent commercial or competition cases in which these torts are raised.[18] To regard the so-called general economic torts as simply industrial torts is, therefore, not helpful.

The better approach (especially when attempting an overall analysis) is to see all of these torts as protecting against the infliction of economic harm, against a background of competition. They impinge on competitive practices generally. So all of the economic torts 'inevitably limit the type

---

[12] This is discussed in greater detail in Ch. 10.

[13] And as Lord Wedderburn, *Clerk and Lindsell on Torts*, 18th edn. (London: Sweet & Maxwell, 2000) notes (para 24–188, n. 14) particularly in industrial action cases the law has been much affected by procedure attaching to interlocutory injunctions when the plaintiff need prove no more than an arguable case or serious question to be tried.

[14] e.g. *Falconer v NUR* [1986] IRLR 331, Judge Henham, Sheffield County Court. The defendants argued that they had intended to harm British Rail (through the industrial action), not the passengers using British Rail, like the plaintiff. However, this argument was rejected by the judge as being 'both naïve and divorced from reality'.

[15] *Emerald Construction Co Ltd v Lothian* [1966] 1 WLR 691, CA: Lord Denning MR noting that 'even if they [the defendants] did not know of the actual terms of the contract but had the means of knowledge—which they deliberately disregarded—that would be enough'.

[16] *Torquay Hotel Ltd v Cousins* [1969] 2 Ch 106. See discussion in Ch. 3.

[17] Elias, P., and Ewing, K. 'Economic Torts and Labour Law: Old Principles and New Liabilities' 41 CLJ (1982) 321. 'Parliament may give immunities to counter the existing common law liabilities but the judges may in turn create new wrongs or reinterpret old principles and thereby frustrate Parliament's intention' (p. 321).

[18] As in, e.g., *Millar v Bassey* [1994] EMLR 44, CA, discussed in Chs. 3 and 10.

of commercial behaviour in which the defendant might indulge'.[19] Thus the main 'industrial' economic tort, inducing breach of contract, dates from a trade competition case, *Lumley v Gye*,[20] while unlawful conspiracy is often alleged against those who participate in commercial fraud.[21] Moreover, the notion of competition can be applied (in a loose sense) not only to commercial endeavour but also to 'competition' in the industrial relations sphere. So Cane accepts that 'industrial action designed to improve wages and conditions is a form of competitive activity in the sense that the aim of the action is to achieve a redistribution of wealth from the employer to the employees, just as traders seek to divert wealth from their competitors to themselves'.[22] Interestingly, Lord Shand in *Allen v Flood* (a trade dispute case) categorized the issue before the court as 'one of competition in labour, which . . . is in all essentials analogous to competition in trade and to which the same principles apply'.[23]

THE HIERARCHY OF INTERESTS AT COMMON LAW

Economic interests come lower in the hierarchy of interests that the common law is willing to protect than physical integrity, property rights/enjoyment and reputation.[24] As Lord Oliver asserted in *Murphy v Brentwood DC*[25] 'the infliction of physical injury to the person or property of another universally requires to be justified. The causing of economic

---

[19] Whish, R., *Competition Law*, 3rd edn. (London: Butterworths, 1993), p. 36. They also encroach into a similar area covered by the commercial law concepts of restraint of trade and economic duress.

[20] Again, *Bowen v Hall* (1881) 6 QBD 333, CA involved the defendant enticing a skilled worker away from the defendant's trade rival. Interestingly, there are French cases being decided at the end of the nineteenth century with facts parallel to English cases involving inducing breach of contract, where such activity was found to be unlawful within the unfair competition, Arts. 1382–3 Code Civil. This development extended protection from enticement of manual servants to enticement of skilled workers in the fashion industries and entertainment industries (like Miss Wagner). See Palmer, V., 'A Comparative Study (from a Common Law Perspective) of the French Action for Wrongful Interference with Contract', 40 Am J Comp L (1992) 297.

[21] For a recent example of this see e.g. *Kuwait Oil Tanker Co SAK v Al Bader (no. 3)* [2000] 2 All ER (Comm) 271.

[22] Above, n. 3, p. 472, n. 72.

[23] [1898] AC 1, p. 164. In *Vegelahn v Guntner* 167 Mass 92 Holmes J asserted that the conflict between employers and employed is competition.

[24] Carpenter, C., 'Interference with Contractual Relations' 41 Har L Rev (1928) 728, p. 746 'in general, the interests in life, reputation and property other than contracts are more fully protected from invasions than is the interest in contract rights'. With defamation, '[common law] liability is absolute: it matters not whether the defendant could have taken steps to discover that the statement was defamatory' (Brazier, M., and Murphy, J., *Street on Torts*, 10th edn. (London: Butterworths, 1999), p. 446.

[25] [1991] AC 398, p. 487.

loss does not.' This hierarchy of interests is very clear in the tort of negligence. The classic view of the tort of negligence was that it allowed recovery of those economic losses consequent on physical damage to person or property, but not pure economic loss. This general approach still applies, though in exceptional cases, usually within the *Hedley Byrne v Heller* principle,[26] pure economic loss may be recoverable. Even with intentionally caused economic harm, however, the courts have (on the whole) resisted imposing liability simply on the basis of the infliction of intended harm.[27] *Dicta* can be found in early cases, indicating wide liability for competitive practices—in *Keeble v Hickeringill*[28] for example, it was stated that 'he that hinders another in his trade or livelihood is liable to an action for so hindering him'. However, the House of Lords in *Allen v Flood*[29] rejected such liability. There is thus no general tort governing the limits of lawful competition practice; rather there are a number of specific torts, liability for which (the torts of passing off and simple conspiracy apart) depends on the presence of unlawful acts.[30]

HISTORY OF THE TORTS

Though most have their origins much earlier[31] the real development of all these torts took place in the late nineteenth and early twentieth centuries. To understand this development it is important to underline the choices made by the judges in this era. These were the result of two antithetical policies.[32]

First, there was a policy of judicial abstentionism, providing the base

---

[26] *Hedley Byrne & Co Ltd v Heller & Partners Ltd* [1964] AC 465. For a detailed discussion see Ch. 9.

[27] Generally, the courts have not developed a tort of intentionally causing harm. 'In regard to the nominate torts, the advantages of the simplicity achievable by working under a single general principle would be far outweighed by the complexity and variety of exceptions that would be necessary to accommodate the various policy considerations at stake', Smith, J. C. and Burns, P., 'Donoghue v Stevenson, The Not So Golden Anniversary' 46 MLR (1983) 147, p. 149. However, Sales, P., and Stilitz, D., 'Intentional Infliction of Harm by Unlawful Means' 115 LQR (1999) 411 argue that there is 'scope for development of general principles of liability in respect of harm inflicted intentionally' (p. 436).

[28] 11 East 574, p. 575.

[29] [1898] AC 1.

[30] The tort of malicious falsehood may impose liability where there is a belief in the falsehood, but the defendant is motivated by spite: see discussion in Chs. 7 and 10. The common law has never, however, accepted liability for harmful representations that are truthful.

[31] The history of each tort is discussed in the individual chapters that follow.

[32] Wedderburn, above, n. 13, para 24–02 'liabilities for the intentional economic torts, being concerned largely with social relations and intangible property rights, tend to attract policy considerations to a high degree, not always pointing in the same direction'.

line of these torts. It was a policy that followed from the decision of the majority of the House of Lords in *Allen v Flood*.[33]

That case arose essentially out of a demarcation dispute. The plaintiffs were workers, dismissed after Allen, a trade union official, had advised their employers of their colleagues' intention to walk out if they remained employed. The walk out would not have been in breach of contract and the plaintiffs were lawfully dismissed. The trial judge found no evidence of conspiracy, intimidation, or breach of contract. No intrinsically unlawful means were employed, therefore, by the defendant, though the intention was clearly to harm the plaintiffs. The plaintiffs alleged a malicious interference with their livelihood. The Court of Appeal were willing on this basis to hold the defendants liable for maliciously procuring the lawful dismissal of the plaintiffs. However, the majority of the House of Lords[34] took a policy decision: motive of itself was not a permissible mechanism for imposing economic tort liability.[35] Lord Watson stated: 'the law of England does not . . . take into account motive as constituting an element of civil wrong . . . the existence of a bad motive, in the case of an act which is not of itself illegal, will not convert that act into a civil wrong.' For Lord Herschell, provided they did not resort to unlawful acts, the defendants would be entitled 'to further their interests in a manner which seems to them best and most likely to be effectual'.

The importance of *Allen v Flood* is that the majority of the House of Lords decided on an abstentionist role for the common law in the area of intentionally inflicted economic harm. The Court of Appeal had appeared to favour an interventionist role, where intentional injury causing loss should be actionable unless public policy, in the guise of the defence of justification, indicated otherwise. Interestingly, it was the interventionist view that gained favour across the Atlantic. This was revealed in the notion of *prima facie* tort liability (where the intention to cause harm is in itself sufficient unless justified) and the development of torts that could loosely be described as the unfair competition torts. So in *Tuttle v Buck*[36]

---

[33] [1898] AC 1. And see *Mogul Steamship v McGregor*(1889) 23 QBD 598 when, in an action brought against a cartel, the House of Lords refused to distinguish between fair and unfair competition. There was no liability in the absence of unlawful acts. At this time, of course, the US Congress was passing the Sherman Act to outlaw conspiracies in restraint of trade.

[34] Lord Herschell [1898] AC 1, pp. 132–3 noted that the judges who had been called on to advise the House of Lords were in favour of *Keeble v Hickeringill* (1707) 103 ER 1127 and the proposition that 'every man has a right to pursue his trade or calling without molestation or obstruction and that anyone who by any act, though it be not otherwise unlawful, molest or obstruct him is guilty of a wrong unless he can show lawful justification or excuse for so doing'.

[35] And note *Bradford v Pickles* [1895] AC 587, where the House of Lords held that the lawful use of property, though inspired by malice, would not lead to liability.

[36] 119 NW 946 (Minn. 1909). This is probably the most famous example of this approach: an approach rejected by Weir who comments that 'disinterested malevolence is so rare that

the court found the defendant, a banker, liable for setting up a barber's shop simply to ruin the rival barber's business, run by his personal enemy. The court based liability on malicious motive. Heydon bemoans the fact that the English courts did not adopt this approach. He contends that the decision in *Allen v Flood* denied the economic torts theoretical consistency, rejecting malice as the focus of liability. It is the aim of this book to show otherwise.

The absence of unlawful means in *Allen v Flood* meant that the defendant was not liable for the intentional economic harm. This approach is of course consistent with the earlier recognition of the tort of inducing breach of contract in *Lumley v Gye*.[37] Liability in that tort resulted from the use[38] of unlawful means.[39] Indeed, this decision was referred to by Lord Watson in *Allen v Flood* when analysing the limited grounds upon which a defendant might be liable for injuring a plaintiff through a third party.[40] Thus after *Allen v Flood* a general tort of unjustified interference with trade was untenable. The general theme of the economic torts was that intentionally inflicted economic harm, even if inspired by malice, would not result in liability unless unlawful means were used[41] against the plaintiff.

This same abstentionist approach can be seen in the torts of deceit and malicious falsehood. The development of these torts has been dictated by the caution of the common law[42] in allowing competitors to control commercial misrepresentations.[43] The basic ingredients of these two torts

it is unwise to develop a rule to combat it which can be used by a disgruntled hairdresser who has lost his profitable local monopoly', Weir, T., *Economic Torts* (Oxford: Clarendon Press, 1997), p. 73.

[37] (1853) 2 E&B 216. Note, however, Lord Herschell in *Allen v Flood* [1898] AC 1, p. 123: 'I am not concerned now to inquire whether the decision in *Lumley v Gye* was right . . . there are . . . arguments the other way and I must not be understood as expressing an opinion one way or the other, whether such an action can be maintained.'

[38] Though in this tort the defendant procures such unlawful means rather than commits them himself.

[39] So it was acknowledged by Lord Herschell that there would be no liability for inducing another not to contract with the plaintiff: [1898] AC 1, p. 121.

[40] [1898] AC 1, p. 96 : liability results either from inducing the third party to commit an actionable wrong or from deliberately causing the third party to act to the detriment of the plaintiff by the use of 'illegal' means. As Sales and Stilitz, above, n. 27, point out (p. 413) 'it is a curiosity of Lord Watson's speech that he appears to regard *Lumley v Gye* as an example of the second principle of liability to which he refers . . . while the case itself is the leading authority establishing the tort of knowingly inducing breach of contract ie one of the main applications of the first principle of liability to which he refers'.

[41] Either by the defendant or through a third party. Weir, Casebook, above, n. 7, p. 599 notes the importance of *Allen v Flood* 'it holds that, whatever morality may say, in law one is free to beggar one's neighbour provided one neither does anything unlawful oneself nor gets anyone else to do anything unlawful'.

[42] Naresh, S., 'Passing-off, Goodwill and False Advertising: New Wine in Old Bottles' (1986) CLJ 97, p. 120.

[43] As Parker J in *Cundey v Lerwill & Pike* (1907–8) 24 TLR 584, p. 586 stressed: 'it is not every false representation that a firm has a right to restrain.'

were formalized around the end of the nineteenth century in key House of Lords' decisions. With deceit—*Derry v Peek*[44]—and malicious falsehood—*White v Mellin*[45]—the sympathy of the House of Lords was with the defendants in their endeavours in the 'hard world of competition for customers', leading to the 'scrupulous limitation of liability for misstatements . . . and for unfair advertising practices'.[46] The decision in *Derry v Peek*, in rejecting liability for careless misrepresentations, represented an instinctive focus on contract as the main mechanism for protecting financial interests,[47] while *White v Mellin* was part of a wider policy to deny responsibility for determining what is fair and unfair in competition.[48] Lord Herschell stressed in that case that the courts of law should not be turned into 'a machinery for advertising rival productions by obtaining a judicial determination which of the two was the better'. Thus the tort of deceit was severely limited by the need to prove fraud, just as the tort of malicious falsehood was emasculated by the requirement of malice and special damage. Moreover, mere puffs and self-commendation would not render the trader liable.

What then is the reason for this abstentionist policy? Cornish notes that a 'complex set of justifications and underlying motives seem to have been at work'.[49] There is of course the natural tendency of the common law to develop slowly by analogy, rather than by generalized rights or liabilities.[50] Further, a policy of supporting competition is also apparent at times in the development of these torts.[51] However, as Letwin has noted, the

---

[44] (1889) 14 App Cas 337.   [45] [1895] AC 154.

[46] Cornish, W., and Clark, G. De N., *Law and Society in England 1750–1950* (London: Sweet & Maxwell, 1989), p. 329, n. 41. Lord Diplock in *Advocaat* [1979] AC 731 noted that 'the market in which the action for passing off originated was no place for the mealy-mouthed'.

[47] Lord Bramwell (1889) 14 App Cas 337, p. 347: 'to found an action for damages there must be a contract and breach or fraud.' Stevens, R., '*Hedley Byrne v Heller*: Judicial Creativity and Doctrinal Possibility' 27 MLR (1964) 121, p. 121 notes that the case represents 'the strongest form of nineteenth-century laissez-faire individualism'.

[48] Lord Herschell LC [1895] AC 154, p. 164 rejected liability for untrue self-commendation as this would lead to the courts being 'constantly employed in trying the relative merits of rival productions'. At this time Fry LJ in *Mogul Steamship v McGregor* (at Court of Appeal level) contended: 'to draw a line between fair and unfair competition . . . passes the power of the courts' (1889) 28 QBD 598, pp. 625–6.

[49] Cornish, W., *Intellectual Property*, 4th edn. (London: Sweet & Maxwell, 1999), p. 15.

[50] See *White v Mellin* [1895] AC 154, p. 164. And note the hierarchy of interests protected by the common law, noted above.

[51] Jones, F. D., 'Historical Development of the Law of Business Competition' 35 Yale LJ (1925–6) 905; continued 36 Yale LJ (1926–7) 351. A preference asserted early in the *Case of Glouster Grammar School* (1410) YB 11 Hen. This policy is, however, not always apparent especially in relation to cartels in the period leading up to the First World War. This was a period that saw a growth of trade associations and restrictive agreements such as price-fixing, market-sharing, and quota agreements. It was in this period that the House of Lords decided that cartels, as conspiracies, could be justified: *Mogul Steamship v McGregor*. See discussion by Cornish, above, n. 49, pp. 15–18. Where aggressive competition is involved, however, there are modern *dicta* in favour of supporting the competitive process: see discussion in Ch. 10.

main justification for the abstentionist policy was that the judges did not wish to assume the role of controlling aspects of the economy: either by curbing aggressive competition[52] or by automatically prohibiting the exclusion of competition.[53] This is clear from the middle of the nineteenth century onwards, especially in developments in the restraint of trade doctrine[54] and the tort of conspiracy. Indeed, there are famous *dicta* which made clear judicial unwillingness to participate in the formulation of economic policy. Thus Lord Davey asserted:[55] 'public policy is always an unsafe and treacherous ground for legal decisions.' This, then, appears to be the main reason why no tort of unfair competition was allowed to develop.[56] Rather, the competitive process was protected in a negative way:[57] the judges decided to avoid regulating such activities and instead to react only to clearly excessive economic behaviour.

But what of the tort of passing off? It developed in the early industrial period 'to meet an evident commercial need'—namely the protection of trade marks and names.[58] Equity played a dominant role in its development as injunctions were the favoured remedy in this area. The effect of this was that it was refashioned from a tort based on deceit into a strict liability tort, with assumed damage.[59] Thus unlike deceit and malicious falsehood, passing off came to focus on the effect of the misrepresentation, rather than the fault of the defendant. The fact that this occurred at an earlier date than the critical development of deceit meant that equity could fashion the tort, a process that was not allowed to happen with the

---

[52] As the torts of deceit and malicious falsehood gained their modern form in the latter part of the nineteenth century, parallel to the rise of the distributive trades, there are *dicta* to the effect that trade rivalry was to be encouraged.

[53] Letwin, W., 'The English Common Law Concerning Monopolies' 21 Univ Chic LR (1954) 355.

[54] So in *Nordenfelt v Maxim Nordenfelt Guns and Ammunition Co* [1893] Ch 630 the doctrine of restraint of trade (originally in essence an attack on the power of the guilds and the king) was tempered by the notion of a permissible 'reasonable' restraint.

[55] [1902] AC 484, p. 500.

[56] Cornish, above, n. 49, p. 17 'over recent decades there has been some modification of the courts' approach, but when compared with developments of unfair competition doctrine in parts of Western Europe and the United States, the continuing attraction of late Victorian attitudes remains apparent'.

[57] Fleming, J., *The Law of Torts*, 9th edn. (Sydney: LBC Information Services, 1998), p. 766 comments that in its heyday the *Allen v Flood* rule—that malice *per se* does not create an actionable wrong even though intentional economic harm is visited on the plaintiff—operated in a policy neutral fashion, sometimes promoting free competition, sometimes monopoly.

[58] Cornish, above, n. 49, p. 12.

[59] The development could have been otherwise: cf. the House of Lords in *Cellular Clothing v Maxton & Murray* [1899] AC 326. Wadlow, C., *The Law of Passing Off*, 2nd edn. (London: Sweet & Maxwell, 1995), p. 25 notes that just as malicious falsehood was severely limited at this time so could the tort of passing off have been if the Court of Appeal decision in *Reddaway v Banham* had been upheld and there are indications in *Cellular Clothing* that the later House of Lords were unhappy with the final decision in *Reddaway*.

tort of deceit itself.[60] So by the end of the nineteenth century when the tort of passing off had established itself as a strict liability tort of great use to traders it was unaffected by the restrictive (common-law) approach to deceit and malicious falsehood. Indeed, this era saw its continued development.[61] The House of Lords in *Reddaway v Banham*[62] acknowledged its potential to protect even descriptive terms against customer confusion. This period also saw plaintiffs beginning to use the tort of passing off where they were not competing with the defendants and where the basis of damage was injury to reputation,[63] rather than the standard allegation of diversion of custom. Having achieved a useful role by the start of the twentieth century—as was acknowledged by the House of Lords in *Spalding v Gamage*[64]—it has been the subject of expansion ever since. In particular, the 1970s witnessed a massive extension of the tort in *Erven Warnink B.V. v Townend & Sons (Advocaat)*,[65] in line with the consumer-centred approach of Parliament at the time. From protecting against source misrepresentations, the tort now also protects against product misrepresentations.

Though the above explains the separate development and unique characteristics of the tort of passing off within the economic torts, that tort does not undermine the abstentionist policy of the common law. The parameters of the tort of passing off have been set by caution, lest the judges be drawn too deeply into the competitive process. The hopes of some commentators who saw the potential in *Advocaat*[66] for the development of a wide economic tort of misappropriation were dashed by the Privy Council a year later in *Cadbury Schweppes Pty v Pub Squash Pty Ltd*.[67] This indicated that there is still judicial opposition to the creation of wide 'competition torts'.[68] Thus passing off has limits provided by the need to

---

[60] So in *Derry v Peek* (1889) 14 App Cas 337, p. 350 Lord Bramwell stifled earlier moves by equity to extend the protection against careless misrepresentations as the imposition of such liability would make 'mercantile men cry out'. See discussion of *Derry v Peek* in Ch. 6.

[61] Wadlow, above, n. 59, p. 29 suggests that the emasculation of malicious falsehood by *White v Mellin* and *Royal Baking Powder v Wright Crossley* (1900) 18 RPC 95, HL, might have prompted plaintiffs to test whether the tort of passing off could be made to fill a gap in liability.

[62] [1896] AC 199.

[63] Or exposure to liability as in *Walter v Ashton* [1902] 2 Ch 282.

[64] (1915) 84 LJ Ch 449, HL.

[65] [1979] AC 731, discussed in detail in Ch. 8.

[66] [1979] AC 731, HL.   [67] [1981] 1 WLR 193.

[68] Indeed, limits on liability for misrepresentations were acknowledged even in *Advocaat* itself, Lord Diplock advising against the risk of 'hampering competition by providing civil remedies to every one competing in the market who has suffered damage to his business or goodwill in consequence of inaccurate statements of whatever kind that may be made by rival traders about their wares'. That said, it has been the subject of continued attempts— some of which sneak through the less rigorous interlocutory process—to extend it into a more general misrepresentation tort or even an unfair competition action. See detailed discussion in Ch. 8.

show an existing customer base and a misrepresentation likely to confuse customers when making their purchasing choice.

This first policy has provided the general approach to the development of the economic torts with only a limited role for the judges. 'In the main, the courts were insisting that . . . the common law would not hold activities to be wrongful merely because they must injure others.'[69] The result was that no general principle of unfair competition emerged. This is in marked contrast to most other European countries and (to an extent) the USA.[70]

However, a separate policy also shaped these torts. This second policy arose from the presence of judicial hostility to the growth of the trade unions,[71] even after the decision of the House of Lords in *Allen v Flood* which had accepted that industrial action could be lawful, though aimed at harming the plaintiff. That hostility was replaced in the twentieth century by concern over the power wielded by trade unions.[72] In no small measure this policy has contributed to the chaos of these torts.

Thus a stimulus towards developing new economic torts appeared to be triggered by Parliament's growing acceptance of the role of the trade unions and their use of collective action as a balance to managerial power. During the first part of the nineteenth century, trade unions were criminal conspiracies both at common law and under statute.[73] Moreover, their activities were subject to prosecution for such vague offences as 'molestation' and 'obstruction'. As Parliament came to recognize the legitimacy of the trade unions and their activities, they were legalized and the threat of criminal sanctions removed by the Trade Union Act 1871 and the Conspiracy and Protection of Property Act 1875. However, the judges reacted by transferring conspiracy liability from the criminal law into the civil law. Thus the tort of conspiracy developed two strands: unlawful conspiracy, a combination to use unlawful means (often involving another economic tort) in order to harm the plaintiff and 'simple' conspiracy, where the presence of the combination to harm rendered the defendants potentially[74] liable, despite no use of unlawful means. In this way Lord Halsbury, who had been in the minority in *Allen v Flood*, circumvented the

---

[69] Cornish and Clark, above, n. 46, p. 329. The authors also point out the 'scrupulous limitation' of liability for misstatements in *Derry v Peek* (1889)14 App Cas 337 and for unfair advertising practices in *White v Mellin* [1895] AC 154.

[70] See Cornish, above, n. 49, pp. 14–17.

[71] See generally Cornish and Clark, above, n. 46, pp. 309–36 (esp. p. 320 onwards).

[72] Lloyd, D., 'The Right To Work' 10 Current Legal Problems (1957), p. 41 and see Denning LJ in *Lee v Showmen's Guild* [1952] 2 QB 329.

[73] For a useful summary of the historical background see Wedderburn, K. W., *The Worker and the Law*, 3rd edn. (London: Penguin, 1986).

[74] Where simple conspiracy is alleged liability can be avoided by showing that the predominant purpose behind the combination was 'legitimate'. See Ch. 2.

logic of that case[75] in *Quinn v Leathem*.[76] Here the facts of the case were similar to those in *Allen v Flood* but with the additional ingredients of combination and threats. By distinguishing the fact of combination in *Quinn*,[77] the House of Lords was able to impose liability for intended harm, even though no unlawful means were used.[78]

Lord Loreburn, commenting during the Parliamentary debates over what became the Trade Disputes Act 1906 said revealingly of *Quinn v Leathem*: '[until then] there never had been any attempt to make out any civil liability for conspiracy . . . [then] came the new world and the new ideas.'[79] At the same time there was a rapid development[80] of the tort of inducing breach of contract. Originally believed to apply only to contracts of service, by the early part of the twentieth century it was acknowledged to apply to all contracts, posing a threat to the legality of secondary industrial action.[81]

Parliament reacted to these developments by providing immunities[82]

---

[75] However, it has to be accepted, as Heuston, R. F. V., has noted in 'Judicial Prosopography' 102 LQR (1986) 90 that it is something of an oversimplification to see certain judges as interventionist and others as abstentionist. Thus though Lord Halsbury did dissent in *Allen v Flood*, he gained the concurrence of Lords Shand, Macnaghten, and Davey in *Quinn v Leathem*, all of whom had been in the majority in *Allen v Flood*. Indeed, Lord Macnaghten in *Allen v Flood* [1898] AC 1, p. 153 drew attention to the vice of 'those forms of terrorism commonly known by the name of boycotting'. In *Quinn v Leathem*, the plaintiff was a butcher boycotted by the members/officials of the Belfast Journeymen Butchers and Assistants' Association.

[76] The case is dealt with in more detail in Ch. 2. As Elias and Ewing point out, above, n. 10, p. 324: 'many statements in *Quinn v Leathem* are simply irreconcilable with *Allen v Flood* and do support the view that it is a tort deliberately to harm another without justification.' Indeed, it was precisely because of this uncertainty created by the apparently conflicting decisions that when Parliament passed the Trade Disputes Act 1906 they included the second limb of s. 3 which provided immunity for any liability there might be (even in the absence of conspiracy or unlawful means) for interference with trade.

[77] This is the accepted explanation of *Quinn v Leathem*: see *Ware and De Freville Ltd v Motor Trade Association* [1921] 2 KB 40, pp. 90–1 (Atkin LJ) and *Sorrell v Smith* [1925] AC 700, p. 723 (Lord Dunedin) and pp. 748–9 (Lord Buckmaster). However, note that in *Rookes v Barnard* [1964] AC 1129 Lord Diplock (p. 1216) doubted whether 'even today it is possible to say with certainty what *Quinn v Leathem* decided'.

[78] Cornish and Clark note, above, n. 46, p. 330: 'never was the law more nakedly the partisan of masters against men.' There was a double whammy: subsequently the House of Lords deemed trade unions to have sufficient legal personality to be sued: *Taff Vale Rly v ASRS* [1901] AC 426.   [79] (1906) 166 Parl Deb Col 693.

[80] Note the comment in Cornish and Clark, above, n. 46, p. 329 : 'the notion of such a tort had emerged in *Lumley v Gye* (1853) 2 E&B 216, but it had scarcely flourished . . . yet in *Temperton v Russell* [1893] 1 QB 715, a secondary trade boycott by a trade union, it was accepted within the canon of common law torts, whether the contracts in question were commercial or for labour.'

[81] i.e. where the trade union attacks the plaintiff trade dispute employer by means of the employees of his commercial partner.

[82] Note this set the scene for labour law to this day: trade unions and their members do not have the right to take industrial action; rather they have immunities from liability in circumstances defined by statute. See n. 94, below.

from the emerging civil liability, in the Trade Disputes Act 1906. This process—the judges extending liability and Parliament reacting by restoring (or attempting to restore) the status quo—is indeed the *leitmotiv* of this period until the Conservative administration that took office in 1979.[83] There had been interludes of non-intervention by the courts, particularly around the war years, typified by *Reynolds v Shipping Federation*[84] in 1924 (which accepted the legitimacy of the closed shop) and *Crofter Handwoven Harris Tweed Co Ltd v Veitch*[85] in 1942 (which accepted that a combination to improve wages and extend trade union membership could be legitimate). However, even of these Lord Wedderburn comments : 'the exceptional "non-interventionist" decisions of judge-made law have tended to occur when the interests of a union coincide, rather than conflict, with the predominant interests of employers and the State.'[86]

So, in the 1960s and 1970s the further growth and development of these torts sprang from judicial alarm at the disruption caused by trade union activity (and indeed by unofficial action).[87] In 1964 the House of Lords created a new tort of intimidation out of an obscure tort that first appeared in the seventeenth century,[88] a tort that as a result imposed liability for threatening to break a contract. This decision of the House of Lords in *Rookes v Barnard*[89] was accordingly described by Kahn-Freund as 'a frontal attack upon the right to strike'.[90] Parliament reacted by providing immunity from this tort in the Trade Disputes Act 1965. However, the continued judicial mistrust of trade union power and concern over the scope of their statutory immunities led to further new economic torts being developed or suggested—in particular the torts of inducing breach of statutory duty[91] and unlawful interference with contract performance.[92] Such torts were methods of circumventing the then extensive

[83] Markesinis, B., and Deakin, S., *Tort Law*, 4th edn. (Oxford: Clarendon Press, 1999), p. 470 'at times it has seemed that the courts (and the Bar) were engaged in a battle of wits with the Parliamentary drafter, to see which side could develop the optimal formula for widening or for narrowing liability respectively.'

[84] [1924] 1 Ch 28.

[85] [1942] AC 435, HL.

[86] Wedderburn, *The Worker and the Law*, above, n. 73, p. 94.

[87] Fleming, above, n. 57, p. 751 'the record is that of alternating passivity and overreaction, . . . repeatedly corrected by legislation'. As Deakin, S., and Morris, G., *Labour Law*, 2nd edn. (London: Butterworths, 1998) note (p. 866) 'by the 1960s . . . there was growing concern about the British industrial relations system and, in particular, the number of unofficial strikes'. This led to the establishment of the Donovan Commission which reported in 1968 (Royal Commission on Trade Unions and Employers' Associations, Cmnd. 3623). See generally Deakin and Morris, pp. 862–72.

[88] See Ch. 4.

[89] [1964] AC 1169.

[90] 14 *Federation News* (1964) p. 30.

[91] *Meade v Haringey* [1979] 1 WLR 637, CA; *Associated British Ports v TGWU* [1989] 1 WLR 939 (reversed on other grounds). This is discussed in Ch. 3.

[92] *Dimbleby v NUJ* [1984] 1 WLR 67: the House of Lords did not consider this point.

statutory immunities that peaceful industrial action attracted. As the various judgments of the Court of Appeal judges in *Associated Ports v TGWU* (the Docks Dispute litigation of 1989) revealed, there were still those who sought an interventionist expansion of this area of the law.[93]

Although trade union dispute immunities still exist, the traditional role of Parliament as restorer of the status quo has now gone. Since 1980, there have been a series of statutes that limit the application of the immunities.[94] The result is that the true nature of the general economic torts is only now being debated. Until 1980, it would tend to be assumed that even if economic torts arose in a dispute, the wide statutory immunities that then existed under the Trade Union and Labour Relations Act 1974 would apply. Therefore, in essence, the definition of these torts was rarely in issue. It is only since the gradual withdrawal of these immunities that the exact definition of these torts has become critical in industrial disputes. It is in this new era that the courts have accepted the economic tort of unlawful interference with trade.[95] The question is whether it extends tort liability (and if so, how) or merely rationalizes some of the existing economic torts.

The second policy, therefore, has created the tort of simple conspiracy (and accepted a tort of unlawful conspiracy) and intimidation. It has also unsettled the development of the tort of inducing breach of contract and left us with a lack of coherence in the economic torts—such being evidenced by the imprecision surrounding the tort of unlawful interference with trade.

[93] See both the CA and HL decisions in *Associated British Ports v TGWU* [1989] ICR 557.

[94] The statutory immunities are now contained in the Trade Union and Labour Relations (Consolidation) Act 1992 (as amended by the Trade Union Reform and Employment Rights Act 1993 and the Employment Relations Act 1999). Where the action takes place within the 'golden formula, i.e. in contemplation or furtherance of a trade dispute (between the workers and their employer, relating wholly or mainly to an employment issue listed in s.244) then immunity is provided for the torts of inducing breach of contract (and any interference variety of that tort); intimidation and simple conspiracy (see s.219). Presumably if inducing breach or intimidation form the 'unlawful means' for the tort of unlawful interference with trade that too would be covered by the immunities. In general terms, this basic immunity is, however, lost if the required ballot is not held (ss.226–35); if there is unlawful secondary action (s.224) or if the action is seeking to enforce trade union membership (s.222) or to impose a union recognition requirement (s.225). It is also lost if there is picketing outside s.220 and if the action is taken because of dismissal for taking unofficial action (s.223). A detailed consideration of the statutory immunities is contained in ch. 24, *Clerk and Lindsell on Torts* (Lord Wedderburn), above, n. 13.

[95] Markesinis and Deakin, above, n. 83, p. 470 'courts are likely to continue the process of developing the common law in novel directions to meet what they clearly see as the needs of plaintiffs for protection. The dynamic quality of the economic torts, which makes them so resistant to synthesis, is undoubtedly a reaction to Parliament's attempts since 1906 to neutralize this area of common law liability.'

CONCLUSION

Interesting though the history and development of the economic torts may be, the real issue for academics and practitioners alike must be their rationale and potential.

The development of all these torts has been well documented and it might be considered that the only uncertainty in this area relates to the 'genus' tort of unlawful interference with trade. However, when the economic torts are closely analysed it is clear that none of them is in fact free from uncertainties and controversy. Indeed, Lord Wedderburn has commented that the economic torts have been at best 'a ramshackle construction for decades'.

Of course, the economic torts play only a residual role in the regulation of competition[96] but it is a role that claimants seek constantly to increase. There is an obvious need to provide clarification: the problem with litigation in this area is that it tends to start and finish at the interlocutory stage, where no detailed analysis of the law is necessary. At the heart of the uncertainty surrounding these torts is the possibility of uncontrolled judicial expansion of such liability, at odds with the caution of the past. The ultimate question is how far should we move in the direction of a policy to protect against unfair competition or economic behaviour?

The aim of this book is to provide a blueprint for understanding this area of the common law. In order to suggest a framework for these torts an analysis of each of the established torts is necessary. It will be seen that such an analysis is not without its difficulty as a complex knot of issues needs resolving. Indeed, Heydon cautions, 'there cannot be any account of the economic torts which is comprehensible without effort'. However, it is hoped that the following will prove both comprehensible and satisfactory.

---

[96] To paraphrase Weir, T., 'Chaos or Cosmos? *Rookes*, *Stratford* and the Economic Torts' 1964 CLJ 225, p. 236 they define the forbidden short cuts in the economic rat race.

2

Conspiracy

THE TWO TORTS OF CONSPIRACY

There are two sorts of conspiracy: 'the *Quinn v Leathem* type which employs only lawful means but aims at an unlawful end, and the type which employs unlawful means.'[1] Thus the tort can take the form of unlawful conspiracy, where the combination uses unlawful means and the form of simple conspiracy, where the 'magic of plurality' renders a combination to injure tortious, despite the lack of unlawful means. Though these two torts obviously have common factors—an agreement or combination involving two or more persons[2] intentionally to harm the claimant—their focal point is different.[3] For this reason they must be analysed separately.[4] In so doing their relationship to the other economic torts will be revealed.

UNLAWFUL CONSPIRACY

HISTORY

Both the crime and tort of conspiracy grew from a common root, the writ of conspiracy, dating from Edward I. This gave a criminal and civil remedy for the abuse of legal procedure. With the development of the action on the case, relief became available in a wider area of combined action, rather than simply abuse of legal process. However, as Oliver J pointed out in *Midland Bank Trust Co v Green (no. 3)*[5] 'in the more normal case of a concerted commission of a tort there was little advantage in an action for conspiracy when an action equally lay for the commission of

---

[1] Lord Devlin, *Rookes v Barnard* [1964] AC 1129, p. 1204.

[2] Spouses may conspire together (Oliver J in *Midland Bank Trust Co Ltd v Green (no.3)* [1979] Ch 496, p. 522; affirmed, Lord Denning M.R., p. 538 and Fox LJ, p. 541). There may also be a conspiracy between a company and its directors but not between an employer and his employees, acting as employees: see Lord Wedderburn, *Clerk and Lindsell on Torts*, 18th edn. (London: Sweet & Maxwell, 2000), paras 24–119.

[3] Sales, P, 'The Tort of Conspiracy and Civil Secondary Liability' 49 CLJ (1990) 491.

[4] See Lord Bridge in *Lonrho v Fayed* [1992] 1 AC 448, pp. 465–6; see also the perceptive article by Sales, above, n. 3.

[5] [1979] Ch 496, pp. 521–5 (in which he reviewed the history of the tort).

the tort itself'.[6] Indeed, the question whether there was a separate tort of conspiracy was still a matter of debate in 1920.[7] Salmond at this time[8] doubted whether the tort existed, contending that the cases on conspiracy were in fact examples of the tort of intimidation, though this was condemned as 'the leading heresy' by Lord Dunedin in *Sorrell v Smith*.[9] In reality it has always been the tort of simple conspiracy which has led to keen academic and judicial debate in the past.

INGREDIENTS

Intention

The issue of intention is controversial in the economic torts. Though they require intentional harm (apart, of course, from the tort of passing off) it has not yet been established whether that concept of intention is the same for them all.[10] So *dicta* can be found requiring only that the act at the heart of the unlawful conspiracy be deliberate and have the effect of injuring the claimant.[11] However, the better view, accepted by the House of Lords in *Lonrho v Fayed* must be that the combination has to be aimed at or directed at the claimant.[12] If so, the conspiracy must aim at the claimant who must suffer harm as a result of that agreement being put into effect.[13] This will be considered more fully later.[14] Motive is irrelevant to liability, unlike the tort of simple conspiracy.[15]

Agreement/common design

The parties to a conspiracy must have a common design,[16] though they

---

[6] Ibid. 523. See later in text for the modern importance of the tort.

[7] Charlesworth, J., 'Conspiracy as a Ground of Liability in Tort' 36 LQR (1920) 38.

[8] *Salmond on Torts*, 6th edn. (London: Sweet & Maxwell, 1924), pp. 576–8.

[9] [1925] AC 710, p. 719

[10] See more detailed discussion in Ch. 10. Of course, with classic deceit it is knowledge of the falsity of the statement that is important, together with intended reliance.

[11] *Ware and De Freville v Motor Traders Association* [1921] 3 KB 40, Bankes LJ, p. 56; Scrutton LJ, p. 67 (harm to the plaintiff as 'the natural consequence').

[12] *Lonrho v Fayed* [1992] 1 AC 448, p. 465: 'when conspirators intentionally injure the plaintiff and use unlawful means to do so.' And see *Kuwait Oil Tanker Co SAK v Al Bader (no. 3)* [2000] 2 All ER (Comm) 271, where Nourse LJ notes that the claimant must be 'aimed at'.

[13] Paraphrasing Lord Denning MR in *Lonrho v Shell Petroleum* [1981] Com LR 74 ('I would suggest that a conspiracy to do an unlawful act—when there is no intent to injure the plaintiff and it is not aimed or directed at him—is not actionable, even though he is damaged thereby').

[14] In Ch. 10.   [15] See discussion, below.

[16] Lord Devlin in *Rookes v Barnard* [1964] AC 1129, p. 1211 'if the necessary coercive power is dispersed, there must be agreement or combination before it can be effectively used'.

need not all join at the same time.[17] It is clear that conspiracy liability does not depend on an explicit plan between the parties—a tacit agreement is adequate. Nor does the claimant have to show that the parties had a common design to commit a tort[18]—it is sufficient that the parties combine to secure the doing of acts which in the event prove to be a tort[19] (though—as in the doctrine of joint tortfeasance—if the tort in question requires a particular state of mind, no party will be liable in the absence of such a state of mind.)[20] The lack of common design in *CBS Songs Ltd v Amstrad*[21] meant there could be no complicity liability. There the defendants sold recording equipment, capable of being used by members of the public for illegal home taping of copyright material. But there was no common design to this end—once the machines were sold, the defendants had no control over or interest in their use. The requirement of a common design (and the related requirement of concerted action, below)—means that 'mere facilitation' is not sufficient for liability.

Concerted action

Agreement alone is not sufficient for liability: there must be concerted action, consequent on that agreement. Thus Stuart-Smith LJ commented in *Credit Lyonnais v ECGD*: 'it is not enough that [the defendant] merely facilitates the commission of the tort unless his assistance is given in pursuance and furtherance of the common design.'[22] The key to understanding the proper scope of the tort is to separate the issues involved in

---

[17] Stamp J in *Torquay Hotel v Cousins* [1969] 2 Ch 106, p. 121 The Court of Appeal made no finding on conspiracy [1969] 2 Ch 106, p. 132. Harman J in *Huntley v Thornton* [1957] 1 WLR 321, p. 343 asserted: 'no doubt it is not necessary that all the conspirators should join at the same time, but it is . . . necessary that they should know all the facts and entertain the same object.' In the case itself, 'an essential fact' had not been communicated to the local trade union officials, viz. that the executive council of the union had refused to act on the resolution to expel the plaintiff.

[18] It is still not clear whether the tort covers a conspiracy to breach a contract. If it does (discussed in Ch. 10), then it is submitted that the parties to the concerted action are only liable in so far as they intended a breach of contract to result, i.e. knowing that the end result would be a breach. This would put the tort on a par with the tort of inducing breach of contract—both torts rendering the defendant liable as a 'secondary' party. See generally Ch. 10.

[19] Paraphrasing the views of Mustill LJ in *Unilever plc v Gillette* [1989] RPC 583, p. 609 (a case on patent infringement): 'nor is there any need for a common design to infringe. It is enough if the parties combine to secure the doing of acts which in the event prove to be infringements.'

[20] *Gardner v Moore* [1969] 1 QB 55, p. 91.

[21] [1988] AC 1013, HL (the case did not involve a conspiracy claim as such).

[22] Stuart-Smith LJ felt that there would be civil liability on the facts of a case such as *Thambiah v R* [1966] AC 37, cited by Atiyah, P., *Vicarious Liability in the Law of Torts* (London: Butterworths, 1967), p. 301: there the accessory opened a bank account in a false name in furtherance of a fraud to be practised by the main fraudster.

this complicity link. Here case law on the doctrine of joint tortfeasance is useful, given (as will be seen later) that doctrine and this tort have clear overlaps. For both, there must be a common design[23] *and* the acts done by the conspirator must be 'in pursuance and furtherance' of that common design. The mere fact of being a party to an agreement is not sufficient for liability. Glidewell LJ in *Unilever plc v Chefaro*[24] noted that in order to show liability[25] emanating from a common design 'it is necessary to show some act in furtherance of the common design, *not merely an agreement*' [emphasis added], while Lord Templeman in *CBS Songs Ltd v Amstrad Ltd* emphasized that liability results from the parties *acting* in concert, pursuant to a common design.[26] Just as in joint liability,[27] furtherance of the unlawful combination appears to demand that the purpose[28] of the defendant in acting as he does, be established. The mere fact that what the party does has the effect of helping the common venture cannot be sufficient: rather he must act 'for the purpose of' forwarding that venture. Thus Pumfrey J in *Sandman v Panasonic UK Ltd*,[29] having found no decision to support a doctrine of responsibility in tort from mere association with a group acting in concert, concluded there must be some evidence that the defendant was actually involved in furthering the common design, that he 'took part' in the unlawful act. There must be concerted action to a common end.[30] It is the presence of this purpose—to further the common venture—that means the conspirator (or, in the case of joint liability, the joint tortfeasor)[31] and the 'prime' tortfeasor are part and parcel of the same process.

---

[23] Ownership of and the ability to control a subsidiary company is not *per se* evidence of joint tortfeasance/complicity: *Unilever plc v Chefaro* [1994] FSR 135, CA. Applied by Laddie J in *Mead Corp v Riverwood International Corporation* [1997] FSR 484: the fact that a parent company regarded itself and its subsidiaries as a single economic entity is neutral: to show a common design more than mere approval of a subsidiary's activities has to be shown. And see *Sandman v Panasonic Ltd* [1998] FSR 651, Pumfrey J.

[24] [1994] FSR 135 (a joint tortfeasance case). [25] In that case, patent infringement.

[26] [1988] AC 1013, HL Widgery J in *Morgan v Fry* [1968] 1 QB 521, p. 548 having found one of the defendants liable for intimidation, held other to be a joint tortfeasor. The fact that he had communicated the threat and commended the proposed intimidation meant that he had played a 'sufficiently active role'.

[27] Stuart-Smith LJ in *Credit Lyonnais v ECGD* [1998] 1 Lloyd's Rep 19, p. 35 Simply 'looking on with approval' will not render that party liable. On appeal, the House of Lords were similarly unwilling to extend liability, though the focus of Lord Woolf's judgment was on the issue of vicarious liability, [1999] 2 WLR 540.

[28] Of course this is a different concept to the motive of such a party: the motive is irrelevant (though in the separate tort of simple conspiracy—which does not involve secondary liability—motive is the key to liability).

[29] [1998] FSR 651, p. 664 (a joint tortfeasance case) Paraphrasing Laddie J in *Mead Corp v Riverwood Multiple Packaging* [1997] FSR 484.

[30] *Petrie v Laman* (1842) Car & M 93, p. 96.

[31] Again, in *Paterson Zochonis v Merfarken Packaging* [1983] FSR 273 Oliver LJ noted that knowingly to supply goods *for the purpose of enabling a tort to be committed* could involve an inference of common design.

Thus only if the purpose is to further the overall common design are the parties acting in concert, pursuant to a common design.[32] The real usefulness of conspiracy liability is that the claimant does not have to prove that the defendant committed the tort as such. Where there is concerted action then there is collective responsibility for the ensuing harm, 'regardless of which hand struck the actual blow'.[33] In *Credit Lyonnais v ECGD* a third party posed as a considerable exporter of commercial goods and induced the plaintiff bank to purchase (fraudulent) bills of exchange, drawn by him on what were in fact fictitious buyers. The banker's guarantees for these were issued by the Export Credit Guarantee Department. To make this scam work, the third party corrupted a senior employee of the ECGD, Mr Pillai, who dealt with the underwriting of the guarantees. Pillai and the rogue had 'a common design to defraud' and were jointly liable[34] though it was the rogue who presented the forged documents on which the bank relied to their disadvantage (and the issuing of the guarantees by the employee, though lawful in itself, was in furtherance of this fraud).[35]

Damage

Damage is an essential element of liability in the tort of conspiracy for 'the tort, unlike the crime, consists not of agreement but of concerted action taken pursuant to agreement'.[36] Pecuniary loss must be shown.[37] There was a detailed consideration of this point in *Lonrho v Fayed (no. 5)*[38] which though a case concerning the tort of simple conspiracy is likely to provide the approach for unlawful conspiracy also. So damages are at large, i.e. not limited to a 'precise calculation of the amount of the actual pecuniary

---

[32] It is clear from this analysis that simply agreeing to buy a product, knowing that the vendor will thereby be in breach of his own contract should not give rise to secondary liability, either for inducing breach or for conspiring to breach. Yet Roxburgh J in *BMTA v Salvadori* [1949] Ch 556 indicated he would be willing to impose liability in such a case, discussed in Ch. 3.

[33] Fleming, J., *The Law of Torts*, 9th edn. (Sydney: The Law Book Co. Ltd., 1998), p. 290.

[34] Stuart-Smith LJ [1998] 1 Lloyd's Law Rep 19, p. 36.

[35] See Stuart-Smith LJ ibid. 35. However, the acts of assistance which took place in the course of his employment were not part of the deceit itself and therefore did not render the employer vicariously liable.

[36] Lord Diplock, *Lonrho v Shell* [1982] AC 173, p. 188 This was an inevitable result of it being an action on the case. As Oliver J notes in *Midland Bank Trust Co Ltd v Green (no. 3)* [1979] Ch 496, p. 522, 'hence it became possible to sue one conspirator alone without joining the others'.

[37] 'Damages follow much the same pattern as that in inducing breach of contract', McGregor, H., *McGregor on Damages*, 16th edn. (London: Sweet & Maxwell, 1997), para 1936. Warner J in *Unik Time Co v Unik Time Ltd* [1983] FSR 121, p. 125 noted that it was common ground 'that the measure of damages for passing off and conspiracy is the same'.

[38] [1993] 1 WLR 1489.

loss actually proved'.[39] Loss of profits[40] and the expense of investigating the conspiracy[41] are clearly recoverable. The court further held that injury to reputation[42] is not covered by the tort of simple conspiracy (see below). Such a policy may well also apply to unlawful conspiracy. It may also be that injury to feelings is not covered, though there appear to be no policy reasons why this should be so.[43]

Unlawful means

With the general tort of unlawful interference with trade, the concept of 'unlawful means' may be as wide as acts the defendant 'is not at liberty to commit' (discussed in Chapter 5). However, in light of recent *dicta*,[44] it would seem that the unlawful means relied on for the tort of unlawful conspiracy must, as Stuart-Smith LJ in *Credit Lyonnais v ECGD* asserted, be 'actionable' in themselves *and* 'at the suit of the plaintiff'.[45] This was accepted as correct by Toulson J in *Yukong Line Ltd v Rendsburg Investments Corp (no. 2)*.[46] Such a view equates this tort with the torts of inducing breach of contract and inducing breach of statutory duty, where there is a need to show that an actionable wrong (i.e. actionable by the claimant) has been induced.[47] If so, this is an important indication that the tort of

---

[39] Dillon LJ ibid. 1494 However, in the case itself the Court of Appeal were critical of the gross inadequacy of a plea that 'by reason of the matters set out above the plaintiffs have suffered loss, damage and injury'.

[40] Dillon LJ, ibid. 1496 'loss of orders, loss of trade'.

[41] Dillon LJ, ibid. 1497 'cost of managerial and staff time spent in investigating or mitigating the consequences of the conspiracy'. See also Roxburgh J in *BMTA v Salvadori* [1949] Ch 556.

[42] Though Evans LJ was keen to distinguish between reputation and goodwill [1993] 1 WLR 1489, p. 1509.

[43] Giliker, P., 'A "new" head of damages: damages for mental distress in the English law of Torts' 20 LS (2000) 19 is critical of this analysis in *Lonrho v Fayed (no. 5)*. The court refused to recognize damages for injured feelings. Giliker comments: 'this is a difficult decision. No real attempt was made to distinguish injured feelings from loss of reputation . . . and therefore the court gave no clear reason for its rejection of this head of damages. On the facts, actual pecuniary loss was not established and so, technically, such comments were obiter.'

[44] Cf. Rogers,W. V. H., *Winfield and Jolowicz on Tort*, 15th edn. (London: Sweet & Maxwell, 1998), pp. 647–8.

[45] [1998] 1 Lloyd's Law Rep 19, p. 32.

[46] [1998] 1 WLR 294, Toulson J, contending that the law is as stated by Stuart-Smith LJ in *Credit Lyonnais v ECGD* 'that in an unlawful act conspiracy, the unlawful act relied upon must be actionable at the suit of the plaintiff' (p. 314). Though note the view of Waller LJ in *Surzur Overseas Ltd v Koros* [1999] 2 Lloyd's Rep 611, p. 617 that it was 'eminently arguable' that the unlawful act need not be actionable by the plaintiff (a view which obviously attracts Nourse LJ in *Kuwait Oil Tanker Co SAK v Al Bader (no. 3)*, [2000] 2 All ER (Comm) 271. However, this is because he believes that unlawful conspiracy is based on the same framework of liability as unlawful interference with trade. The thesis of this book is that that is fundamentally wrong.

[47] So it is clearly the view of the Court of Appeal in *Associated British Ports v TGWU* [1989] 3 All ER 796 that the unlawful means must be independently actionable *by the plaintiff himself*

unlawful conspiracy performs a role different to that of the tort of unlawful interference with trade. What we have, as Sales has identified,[48] is a form of secondary action, extending the range of defendants for the claimant (discussed below).

Unlawful means for this tort would usually mean other torts. However, drawing parallels with inducing breach of contract it would appear arguable that a conspiracy to breach contract could also amount to the tort of unlawful conspiracy, though Lord Devlin in *Rookes v Barnard* expressly noted that this might not necessarily be the case.[49]

Indeed, some would contend that the concept of 'unlawful means' goes beyond torts or even breaches of contract to include equitable wrongs and breaches of trust/fiduciary duty. Wedderburn,[50] suggests that where a combination uses a breach of confidence as part of the method of achieving its objective, that may be sufficient. Since it is a tort to induce breach of an equitable obligation,[51] a combination to do so would appear to be a conspiracy to use unlawful means. At issue here is whether the economic torts can be used to 'tortify' other areas of the civil law.[52] However, if unlawful conspiracy is an example of secondary liability, mere crimes cannot be sufficient, for, as Sales points out, such liability demands that the claimant show the defendant has encouraged his co-conspirators to wrong the claimant 'in a manner in respect of which the civil law permits the plaintiff to recover compensation'.[53]

Justification

It is clearly arguable that where unlawful means are deliberately used to harm a defence of justification should rarely if ever apply. Indeed, it is hard to see why this special defence would apply in unlawful conspiracy

---

and Hoffmann LJ in *Law Debenture Trust Ltd v Ural Caspian Oil Corp* [1995] Ch 152 noted that the actionable wrong must involve actual breach of contract, breach of statutory duty or breach of equitable obligation. And see *Michaels v Taylor Woodrow Developments Ltd* [2000] 4 All ER 645, Laddie J.

[48] Above, n. 3., p. 491 'the tort of conspiracy to injure by unlawful means (but not the tort of conspiracy to injure by lawful means) is a form of secondary liability in civil law'.

[49] This is all the more puzzling, given *Rookes v Barnard* [1964] AC 1129 itself held that a threat to breach a contract could be an unlawful threat and constitute the tort of intimidation. Wedderburn, K. W., 'Intimidation and the Right to Strike' 27 MLR (1964) 257, p. 268 suggests 'perhaps it is because of some vision of the limitless consequences of treating breach of contract as fully "unlawful" that Lord Devlin draws back'. This is discussed in Ch. 10. Nourse LJ in *Kuwait Oil Tanker Co. SAK v Al Bader (no. 3)*, [2000] 2 All ER (Comm) 271, implies that a breach of contract (and indeed a crime) would be sufficient unlawful means.

[50] *Clerk and Lindsell*, above, n. 2, paras 24–98, 24–121. But see also 24–38.

[51] Though this writer queries whether this is established. See discussion in Ch. 10.

[52] Discussed more fully in Ch. 10.

[53] Sales, above, n. 3, p. 494. However, Nourse LJ in *Kuwait Oil Tanker Co. SAK v Al Bader (no. 3)*, *The Times*, 30 May 2000, implies that crimes may be sufficient unlawful means.

if the unlawful means need to be independently actionable—unless something like the defence of justification applies to the 'primary' tort.[54]

MODERN IMPORTANCE

It is common to assert that this version of the tort of conspiracy 'verges on the redundant'.[55] Lord Devlin stated in *Rookes v. Barnard*[56] that 'the element of conspiracy is usually of only secondary importance, since the unlawful means are actionable by themselves'.

Yet Rogers and Eekelaar comment that the tort can add a useful weapon in the claimant's armoury against unlawful, intended economic harm. So it is useful to plead the combination in its own right by way of 'fortification'[57] of an allegation of intentional harm. Rogers[58] notes that the fact of a combination may lead the court 'to be more ready to grant an injunction or larger damages'.[59] Also, in a case founded on conspiracy the acts and admissions of one conspirator (in pursuance of a conspiracy) are admissible against the others.[60] Moreover, Eekelaar stresses the evidential advantage that may result from framing the action in conspiracy, given 'in a complex case, it may not be easy to show which individual defendant adopted the specific unlawful procedures alleged'. Indeed, the usefulness of the tort was revealed in *Rookes v Barnard*[61] where two of the plaintiff's colleagues and their union organizer instigated and relayed to the employer the threat of strike action, to enforce a closed shop agreement. It was held that this was a combination involving the use of unlawful means: the threat to break contracts of employment.[62] As the combination was aimed at causing harm to the plaintiff—to force the employer to

---

[54] Otherwise all the defendants would not be liable in conspiracy but some could still be liable for the primary tort

[55] Rogers, above, n. 44, p. 545.

[56] [1964] AC 1129, p. 1204.

[57] Eekelaar, J, 'The Conspiracy Tangle' 106 LQR (1990) 223.

[58] Above, n. 44, p. 648. Heydon, J. D., *Economic Torts*, 2nd edn. (London: Sweet & Maxwell, 1978), p. 77 cites *Denison v Fawcett* (1958) 12 DLR (2d) 537 and *NCB v Galley* [1958] 1 WLR 16 as examples of this.

[59] See *Sorrell v Smith* [1925] AC 700, p. 713, V Cave LC; *Pratt v BMA* [1919] 1 KB 244, p. 254, McCardie J.

[60] *Derby & Co. v Weldon (no. 5)* [1989] 1 WLR 1244, p. 1254 Sales also suggests (above, n. 3) that the loss may have only resulted from the combination of the wrongful acts of the defendants as in e.g. a strike where it is the concerted action which causes the loss (p. 511). In *Kuwait Oil Tanker Co. SAK v Al Bader (no. 3)*, [2000] 2 All ER (Comm) 271, the Court of Appeal accepted that the use of this tort may enable the double actionability rule to be applied easily and more sensibly.

[61] [1964] AC 1129.

[62] That there would have been a breach of the individual contracts of employment was a concession by counsel.

dismiss him when he left the union—the tort was made out. By pleading unlawful conspiracy, all the defendants could be held liable even though it would be difficult to attribute the harm to any 'particular' act of the defendants.[63] Moreover, by using conspiracy it was possible to add the trade union official to the list of defendants even though he was not bound by contract to the employer and, therefore, could not be liable for the threat to break the contract as such. He was liable as a party to a conspiracy to intimidate.[64]

Overall, the Court of Appeal in *Kuwait Oil Tanker Co SAK v Al Bader (no. 3)*[65] accepted that conspiracy may be a more appropriate allegation than an allegation that the defendant had committed a particular tort, 'especially if . . . it expresses the true nature and gravamen of the case against the defendants'. They did stress, however, that the claimants would not be allowed to gain an illegitimate advantage by using the tort of unlawful conspiracy.

Of course, these useful effects would also arise were the doctrine of joint tortfeasance applied to the same conspirators. Indeed, Rogers notes[66] 'it may be that the primary significance of unlawful means conspiracy is to make each party a joint tortfeasor, though it hardly seems necessary to have a free-standing tort to achieve this'.

RATIONALE

This last aspect of unlawful conspiracy, the facility to join defendants not necessarily able themselves to commit the unlawful act in question, raises the relationship of the tort to the doctrine of joint tortfeasance. Here the uncertainty of the economic torts is matched by the 'obscure and under-theorized'[67] law governing parties to a tort. The doctrine of joint tortfeasance encompasses vicarious liability and liability for agents. However, a further important area involves joint liability for tortfeasors who act in pursuit of a common design, where there is 'concerted action to a common end'[68]—the Court of Appeal in *The Koursk* clearly acknowledging combination as a relevant link for the imposition of joint liability.[69]

---

[63] Eekelaar, above, n. 57, p. 224.

[64] Lord Reid [1964] AC 1129, p. 1166; Lord Devlin, pp. 1210–11 Hence the defendant was unable to attract the immunities from liability that would have applied had he been liable simply for inducing breach of contract.

[65] [2000] 2 All ER (Comm) 271.

[66] Rogers, above, n. 44, p. 648.

[67] Birks, P., 'Civil Wrongs: a New World' in *Butterworths Lectures 1990–1* (London: Butterworths, 1992), p. 100.

[68] *The Koursk* [1924] P. 140, p. 156.

[69] Of course, the actual decision of the Court of Appeal in *The Koursk* [1924] P. 140 was as

According to *The Koursk*, concerted action, where 'two persons . . . agree on common action, in the course of, and to further which, one of them commits a tort',[70] would make each combiner a joint tortfeasor. Thus as Lord Wedderburn notes 'it would appear that the question whether a person is a party to a combination constituting a conspiracy is essentially the same whether he is liable as a joint tortfeasor or for procuring a wrong, by reason of a common design'.[71]

Both the doctrine of joint tortfeasance and the tort of unlawful conspiracy have a tort central to the liability. Without the independent tort, actionable by the claimant, there is no liability for unlawful conspiracy and there is nothing in relation to which the participator could be jointly liable. Indeed, the courts see the allegation of liability for unlawful conspiracy as a gloss on the tort which constitutes the unlawful act.[72] Obviously, the tort of conspiracy is narrower than the doctrine of joint tortfeasance, demanding as it does an intention to harm the claimant on the part of the conspirators.[73] However, as Wedderburn points out, the distinction in case law between liability as a joint tortfeasor and liability as a conspirator is not always maintained.[74]

The tort and the doctrine of joint tortfeasance perform the same function: they focus on a complicity link to render a wider group of defendants liable to the claimant. They both widen the circle of liability from the central tortfeasor to those involved in the concerted action. The tort and the doctrine make the defendants jointly responsible for the acts done

to the *form* that liability should take, rather than the *creation* of liability There the defendants were clearly liable separately for the independent acts of negligence that led to the sinking of the plaintiffs' ship. The issue of joint liability arose when the judgment against one of these tortfeasors was unsatisfied. However, it became clear in the decision of the Divisional Court in *Brooke v Bool* [1928] 2 KB 578, Div C some four years later, that the fact of combination can be used to *extend* liability to a participator, where no independent tort is committed by that participator. See for a more detailed analysis, Carty, H., 'Joint Tortfeasance and Assistance Liability', 19 Legal Studies (1999) 489.

[70] Scrutton LJ [1924] P 140, p. 155.

[71] *Clerk and Lindsell on Torts*, above, n. 2, paras. 24–120.

[72] So for Lord Dunedin 'if a combination of persons do what is done by one would be a tort, an averment of conspiracy so far as founding a civil action is mere surplusage' *Sorrel v Smith* [1925] AC 700, p. 716 while Lord Denning asserted in *Ward v Lewis* [1955] 1 WLR 9, p. 11 that: 'the prior agreement merges in the tort . . . conspiracy adds nothing when the tort has in fact been committed.' Stuart-Smith LJ in *Credit Lyonnais Bank Nederland NV v ECGD* [1998] 1 Lloyd's Rep 19, p. 32 'the claim in conspiracy added nothing to the claim in deceit'. However, the force of such dicta should now be doubted, given the decision of the C.A in *Kuwait Oil Tanker Co SAK v Al Bader (no. 3)*, [2000] 2 All ER (Comm) 271. There the C.A rejected the defendants' assertion that there existed a 'doctrine of merger' (so that the conspiracy merges with the tort and cannot be pleaded). Rather the C.A accepted that there may be reasons why the tort of conspiracy can legitimately be pleaded (see earlier in text).

[73] So the doctrine could apply to the tort of negligence, as it did in *Brooke v Bool* [1928] 2 KB 578.

[74] *Clerk and Lindsell on Torts*, above, n. 2, para 23–09.

in pursuance of the combination.[75] Here the responsibility is justified for 'there is one tort committed by one of them on behalf of, or in concert with another'.[76]

CONCLUSION

It is clear, therefore, that the tort of unlawful conspiracy is not in fact part of the general tort,[77] unlawful interference with trade. Rather Sales has correctly identified it as a form of secondary civil liability—secondary involvement (through combination) in another's tort (or perhaps any civil wrong) attracting liability.[78] For him, 'there is an underlying connection defined by law between the plaintiff's loss and the actions which caused it (i.e. the primary wrong) and the defendant conspirator is simply treated as jointly responsible for that underlying wrong'.[79] Given the wider scope of the doctrine of joint tortfeasance, the need for a separate tort of unlawful conspiracy may as a result be questioned (discussed later).[80]

SIMPLE CONSPIRACY

Here there is liability for an agreement to do acts, lawful in themselves, for the sole or predominant purpose of causing injury to the claimant and which causes injury to him. Simple conspiracy is an exception to *Allen v Flood*:[81] the fact of combination can render action tortious that would not be tortious if done by one alone.

---

[75] Note that Hobhouse LJ in *Credit Lyonnais v ECGD* expressed the view that there could be vicarious liability for unlawful conspiracy in only the exceptional case, [1998] 1 Lloyd's Law Rep 19, p. 41.

[76] *The Koursk* [1924] P 140, p. 151 Bankes LJ: 'there must be some connection between the act of the one alleged tortfeasor and that of the other.'

[77] Sales, above, n. 3, p. 494, n. 19 [it] 'cannot be explained simply as an example of the tort of interference with business by unlawful means'.

[78] However, care needs to be taken here. What exactly is the scope of such 'secondary liability' in the law of tort needs to be addressed. Sales claims that the civil law generally has a latent doctrine of secondary liability, mirroring the criminal concept of accessory to a crime. So when a person assists another in the commission of a civil wrong he will be liable as a secondary party (on a par with an aider and abetter in crime). This is debated in Ch. 10. However, it should be noted that if he is right, such an extension of joint liability undermines the limits on economic tort liability.

[79] Above, n. 3, p. 513. At p. 500 he asserts: 'the conspirators who do not themselves carry out [the unlawful acts] should be treated as liable for the tort of conspiracy in respect of those acts, because by entering the conspiracy they have created a sufficient nexus between themselves and the wrong done to the plaintiff so that the plaintiff should be entitled to hold them responsible for damage suffered as a result of that wrong.'

[80] Ch. 10.

[81] [1898] AC 1, discussed in Ch. 1.

HISTORY

Lord Denning MR found simple conspiracy to be 'a modern invention altogether'.[82] Simple conspiracy was established in a modern form in *Mogul Steamship Co v McGregor*[83] and nurtured in *Quinn v Leathem*.[84]

In part it owed its existence to the 'legalization' of the trade unions and the withdrawal of the threat of criminal conspiracy. Thus the Trade Union Act 1871 provided that the purposes of unions were not to be deemed unlawful, and thereby render members liable for criminal conspiracy, simply because they were in restraint of trade. More specifically, the Conspiracy and Protection of Property Act 1875 provided that there would be no indictment for criminal conspiracy where an agreement in contemplation and furtherance of a trade dispute[85] involved acts, which if committed by one alone would not involve crime. Although the crime of conspiracy, frequently used against the trade unions was thereby emasculated, the civil wrong of conspiracy took its place. Thus in *Quinn v Leathem*, decided some three years after *Allen v Flood*, the House of Lords[86] failed to build on the logic of *Allen v Flood*[87] and instead unsettled the development of this area of tort law. Though a case similar to *Allen v Flood* it contained the added features of combination and threats. The case involved a dispute between the defendants, trade union officials, and the plaintiff, a butcher, over the employment of non-union workers. The defendants threatened the plaintiff's chief customer that his workers would leave his employ unless he ceased dealing with the plaintiff. When the customer acceded to this demand (with no breach of contract involved) the plaintiff alleged conspiracy to injure. The jury found that the defendants had maliciously conspired to induce the customer not to deal with the plaintiff and the House of Lords accepted that the defendants were liable. Lord Macnaghten asserted that conspiracy to injure might give rise to civil liability even though the end were brought about by conduct and acts, which in themselves, and apart from the element of combination or concerted action, could not be regarded as a legal wrong.[88]

---

[82] *Midland Bank Trust Co Ltd v Green (no. 3)* [1982] Ch 529, p. 539.

[83] [1892] AC 25.　　　　　　　　　　　　　　　　　　　　　[84] [1901] AC 495.

[85] s. 3 Conspiracy and Protection of Property Act 1875 was the first statutory use of the so-called 'golden formula': the key to immunity for peaceful industrial action.

[86] Lead by Lord Halsbury.

[87] *Allen v Flood* was decided between the trial at first instance of *Quinn v Leathem* and the time the motion to set aside the verdict came before the Divisional Court. The uncertainty of the law was stressed by the Royal Commission on Trade Disputes and Trade Combinations, which reported in 1906 (1906 RC Cmnd. 2825). Sir Godfrey Lushington in his report noted that the coexistence of *Allen v Flood* and *Quinn v Leathem* had created a situation 'which is bound to produce contradiction and uncertainty'.

[88] [1901] AC 495, p. 510. In the *Taff Vale* decision ([1901] AC 426) the House of Lords had

Simple conspiracy, therefore, runs counter to the general theme of the economic torts, which depend on unlawful means.[89] The orthodox explanation for this anomalous tort is the oppressive nature of conspiracies, as contrasted to individual action. Lord Lindley in *Quinn v Leathem* remarked that: 'numbers may annoy or coerce where one may not.'[90] That this is a weak justification has received judicial recognition. Thus Lord Diplock remarked in *Lonrho Ltd v Shell Petroleum Ltd*: 'to suggest . . . that a multinational conglomerate . . . does not exercise greater power than any combination of small businesses is to shut one's eyes to what has been happening in the business and industrial world since the turn of the century, and in particular since the end of the 1939–1945 War.'[91] Of course some, including Heydon,[92] would argue that the way round this rather weak explanation of the tort would be to render tortious all intentional and unjustified economic harm, whether done by one or many. So there is no tort of simple conspiracy in America,[93] rather the courts are prepared to penalize certain practices as exceeding the desirable bounds of business practices, *Tuttle v Buck*[94] being the classic example.

INGREDIENTS

As with unlawful conspiracy, the tort requires an agreement and concerted action, causing harm. However, the tort does not require unlawful means, basing liability on the fact of the 'magic of combination' and that very nineteenth-century allegation 'malice', reworked as 'illegitimate purpose'. That being so, it becomes unnecessary to consider

allowed a union to be sued, despite the problem over legal personality, so that having created a new civil offence (civil conspiracy) they created the obvious defendant for that offence.

[89] Either committed by the defendant or a third party, with participation in that third party's unlawful act by the defendant. See Ch. 10. Again, the tort of passing off is different.

[90] [1901] AC 495, p. 538. See also Bowen LJ in *Mogul v McGregor* (1889) 23 QBD 598, p. 616 'the distinction is based on sound reason, for a combination may make oppressive or dangerous that which if it proceeded only from a single person would be otherwise' (affd [1892] AC 25); and Lord Wright in *Crofter Hand Woven Harris Tweed Co v Veitch* [1942] AC 435, p. 468: 'it is easier to resist one than two', though he admitted that this explanation of the rule was hardly satisfactory.

[91] [1982] AC 173.

[92] Heydon, J. D., *Economic Torts*, 2nd edn. (London: Sweet & Maxwell, 1978), p. 28.

[93] A useful summary of the American position can be found in 'The Competition Torts' 77 Har L Rev (1963–4) 923. At p. 929 the commentator (not named) states that concerted action may be a suspect practice for 'the very purpose of the concert is to evade the competition system's internal checks by making impossible or more difficult the substitution of alternative suppliers or customers and since any advantages forgone by one will be forgone by all, none need fear that his refusal puts him at a competitive disadvantage'.

[94] 119 NW 946 (Minn 1909).

separately a defence of 'justification' as the tort itself is based on an allegation of unjustified harm.

Illegitimate purpose

As an anomalous economic tort,[95] simple conspiracy in fact only applies in the most extreme cases of oppressive combination. This is because of the need to prove that the combination is motivated by an illegitimate purpose. Given this tort can render a defendant liable, even though no unlawful means have been employed, this proviso to liability is an attempt: 'to hold the balance between the defendant's right to exercise his lawful rights and the plaintiff's right not to be injured by an injurious conspiracy.'[96] Thus this proviso does not apply to the tort of unlawful conspiracy, a point reaffirmed by the House of Lords in *Lonrho v Fayed*,[97] after a short period of uncertainty created by *dicta* in Lord Diplock's judgment in *Lonrho v Shell*, as interpreted by the Court of Appeal in *Metall und Rohstoff v Donaldson Lufkin & Jenrette Inc*.[98] With simple conspiracy the ingredient of illegitimate purpose can be seen as necessary to fill the gap when no unlawful means are involved.[99] In an unlawful conspiracy, by definition, unlawful acts are involved and it would be bizarre if a 'legitimate purpose' such as self-interest could excuse the unlawful actions used by the defendants.

Aggressive trade competition early received recognition as a legitimate purpose in *Mogul Steamship Co Ltd v McGregor Gow*.[100] In this case a cartel of shipowners sought to regulate a carrying trade exclusively for themselves. To rid themselves of competition from the plaintiff, they undercut the plaintiff to such an extent that he was obliged to carry at unremunerative rates; agents who dealt with him were threatened with dismissal and shippers warned that they would lose their rebate from the cartel if they dealt with the plaintiff. The plaintiff alleged tortious conspiracy: namely a combination to prevent the plaintiff from trading in the relevant ports. But the House of Lords held this to be a justified cartel. Lord Hals-

---

[95] Stressed again by Lord Bridge in *Lonrho v Fayed* [1992] 1 AC 448.

[96] Lord Wright, *Crofter v Veitch* [1942] AC 435, p. 462.

[97] [1992] 1 AC 448, see Lord Bridge, pp. 463–8. Thus reasserting 'the fundamental distinction' between simple and unlawful conspiracy: Sales, above, n. 3, p. 493. Hence in *Lonrho v Fayed* the plaintiffs' acceptance that injury to them was not the predominant purpose of the defendants' alleged unlawful act was not fatal to the action pleaded.

[98] [1990] 1 QB 391.

[99] Lord Bridge, *Lonrho v Fayed* [1992] 1 AC 448, p. 465: 'where conspirators act with the predominant purpose of injuring the plaintiff and in fact inflict damage on him, but do nothing which would have been actionable if done by an individual acting alone, it is in the fact of their concerted action for that illegitimate purpose that the law, however anomalous it may now seem, finds a sufficient ground to condemn that action as illegal and tortious.'

[100] [1892] AC 25.

bury LC commented that if the plaintiff was right in alleging a tortious wrong: 'all competition must be malicious and consequently unlawful', a sufficient *reductio ad absurdum* in his view to dispose of the matter.[101] As Fleming notes:[102] 'the defendants had done nothing more than pursue to the bitter end a war of competition waged in the interests of their own trade and it was not the proper function of the courts to police prices at which traders could sell or hire, for the purpose of protecting or extending their business.'

In establishing what is or is not a legitimate purpose some of the judges at the turn of the century were unable to equate the 'legitimacy' of the harm caused in trade competition with the harm caused in trade disputes.[103] Competition was seen as justification for a conspiracy; all else was uncertain.[104] However, by 1942[105] the House of Lords was prepared to accept a more realistic and balanced approach in interpreting the bona fide and legitimate interests of those who combine. In *Crofter Hand Woven Harris Tweed Co Ltd v Veitch*[106] a combination to create a better basis for collective bargaining (by driving a rival trader out of business) did not render the union officials involved liable in tort.[107] The plaintiffs were cutting costs by importing yarn from the mainland to be woven on the island of Lewis. The defendants, trade union officials, were told by the island mill owners that their spinners' pay claims could not be met because of this competition from the plaintiffs. The defendants thereupon instructed dockers not to handle the plaintiffs' yarn (no breach of contract thereby resulting). The plaintiffs alleged conspiracy between the union

---

[101] [1892] AC 25, p. 37 and note Holmes J (dissenting) in *Vegelahn v Guntner* Supreme Judicial Board of Massachusetts 44 NE 1077 (1896) 'it is plain from the slightest consideration of practical affairs, or the most superficial reading of industrial history that free competition means combination . . . it seems to me futile to set our faces against this tendency.'

[102] *The Law of Torts*, 9th edn. (Sydney: LBC), p. 705. Weir, *A Casebook on Tort*, 9th edn. (London: Sweet & Maxwell, 2000) underlines the fact that 'the tactics used by the Conference were implacably used and cripplingly effective—predatory price-cutting, "fighting ships", and pressure on agents.'

[103] This was noted by Oliver Wendell Holmes in 8 Har L Rev (1894) 1, p. 7. He contrasted the view of the House of Lords in *Mogul Steamship v McGregor* [1892] AC 25 with the view of the Court of Appeal in *Temperton v Russell* [1893] 1 QB 715.

[104] See 1906 RC Cmnd. 2825, pp. 87–8, Sir Geoffrey Lushington: 'otherwise the justification required is what the judges and jury may think in their discretion amounts to justification, in other words it is moral justification.'

[105] See earlier decisions which adopted a more liberal approach e.g. *Reynolds v Shipping Federation Ltd* (1924) 1 Ch 28: an agreement by an employers' association and the trade union to employ only members of that trade union was attacked by the plaintiff, a member of a rival trade union, who had been refused employment. Held however, this was a legitimate agreement, to advance the interests of the employers and employed alike by maintaining the advantages of collective bargaining.

[106] [1945] AC 435.

[107] Markesinis, B., and Deakin, S., *Tort Law*, 4th edn. (Oxford: Clarendon Press, 1999), p. 487, *Crofter* 'represents the high-water mark of judicial abstentionism in industrial disputes and of the courts' acceptance of the essential legitimacy of trade union organisation'.

and the mill owners. However, the House of Lords held that even if such a conspiracy existed, the defendants were motivated by self-interest, the interest of their members, and therefore the conspiracy was justified. As Kahn-Freund has pointed out, the importance of the *Crofter* decision was that it extended the principle of *Mogul* from the concerted action of traders to the concerted action of workers.[108]

Self-interest is the clearest case of a legitimate motivation.[109] Those induced to enter a conspiracy for payment, having no other interest in the cause, would not be protected; nor, probably, would busybodies. An important but as yet unresolved question is whether the defendant must aim to protect himself or his business interests or whether altruism, acting to protect another, would be sufficient. It would appear arguable that the latter is a legitimate interest and that the proviso is not therefore limited to the furtherance of a material interest. So in *Scala Ballroom (Wolverhampton) Ltd v Ratcliffe*[110] when the plaintiff excluded coloured people from their dance hall, the Musicians' Union retaliated by barring members from performing in the orchestra. Although *dicta* in the case suggest that altruism may be a legitimate purpose, and material interests may not have to be affected, the Court of Appeal accepted that the trial judge had found evidence beyond altruism: that a colour bar eventually endangered the livelihood of the musicians, lowered the standard of their profession, and could cause friction (as some of the musicians involved were coloured).[111] The exact state of the law on this matter is, therefore, not certain.[112] Cane argues that the true basis of self-interest (given it provides a legal justification)[113] may be that it furthers some wider public interest so that the line between self-interest and altruism becomes 'logic-ally indefensible'.[114] However, he does accept that the courts 'are unlikely to relish the prospect of being expressly asked to decide which political or social causes justify conspiracies to injure'.

What is certain is that the court will have regard to the predominant motive: there may be more than one purpose activating a combination but provided 'the predominant purpose is the lawful protection or promotion

---

[108] Kahn-Freund, O., 'Attacking the Colour Bar—A Lawful Purpose' (1959) 22 MLR 69.

[109] *Crofter v Veitch* [1942] AC 435, pp. 477–8; *Rookes v Barnard* [1964] AC 1129, p. 1232.

[110] [1958] 1 WLR 1057.

[111] Markesinis and Deakin, above, n. 107, p. 487, assert that the aim must be an economic one, though they acknowledge that this is sufficiently broad a concept to encompass *Scala Ballroom v Ratcliffe* [1958] 1 WLR 1057.

[112] The position of the law is open, according to Lord Porter in *Crofter v Veitch* [1942] AC 435, p. 491. Lord Bridge in *Lonrho v Fayed* [1992] 1 AC 448 refers to the purpose 'to further or protect their own interests'.

[113] Cane, P., *Tort Law and Economic Interests*, 2nd edn. (Oxford: Clarendon Press, 1996): 'For self-interest to be legitimate it is arguably necessary for the furtherance of self-interest to be, in some sense, in the public interest' (p. 259).

[114] Ibid. 260.

of any lawful interest of the combiners',[115] the combination is legitimate. Indeed, once the predominant purpose is deemed legitimate, the quantum of damage inflicted is irrelevant as is 'glee' at the expected upset to the claimant:[116] there is no tortious liability. What the predominant motive is, in a given conspiracy, is a question of fact. Presumably, the jury found that in *Quinn v Leathem* the predominant object of the combiners was punishment of the plaintiffs rather than their own self-interest.[117] Moreover, 'the courts have repudiated the idea that it is for them to determine whether the object of the combination is reasonably calculated to achieve [the benefit claimed]', the issue being a subjective one, according to Lord Wright in *Crofter*.[118] Of course where some in a combination have legitimate motives, others may have illegitimate motivation.[119] However, where only one has an illegitimate motive, it would appear that there can be no liability.[120]

MODERN IMPORTANCE

Sales[121] notes that the scope of simple conspiracy is limited 'to conspiracies to injure others out of spite, where no commercial purpose of the conspirators was furthered thereby'. Thus in *Huntley v Thornton*,[122] the actions of a branch committee of a trade union, in seeking to ensure that the plaintiff did not obtain work, were held to be motivated by 'their own ruffled dignity'. This personal vendetta meant that the committee 'grossly abused the quite frightening powers at their command' (underlining the fact that gross abuse of power is the rationale of the tort). Overall it is important to realize that this tort is of little practical importance: the need to show illegitimate motive/purpose robs it of major impact.[123] Given the scope of justification, it is hardly surprising that Lord Diplock should

---

[115] Viscount Simon, *Crofter v Veitch* [1942] AC 435, p. 445 and note the different self-interest involved in the case itself: the mill owners wanted higher profits; the union wanted higher wages and a closed shop.

[116] Viscount Simon, *Crofter v Veitch* [1942] AC 435, p. 445; pp. 469– 71.

[117] Though McCardie J in *Pratt v BMA* [1919] 1 KB 244 commented: 'in *Quinn v Leathem*, the defendants were subject to heavy damages, although the substantial object of the defendants was the advancement of their trade interests.'

[118] [1942] AC 435, p. 469.

[119] As in *Huntley v Thornton* [1957] 1 All ER 234: two of the defendants were not liable because they were not motivated by 'ruffled dignity'. Some of the defendants were held not liable in *Jarman and Platt v Barget* (1977) 3 FSR 260 because they were not motivated by the malice of the other defendants.

[120] Evatt J in *McKernan v Fraser* (1931) 46 CLR 343, p. 407.

[121] Above, n. 3, p. 492.

[122] [1957] 1 All ER 234.

[123] As Weir notes (Weir, T., *Economic Torts* (Oxford: Clarendon Press, 1997), p. 73) disinterested malevolence is rare.

comment that simple conspiracy during its chequered history has attracted more academic controversy than success in its practical application.[124] Moreover, given it is out of step with the other economic torts, Lord Diplock in *Lonrho Ltd v Shell Petroleum Ltd*[125] refused to extend 'this already anomalous tort beyond those narrow limits that are all that common sense and the application of the legal logic of the decided cases require'.

The tort did provide interlocutory relief to the plaintiff in *Gulf Oil (GB) Ltd v Page*.[126] In that case a contractual dispute arose between the plaintiffs and defendants, with the ensuing High Court decision finding the plaintiffs to have been in breach of contract. Pending the appeal, the defendants began a campaign against the plaintiffs, circulating leaflets to several of the plaintiffs' customers, giving an account of the litigation and flying a banner over the plaintiffs' hospitality tent during a race meeting. The banner read: 'Gulf exposed in fundamental breach.' The truth of the words was not in issue and, if this had been a defamation case, the court, applying the principle in *Bonnard v Perryman*,[127] would not have granted an interlocutory injunction. However, the plaintiffs alleged conspiracy to injure. Here there was a serious question of conspiracy, motivated by revenge.[128]

However, there is an obvious need to be wary of applying the tort of simple conspiracy to cases where the combination to injure uses words, rather than acts. The tort could place the courts in a dilemma if it allowed claimants too easily to circumvent the requirements of a defamation action and gain damages for injury to reputation where the basis of the action was that the defendants had conspired to tell the truth.[129] Hence the Court of Appeal in *Lonrho v Fayed (no. 5)*,[130] mindful of the free-speech implications of their decision, held that as injury to reputation was in a field of its own, the special ingredients of defamation or malicious falsehood[131] should be required. In essence, therefore, they held that the tort of simple conspiracy is not complete without pecuniary loss.[132] Further-

---

[124] It may be useful as a tort where previous tort liability has been removed see e.g. *Lonrho v Fayed (no. 5)* [1993] 1 WLR 1489 where Dillon LJ suggested that though the tort of maintenance had been abolished by s.14 Criminal Law Act 1967, the plaintiffs could use an action for simple conspiracy to attack an illegitimate instance of maintenance. Stuart-Smith LJ, however, disagreed, p. 1505.

[125] [1982] AC 173.   [126] [1987] 2 Ch 327.

[127] [1891] 2 Ch 269, CA.

[128] Now of course the claimant would have to allege actual pecuniary harm.

[129] There being a defence of justification (truth) in the tort of defamation.

[130] [1993] 1 WLR 1489.

[131] Though that tort does not protect personal reputation as such: see Ch. 7.

[132] Cane, above, n. 113, p. 103 'this qualification seems sound because it rests on a specification of the interests which the different torts are designed to protect. The elements of the tort of defamation are designed to strike a balance between the individual's interest in good

more, Dillon LJ[133] warned that the courts would deny the validity of 'some airy-fairy general reputation in the business or commercial community which is unrelated to the buying or selling or dealing with customers'.

RATIONALE

The foundation of liability for simple conspiracy is the fact that 'steps are taken in pursuance of an agreement between the defendants'.[134] The tort of simple conspiracy is an anomaly born out of a desire to monitor the oppressive abuse of economic power. That that is its true role is underlined by the need for the claimant to show not just intentional harm aimed at him, but an illegitimate purpose on the part of the defendant. Abuse of market power would appear to be a concern of any economy based on free competition. The control of monopolies and restrictive trade practices may seem central to a free market.[135] The tort of simple conspiracy is a minor weapon in the policy to promote competition, minor because it focuses on protecting private interests, though happy thereby to attack anti-competitive action.

The same can broadly[136] be said of the restraint of trade doctrine,[137] the main effect of which is to render unenforceable a contract in unreasonable restraint of trade.[138] This doctrine is the other side of the same coin as the tort. Indeed, in the days prior to statutory intervention the relationship

---

reputation and society's interest in freedom of speech and people should not be allowed to upset this balance by suing for injury to reputation in any other cause of action than defamation.' They tagged on the view that injury to feelings could also not be recovered, but this has been criticized by McGregor, see n. 37, above.

[133] [1993] 1 WLR 1489, p. 1496.   [134] Sales, above, n. 3, p. 500.

[135] Of course, at various stages in the development of an economy the exact weight afforded to the prevention of such anti-competitive practices may differ. As Whish, *Competition Law*, 3rd edn. (London: Butterworths, 1993) notes: 'competition law is an aspect of the social and economic policy of the system to which it belongs, and as such it reflects the tensions and the preoccupations of that system at any time' (p. 9).

[136] The traditional focus of the restraint doctrine has been on the attack on private interests, with the public interest, although claimed as its justification, in fact playing a shadow role. Treitel, G. H., *The Law of Contract*, 9th edn. (London: Sweet & Maxwell, 1999), p. 425: 'In the common law relating to restraint of trade, the public interest refers to legally recognized interests, and in particular to the interests of the public that a person should not be subjected to unreasonable restrictions on his freedom to work or trade. An agreement is unlikely to be invalidated because it is alleged to infringe some wider public interest e.g. because it might lead to an improper allocation of economic resources or prove inflationary.'

[137] Heydon, J. D., 'The Restraint of Trade Doctrine', 50 ALJ (1970), p. 290.

[138] Rodger, B., and MacCulloch, A., *Competition Law and Policy in the European Community and United Kingdom* (London: Cavendish, 1999), p. 21 note that in recent years this 'fairly limited doctrine' has been used by those involved in long-term contractual relationships who claim that the agreements they entered into at the start of such relationships were in

between the conspiracy tort and the restraint doctrine was highlighted in cartel and trade association cases.[139] In the cartel and trade association cases adversely affected third parties would seek redress through the tort of conspiracy while disaffected members would seek to avoid the agreement through the restraint doctrine.[140] However, judicial decisions at the turn of the nineteenth century reflected the concern of British industry over the growth of protectionism in America and Germany. There was a lack of belief in competition which fostered the growth of cartels and other restrictive practices. The courts reacted sympathetically to this development: the *Mogul* case saw the end of the threat of 'simple' conspiracy against cartels. Such a combination was easily justified. Although there were some successful applications of the restraint doctrine—indeed, as Cornish and Clark point out, when it came to labour relations a cartel would be held in restraint[141]—yet the courts appeared to be more willing to accept the argument that certain restraints were reasonable and therefore valid. This approach was highlighted in the *Nordenfelt*[142] case where a worldwide restraint was held to be valid in the circumstances. Thus Letwin has remarked: 'the *Mogul Steamship* case was decided two years before the *Nordenfelt* case: these two are among the chief reasons for the subsequent inability of the common law substantially to deter the growth of monopolies.'[143] As competition came back into favour *post*-1945 and as Parliament reacted to the domination of cartels in

---

restraint of trade because of the inequality of bargaining power see e.g. *Panoyiotou v Sony Music UK Ltd* [1994] 1 All ER 755 (where the action failed).

[139] The restraint must also seek to protect a legitimate interest, rather than simply seek to prevent competition. However, in the case of restrictive trading agreements an attempt to prevent competition *per se* may be permitted, provided the right terminology is used: in *McEllistrim v Ballymacelligot Co-Operative Agricultural and Dairy Society* [1919] AC 548, Lord Birkenhead accepted that the agreement did not seek to stop competition as such, but rather ensure 'stability in their list of customers' (p. 564). (In fact this is one of the few cases where a cartel was successfully challenged by a member.)

[140] See Simpson, F. D., 'How Far Does the Law of England Forbid Monopoly?' 41 LQR (1925) 393; Heydon, J. D., 'The Defence of Justification in Cases of Intentionally Caused Economic Loss', 20 U Tor LJ (1970) 139.

[141] In *Hilton v Eckersley* (1855) 8 E&B 47 a combination amongst masters to fix wages and conditions of employment was held void as an illegal restraint of trade 'otherwise, by simple reciprocity, the courts would have to entertain questions of trade union agreement', Cornish, W., and Clark, G. De N., *Law and Society in England 1750–1950* (London: Sweet & Maxwell, 1989), p. 265; in *Mogul* itself most of the Law Lords suggested that the agreement between the shipowners would not be enforceable at law.

[142] *Nordenfelt v Maxim Nordenfelt* [1894] AC 535.

[143] Letwin, W., 'The English Common Law Concerning Monopolies' 21 Univ Chicago LR (1954) 355, p. 382. It was at this time, and in response to the perceived weakness of common law protection that the US Anti-Trust laws were passed enabling triple damages for unlawful conspiracies in restraint of trade. Laker attempted to use the US laws to gain substantial compensation against an alleged conspiracy between IATA airlines in the USA to drive out his Skytrain business by, *inter alia*, 'predatory pricing'. In *BA v Laker* [1985] AC 58, Lord Diplock accepted that Laker would have no success with the English tort of

British manufacturing industry by enacting legislation to regulate restrictive trade practices,[144] so the common law appeared to signal that the restraint doctrine still has potential: this was the thrust of the House of Lords' decision in *Esso Petroleum Co Ltd v Harper's Garage (Stourport) Ltd*.[145]

Indeed, there have been indications of an extended protection under the restraint doctrine available to third parties, adversely affected by a restraint agreed between others. The most famous examples of these are the sporting bodies cases.[146] However, the scope of this protection is limited to the most extreme cases, to protect those whose work prospects have been affected by the monopoly power of a trade association or indeed a trade union. Whish notes:[147] 'it remains to be seen whether the courts would be prepared to go further and grant a remedy to a plaintiff whose commercial interests were harmed by a contract in restraint of trade rather than whose employment prospects were eradicated altogether.' Treitel shares in these doubts, noting 'it seems unlikely that a buyer of goods or services could at common law get an injunction against

simple conspiracy on the same alleged facts, given the defendants' predominant purpose was self-interest.

[144] Restrictive Trade Practices Act 1956, to attack cartels, price-fixing, and market division. By this time, the Monopolies Commission existed to investigate structural monopoly. There was a consolidation of subsequent amending legislation in the RTPA 1976, with a Resale Prices Act and Restrictive Practices Court Act in the same year. Investigation of anti-competitive practices was introduced in the Competition Act 1980. Now of course see the Competition Act 1998.

[145] Although Lord Wilberforce stressed that the mere allegation that a contract limits a trader's freedom of action will not always raise the doctrine, the House of Lords were willing to accept that the restraint doctrine is not simply limited to its typical territory of employment contracts and sale of business goodwill. Rather 'the classification must remain fluid and the categories can never be closed'. As Atiyah, remarked 'by the 1960s the courts were ready to take the plunge and re-enter the waters of restrictive agreements even as a matter of common law', Atiyah, P., *The Rise and Fall of Freedom of Contract* (Oxford: OUP, 1979), p. 707.

[146] In *Eastham v Newcastle United FC* [1964] Ch 413 the court was asked to judge the validity of the retain and transfer system then current amongst Football League clubs. The plaintiff successfully sought a declaration that the system was in restraint of trade, the court stating that the defendants were bodies of considerable standing and repute, who would, therefore, change their system as a result of the court's decision. See also *Blackler v New Zealand Rugby Football League* [1968] NZLR 547 NZCA—declaration granted that the rules of the association that *de facto* prevented him from seeking employment oversees were void; *Buckley v Tutty* (1971) 125 CLR 353 and *Greig v Insole* 1978 1 WLR 382; *Hall v Victoria Rugby League* [1982] VR 64; *Cooke v FA, The Times*, 24 March 1972. These cases make it clear that the restraint doctrine is not tied to contract partners but may protect those subject to a restraint imposed by a cartel/trade association. Note also *Pharmaceutical Society of GB v Dickson* [1970] AC 403, the professional body of registered pharmacists proposed a new ethical rule to restrict the range of goods which could be sold in existing pharmacies. Although the relevant code of practice was not a contract, Wilberforce J had regard to the practical working of the restraint, rather than its legal form; see also the controversial decision in *Nagle v Feilden* [1966] 2 QB 633.

[147] Above, n. 135, p. 56.

a price-ring merely because it operated to his prejudice'.[148] Moreover, a declaration may be all that is achieved,[149] though injunctions have been awarded against professional associations which control the freedom to trade or work.[150]

If the real role of simple conspiracy arises from the need to monitor oppressive abuse of economic power, it becomes apparent that the tort is largely overshadowed by EC and national competition laws.

So the problem of powerful and abusive conspiracies appears to be addressed by Articles 81 and 82 of the Treaty of Rome (formerly Articles 85 and 86).[151] Article 81 prohibits agreements which have the effect of restricting or distorting competition while Article 82 prohibits an abuse of a dominant market position (with collective dominance through oligopolies apparently also covered).[152] Of course, to fall within the Treaty provisions the anti-competitive practice must have an EC dimension and impact on the single market: trade between the member states must be affected.

The effect of these Articles is to create a new framework for bureaucratic intervention: victims of such anti-competitive practices can complain to the Commission which can order an end to any infringement and impose fines. However, the most interesting fact about these Articles, in relation to the economic torts, is the fact that they are directly effective.[153] Therefore, they could give rise to civil liability, leading to the possible award of damages, a proposition accepted by Lord Diplock in

---

[148] Above, n. 136, p. 429.

[149] Should the courts decide to take a more interventionist, pro-competition stance with the restraint doctrine, especially in its protection of third parties, then the range of remedies for that doctrine will have to be carefully limited, to avoid a new form of *de facto* economic tort liability, in conflict with *Allen v Flood* (the view of Foster J in *Cooke v FA*, *The Times*, 24 March 1972). However, Lord Denning in *Hadmor v Hamilton* [1982] ICR 112, when plaintiff's counsel suggested that the Court of Appeal 'introduce' a new tort of unjustifiable interference in restraint of trade, commented that he would leave this point until another day. Note Heydon, above, n. 92, would seek more coercive relief.

[150] Lord Upjohn in *Pharmaceutical Society of GB v Dickson* [1970] AC 403, p. 433; Slade J in *Grieg v Insole* appeared to believe he had the power to grant an injunction in a non-contractual arrangement. An interlocutory injunction was awarded by Jacob J in *Newport Association FC Ltd v Football Association of Wales Ltd* [1995] 2 All ER 87 on the basis that the doctrine gave rise to a 'cause of action'. This cannot, with respect, be right. Some of these cases involve bodies with a high public profile, leading one judge to suggest that judicial review might be more appropriate: *R v Jockey Club ex p RAM Racecourses* [1993] 2 All ER 225, p. 243. However, cf. *ex p Aga Khan* [1993] 1 WLR 909, p. 933.

[151] Sales, above, n. 3, p. 501; n. 30 notes that this dual prohibition (of cartels and abuse of a dominant position) avoids the criticism that Lord Diplock aimed at simple conspiracy, viz. 'that a single large commercial entity may be capable of causing more harm acting alone than a number of small entities acting together'.

[152] *Societa Italiano Vetro v Commission* (Italian Flat Glass) Cases T-68, 77 & 78 (1989) [1992] ECR II-1403; [1992] 5 CMLR 302.

[153] *Belgische Radio Television v SABAM* Case 127/73 [1974] ECR 51; [1974] 2 CMLR 238.

Garden Cottage Food Ltd v Milk Marketing Board[154] or an injunction, should damages be inadequate.[155]

A major uncertainty is as to how such an action in tort should be framed. Lord Denning suggested that the Articles gave rise to new torts which he christened 'undue restriction of competition within the Common Market' and 'abuse of a dominant position within the Common Market'.[156] This view has found little judicial favour. Hoskins[157] has suggested that the scope of the 'EC torts' could be limited by incorporating them into the general tort of unlawful interference with trade (the EC contravention providing the unlawful means). He believes that the use of unlawful interference with trade as a 'host' tort would provide 'a more discriminating cause of action . . . since liability there requires an intention on the part of the defendant to harm the plaintiff'. However, it is extremely unlikely that this suggestion will prove acceptable. For Jones[158] 'none of [the economic torts] really gets to the heart of the economic concepts underlying the competition rules'.[159] The requirement of intentional harm in particular means that the tort of unlawful interference with trade is 'under-inclusive' and its use as host would, therefore, fail to meet EC obligations. Whish[160] notes 'there is a possibility that a requirement of super-added fault as a determinant of liability to damages could in itself be inconsistent with Community law'.

[154] Lord Diplock (giving the main speech) indicated that damages were also available to victims in the national courts, at least under Article 86 (now Article 82). Lord Wilberforce dissented, asserting that an interlocutory proceeding was inappropriate for such a important issue: he appeared to favour the view that only an injunction would be appropriate. Parker LJ in *Bourgoin SA v MAFF* [1986] QB 716 stated *obiter* that damages would be available in an action based on Article 86, while in *Plessey Co plc v General Electric Co plc and Siemens* [1990] ECC 384 Morritt J asserted that Article 85 infringements (now Article 81) could also give rise to civil liability. See also *An Bord Bainne Co-operative Ltd v Milk Marketing Board* [1984] 1 CMLR 519; *Cutsforth v Mansfield Inns* [1986] 1 WLR 558 the court held it to be clear that Article 85 gave rise to a cause of action in the member states.

[155] Though this has been little used to date. In *Argyll Group v Distillers Co plc* [1986] 1 CMLR 764, Court of Session, an injunction was refused as there was no arguable case that a proposed merger would be an infringement of Article 86 (now Article 82). See also *Budgett v British Sugar* noted (1979) 4 EL Rev 417; *Iberian UK Ltd v BPB Industries plc* [1996] 2 CMLR 601.

[156] In *Application des Gaz v Falks Veritas Ltd* [1974] Ch 381. Support for the 'new tort' theory can be found in Staines, M., 'The Right to Sue in Ireland for violation of the EEC Rules on Competition', 2 Legal Studies of European Integration (1977) 53 and in Jones, C., *Private Enforcement of Antitrust Law* (Oxford: Oxford University Press, 1999).

[157] Hoskins, M., 'Garden Cottage Revisited: the Availability of Damages in the National Courts for Breach of the EEC Competition Rules' 13 ECLR (1992) 257. And see Steiner, J., 'How to Make the Action Suit the Case: Domestic Remedies for Breach of EEC Law' 12 Eur L Rev (1987) 102.   [158] Above, n. 156, p. 118.

[159] Though he acknowledges that they may be useful at times.

[160] Whish, R., 'The Enforcement of EC Competition Law in the Domestic Courts' [1994] 2 ECLR 60, p. 65. Jones (above, n. 156) comments that the view 'that EC antitrust provisions can *only* give rise to an action for damages where they form the underpinnings (e.g. unlaw-

Rather, it is Lord Diplock's 'breach of statutory duty' theory which is most likely to prove acceptable for framing tort liability based on these Articles. Lord Diplock categorized breach of Article 86 (now Article 82) as breach of a statutory duty (i.e. breach of the duty under the European Communities Act 1972, to observe enforceable community rights) 'imposed not only for the purpose of promoting the economic prosperity of the Common Market but also for the benefit of private individuals to whom loss or damage is caused by a breach of the duty'. The same principle could be applied to breach of Article 81. Of course, concern has been expressed as to the possible indeterminate nature of liability based on such a statutory tort, as it would appear that the claimant has only to show a factual link between the breach and his loss.[161] Moreover, there would be major problems for the court in analysing the relevant market to find whether the causal link is proved.[162] Such suggestions raise 'floodgate arguments'.[163]

The need to resolve the nature of this cause of action (and its extent) in competition claims is even more pressing, in light of the Competition Act 1998.[164] This has reshaped national competition laws, first enacted in 1956,[165] in line with the main EC competition rules. So new controls are introduced 'modelled essentially on Articles 85 and 86' (now Articles 81 and 82).[166] The Act creates Chapter I prohibitions in respect of concerted practices implemented in the UK the object or effect of which distort competition within the UK[167] and Chapter II prohibitions to cover an abuse (by an undertaking or undertakings) of a dominant position within

---

fulness) of a narrow and unrelated domestic head of claim clearly is an even more flagrant case of superimposing domestic rules on directly effective Community rights than was struck down in *Dekker* ([1990] ECR I-3941) or *Factortame III* ([1996] ECR I–1029). This does considerable violence to the principle of supremacy of Community law.'

[161] See Whish, above, n. 160, p. 64 and Hoskins, M., 'Garden Cottage Revisited: the Availability of Damages in the National Courts for Breach of the EEC Competition Rules' 13 ECLR (1992) 257 who notes (p. 260): 'the nature of anti-competitive behaviour is that it affects the proper operation of the market. Thus, in many cases, the number of people and companies affected by anti-competitive behaviour would indeed be indeterminate.'

[162] Hoskins, above, n. 157, rejects a test of remoteness—reasonably foreseeable—to overcome this difficulty: 'it could be said that a reasonable man could foresee that anti-competitive behaviour which affected the normal operation of the market would cause very wide scale loss to all those who operated within that market. Such foreseeable loss could be said to extend right down the chain of causation to ultimate consumers' (p. 261).

[163] Whish, above, n. 160, p. 65.

[164] In force, 1 March 2000.

[165] For the history of the development of UK competition law see Rodger, B., and MacCulloch, A., *Competition Law and Policy in EC and UK* (London: Cavendish, 1999). Concern over the activities of trade associations led to the Restrictive Trade Practices Act 1956. This was followed by the Fair Trading Act 1973, RTPA 1976 and Competition Act 1980. The Competition Act 1998 repeals the 1976 Act and the Competition Act 1980.

[166] Ibid. 23.

[167] s. 2 Competition Act 1998.

the United Kingdom.[168] Though the Act is silent on the matter,[169] it was the clear view of the Government that the Act should confer rights on third parties to sue for breaches of Chapter I and Chapter II prohibitions in the civil courts.[170] 'This is a major development in United Kingdom competition law enforcement which under the previous framework was almost always exclusively the preserve of the administrative bodies involved.'[171] But the question still remains as to the shape such civil liability will take.[172]

CONCLUSION

What the common law appears to have done, mistrusting group power, is use conspiracy/combination as a crude (and arbitrary) method of attacking an abuse of market power (in its widest sense).[173] Combine the power of a conspiracy with illegitimate purpose and the courts are willing to protect the victim of this group power: 'effectively it [simple conspiracy] creates liability for the abuse of the right to combine.'[174] So there are occasions when the common law accepted that the defendants' action is so unjustified/unfair that they should be liable. However, any intervention

[168] s.18 Competition Act 1998.

[169] The normal principles of statutory interpretation demand that the obligation or prohibition created be for the benefit or protection of a particular class of individuals or that a public right is created and the plaintiff suffers particular damage (see *Cutler v Wandsworth* [1949] AC 398; *Lonrho v Shell* [1982] AC 173) s.2(4) provides that a prohibited agreement is void.

[170] Lord Simon of Highbury 'we are including provision to facilitate rights of private action in the courts for damages' (Hansard HL Vol. 582 col. 1148). See also Turner, J., 'The UK Competition Act and Private Rights' 20 ECLR (1999) 62 who points out that under s.60, the court must determine issues consistently with EC law and that Articles 85 and 86 (now Articles 81 and 82) are directly effective.

[171] Rodger and MacCulloch, above, n. 165, p. 51.

[172] It is likely that the courts will not be able to continue for much longer with the cautious approach they have so far displayed in cases where Articles 85 and 86 (now Articles 81 and 82) have been raised (e.g. though damages can be recovered for breach of Article 85—now Article 81 and its UK equivalent, Chapter I—the Court of Appeal in *Gibbs Mew v Gemmell* [1998] EuLR 588 held that they cannot be claimed by a party to an agreement, since such a party would have to rely on its own illegality and see *Crehan v Courage LT* unreported 27 May 1999 in which a reference on this issue was made to the European Court). As far as private litigation is concerned, the fact that confidential information acquired by the Director-General of Fair Trading may be made available for civil proceedings (see ss.55–6 Competition Act 1998) and that the Director's findings are binding (s.58 (1)) will obviously prove useful.

[173] Thus Lord Wright commented in *Crofter v Veitch* [1942] AC 435, p. 468 that the tort of simple conspiracy may owe its existence to the view of the common law 'that there is always the danger that any combination may be oppressive'.

[174] Elias, P., and Ewing, K., 'Economic Torts and Labour Law: Old Principles and New Liabilities' 41 CLJ (1982) 321, p. 325.

was aimed at protecting the individual and his private interests: the courts have on the whole rejected the role of regulating competition in the public interest, just as they have also rejected a general power to adjudicate on unfair commercial practices. This is summarized in the often quoted remark of Fry LJ in *Mogul Steamship Co v McGregor* (at Court of Appeal level) that 'to draw a line between fair and unfair competition . . . passes the power of the courts'.[175] Of course, the courts could have determined on a more interventionist approach as appeared to happen in America with the rise of the *prima facie* tort doctrine.

Simple conspiracy exists but is of little practical value. It presents the opportunity for protection only in the most extreme cases of hostility and vendetta. It will rarely be useful for victims of others' use of market power. A tort based on reviewing the interests and motivation of only the parties before the court would appear of little value in the process of market regulation. In the modern world it is the national and European competition laws that regulate restrictive practices and abuse of market power. This regulation is based on the public interest and administrative as well as judicial regulation. It is in this area that the courts will become embroiled in competition policy, though only as it relates to anti-trust matters. They will have to cast aside the principle of *Mogul* and the caution of the restraint of trade policy (though cases on the EC equivalents in Articles 81 and 82 show that this will not be an easy process for them[176]).

Moreover, as an 'anomalous' economic tort, 'simple' conspiracy offers no clues as to the true potential of the other economic torts.

---

[175] (1989) 28 QBD 598, pp. 625–6; a matter for Parliament according to Lord Wright, *Crofter v Veitch* [1942] AC 435, p. 472. The French courts, however, developed the concept of 'concurrence déloyale'.

[176] As is evidenced in the cases discussed in n. 172, above.

3

Inducing Breach of Contract

HISTORY AND COMPLEXITY OF THE TORT[1]

The common law protected interference with the master–servant relationship from medieval times. Thus the action for enticement of a servant contained in the Statute of Labourers 1349[2] sought to deal with the problem of labour shortage, following the devastating effect of the Black Death. However, modern liability for inducing breach of contract dates from 1853 and the decision in *Lumley v Gye*.[3] There, a singer who had an exclusive performing contract with the plaintiff was persuaded by the defendant to break her contract and sing for him instead. The court, Coleridge J dissenting,[4] held that the defendant's action, with knowledge of the plaintiff's contract,[5] was tortious. The decision eventually 'freed the old enticement action from its roots in status relations',[6] though it took some thirty years for it to become established[7] that the principle extended

---

[1] See in particular Sayre, F. B., 'Inducing Breach of Contract', 36 Har L Rev (1923) 663; Weir, T., *Economic Torts* (Oxford: Clarendon Press,1997); and Lord Wedderburn, *Clerk and Lindsell on Torts*, 18th edn. (London: Sweet & Maxwell, 2000), ch. 24—Economic Torts.

[2] See Jones, G., 'Per Quod Servitium Amisit' 74 LQR (1958) 39. This statutory action in effect strengthened an earlier common law action, developed from the writ of trespass for abducting a servant. There was an associated tort of harbouring a servant. Note Partlett, D., 'From Victorian Operas to Rock and Rap' 66 Tulane L Rev (1991–2) 771, p. 785, *Lumley v Gye* 'was an equally well-suited solution to the farm labor shortage that troubled the American South during the Reconstruction. The Civil War and the emancipation of slaves in the American South had the same effect as the plague had produced in England.' Sayre (above, n. 1) sees the origins of the tort in the recognition in Roman law of a cause of action of a paterfamilias, based on injury to family, slaves, or other household members.

[3] [1853] 2 E&B 216; there was parallel action brought against the singer herself: *Lumley v Wagner* (1852) 42 ER 687.

[4] Partlett, above, n. 2., p. 779, n. 34 comments: 'the very real debate between legal formalism and broad substantive judicial activism is well-exemplified in this case.'

[5] Note, however, that at the trial the jury subsequently found that the defendant did not have knowledge of the plaintiff's contract and was not therefore liable: Brazier, M., and Murphy, J., *Street on Torts*, 10th edn. (London: Butterworths, 1999), p. 148.

[6] Danforth, J., 'Tortious Interference with Contract: A Reassertion of Society's Interest in Commercial Stability and Contractual Integrity' 81 Col LR (1981) 1491, p. 1495; Erle J suggested a 'larger doctrine' according to Brett J in *Bowen v Hall* (1881) 6 QBD 333, Crompton and Wightman JJ based their decision on the narrower ground of an extension to the enticement action. Palmer, V., 'A Comparative Study (from a Common Law Perspective) of the French Action for Wrongful Interference with Contract' 40 Am J of Comp Law (1992) 297 notes a similar development in French law at about this time, again extending protection against enticement (debauchage) of menial servants to enticement of skilled workers in the fashion industry and those in the entertainment industry (like Miss Wagner).

[7] As Cornish, W. R., and Clark, G. de N., *Law and Society in England, 1750–1950* (London:

to the knowing procurement of all kinds of contracts.[8] Although malice appeared to be an important issue in the judgments in *Lumley v Gye* and *Bowen v Hall*[9] the inclusion of this ingredient in the tort was rejected by Lord Macnaghten in *Quinn v Leathem*.[10] This was in line with the late nineteenth-century distaste for inquiry into the subjective state of mind, for liability purposes.[11] However, at one point it appeared that the tort would provide protection against interference with prospective contracts, as the Court of Appeal in *Temperton v Russell*[12] were prepared to extend the tort to protect against persuasion not to contract. Though this was later rejected by the House of Lords in *Allen v Flood*[13]—Lord Herschell stressing the 'chasm' between inducing breach and merely persuading another not to enter into a contract—*Temperton v Russell* had a profound effect on the development of the tort in America, leading to the protection of commercial expectations generally.[14]

All contracts, then, are protected by this tort. Indeed, it has even been accepted that the tort applies to contracts affecting land, though it is apparent that principles developed in land law and the tort of inducing breach of contract may collide. A contract, registered as a land charge may have priority over an earlier, unregistered deal, but that would not prevent an action in this tort, provided the circumstances of the later transaction met its requirements. Thus, Gardner[15] warns that the tort could 'provide a means for completely circumventing conventional property law, in which there are known proprietary obligations of defined content'.

Sweet & Maxwell, 1989), note, pp. 329–30 'the notion of such a tort had emerged in *Lumley v Gye*, but it had scarcely flourished in face of the disapprobation of Willes J and several other judges'. This was due to the perceived erosion of the privity doctrine.

[8] In *Lumley v Gye*, the majority of the four judges categorized the singer as a 'servant'. *Bowen v Hall* (1881) 6 QBD 333 (Lord Coleridge CJ dissenting) and *Temperton v Russell* [1893] 1 QB 715 removed the doubts that the doctrine of *Lumley v Gye* would be extended to include contracts where no personal services were involved. For a review of this development see Carpenter, C., 'Interference with Contract Relations' 41 Har L Rev (1928) 728.

[9] Which stressed that malicious interference, rather than enticement, was the foundation of the tort.

[10] [1901] AC 495, p. 510.

[11] Partlett, above, n. 2, p. 781, n. 40 notes that the focus on the vague concept of malice did not fit well with emerging case law 'in an era when firm rules were favoured and the orthodoxy was higher formalism'. This was articulated most strongly in *Allen v Flood*. The exception to this was of course the tort of simple conspiracy.

[12] (1893) 1 QB 715.   [13] [1898] AC 1.

[14] In *Temperton v Russell* [1893] 1 QB 715 Lord Esher MR was unable to see the distinction between inducing breach of contract and inducing people not to enter into contracts or deal with the plaintiff. See *Brekkes v Catel* [1972] Ch 105, 114; *Gersham v Manitoba Vegetable Producers Marketing Board* (1977) 69 DLR (3d) 114, pp. 117–20.

[15] Gardner, S.,'The Proprietary Effect of Contractual Obligations under *Tulk v Moxhay* and *De Mattos v Gibson*' 98 LQR (1982) 279, p. 322 and see Smith, R. J., 'The Economic Torts: their Impact on Real Property' 41 Conv NS (1977) 318.

Though the tort has been around since 1853,[16] it is surrounded by uncertainty and complexity. In 1923, Sayre commented that the tort was still an 'ingénue' in the law whose characteristics and limitations had yet to be determined or agreed upon.[17] Some seventy years later, Ralph Gibson LJ[18] referred to it as a 'comparatively new tort of which the precise boundaries should be established from case to case'. Indeed, the uncertainty surrounding the scope of the tort even led to the plaintiffs in *Lubenham Fidelities Co Ltd v S. Pembrokshire DC*[19] alleging *inter alia* (without success) that the defendant was liable for *negligently* causing interference with his contract.

The analysis of this tort has been less than rigorous. As we have seen, this is partly because it is usually alleged in interlocutory proceedings during industrial action (indeed, the tort was a useful tool against the emerging trade unions). But a further reason for the uncertain ambit and the overcomplicated judicial approach to the tort is the misconception surrounding the extent of the tort, compared to the area covered by the wider tort of unlawful interference with trade. This would appear to emanate from the impressive, but as Weir reminds us, *extempore*, judgment of Jenkins LJ in *Thomson v Deakin*.[20] There he sought to identify 'varieties' of the tort, to include direct and indirect interference with a contract as well as the classic form of inducing breach. Consequently, it has become common to analyse the tort as involving all intentional harm by a third party to the claimant's contract, as if it mattered not whether that interference is by way of persuasion or prevention. Thus it is not uncommon to find the tort paraphrased as interference with contract.[21]

Yet this approach is fundamentally flawed. The tort of inducing breach needs to be clearly limited to cases where the defendant directly induces breach of contract. All other so-called varieties of the tort are not focused on breach at all. Rather, liability for direct and indirect intervention in contracts is part of the wider tort of unlawful interference with trade. Here, it is not interference with contract that is the key aspect, but rather the intentional use of unlawful means to harm the economic interests of the claimant. Rather than protecting contract rights, these 'varieties' condemn the use of unlawful means. Failure to realize and apply this has led, in Weir's words, to 'baleful consequences'.[22]

---

[16] *Lumley v Gye* [1853] 2 E&B 216.   [17] Above, n. 1, p. 671.

[18] *Millar v Bassey* [1994] Entertainment and Media Law Reports 44.

[19] (1986) 33 BLR 39, CA.

[20] [1952] Ch 646.

[21] Neill LJ termed it 'direct interference with contractual relations' in *Middlebrook Mushrooms Ltd v TGWU* [1993] ICR 612; Hoffmann J termed it 'interference with the plaintiff's contractual relations' in *Law Debenture Trust Corp v Ural Caspian Oil Corp* [1993] 1 WLR 138, p. 148.

[22] Weir, above, n. 1, p. 41.

This chapter attempts to build on this analysis of the tort and distinguish it from similar tortious liability which in fact arises from the general tort of unlawful interference with trade. To this end two categories of liability—both often claimed to arise from *Lumley v Gye*—are identified and clearly separated. These categories are: classic inducement to breach liability and unlawful interference liability. As will be seen, unless these two categories are separated, error and the tendency for overbroad liability creep in. However, though these categories focus on different elements for liability, the need for coherence in the (limited) control by the common law of excessive competitive behaviour demands that the intention required for the tort of inducing breach of contract be the same as that required for the tort of unlawful interference with trade.[23] By accepting these two propositions, the endless citation of irreconcilable and misunderstood dicta in litigation surrounding this tort[24] would be avoided.

Category 1: Classic inducing Breach of Contract

INGREDIENTS

The classic form of the tort established by *Lumley v Gye* is direct inducement[25] to breach of contract. It was defined by Jenkins LJ in *Thomson v Deakin*[26] as: 'direct persuasion, procurement or inducement applied by the third party to the contract breaker, with knowledge of the contract and the intention of bringing about its breach.'[27] Thus procurement, knowledge, intention, and actual breach are the vital ingredients. Though Porter J in *De Jetley Marks v Greenwood*[28] asserted that only breaches that went to the root of the contract were actionable in the tort, Lord Evershed MR was not convinced of this in *Thomson v Deakin*.[29] Inducing breach of a negative covenant e.g. a restrictive covenant in an employment contract is

---

[23] This is further discussed in Ch. 10.

[24] *Millar v Bassey* [1994] Entertainment and Media LR 44 is a clear example of this confusion and tangled *dicta*.

[25] Where the inducement is by a servant of the contract breaker, acting within the scope of his authority or employment, the servant is not liable for this tort (at least if he acts *bona fide*) as he is acting as the *alter ego* of the contract breaker: *Said v Butt* [1920] 3 KB 497. This principle also protects company directors. However, the servant or agent can be liable for acts done outside their authority: see May LJ in *Lubenham v S Pembrokeshire DC* 33 BLR 39, p. 74.

[26] [1952] Ch 646.

[27] [1952] Ch 646, p. 694.

[28] [1936] 1 All ER 872.

[29] [1952] Ch 646, p. 690. Interestingly, Weir, above, n. 1, p. 75 is willing to acknowledge that formalism may lead to liability where it should not and cites as a possible answer to this the German view that not every induced breach of contract is relevant, but only breaches of principal obligations.

covered by the tort: see *Rickless v United Artists Corporation*[30] where all
that remained of the contract in question (which had otherwise been fully
performed) was the negative covenant. As with all the economic torts,
damage must result. It would appear that the claimant has to show that
he was able and willing to perform the contract[31] and that the contract
breaker cannot himself sue the inducer.[32] Unlike the other 'varieties' of
this tort identified by Jenkins LJ, no unlawful means on the part of the
defendant are necessary, in order to persuade or induce the contract
breaker to act. Given this, the tort is subject to an uncertain defence of
justification. As that defence can only be understood and defined in relation to the rationale of the tort, the concept of justification is dealt with,
together with the discussion of the tort's rationale, below.

Procurement

This direct form of the tort requires an element of inducement, persuasion, or other form of procurement. No individual contact, however, is
necessary: in *Greig v Insole*,[33] the resolutions and press statements made
by the cricket governing body were inducements. Communication may
also be through the agent of the inducer.[34]

Moreover, there must be direct persuasion: 'if the case is to fall within
the *Lumley v Gye* category, the persuasion has to be directed at one of the
parties to the contract.'[35] Where the persuasion or inducement is brought
to bear on strangers to the claimant's contract[36] the effect on the
claimant's contracting party is indirect. And where indirect means are
used, the better view is that the tort of unlawful interference with trade is
involved, requiring unlawful means to achieve the ultimate breach of the
claimant's contract. For Neill LJ in *Middlebrook Mushrooms Ltd v TGWU*[37]
it was important that the *Lumley v Gye* principle should not be extended
outside its proper limits.

---

[30] [1988] QB 40.

[31] *Long v Smithson* (1918) 88 LJ KB 223.

[32] See Upjohn J in *Boulting v Association of Cinematograph, Television and Allied Technicians*
[1963] 2 QB 606, pp. 639–40 and May LJ in *Lubenham v S Pembrokeshire DC* 33 BLR 39, p. 76.
However, where indirect attack on the contract is involved see *Dimbleby v NUJ* [1984] 1 WLR
427. Here the 'piggy in the middle' was allowed to sue and see *Hersees of Woodstock Ltd v
Goldstein* (1963) 38 DLR (2d) 449.

[33] [1978] 1 WLR 302.

[34] *Daily Mirror v Gardner* [1968] 2 QB 762.

[35] Neill LJ in *Middlebrook Mushrooms Ltd v TGWU* [1993] IRLR 232, p. 235. Cf. the views of
Hoffmann LJ in the same case, that a procurement is 'direct' if the defendant is responsible
for the effective pressure. Such an analysis is fraught with dangers.

[36] Wedderburn, above, n. 1, para 24–58 summarizes the orthodox distinction as 'whether
the inducement was directed to strangers to the contract or to a party to it'.

[37] [1993] ICR 612, p. 620, CA.

'Mere advice' is not sufficient to constitute persuasion.[38] For Lord Evershed MR in *Thomson v Deakin*[39] 'a mere statement of or a drawing of attention of the party addressed to the state of the facts as they were' would not lead to liability. Hart and Honoré[40] define advice as drawing attention to facts 'which show how eligible or desirable a given course of action is'; whereas inducement '[makes] a given course of action more eligible or desirable in the eyes of the other than it would otherwise have been, or seem more eligible or desirable than it really is'. Indeed, this distinction between advice and persuasion attempts to limit the potential restriction on free speech posed by the tort, a fact acknowledged by Neill LJ in *Middlebrook Mushrooms Ltd v TGWU*,[41] where there is a passing reference to Article 10 of the ECHR.[42]

However, at times it may be difficult to distinguish between advice and persuasion,[43] particularly where the tort is alleged in an industrial action setting. Thus though in *Thomson v Deakin*[44] a notification to the plaintiff's contractual partner, Bowater, that the plaintiff was boycotted was treated as mere 'information', the House of Lords in *Stratford v Lindley* treated a similar notification as an inducement, Lord Pearce asserting: 'the fact that an inducement to break a contract is couched as an irresistible embargo rather than in terms of seduction does not make it any the less an inducement.' In *Square Grip Reinforcement Co Ltd v Macdonald*[45] Lord Milligan noted that if the defendant were shown to be 'desperately anxious' that something should happen, then it is likely that he will have gone beyond mere advice, compared to the typical disinterested adviser. So that 'a remark which might in the former case have been construed as an inducement would fall to be treated as of relatively minor importance' in the latter example. Thus, if there is a trade dispute in the background any

---

[38] Note, however, the view of Bagshaw, R., ch. 7 'Inducing Breach of Contract', in *Oxford Essays in Jurisprudence*, 4th Series, ed. Horder, J. (Oxford: OUP, 2000). He bases his view on an analogy between contract rights and property rights so 'directing a party's attention to a reason for not performing of which the party was previously unaware does damage the "property" created by a contract, since it may well make the party less willing to perform. Thus if advice is given with the knowledge that it is likely to make a party unwilling to perform his or her contract then it is arguable that this should be actionable unless justified' (p. 144).

[39] [1952] Ch 646, p. 686.

[40] Hart, H. L. A. and Honoré, T., *Causation in the Law*, 2nd edn. (Oxford: Clarendon Press, 1985), p. 54.

[41] [1993] ICR 612, p. 620, CA.

[42] And of course clearly present in the provisos to liability contained in the Restatement (Second) of Torts s.767. However, rather than see it as a justification it should be seen as outside the tort.

[43] Coleridge J in *Lumley v Gye* complained that 'to draw a line between advice, persuasion, enticement and procurement is practically impossible' (1853) 118 ER 749, p. 762.

[44] [1952] Ch 646, p. 686.

[45] [1968] SLT 65.

advice or information given by defendants connected to the workers in dispute to the dispute employer or his suppliers/customers is likely to be adjudged persuasion.[46]

Persuasion, then, is the necessary link between the broken contract and the defendant, a third party to that contract: 'if I persuade someone, whether by stick or carrot, to conduct himself at variance with his duties under a contract, I have altered his conduct, I have perverted him, or converted him to my use as a means of inflicting harm which would otherwise not occur.'[47] No 'extra' unlawful means are necessary for liability. Where the real issue is not that the defendant has persuaded the claimant's partner into breach but rather has prevented the performance of the claimant's contract, a different focus for the analysis of potential liability follows. Prevention may be the result of acceptable (if ruthless) competitive practice: an example of such being a deliberate cornering of the market, in order to prevent a contract from being performed.[48] For this reason, where prevention is concerned, independently unlawful means are required for liability, and that liability will arise from the general tort of unlawful interference with trade. This crucial distinction between the two categories has not always been clearly realized by the courts: Beldam LJ in *Millar v Bassey* commenting that he failed to see the distinction between causing and procuring.[49] Yet the difference is fundamental to a clear understanding of this tort and its proper scope. Prevention, to give rise to liability, requires unlawful means; persuasion to breach, effectively directed at the claimant's contractual partner, requires no separate unlawful act on the defendant's part for liability to ensue. As Jenkins LJ noted in *Thompson v Deakin*[50] direct persuasion, with the requisite knowledge and intention, 'is clearly to be regarded as a wrongful act in itself'.[51]

Knowledge and intention

Liability under the tort requires both that the defendant know of the existence of the claimant's contract and that he have an intention to cause a

---

[46] *Union Traffic Ltd v TGWU* [1989] IRLR 127, p. 130. However, note the view of Megaw LJ in *Camellia Tanker Ltd v ITF* [1976] ICR 274, p. 296 'it would be unjust and unfair to allow an injunction to be granted against the defendant on the basis, not of direct evidence, but of an inference as to his past and future conduct, without taking into account his own categorical denial of such conduct'.

[47] Weir, above, n. 1, p. 34.

[48] *Torquay Hotel v Cousins* [1969] 2 Ch 106, p. 138.

[49] [1994] EMLR 44, CA.

[50] [1952] Ch 646, p. 694.

[51] Bagshaw, R., 'Can the Economic Torts be Unified?' 18 OJLS (1998) 729, p. 735 finds it difficult to accept that 'the plaintiff has some interest in a contracting party not being corrupted which is separate from his interest in obtaining performance' but the tort is based on this premise, as Weir implies in *Economic Torts*, above, n. 1, esp. p. 35.

breach of that contract. Obviously these ingredients are connected, forming a 'twofold' requirement.[52] Slade J in *Greig v Insole*[53] asserted that the defendant's ignorance of the precise terms of the contract may, in particular circumstances, enable him to satisfy the court that he did not have the necessary intent. However, he went on to stress that ignorance alone would not suffice to show an absence of intent.

(i) Knowledge of contract

There must be knowledge of the contract which the defendant seeks to persuade or induce[54] the claimant's partner to breach. 'If the *Lumley v Gye* tort intended to offer a special degree of protection to contract interests, the focus on knowledge of the contract interests is, of course, wholly understandable.'[55] An honest doubt whether a contract exists should be sufficient to avoid liability,[56] though not a mistake as to 'the legal result of known facts'.[57]

Though Wedderburn has noted[58] that in *Thomson v Deakin* and earlier cases 'the demand for full knowledge of the contract broken was often strict', it has become clear since that it is not necessary to have knowledge of the precise terms, provided the defendant knew of its existence.[59] Indeed, the more modern tendency in cases involving industrial action is to find presumed knowledge sufficient (at least for interlocutory purposes).[60] The House of Lords in *Stratford v Lindley*[61] (1965) were prepared to grant interlocutory injunctions even though the Court of Appeal found that the plaintiff had not shown that the defendants knew of the relevant terms of the plaintiff's contracts. The House of Lords held that the requisite knowledge lay in the fact that the contractual requirement in issue 'must have been obvious to them' and it was 'reasonable to infer' that they knew that they would cause a breach of those contracts.[62] This concept of deemed knowledge has been applied again and again in

---

[52] Lord Diplock in *Merkur Island Shipping Corp v Laughton* [1983] AC 570, p. 608.

[53] [1978] 1 WLR 302, p. 336.

[54] *Time Plan Education Group Ltd v NUT* [1997] IRLR 457, CA.

[55] Bagshaw, above, n. 51, p. 737.

[56] An honest doubt as to which of inconsistent agreements should prevail may not be sufficient, however. There may be a need to show advice was taken and honestly believed: *Swiss Bank Corp v Lloyds Bank Ltd* [1979] Ch 549, p. 580.

[57] *Solihull MB v NUT* [1985] IRLR 211, p. 213 (Warner J).

[58] Wedderburn, K. W., 'Stratford & Sons v Lindley' 28 MLR (1965) 205, p. 206.

[59] *Time Plan Education Group Ltd v NUT* [1997] IRLR 457 Peter Gibson LJ, p. 460.

[60] Though cf. Lord Devlin in *Rookes v Barnard* [1964] AC 1129, p. 1212 (discussing the requisites for a cause of action for inducing a breach of contract): 'there must be, besides the act of inducement, knowledge by the defendant of the contract in question and of the fact that the act induced will be a breach of it .'

[61] [1965] AC 269.

[62] Lord Pearson felt that there were 'considerable indications' the defendants knew they were inducing breaches (ibid. 332).

cases concerning industrial disputes since *Stratford v Lindley*.[63] In particular experienced trade union officials are anticipated to know the normal
contract links in their industry.[64] Thus, Lord Diplock in *Merkur Island
Shipping v Laughton*[65] approved the view of Sir John Donaldson MR in the
case, that the trade union official must be deemed to have known of the
'almost certain' existence of the contracts in issue and in *Associated Newspaper Group v Wade*,[66] the Court of Appeal held that the union officers
concerned 'must have known' of the potential breaches of contract.
Indeed, in such cases, at the interlocutory stage (where the vast majority
finish) the precise contract terms may not be available even to the court
itself. In *Dimbleby v NUJ*,[67] Lord Diplock acknowledged that the evidence
before the judge as to the specific contract terms was 'scanty'. However,
since the avowed intention of the NUJ was to prevent the printing
contract from being performed at all, the likelihood of the NUJ's succeeding at the trial on this argument was small.[68]

Lord Denning MR in *Emerald Construction v Lothian*[69] even went so far
as to suggest that liability would ensue where the defendants had the
means of knowledge which they had deliberately disregarded. However,
there must be limits to the extent to which knowledge will be imputed. In
Middlebrook Mushrooms Ltd v TGWU,[70] where dismissed strikers protested
outside a supermarket supplied by their employer, the High Court
judge[71] awarded an interlocutory injunction to prevent the picketing on
the basis that there might be contracts (although there was no evidence of

---

[63] The possibility of 'constructive' knowledge was raised by the House of Lords in *British
Plastics v Ferguson* [1940] 1 All ER 479, pp. 482–3. However, Browne-Wilkinson J in *Swiss Bank
Corp v Lloyds Bank Ltd* [1979] 1 Ch 548, p. 572 was not prepared to 'bedevil' the tort with 'such
equitable refinements' (reversed on other grounds [1982] AC 584, HL).

[64] See e.g. *Merkur Island Shipping Corp v Laughton* [1983] 2 AC 570, p. 608 (Lord Diplock).

[65] [1983] 2 AC 570, pp. 608–9.

[66] [1979] ICR 664.

[67] [1984] 1 WLR 427.

[68] However, even on this analysis, Winn LJ must be wrong in *Torquay Hotel v Cousins*
[1969] 2 Ch 106 , p. 146 when he criticized the defendants for acting without investigating
whether a contract existed; though if there are circumstances creating doubts as to whether
the contract rights of another might be impaired, it might be wise to check: see *Daily Mirror
Newspapers Ltd v Gardner* [1968] 2 QB 702 and *Emerald Construction Co Ltd v Lothian* [1966]
1 WLR 691. See generally, Wedderburn, K. W., 'Inducing Breach of Contract and Unlawful
Interference with Trade' 31 MLR (1968) 440, pp. 442–3.

[69] [1966] 1 WLR 691, pp. 700–1.

[70] [1993] IRLR 232. Though Neill LJ accepted (p. 236) that 'a third party may be deemed
to know of the almost certain existence of a contract and indeed of some of its likely terms',
in this case there was no evidence of the existence of any contracts between the supermarket (being picketed) and the employer (with whom the pickets were in dispute).Given the
short shelf life of the commodity in question and the conditions of oversupply, it might well
have been that no long-term contracts or even short-term ones were involved.

[71] Blofeld J.

such) that might, in consequence, be breached by effective picketing.[72] The Court of Appeal rejected this view.[73]

(ii) Intention to induce breach

There must be an 'intentional invasion' of the claimant's contract rights: it is a key requirement of the tort. Though in *Emerald Construction v Lothian*,[74] Lord Denning asserted that a deliberate indifference to the plaintiff's contract rights could be sufficient, this has been criticized by Hughes as reducing the intention required to 'an intention to bring the contract to an end, by breach if necessary'.[75] Rather, as Lord Devlin noted in *Rookes v Barnard*[76] there must be 'an intention to cause breach'.

Of course, malice is not necessary for this tort: a desire to injure is not required. Rather, the claimant must show that his contract right was intentionally attacked—for whatever reason[77] the defendant intended to procure the breach of the claimant's contract.[78] The best way to avoid misunderstandings of the intention requirement in the tort is to focus on the notion of intended *breach* rather than intended *injury*.[79] As with the tort of unlawful interference with trade, the claimant must show he was targeted by the defendant: but with this tort the target specifically must be the claimant's contract.[80] In this sense the claimant is 'aimed at'—the contract must be breached to secure the defendant's intended goal. So an intention to procure the breach[81] must be shown; mere consequential harm, however foreseeable or even inevitable is not sufficient.

---

[72] The High Court judge appeared to accept that this could be the direct form of inducing breach of contract: that the defendants intended, through leafleting, to put pressure on the supermarket to stop dealing with the plaintiff. However, there was no direct pressure on the supermarket.

[73] [1993] IRLR 232, p. 236 Hoffmann LJ 'the court . . . is being asked to invent hypothetical contracts which the union campaign might disrupt. I do not think that it should do so.'

[74] In *Lubenham v S Pembrokeshire DC* 33 BLR 39 an allegation of negligent interference was held not to constitute the tort. In interlocutory proceedings, the intention requirement has at times been reduced to an intention to bring the contract to an end by breach, if necessary: see Diplock LJ in *Emerald Construction v Lothian* [1966] 1 WLR 691, p. 704 and note by O'Higgins, P., 'When is an employee not an employee: inducing breach of contract' (1967) CLJ 27.

[75] 86 LQR (1970) 181, p. 187.

[76] [1964] AC 1129, p. 1212.

[77] And that may be self-interest, as in *Lumley v Gye*.

[78] Beldam LJ in *Millar v Bassey* [1994] EMLR 44: '[it was not alleged in *Lumley v Gye*] that the defendant Gye had any intention to cause harm to the plaintiff beyond an intention that Miss Wagner should break her contract with him.'

[79] Weir, *Economic Torts*, above, n. 1, p. 13 appears, however, to prefer harm to breach.

[80] See Weir, above, n. 1, and Wedderburn, above, n. 1, para 24–18 'the better view may be . . . that the levels of knowledge and intention required are not in principle different in the torts of procuring breach of contract and unlawful interference'.

[81] Jenkins LJ in *Thomson v Deakin* [1952] 1 Ch 646, p. 695 'with knowledge of the contract and *the intention of bringing about its breach*' [emphasis added].

There are strong policy reasons why the law should restrict the ambit of the tort in this way. Freedom of competitive action should not be unduly restricted by liability for incidental consequences. And the ability to take effective industrial action should also not be thwarted by the prospect of limitless liability. Thus 'interference with contracts may flow from competition and is the normal and expected consequence of industrial action. It would not be right for the law to discourage competition by encouraging actions by unsuccessful competitors or to allow tort actions by those who suffer only incidentally from another person's activities.'[82] The better view must be that expressed by Henry J in *Barretts & Baird v IPCS* that those inevitably harmed by strike action are not able thereby to prove that the defendant intended to cause the breaches of contract of which they complain.[83]

It has to be admitted, however, that this definition of intention has yet to gain universal approval, so that uncertainty still surrounds the fault necessary to constitute the tort. In *Edwin Hill and Partners v First National Finance Corporation*[84] Stuart-Smith LJ did not accept the defendant's contention that the necessary intention in the tort was that the defendant's conduct should be 'aimed at' the plaintiff. His views were cited with approval by Beldam LJ in *Millar v Bassey*.[85]

Of course, it should be stressed that not only were Stuart-Smith LJ's remarks *obiter* in *Edwin Hill*, he was in fact reacting to a specific submission by the defendant's counsel. This submission was to the effect that the plaintiff must establish that the defendant's conduct was 'aimed at the plaintiff *and there is a desire to injure him*'[86] [emphasis added]. The second element in this submission is clearly wrong.[87] Similarly, there are *dicta* from Stuart-Smith LJ in *Associated British Ports Ltd v TGWU*[88] that it is not necessary in the *Lumley v Gye* tort that there should be an intention *to injure the plaintiff*.[89] However, it appears clear from later in his judgment that he is content to define intention for this tort as less onerous than that required for the tort of unlawful interference with trade, which he

---

[82] Peter Gibson LJ in *Millar v Bassey* [1994] EMLR 44.

[83] Thus *Falconer v ASLEF and NUR* [1986] IRLR 331 is wrong (H. H. Judge Henham allowed a disappointed British Rail passenger to sue successfully the unions who had called the industrial action that prevented British Rail from fulfilling its contract obligation to him).

[84] [1989] 1 WLR 225, p. 234.

[85] [1994] Entertainment and Media Law Reports 44.

[86] [1989] 1 WLR 225, p. 234.

[87] In *Smithies v NAOP* [1909] 1 KB 310, p. 316 the defendants were liable despite the express finding that they did not intend to injure the plaintiff (or the dismissed worker) but rather intended to enforce a national collective agreement. However, they clearly intended to procure breaches of the workmen's contracts.

[88] Reversed on other grounds.

[89] Though compare his views in *F v Wirral MBC* [1991] Fam 61, pp. 114–15.

accepted required 'deliberate and intended damage'.[90] On this view, to establish liability the claimant simply proves the existence of his contract and that the defendant interfered so as to impair or prevent performance with knowledge of the existence of that contract. Again, Beldam LJ in *Millar v Bassey* was willing to accept that the inevitable breach of the plaintiffs' contracts could lead to liability, even in the absence of an assertion of a specific intention to interfere with that contract.

Yet such views are hard to square with the assertion of Jenkins LJ in *Thomson v Deakin*[91] that the defendant must have acted 'with . . . the intention of bringing about [the contract's] breach'. He clearly did not envisage that a breach of contract which was merely consequential would be sufficient.[92] The sense in requiring such a tight 'nexus' between the act of the defendant and the breach is highlighted in the 'unfortunate'[93] decision of the Court of Appeal in *Millar v Bassey*. Here, the defendant had agreed to sing for a recording company who had contracted with the plaintiffs for them to provide the necessary technical and musical services for this recording. When the defendant refused to record, the plaintiffs found that their contract was worthless. Rather than sue the recording company, they sued the defendant. They argued that though the defendant had not targeted them in her (alleged) breach of contract, her deliberate action inevitably led to the recording company's breach of their contract with the plaintiffs. The Court of Appeal (Peter Gibson LJ dissenting)[94] were persuaded that it was arguable that the tort[95] only required proof of such inevitability, consequent on the defendant's deliberate action.[96] Of course this decision can also be objected to on the ground that no procurement was involved: the defendant caused a breach but did not induce it. As will be argued below, the tort does not extend beyond procurement.[97]

---

[90] Suggesting a 'difference in the nature of the intention required in the torts of inducing breach of contract and unlawful interference with trade', *Associated British Ports v TGWU* pp. 965–6.   [91] [1952] Ch 646, p. 697.

[92] See Peter Gibson LJ in *Millar v Bassey* [1994] EMLR 44 and the views of Lord Devlin in *Rookes v Barnard* [1965] AC 269.

[93] Weir, above, n. 1. The case involved a successful appeal against striking out.

[94] He highlighted the folly of this approach: 'I venture to suggest that deliberate interference with the plaintiff's contract with a view to bringing about its breach is conduct "aimed at" or "directed against" the plaintiff in the sense in which those terms have been used in the authorities.'

[95] Designated 'interference with contract' in that case.

[96] For Beldam LJ, [1994] EMLR 44, given the defendant knew of the plaintiffs' contracts that would inevitably be breached when she broke her own contract with their contract partner, 'in such circumstances it seems to me unnecessary to assert a specific intention to interfere with the performance of the appellants' contracts which must necessarily follow from her own refusal to perform her obligations [to the appellants' contract partner]'.

[97] And again, the need to show a deliberate procurement of a deliberate breach means that foreseeable or inevitable breach is not sufficient. This is discussed in greater detail in Ch. 10.

Causation of contract breach[98]

Obviously, if there is no breach of contract, the defendant cannot be liable. Therefore the tort is not committed, despite intended harm and persuasion, if the plaintiff's contract is void, nor it is submitted, where the contract is voidable.[99] Certainly, Slade J was prepared to accept this as correct in *Greig v Insole*,[100] of which Weir comments 'it is right that the plaintiff's tort claim lies only if the middleman could be sued for what the defendant got him to do'.[101] *A fortiori* it is not tortious to persuade the claimant's co-contractor to terminate the contract lawfully, even though he would not have done so, but for the defendant's intervention.

However, this aspect of the tort has become muddled in recent years. The different focal points of this tort and the general tort of unlawful interference with trade have been obscured at times, so that a 'half-way' tort of unlawful *interference* with contract has emerged (discussed in Category 2 below). Moreover, there are *dicta* that recur in recent cases that support liability for mere interference with contract, even in the absence of unlawful means. Lord Denning was keen to develop the tort beyond contract rights as such and suggested in *Torquay Hotel Co Ltd v Cousins*[102] that the time had come for the tort to be extended 'to cover deliberate and direct interference with the execution of a contract without that causing any breach'—a view with which Lord Diplock in *Merkur Island Shipping Corp v Laughton* appeared to agree.[103] Though the orthodox view is that

---

[98] Sir Thomas Bingham MR accepted in *Law Debenture Trust Corp v Ural Caspian Oil Corp Ltd* [1995] Ch 152, p. 165 that a secondary right in contract might be sufficient for the tort: 'for example, if, following default by the principal debtor, a third party induced a guarantor to dishonour his secondary obligation to pay the creditor, I would need much persuasion that the third party was not liable in tort'. However, the same would not apply where any such secondary right was contingent. In the case itself the transfer of shares to defendant number 6 by defendant number 5 (who was clearly liable for an earlier procurement of breach of the plaintiff's contract with yet another company, in relation to those shares) gave rise to no liability in tort. Though the series of transfers defeated the plaintiffs' remedy against the procurer of the breach (for a retransfer of those shares) no wrong was committed by defendant number 6. At the time of the transfer, defendant number 5 was the owner of the shares and had no contract relationship with the plaintiff.

[99] Cf. America: see Fine, B., 'An Analysis of Property Rights Underlying Tortious Interference with Contract and other Economic Relations' 50 U Chicago LR (1983) 1116.

[100] [1978] 3 All ER 449.

[101] Above, n. 1, p. 36, n. 44.

[102] [1969] 2 Ch 106, CA. He laid the ground for this startling suggestion in *Emerald Construction Co v Lothian* [1966] 1 All ER 1013, p. 1017.

[103] Lord Diplock cited with approval part of Lord Denning's judgment in *Torquay Hotel Co Ltd v Cousins* [1969] 2 Ch 106 and rewrote the essential elements of the tort, as stated by Jenkins LJ in *Thomson v Deakin* [1952] Ch 646 by substituting 'interference with performance' for 'breach'. For Weir, above, n. 1, the fruit of this 'wretched development' is *Millar v Bassey* [1994] EMLR 44, a striking out action but rightly noted by Weir as having alarming implications.

for the classic form of the tort (and in fact the only true form of this tort) a breach must arise, these *dicta* still promote uncertainty, particularly in interlocutory proceedings. So Beldam LJ in *Law Debenture Trust Corp v Ural Caspian Oil Corp Ltd*[104] built on these *dicta* to assert: 'it is an actionable tort knowingly to interfere with another's right to performance of a contractual obligation by preventing or hindering the other party from performing his obligations under the contract.' And in the New Zealand case, *Mackenzie v MacLachlan*[105] the court refused to strike out an allegation of interference with contract (based on the Lord Denning's *dicta* in *Torquay Hotel v Cousins*) where the issue related to harassment of an employee by a manager, but with no direct effect on the plaintiff's contract of employment at all! It was accepted that the harassment could amount to 'interference'.

The time has come to abandon Lord Denning's suggested extension and recognize that there is no tort—and there should be no tort—of simple interference with contract. Only if unlawful means are used could such an interference be prevented and then by means of the separate tort of unlawful interference with trade. The nature of the wrongdoing in the tort of inducing breach of contract is the procurement of a breach of the claimant's contract. For Sayre[106] to abandon the need for a breach of contract in this tort 'would be as preposterous as it would be unjust'.

Damage

The claimant must suffer damage—and more than nominal damage[107]—as a result of the intended breach of his contract.[108] In *Jones Brothers (Hunstanton) Ltd v Stevens*[109] no damage was suffered as it was clear that the plaintiff's servant (whom the defendant had continued to employ after he realized that the servant had broken his contract with the plaintiff), would not return to the plaintiff's employment.

However, it is clear that damage may be inferred if the breach be such as must 'in the ordinary course of business' inflict damage on the claimant.[110] Lost profits will often be the centre of this allegation,[111]

---

[104] [1995] Ch 152, p. 167.   [105] [1979] 1 NZLR 670, Moller J.
[106] Above, n. 8, p. 700.
[107] Lord Devlin in *Rookes v Barnard* [1964] AC 1129, p. 1212; Slade LJ in *Greig v Insole* [1978] 1 WLR 302, p. 332; Peter Gibson LJ in *Time Plan Education Group Ltd v NUT* [1997] IRLR 457, CA.
[108] Of course, where a *quia timet* injunction is sought, it will be the likelihood of harm that is important: Slade LJ in *Greig v Insole* [1978] 1 WLR 302, p. 332.   [109] [1955] 1 QB 275.
[110] Neville J in *Goldsoll v Goldman* [1914] 2 Ch 603, p. 615.
[111] Either loss on the contract in issue or loss due to prospective contracts: *Jones v Fabbi* (1973) 37 DLR (3d) 27. In *Bent's Brewery Co v Hogan* [1945] 2 All ER 570 where the trade union requested the plaintiff's pub managers to reveal confidential information on wages, the potential harm was that of having to pay increased wages.

though the claimant may also be able to recover for expenses incurred in establishing his claim. Thus in *BMTA v Salvadori* the expenses incurred in investigating the defendants' organized undermining of the plaintiffs' resale conditions were recoverable as 'directly attributable to the tort', while in *The Nadezhda Krupskaya* [112] the additional cost of substituting an alternative vessel, to replace the one denied by the defendant's action, was recovered.

All intended damage will be recoverable, as will non-remote consequences. So in *Boxfoldia Ltd v NGA (1982)* [113] the strike induced by the union led to the company being forced to make some of their non-striking workers redundant. These redundancy payments were held to be losses reasonably foreseeable as a consequence of the tort. According to McCardie J in *Pratt v BMA* [114] once pecuniary loss is shown, injury to feelings could be compensated. In that case the court found there had been a period of 'humiliation and menace' in an attempt to inflict 'complete ruin'. However, it is likely that injury to reputation is not compensatable under this tort, in line with recent decisions in conspiracy [115] and malicious falsehood. [116]

THE INCONSISTENT TRANSACTION FALLACY

The tort of inducing breach of contract requires an unlawful end (the breach), caused by the defendant's persuasion or inducement. The defendant is liable for being instrumental in the decision to breach. The requirement of persuasion justifies liability (on which see below), while reducing the potential scope of the tort, so that mere prevention of the contract is not tortious.

However, apart from persuasion, Jenkins LJ in *Thomson v Deakin*, asserted that 'inconsistent dealings' could give rise to liability for the tort of direct inducement to breach [117] (the other members of the court did not consider this point). He stated: 'if a third party, with knowledge of a contract between the contract breaker and another, had dealings with the contract breaker which the third party knows to be inconsistent with the contract, he has committed an actionable interference.' [118] He accepted that this means liability, even though: 'the contract breaker may himself be a willing party to the breach without any persuasion by the third

---

[112] [1997] 2 Lloyd's Law Reports 35, Rix J.   [113] [1988] IRLR 383, Saville J.
[114] [1919] 1KB 244, p. 281.   [115] *Lonrho v Fayed (no 5)* [1993] 1 WLR 1489.
[116] *Joyce v Sengupta* [1993] 1 WLR 337; *Khoraparast v Shad* (2000) 1 All ER 545.
[117] See Lauterpacht, H., 'Contracts to Break a Contract' 52 LQR (1936) 494.
[118] [1952] Ch 646, p. 694; Lord Evershed MR did not mention 'inconsistent transactions'.

party.'[119] If this be correct,[120] knowingly entering into a conflicting transaction could constitute the tort of inducing breach of contract. Facilitating a breach would suffice. On such an analysis the causal connection between the defendant's act and the breach of contract is reduced to the defendant saying 'yes' to the contract breaker, who has already decided to break his contract.

Jenkins LJ drew support for his assertion from the judgment of Roxburgh J in *BMTA v Salvadori*.[121] In *Salvadori* the defendant bought a car from the plaintiff's co-contractor knowing that this sale constituted a breach by the co-contractor of his obligation not to sell the car within a year.[122] At one point in his judgment Roxburgh J stated that inducement to breach of contract included offering a price high enough for the contract breaker to agree.[123] He also later referred to the active steps the defendant must take, before he will be liable. As such this would appear to be a run-of-the-mill direct persuasion case. The fact that the defendant did not take the initiative is irrelevant. However, later in his judgment Roxburgh J asserted that simply by agreeing to buy the car, known by him to be on offer in breach of contract, the defendant was taking active steps by which he facilitated the breach of contract.[124] Indeed, Jenkins LJ also asserted: 'inconsistent dealing . . . may, indeed, be commenced without knowledge by the third party of the contract thus broken; but if it is continued after the third party has notice of the contract, an actionable interference has been committed by him.'[125] In support of this proposition he cited *De Francesco v Barnum*[126] where a theatre manager continued to employ showgirls, after being informed of their prior inconsistent contract with the plaintiff. The plaintiff succeeded, liability depending on the defendant's after-acquired knowledge of the prior inconsistent contract.

The relevant *dicta* from Roxburgh J's judgment in *BMTA v Salvadori* have been cited with approval by Bingham LJ in *Rickless v United Artists*

---

[119] Ibid. 694.

[120] Roxburgh J in *BMTA v Salvadori* [1949] Ch 556, p. 565 stated 'any active step taken by the defendant having knowledge of the covenant by which he facilitates . . . a breach of that covenant is enough'.

[121] [1949] Ch 556.

[122] The background to the case was the post-war shortage of new cars. For a similar Scottish case see *BMTA v Gray* 1951 SLT 247.

[123] See also *BIP v Ferguson* [1940] 1 All ER 479 where although the contract breaker originally approached the defendants the court stressed that the issue was the price offered by the defendants for the information offered.

[124] See also Stamp J in *Sefton v Tophams* [1965] Ch 1140, p. 1160 (reversed on other grounds [1967] 1 AC 50) where he accepted Roxburgh J's view that inducement is no longer necessary, although adding that the purchase price is a sufficient inducement.

[125] [1952] Ch 646, p. 694.   [126] (1890) 45 Ch D 430.

Corp,[127] while Hoffmann LJ in *Law Debenture Trust Corp v Ural Caspian Oil Corp Ltd*[128] asserted that 'knowingly entering into a transaction inconsistent with the contracting party's obligation' was well established to be within the tort.

But can this minimal degree of interference be sufficient to render the defendant liable in tort? Arguably, the only legitimate reason for adding tort liability to the contract breaker's already existing liability in contract is precisely because the defendant has played an important part in persuading (procuring/inducing) the co-contractor to break his contract. In Weir's phrase, he has 'seduced' the claimant's contract partner.[129] It would appear justifiable to demand a causal link before facilitation could lead to liability. Certainly 'procure' has clearly been so defined in the intellectual property cases where suppliers have been held not liable for the supply of innocent goods, knowing of their intended unlawful use (to infringe the plaintiff's patent or copyright).[130] Hart and Honoré contend that the plaintiff should prove that the defendant's conduct 'was at least one factor which influenced the third party to make up his mind to breach his contract'.[131] If the defendant has simply said 'yes' he is better regarded as the tool of the contract breaker, rather than vice versa. Some support for this view can be gleaned from *Batts Combe Quarry Ltd v Ford*.[132] There the plaintiff's contract partner breached his contract not to assist in carrying on a rival quarry business. The breach involved the provision of a sum of money to his sons to enable them to purchase a rival quarry. The Court of Appeal agreed with the trial judge that the mere acceptance by the sons of the gift did not amount to a procuring by them of the breach of contract.

Furthermore, none of the cases cited in support of the 'inconsistent

---

[127] [1988] 1 QB 40, p. 59 Bingham MR 'I regard it as good law'. The case was also cited as authority for a cause of action based on inconsistent transactions by Jacobs J in *Oren v Red Box Toy Factory* [1999] F.S.R. 785.

[128] [1993] 1 WLR 138, p. 151.

[129] Weir, above, n. 1, p. 42 n. 54. And see Ch. 10 for the proposed rationale of the tort, based on the principle of secondary civil liability.

[130] In *Townsend v Haworth* (1875) 48 LJ Ch 770 the defendant was not jointly liable with the infringer of the plaintiff's patent though he sold (commonplace) chemical substances to the infringer, knowing that he intended to use those substances to infringe the patent. This dichotomy was underlined more recently in *Belegging-en Shappij Lavender v Witten Inds Diamonds Ltd* [1979] FSR 59. Buckley LJ noted that 'facilitating the doing of an act is obviously different from the procuring of the doing of the act'.

[131] Above, n. 40, p. 191.

[132] [1942] 2 All ER 639. *Batts v Combe Quarry* was not referred to in either decision. Cohen-Grabelsky, N., 'Interference with Contractual Relations and Equitable Doctrines' 45 MLR 241 (1982), p. 251 agrees that the cases cannot be reconciled but concludes that *Batts* is wrong, a part of the evolution of the tort, superseded by *Salvadori*. Burns, P., 'Tort Injury to Economic Interests: Some Facets of Legal Response' 58 Can Bar Rev (1980) 103, p. 109 argues that the case can be explained on the basis that inconsistent dealings will not be actionable if the third party accepts the benefits of an inconsistent transaction at the insistence of the contract breaker. However, Roxburgh J in *Salvadori* does not make such a distinction.

transaction' doctrine are solid authority for its existence. Thus *De Francesco v Barnum*[133] draws on the old action for harbouring another's servant, a species of the action for enticing away a servant, abolished by s.2 Administration of Justice Act 1982. In the later case of *Jones Brothers (Hunstanton) Ltd v Stevens*[134] the court did stress that to be liable for after-acquired knowledge the causal link has to be established—in that case it could not be shown that the employees concerned would have returned to their original employer but for the defendant, indicating that a continued 'inducement' to breach must be shown. *BMTA v Salvadori* can be seen as an organized attack by the defendants on the plaintiff association's covenanting system which sought to prevent the immediate resale of new cars. Actual inducement appears to have been present, as well as a conspiracy.[135] Nor were either *Rickless* or *Law Debenture* cases involving inconsistent transactions, in the Jenkins LJ sense.[136]

A rejection of the 'inconsistent transaction fallacy' is also in line with the parallel drawn (and rightly drawn) between the tort of inducing breach of contract and the doctrine of joint tortfeasance. This is discussed later in this chapter.

Moreover, *dicta* that support liability in the tort for 'mere' inconsistent transactions only obscure those equitable principles which may provide a limited but effective remedy where such transactions have harmed the claimant's contract rights. Part of the reason why the 'frontiers of tort and equity liabilities cannot . . . be regarded as finally settled'[137] is precisely because the more obvious limits of tort liability have been overlooked. Only by rejecting the application of the tort to 'inconsistent transactions' does it become necessary to clarify the basis and extent of these equitable principles—which represent 'an old but vexed question in the law of obligations'.[138] Equity has been prepared to enhance the protection of

---

[133] This was applied in *Wilkinson v Weave* [1915] 2 Ch 323, p. 325 where the allegation was that the employer by continuing to employ 'knowingly assisted' the breach.

[134] [1955] 1 QB 275.

[135] In *Thomson v Deakin*, Lord Evershed MR said that in the *Salvadori* case the defendant's conduct was tortious in itself as it amounted to a conspiracy with the plaintiff's co-contractor: see [1952] Ch 646, p. 678. Weir, above, n. 1, p. 36 argues that the decision, which he categorizes as an 'anti-postwar-spiv' decision, was wrong anyway, on the basis that the contract was unenforceable as between the parties (being in restraint of trade): however, in *BMTA v Gray* 1951 SLT 247, a similar contract was held not to be in restraint of trade.

[136] Indeed, in *Rickless v United Artists* there was an unlawful act by the defendant—a reproduction of a performance without the consent of the performer, a statutory tort under the Dramatic and Musical Performers Protection Acts. The result was an unlawful interference with the plaintiff's contract. Moreover, at other times in his judgment Bingham LJ contended that the defendants were liable for *inducing* breach. He compared their position to that of a defendant inducing the plaintiff's ex-employee to breach a restrictive covenant by working for him.

[137] Wedderburn, Clerk and Lindsell on Torts, 17th edn. (1995) 23–23. A fuller discussion appears in the 18th edn. (above, n. 1), 24-36–24-42.

[138] Tettenborn, A., 'Covenants, Privity of Contract and the Purchasers of Personal Prop-

contract performance, even though that may mean that strangers to a contract (with notice) have the imposition of equitable remedies 'extended' to them—as was the case in *Manchester Ship Canal Co v Manchester Racecourse Co*[139] and *Sefton v Tophams Ltd*.[140] That process, however, should not be allowed to obscure the tort and lead to a sloppy equating of tort and equitable principle. Contract rights may be protected by equity without a tort arising—as Lauterpacht remarked: 'the law has found manifold means of discouraging [inconsistent transactions] by giving adequate protection to the provisions of the first contract.'[141]

Thus there is an uncertain principle with a 'chequered history' that may bind third parties, on equitable principles, where a contract imposes conditions on the use of a chattel.[142] This is sometimes referred to as the *De Mattos v Gibson*[143] principle. In that case Knight Bruce LJ asserted that where 'by gift or purchase' property is acquired by another with knowledge of a previous contract restricting the use of the property, the acquirer will be prevented from acting inconsistently with that previous contract. In essence the principle seems to provide that if an injunction[144] could have been obtained against the person in breach of contract, then an injunction may be sought against a subsequent acquirer of the chattel who has notice of the relevant restrictive stipulations.[145] So equity may intervene to support a covenant by way of a negative injunction, restraining the purchaser from acting inconsistently with the covenant.[146] The principle

---

erty' 41 CLJ (1982) 58. See also Treitel, G., 'Limited Interests in Chattels' 21 MLR (1958) 433; Chafee, Z., 'Equitable Servitudes as Chattels' 41 Har L Rev (1927–8) 945, esp. pp. 969 onwards. Note also *British Homophone v Kunz* 1935 152 LT 589, p. 593.

[139] [1901] 2 Ch 37.

[140] [1965] Ch 1140 where the majority of the Court of Appeal applied the *Manchester Ship Canal* case (though Sellers LJ held the tort to apply). The House of Lords reversed the decision on other grounds: [1967] 1 AC 50.

[141] Above, n. 117, p. 509.

[142] An even more obscure doctrine, arising from equity's protection of 'property' is based on *Springhead Spinning Co v Riley* (1868) LR 6 Eq 551, where property was taken to include business interests/profit expectations. In *Ex parte Island Records* [1974] Ch 122 Waller LJ relied on this to protect the economic advantages to be obtained from an exclusive recording contract. Though this definition of 'property' was rejected by the Court of Appeal in *RCA v Pollard* [1983] Ch 139, the existence of the 'property injunction' was not disputed. See discussion in Chs. 5 and 10.

[143] (1858) 4 De G & J 276.

[144] A contract that was specifically enforceable would present no problems: see Tettenborn, above, n. 138.

[145] Tettenborn (ibid.) suggests that the doctrine is based on the idea of unjust enrichment: where contract rights are enforceable by injunction against the contract partner, these rights will be ineffective unless enforceable against anyone into whose hands the property may have come.

[146] Hoffmann J in *Law Debenture Trust Corpn v Ural Caspian Oil Corp* [1995] Ch 152 noted that the *De Mattos* principle only applied to the grant of a negative injunction, restraining a purchaser from acting inconsistently with covenants. The principle was not discussed by the Court of Appeal in that case.

was 'enthusiastically endorsed' by Lord Shaw in *Strathcona SS Co v Dominion Coal Co.*[147] Though Browne-Wilkinson J contended in *Swiss Bank Corp v Lloyds Bank Ltd*[148] that the *De Mattos* principle was the equitable counterpart of the tort of inducing breach, the principle is in fact separate from the tort. As Tettenborn points out, there was no participation between the co-contractor and the defendant in *De Mattos v Gibson*, although the plaintiff's contract rights were denied by the defendant. Furthermore, the principle existed considerably earlier than *Lumley v Gye*, being employed, as Gardner[149] points out, some nine months before that case to give an injunction against Gye.

Inconsistent transactions are not *per se* tortious. Unless this is accepted, an attempt to provide a coherent framework for the tort is undermined. The acceptance of inconsistent transactions as tortious places liability in the area of facilitating a breach. This appears to downgrade the need for causal and intentional harm, emanating from the defendant. Yet, 'liability should attach under *Lumley v Gye* only when the defendant has persuaded the plaintiff's contractor deliberately to break his contract, where the defendant has used the contractor as a means of harming the plaintiff'.[150] This requires accepting *Batts* as correct and rejecting the wider *dicta* in *Salvadori*.[151]

INTENTIONAL INDUCEMENT OF OTHER WRONGS[152]

Though *Lumley v Gye* established the tort of inducing breach of contract, in fact *dicta* from that case have led to a wider principle of tort liability that may protect other than contract rights. Erle J asserted[153] '[the class of case] rests upon the principle that the procurement of the violation of the right is a cause of action . . . it is clear that the procurement of the violation of a right is a cause of action in all instances where the violation is an actionable wrong'. This more general principle of liability was summarized by Lord Macnaghten (in *Quinn v Leathem*) as based on 'a violation of a legal

---

[147] [1926] AC 108, though admittedly, Diplock J in *Port Line v Ben Line* [1958] 2 QB 146 did not believe that the decision was right: for a full discussion see Tettenborn, above, n. 138.

[148] [1979] Ch 548 (the case was reversed in the House of Lords on other grounds [1982] AC 584).

[149] Gardner, S., 'The Proprietary Effect of Contractual Obligations' 98 LQR (1982) 279.

[150] Weir, above, n. 1, p. 35. However, he goes on to conclude that the rules are therefore in no way different from those of the general tort of unlawful interference with trade.

[151] According to Cohen-Grabelsky, above, n. 132, p. 251, this would appear to represent the American view.

[152] For reasons which should become clear in the text, this title is preferred to 'intentional invasion of legal rights'.

[153] (1853) 2 E&B 216, p. 232.

right committed knowingly'. The Court of Appeal in *Associated British Ports v TGWU* accepted its validity, as an extension from *Lumley v Gye*,[154] as did Sir Thomas Bingham MR in *Law Debenture Trust Corp v Ural Caspian Oil Corp*[155] who pointed out that Erle J's original formulation was not limited to inducing breach of contract alone. More recently, it has been accepted by the House of Lords in *Credit Lyonnais Nederland N.V. v Export Credits Guarantee Department*[156] (discussed below).

Clearly, the principle of *Lumley v Gye*—liability based on procuring a legal wrong—is capable of applying beyond breach of contract. However, care must be taken in this area. Read in isolation, Lord Macnaghten's statement in *Quinn v Leathem* fails to include two important elements from the principle of *Lumley v Gye*: the need for procurement and the need for an actionable wrong.[157]

So any analogous civil liability based on *Lumley v Gye* must involve inducement. Erle J used the word 'procurement' in relation to this extended liability while subsequently Lord Watson in *Allen v Flood* noted that the defendant 'will incur liability if he knowingly and for his own ends induces that other person to commit an actionable wrong'.[158] In *Credit Lyonnais Nederland BV v ECGD*[159] the plaintiffs attempted to impose liability on the defendant employer where their employee had assisted a rogue to swindle the plaintiffs. None of the acts of deceit took place within that employee's course of employment. The acts that the employee did perform within his employment, though they set the scene for the deceit, were not themselves unlawful and in themselves had no adverse consequences for the plaintiffs. The plaintiffs argued, *inter alia*, that there was a tort of assisting another in the violation of another's right, provided there was an intention to bring about that result. If this argument were correct, the employer would be vicariously liable for the employee's undoubted assistance of the rogue. Authority for this tort was alleged to be derived from the tort identified in *Lumley v Gye*. This argument was rejected by

---

[154] Neill LJ [1989] 1 WLR 939, p. 952 'the inducement of a breach of statutory duty is, of course, akin to the inducement of a breach of contract'; Stuart-Smith LJ, p. 963 accepted the general tort of intentional interference with rights, with inducing breach as the 'commonest example of the tort'; Butler-Sloss LJ recognized the extension, labelling it 'interference with legal rights' or 'direct invasion of legal rights'.

[155] [1995] Ch 152.

[156] [1999] 2 WLR 540.

[157] Indeed, it was Hoffmann LJ's focusing on the 'right' in *Law Debenture Trust Corp v Ural Caspian Oil Corpn* [1995] Ch 152 that led to error, according to Sir Thomas Bingham MR: 'in concentrating on the right, it seems to me that the judge did take his eye off the wrong' (p. 166).

[158] [1898] AC 1, p. 96. In *Quinn v Leathem*, [1901] AC 495, p. 509, Lord Macnaghten asserted that Lord Watson's speech was to be regarded as the leading speech in *Allen v Flood*.

[159] [1999] 2 WLR 540, HL.

Lord Woolf,[160] liability in the tort requiring direct procurement, rather than mere facilitation.[161]

Further, an actionable wrong must be involved. Just as the tort of inducing breach protects valid contracts, the majority of judicial opinion accepts the need to show that the legal right at the centre of this action is capable of forming the basis of a cause of action—that there has been an actionable wrong induced.[162] Indeed, this was the view of Henry J in *Barretts v Baird*[163] and the Court of Appeal in *Associated British Ports v TGWU*.[164] In *Law Debenture Trust Corp v Ural Caspian Oil Corp*, Hoffmann LJ suggested interference with a contingent equitable right could suffice for liability but this was rejected by the Court of Appeal. In that case, though the intended effect of the series of transactions involved was to deny the plaintiff his potential claim for a retransfer of shares (the subject of his original contract right) there was no actionable wrong when shares were transferred on to the final defendant, prior to the plaintiff obtaining any injunctive relief to stop that happening. Though the transferor was liable for an earlier breach of contract that he had induced (in order to obtain those shares), at the time of the transfer to the final defendant he was the owner of the shares and no contract right of the plaintiff was thereby infringed. No liability could ensue, given the onward transfer was not an actionable wrong.[165]

---

[160] On the basis that the liability for such a procurement as is discussed in that case is secondary (hence the plaintiff still could not show that the ECGD would be vicariously liable) and that the speech of Lord Templeman in *CBS Songs Ltd v Amstrad plc* [1988] AC 1013 'strongly suggests that there is little scope for the creation' of such a tort. Lord Woolf: 'this statement of Erle J is capable of being treated as saying no more than that if you procure the commission of an actionable wrong by another then you are liable for that actionable wrong. The responsibility for the actionable wrong is a form of secondary liability.' This is discussed more fully later and see Ch. 10.

[161] This of course feeds into a wider debate on the framework for accessory liability in the civil law and whether there is a unified concept of secondary liability. See Ch. 10 and Carty, H., 'Joint Tortfeasance and Assistance Liability', 19 Legal Studies (1999) 489.

[162] Hoffmann LJ [1993] 1 WLR 138, p. 151 the actionable wrong must involve actual breach of contract; breach of statutory duty or breach of equitable obligation. Without such an emphasis on actionable wrongs this principle could easily be reworked into general protection against interference with 'rights'. This appeared to be the aim of plaintiffs in certain family law litigation: so in *Frame v Smith* 42 DLR (4th) 81 (1987) there was an attempt to use the principle to uphold the rights of parental access in a custody dispute and in *F v Wirral MC* [1991] 2 All ER 648 there was an attempt to query the actions of the local authority in relation to care proceedings by relying on an alleged tort of interference with parental rights. In both cases the action failed, no actionable wrong being involved.

[163] [1987] IRLR 3. There, no breach of statutory duty arose.

[164] Though bizarrely they accepted that a breach of a statutory provision that did not amount to an actionable tort could be sufficient to constitute 'unlawful means' in the general tort of unlawful interference with trade. See Ch. 5.

[165] Cane, P, 'Tortious Interference with Contractual Remedies' 111 LQR (1995) 400, p. 401 'knowingly depriving a person of the opportunity to claim a remedy for interference with contract' is not the tort of inducing breach of contract. However, he questions whether the

Once the true basis of the *Lumley v Gye* principle is identified it is clear that it applies to inducing breach of statutory duty (on the basis that breach of such duty gives rise to tort liability). The possibility of such a tort of inducing breach of statutory duty was raised in *Meade v Haringey BC*[166] and in *Associated Newspapers Group v Wade*,[167] with Lord Denning a member of the Court of Appeal in both cases. For liability, as we have seen, the breach must itself be actionable. The importance of this proviso was apparent in *Wilson v Housing Corporation*.[168] Here an unfairly dismissed worker alleged inducing breach of contract and intimidation against the defendant, who he alleged 'procured' that dismissal. He sought to add an allegation that the defendant had induced his employer to unfairly dismiss him, arguing that this fell within the tort of inducing breach of statutory duty. However, Dyson J denied the existence of this liability, as the wrong alleged was not actionable in the ordinary courts and attracted its own special rules (including compensation limits). Indeed, more generally, by demanding that an actionable wrong result from the persuasion, no special economic tort liability is created for those employed in the public sector, or the trade unions who represent them, where the employers concerned have statutory duties to perform. In reality, liability for inducing breach of statutory duty can arise under this tort or under the doctrine of joint tortfeasance, underlining the close relationship between the principle behind *Lumley v Gye* and the doctrine of joint tortfeasance. This is explored more fully later in this chapter and in Chapter 10.

Indeed, the pattern of liability established by *Lumley v Gye* appears to apply beyond torts and breaches of contract. So the courts may provide redress where the defendant induces a breach of an equitable obligation. Liability for inducing a breach of fiduciary or equitable obligation[169] does exist, as is clear from *Prudential Assurance Co Ltd v Lorenz*.[170] There, insurance agents withheld payment of their premiums to their employer, as part of an industrial dispute. This was held to be a breach of their fiduciary duty to account and the inducers were liable for procuring this breach of trust.[171] But logically such procurers should not be liable in *tort*.

---

common law should develop to include certain forms of intentional economic harm, beyond simple conspiracy and inducing breach, though no unlawful means as such be used.

[166] [1979] 1 WLR 637.

[167] [1979] ICR 664.

[168] [1997] IRLR 345.

[169] Where confidential information is in issue the courts are willing to impose liability on third parties on wider principles.

[170] (1971) 11 KIR 78, Plowman J., Lord Denning MR in *Boulting v ACTAT* [1963] 2 QB 606, p. 627 asserted 'it is wrong to induce another to act inconsistently with the duty of fidelity which he has undertaken by contract or trust to perform'.

[171] Liability followed the pattern of the doctrine of joint tortfeasance.

Though such an action mirrors the general principle, it should be limited to giving rise to equitable relief, in line with the policy that there is no tort of procuring a breach of trust.[172]

Presumably for liability under the *Lumley v Gye* principle intention and knowledge of the legal rights harmed are required.[173] Again, it is likely that damage must result. Moreover, it is arguable that this extended principle of tortious liability only arises where there has been a direct attack (by persuasion) on the right in question:[174] Stuart-Smith LJ in *F v Wirral MC*[175] asserted that the tort required 'direct and unjustifiable interference'. Indeed, Butler-Sloss LJ in *Associated British Ports* labelled the principle the 'direct invasion of legal rights' tort. What would constitute justification is more problematic. Indirect interference[176] would be covered (if unlawful means were used) by the tort of unlawful interference with trade, on a par with the so-called varieties of inducing breach of contract.

RATIONALE[177]

To clarify the rationale of this tort, it is again vital to note that the two categories of this tort must be analysed separately. Here an attempt is made to identify the rationale of the classic form of the tort: inducing breach, in an absence of other unlawful means.[178] Having identified the rationale, it is possible to explore the concept of justification in the tort.

---

[172] *Metall und Rohstoff AG v Donaldson Lufkin Jenrette Inc* [1990] 1 QB 391, CA, Slade LJ stressed that he could see no justification for a new tort of procuring a breach of trust as liability for such behaviour already existed in equity. However, it has to be said that Plowman J in *Prudential Assurance v Lorenz* (1971) 11 KIR 78 seemed to assume that the action was tortious. His judgment was not referred to in *Metall und Rohstoff*. See also discussion in Ch. 10.

[173] This is implicit in Erle J's *dicta*.

[174] And, of course, where there was such a connection inducing a statutory tort, the parties would anyway be jointly liable: see discussion of joint tortfeasance liability in Ch. 10.

[175] [1991] 2 All ER 648, CA.

[176] Though probably only re economic interests.

[177] Throughout the 1980s and 1990s there was an academic debate in America as to the correct definition and role of this tort: see Danforth, above, n. 6; Perlman, H., 'Interference with Contract and Other Economic Expectancies: A Clash of Tort and Contract Doctrine' 49 U Ch LR (1982) 61; Epstein, R., 'Inducement of Breach of Contract as a Problem of Ostensible Ownership' 16 J Legal Studies (1987) 1; Partlett, above, n. 2; Palmer, above, n. 6. This appears to have been provoked by the reformulation by the American Law Institute of the tort in the Restatement (Second) of Torts. Dean Prosser's proposal—that intentional interference with knowledge of the contract was actionable unless justified was rejected as creating too great a restraint on free competition and commercial enterprise. Dean Wade's subsequent draft, adding the further element of 'impropriety', measured by way of a factor-balancing test, was ultimately accepted, though Partlett (p. 787) notes that there was less than wholehearted approval.

[178] There has been little debate on the rationale of the 'extended' tort.

It is clear that contract rights are central to the tort of inducing breach of contract. This tort does not require 'extra' unlawful means, provided the defendant has procured the breach.

So, Weir together with Lord Diplock (in *Merkur Island Shipping v Laughton*)[179] is wrong to place this tort within the general tort of unlawful interference with trade.[180] Unlike the varieties of unlawful interference with trade, this tort focuses on the claimant's contract rights and seeks to protect them against breach caused by the defendant's direct interference through persuasion or inducement. Though the persuasion or inducement are lawful acts in themselves, the law penalizes such acts where they target contract rights. Thus the modern tort emerged (or, as Wedderburn puts it, 'was invented')[181] as the importance of contract emerged.[182] Danforth concludes that the focus of the tort is on promoting contract rights[183] while Bagshaw accepts that 'the orthodox understanding of the tort recognized in *Lumley v Gye* regards it as offering special protection to the contract relationship'.[184] Indeed, some American commentators, while accepting the legitimacy of tort liability for the infliction of economic harm through independently unlawful means, reject the validity of the tort of inducing breach of contract, precisely because it protects contract rights through tort.[185] In effect the tort enhances the claimant's contract rights by allowing him to sue the real cause of the intended harm.

The question thus becomes why this tort should 'create rights against the world to protect and reflect the rights and duties that contracting parties create among themselves'.[186] Coleridge J dissented in *Lumley v Gye* because he saw the tort that was being proposed as undermining privity of contract.[187] In recent years commentators such as Dobbs[188] have reiterated

---

[179] [1983] 2 AC 570.

[180] This is the main assertion of *Economic Torts* (above, n. 1). By defining the tort as part of unlawful interference with trade, Weir seeks to establish once and for all that every 'general' economic tort requires the infliction of targeted economic harm. As we have seen there are still some who doubt this for the tort of inducing breach of contract. For Weir, this is because they focus on the right not the wrong involved.

[181] Wedderburn, K. W., 'Intimidation and the Right to Strike' 27 MLR (1964) 257, p. 258.

[182] 'Tortious Interference with Contractual Relations in the 19th Century: the Transformation of Property, Contract and Tort' [anonymous note] 93 Har LR (1980) 1511, p. 1523, 'the court advanced a general theory of contractual property in which the procurement of a breach, and not the loss of service, provided the basis for recovery'.

[183] Against intentional interference.

[184] Bagshaw, R., 'Can the Economic Torts be Unified?' 18 OJLS (1998) 729, p. 735.

[185] See in particular Perlman, above, n. 177.

[186] Danforth, above, n. 6, p. 1492.   [187] 118 ER 749, p. 760.

[188] Dobbs, D., 'Tortious Interference with Contractual Relationships' 34 Ark L Rev (1980) 335.

this objection.[189] A further objection against the tort has been raised by those who support the 'efficient breach' doctrine.[190] For these commentators, the law is indifferent to breach or performance and provides the contractors with a choice whether to perform the contract or pay damages[191]—to encourage non-performance where efficiency gains would result. For them, the tort of inducing breach of contract lacks validity as it 'inhibits the contracting parties from competing once a contract has been consummated'.[192] So Perlman[193] contends 'contract rules seem designed to facilitate breach where efficiency gains result; the inducing liability rule, in contrast, seems designed to reduce the number of such breaches'.[194] Other supporters of the 'efficient breach' doctrine such as BeVier[195] and Landes and Posner[196] are willing to accept only a limited validity for the tort, primarily where there are legal or practical problems[197] preventing the contract from providing full compensation for the breach.

However, neither the privity argument nor the 'efficient breach' doctrine in fact undermine the validity of the tort. The tort of inducing breach of contract does not as such enforce the contract.[198] Nor does it provide protection against all breaches in which the defendant has had a part to play. Only those intentional breaches where the defendant has himself deliberately persuaded the contractual partner into breach are covered. Again, the theory of 'efficient breach' can itself be attacked as undermining contract certainty[199] and in particular denying the importance of long-term contractual relationships. As Partlett notes, most of the contracts at the heart of the case law on this tort are 'peculiarly relational—

---

[189] Dobbs (above, n. 188) also objects to the tort on the basis that it appears to imply that the party induced is not an autonomous person, making the defendant responsible for the actions of others.

[190] Indications of which appear in Holmes, O. W., 'The Path of the Law' 10 Har L Rev (1897) 457, p. 462.

[191] Though Perlman would allow restrictive covenants to be enforced, above, n. 177, p. 86.

[192] Above, n. 2, p. 774.

[193] Above, n. 177, p. 83.

[194] In ibid. 75 he argues that only the presence of unlawful acts should render the defendant liable, though where the defendant's motivation is incompatible with competition, as in *Tuttle v Buck* 119 NW 946 (1909), the anti-trust doctrine should apply: 'by confining the tort to cases of independent unlawful acts or cases where improper motive can be discerned from objective facts, social welfare can be enhanced' (p. 128).

[195] BeVier, L., 'Reconsidering Inducement' 76 Va L Rev (1990) 877.

[196] Landes, W., and Posner, R., 'Joint and Multiple Tortfeasors: An Economic Analysis' 9 J. Legal Stud (1980) 517, 552–5 (App II).

[197] e.g. the contract breaker is insolvent

[198] For Weir, T., 'Chaos or Cosmos: *Rookes*, *Stratford* and the Economic Torts' [1964] CLJ 225, p. 229, contractual promises decrease the promisor's liberty of action. So 'in tort, contracts must be looked at from the passive side, from the side of the debtor, in order to discover, not what he must do (for only a creditor can rely on this) but what he is not at liberty to do'.

[199] Friedmann, D., 'The Efficient Breach Fallacy' 18 J Legal Studies (1989) 1, p. 11.

they have to do with employment, leases, professional and long-term business relationships'.[200] Moreover, Weir[201] points out that the tort of inducing breach of contract is justified by some law and economics commentators on the basis that the threat of such liability could save transaction costs given it provides an incentive '[for a potential inducer] to go to the promisee and bargain with him rather than seducing or browbeating the promisor'.

But if the doctrine of privity and the doctrine of 'efficient breach' do not undermine the validity of the tort, what is the rationale for its existence? There are three rationales offered by those who support the tort: the property theory (or variations on this theme), the social policy theory, and the secondary civil liability theory.

For Epstein[202] the tort is best understood 'as an unsuspected manifestation of the problem of ostensible ownership'.[203] Thus the subject matter of contract—the promised performance—constitutes property.[204] As it gives rise to an equitable interest, liability is based on notice. So bona fide, innocent parties who cause interference with the claimant's contract will not be liable. However, though it may be possible to compare the protection given by this tort to at least some of the protection given by the law to property[205] the contract does not as such give rise to property rights.[206] As Cane notes[207] 'actionability *per se* and strict liability which are central

---

[200] Partlett, 'From Victorian Opera to Rock and Rap: Inducement to Breach of Contract in the Music Industry' 66 Tulane LR (1991–2) 771, p. 798. He contends (p. 772) that the effect of the tort is to 'alleviate long-term relational problems due to changing circumstances or opportunistic behaviour and therefore of encouraging cooperation between parties with its attendant social benefits'. For him, the tort is justified on the basis of the maintenance of 'cooperative relationships', so that the tort imposes constraints on the contracting parties which tend to ensure 'constancy and security' in the relationship.

[201] *Economic Torts*, above, n. 1, p. 5. See also the criticism by Bagshaw, R., 'Inducing Breach of Contract', ch. 7 in *Oxford Essays in Jurisprudence*, 4th series, ed. Horder, J. (Oxford: OUP, 2000), pp. 135–6: 'if non-performance of the contract between Lumley and Wagner really would be efficient . . . then Gye should be capable of persuading Lumley, if Lumley is economically rational, to trade his contractual rights.'

[202] Epstein, above, n. 177. See also McChesney, F. S., 'Tortious Interference with Contract Versus "Efficient" Breach: Theory and Empirical Evidence' 28 JLS (1999) 131.

[203] Inducement of breach of contract is used to fill the gaps in the law of trespass or conversion . . . to fill the void that the more traditional notions of property may not reach': above, n. 177, pp. 19–20.

[204] Pollock, F., *The Law of Torts*, 1st edn. (London: Stevens & Sons, 1887), p. 451 thought that *Lumley v Gye* suggested an interest analogous to ownership though he was not happy with this conclusion.

[205] Rogers, W. V. H., *Winfield and Jolowicz on Tort*, 15th edn. (London: Sweet & Maxwell, 1998) notes, of the decision in *Lumley v Gye*: 'commercial contractual relations had become valuable rights which could be regarded as entitled to at least some of the protection given by the law to property' (p. 621).

[206] Palmer, above, n. 6, p. 332 is critical of this abuse of ideas.

[207] Cane, P., *Tort Law and Economic Interests*, 2nd edn. (Oxford: Clarendon Press, 1996), p. 124, n. 95.

features of tortious protection of property rights are not a feature of the torts which protect contracts from interference'.[208]

Bagshaw[209] suggests that rather than see the contract as property, the law 'borrows' well-tested arguments for protecting private property rights against the world and that this provides a secure foundation for the *Lumley v Gye* tort. The fact that contracts extend the choices open to those who choose to contract, ensure that scarce commodities are allocated so as to maximize social wealth and provide a suitable reward for productive behaviour requires that contracts should be protected against third parties.[210] The 'protectable interest' that emerges from this analysis involves the interest in the contract partner's willingness to perform *and* his capacity to perform. This variation on the property right theme breaks down the distinction between procuring breach and preventing perform-ance (at least where that is due to a direct and positive act). It also leads Bagshaw to support a dilute form of intention: inevitable consequences being sufficient for liability.

Yet it is hard not to suspect that this analysis which supports the secur-ity of contracts proceeds from the same base as the second policy justify-ing the tort. This relies on the policy benefits of the tort, 'establishing norms to encourage private order'.[211] Thus Danforth identifies the ratio-nale of the tort as the protection of the integrity of contract, the law reflect-ing 'the important role of contractual relations as a reliable, structure-giving element in any market economy'.[212] Indeed, he suggests that just as the enticement action evolved in response to a social problem (labour shortage, consequent on the ravages of the Black Death) and provided 'a much needed reinforcement for the underlying foundations of the English political economy', the extension of liability to allow protection of all contracts demonstrated that the court in *Lumley v Gye* 'implicitly recog-nized that in 1853 society's interest in a stable foundation for economic activity had shifted from a concern for stability in status relations to a concern for stability in contract relations'. Thus at the height of the Indus-trial Revolution, a tort to protect the integrity of contract relations 'would help stabilize the underlying structure of a rapidly developing market

---

[208] Danforth, above, n. 177, p. 495, n. 34 notes that the tort did not develop from an equa-tion of contract expectations and property rights, though such an equation is suggested by Erle J in *Lumley v Gye*. Of course Dobbs, above, n. 188 and Perlman, above, n. 177 also criti-cize the characterization of contract rights as property.

[209] Bagshaw, above, n. 201.

[210] He rejects a narrow mental element on the basis that it would offer insufficient protec-tion to an interest 'in some way akin to a property interest' (above, n. 201, p. 143). He also would include advice within the tort (with disinterested advisers forced to look to the defence of justification) and inconsistent dealing within the tort (on the basis that such may cause or lead to a continuation of the breach).

[211] Partlett, above, n. 177, p. 809.

[212] Above, n. 177, p. 1493.

economy'.[213] So, married to the individual interest in contract integrity is the public interest in stable contract relations. Where competitive practices are concerned, 'without stability of contracts, markets could not operate properly; and stability of contracts can be undermined just as much by inducement of breach as by breach itself'. Of course, as Cane goes on to note[214] this tort is also frequently used as between employers and trade unions and here 'tort law has been at the forefront of bitter arguments about the (ab)use and control of economic power in society'.

However, any policy that simply focuses on the protection of contract rights runs the risk of being too wide. Contract rights are clearly important but so is free competition—to buy up all the commodity in the free market, knowing and intending that that will wreak a rival's contract will not render the purchaser liable in tort and should not do so. Moreover, the focus on contract rights as such has certainly led to unfounded extensions of liability in case law—the 'tort' of interference with contractual relations being the prime example.[215] For this reason it is misleading to rely on Lord Macnaghten's summary of the tort in *Quinn v Leathem*[216] as: 'a violation of a legal right to interfere with contractual relations recognized by law.'

Simply to focus on the 'protected interest' misses the point of *Lumley v Gye* liability. The contract right is only protected against the defendant in certain circumstances by this tort. There have to be special reasons for making the defendant liable where the wrong concerned is the wrong of another and these special reasons must link the defendant with the contractor's breach. *In this sense* Weir is right to argue that a wrongful act is required. For Weir, what is crucial is the fact that the defendant 'got something unlawful done'.[217]

The true principle that lies behind *Lumley v Gye* is much narrower than that advanced by either the property theory or social policy theory, discussed above. The tort does support contract rights but not in a general way. It does not require a 'quasi-property' right as its base. Rather this tort follows the same pattern as the established doctrine of joint tortfeasance. To procure another's tort will render the procurer jointly liable in tort. By

---

[213] Above, n. 177, p. 1508.

[214] Cane, P., *The Anatomy of Tort Law* (Oxford: Hart Publishing, 1997), p. 151.

[215] In *Economic Torts*, above, n. 1, Weir voices this concern. This error still emerges in case law, as is discussed above. Bagshaw, above, n. 201, p. 149 admits that 'some of the arguments borrowed from private property could be deployed to support such an interest [interference with contract, in the absence of breach]' but concludes 'there is a strong case for saying that such an interest is too indeterminate and should therefore only be protected by the general tort of interference with trade by unlawful means'.

[216] [1901] AC 495, p. 535.

[217] Above, n. 1, p. 23.

the doctrine of joint tortfeasance, the procurement leads the law to 'impute' the commission of the same wrongful act to two or more persons at once.[218] Lord Templeman in *CBS Songs v Amstrad Consumer Electronics plc*[219] asserted that procure involves 'incite or induce or persuade'.[220] For such procuring to lead to liability 'generally speaking', it must be directed 'to an individual infringer and must identifiably procure a particular infringement'.[221] In the case itself, it was sought to make manufacturers liable for advertising and selling a high-speed twin tape recorder that could enable recording at high speed from prerecorded cassettes onto blank tapes. Obviously some ultimate purchasers would use this machine to make pirate or unlicensed copies of the copyright works of those in the music business who brought the action. However, the House of Lords held that though they were providing the means whereby unlawful copying of works could be made, they were not procuring such tortious acts. Thus it is clear that some influence on the decision of the main tortfeasor is required. There must be a causal connection between the procurement and the tort. Hence the concept is in theory to be distinguished from 'mere' advice.[222]

The parallel between this doctrine and the tort of inducing breach is clear. Indeed, Erle J noted in *Lumley v Gye* itself 'it is clear that the procurement of the violation of a right is a cause of action in all instances where the violation is an actionable wrong . . . he who procures the wrong is a joint wrongdoer'.[223] Lord Templeman in *CBS Songs v Amstrad Consumer*

---

[218] According to Scrutton LJ in *The Koursk* [1924] p. 140, p. 155.

[219] [1988] AC 1013, p. 1058. A judgment which, according to Knox J in *Grower v BBC* [1990] FSR 595, p. 607, contains the authoritative statement on 'the law on what activities will make a person a joint tortfeasor'.

[220] And, indeed, this is a typical definition, though it might be noted that Lord Macnaghten in *Allen v Flood* [1898] AC 1 drew a distinction between procuring and inducing (p. 149).

[221] Lord Templeman [1988] AC 1013, p. 1058. Weir, T., 'Liability for Knowingly Facilitating Mass Breaches of Copyright' 47 CLJ (1988) 348, p. 349 notes that the need for the procurement to be directed at a particular individual rather than the general public is 'consistent with inducing breach of contract and reminiscent of negligent misrepresentation'.

[222] One who merely advises another may do no more than draw attention to facts which show how eligible or desirable a given course of action is; whereas one who induces and *a fortiori*, one who makes or causes another to act, does something, if only by his words, to make a given course of action more eligible or desirable in the eyes of the other than it would otherwise have been, or seem more eligible or desirable than it really is.' (Hart and Honoré, above, n. 40.)

[223] [1853] 2 E&B 216, p. 232. In fact this 'mixed joint liability' provides better tort protection, based on the breach of contract: the court in *Lumley v Gye* saw a need to protect the plaintiff where the contract rights involved might not be adequate. Higher damages may be recoverable in this tort than could be obtained in an action for breach of contract against the contract breaker: Erle J noted in *Lumley v Gye*, that 'he who procures the damage maliciously might justly be made responsible beyond the liability of the contractor' (1853) 118 ER 749, p. 756. Moreover, the tort avoids the contract principle of 'limited liability and neutrality toward wilful breach', Chutorian, S., 'Tort Remedies for Breach of Contract' 86 Columbia L

Electronics plc referred to the general principle extracted by Erle J in *Lumley v Gye*[224] as 'he who procures the wrong is a joint wrongdoer and may be sued, either alone or jointly with the agent, in the appropriate action for the wrong complained of'. In reality, therefore, this principle draws on the doctrine of joint tortfeasance, with the twist that the primary wrong is breach of contract, rather than a tort—'mixed joint liability' as Glanville Williams termed it.[225]

This rationale ties in well with the scope of the tort. The underlying purpose of the tort is narrow: only protection against contract breach is granted.[226] Moreover, the tort only protects against the most obvious and premeditated interference, involving corruption of the claimant's contract partner. Mere facilitation or interference, therefore, cannot be sufficient for liability. Commercial freedom of action is only curtailed in these extreme circumstances, in line with the general economic torts as a whole. If all actions (however lawful in themselves) which caused a contract to be broken were to be tortious, 'the flood of liability would engulf not only trade union officials but also the most innocent competitive, profit-seeking trader'.[227]

DEFENCE OF JUSTIFICATION

As unlawful means are not part of the tort, it is likely that the defence will be different (and certainly wider) in this tort than any defence of justification that might apply to the general tort of unlawful interference with trade. Conversely, the protection of contract rights (rather than mere contractual expectancies or performance) means that the concept of legitimate purpose, found in the tort of simple conspiracy, cannot apply. So, as Slade J remarked in *Greig v Insole*: 'good faith and absence of malice on the part of a defendant do not as such provide any defence to an action based

---

Rev (1986) 377, p. 377: damages are at large and any intended damage is recoverable, while the damages will be assessed at the date of breach not the time the contract was made. For McChesney, above, n. 202, 'inducement involves gains to both [contract breaker] and inducer and so (since side payments between the two are always possible) optimal remedies must negate the aggregate gain received by both' (p. 166).

[224] (1853) 2 E&B 216, p. 232.

[225] Williams, G., *Joint Torts and Contributory Negligence* (London: Stevens, 1951), p. 3. Note that Waller J in *The Leon* [1991] 2 Lloyd's Law Reports 611 wished to distinguish between procuring a contract breach and procuring a tort, at least where the inducer is an employee.

[226] Danforth, above, n. 6, p. 1517 notes that it is difficult to imagine that 'prospective relations, no matter how potentially advantageous, have the same structural importance as contractual relations'.

[227] Wedderburn, K. W., 'Inducing Breach of Contract and Unlawful Interference with Trade' 31 MLR (1968) 440, p. 445.

on inducement of breach of contract'.[228] If it did the whole market system would be undermined.[229]

Exactly what is involved in the defence is not clear.[230] Two 'tests' to assess whether justification arises in this area have been suggested, but they are both vague. Porter J in *De Jetley Marks v Greenwood* stated that justification must involve 'an action taken on as a duty, not the mere protection of the plaintiff's own interests', while Romer LJ in *Glamorgan Coal Co v S Wales Miners' Federation* defined a wider defence. He stated: 'regard might be had to the nature of the contract broken; the position of the parties to the contract; the grounds for the breach; the means employed to procure the breach; the relation of the party procuring the breach to the person who breaks the contract; and . . . to the object of the person in procuring the breach.'[231] However, he undermined the usefulness of his own test by agreeing with earlier *dicta*[232] that the question would be for the good sense of the tribunal, so that most attempts to give a complete and satisfactory definition would be 'mischievous'.

Though recently it has been accepted that the defence is a flexible one and 'should not be regarded as confined to narrow straitjackets',[233] if the defence is left vague—Gardner comments that the law on the defence is 'notoriously unstable'[234]—it compounds the uncertainty surrounding the tort as a whole. Moreover, at times the tort and its justification are mixed together to provide an unsatisfactory analysis.

A consideration of case law reveals a framework for the defence, in line with the rationale of the tort. Thus the 'sanctity' of contract will be preserved against procured breaches unless there are compelling reasons otherwise. Those compelling reasons may involve the private interest of the defendant or the public interest, but the essential point, as in tort generally, is whether 'the defendant is able to point to some competing interest which outweighs that of the plaintiff'.[235]

---

[228] [1978] 3 All ER 449, p. 491.   [229] Cane, above, n. 214, p. 151.

[230] The former almost total immunity from economic tort liability granted by Parliament for those engaged in peaceful industrial action provided 'a statutory immunity which in effect fulfilled the function of the defence of justification in the labour context'. It may well be, of course, that the existence of these statutory immunities 'made unnecessary further judicial consideration or development of the common law doctrine', O'Dair, R., 'Justifying an Interference with Contractual Rights', 11 OJLS (1991) 227. Now, of course, those immunities are severely curtailed.

[231] According to Partlett, above, n. 177, p. 790 this dictum 'has found favour throughout the common law world'.

[232] Bowen LJ *Mogul Steamship* (1889) 23 QBD 598, pp. 618–19.

[233] Slade J *Greig v Insole* [1978] 3 All ER 449, p. 493.

[234] Gardner, S., 'The Proprietary Effect of Contractual Obligations under *Tulk v Moxhay* and *De Mattos v Gibson*' 98 LQR (1982) 279, p. 290. Fine, above, n. 99, p. 1117 notes that the defence of justification or privilege is still unclear in America.

[235] Cane, above, n. 207, p. 222.

Certain ground rules become apparent: there must actually be a compelling reason rather than an honest but mistaken belief: 'no one can legally excuse himself . . . on the ground that he acted on a wrong understanding of his own rights.'[236] An absence of ill will[237] or the proof of 'impersonal' or 'disinterested motives'[238] is not sufficient. Vague notions such as altruism,[239] community of interests,[240] inequality in wealth or position[241] or the freedom to compete hardly rank as compelling. Moreover, revenge is not a compelling reason: Buckley LJ in *Smithies v NAOP* rejected the defendants' contention that: 'where there are two independent contracts, the breach of the one by the one party entitles a breach of the other by the other party.'[242] Again, there is no defence of 'partial' justification, based on contributory negligence. This issue was raised before Smellie J in the New Zealand High Court in the case of *Dellabarca v Northern Storemen and Packers Union*.[243] There, the plaintiff manager had, on behalf of his employer, bribed union delegates over a period of time to prevent strikes. When this fact was revealed, the union threatened to strike unless the plaintiff was dismissed. The union argued that, though liable for inducing breach of the plaintiff's contract, the plaintiff had been contributorily negligent in paying the bribes. The court rejected this claim, citing Lord Lindley in *Quinn v Leathem*,[244] 'the intention to injure the plaintiff negatives all excuses'.[245]

On analysis, case law reveals that the defence covers three areas: protecting private rights; protecting private interests; protecting the public interest.

---

[236] Darling J in *Read v Operative Society of Stonemasons* [1902] 2 KB 88. Honest belief whether (in law) contract rights would be breached could still lead to liability in the tort: see *Metropolitan Borough of Solihull v NUT* [1985] IRLR 211 Warner J. However, note Dixon J in *James v The Commonwealth* (1939) 62 CLR 339, p. 370 asserted: 'assuming bona fides, the law always countenances resort to the courts . . . an intention to put the law in motion cannot be considered as wrongful procurement or inducement simply because it turns out that the legal position maintained was ill-founded.'

[237] Lord Halsbury LC *S Wales Miners' Federation v Glamorgan Coal Co* [1905] AC 239, p. 244.

[238] Slade J in *Greig v Insole* [1978] 3 All ER 449, p. 492.

[239] Darling J in *Read v Operative Society of Stonemasons* [1902] 2 KB 88, p. 95 'nor even that he acted as an altruist, seeking only the good of another and careless of his own disadvantage'.

[240] Rejected as a defence by Simonds J in *Camden Nominees v Forcey* [1940] 1 Ch 352, p. 362 and McCardie J in *Pratt v BMA* [1919] 1 KB 244, p. 266: no justification that the defendants had acted for the advancement of the interests of those with whom they were associated.

[241] A 'dangerous proposition' *per* Simonds J in *Camden Nominees v Forcey* [1940] 1 Ch 352, p. 366.   [242] [1909] 1 KB 310, p. 337.

[243] [1989] 2 NZLR 734, NZHC.   [244] [1901] AC 495, p. 537.

[245] Wedderburn, above, n. 1 para 24-64 contends that the defence is not available in this tort, at any rate where the defendant has engaged in dishonest means. He cites *Alliance and Leicester BS v Edgestop Ltd* [1993] 1 WLR 1463 (deceit) and *Corporacion Nacional del Cobre de Chile v Sogemin Metals Ltd* [1997] 2 All ER 917 (bribery excluded defence both in law and equity).

(i) Private right as justification

It would appear that the defendant who asserts a legally enforceable right has the most chance of success in justifying what would otherwise be the tort of inducing breach of contract. A notion of self-help seems to apply. The most useful judicial acknowledgement of this appears in the often-cited *dicta* of Darling J in *Read v Operative Society of Stonemasons*[246] that the justification for interference with the plaintiff's right 'must be an equal or superior right in themselves'. Stuart-Smith LJ in *Edwin Hill and Partners v First National Finance Corporation*[247] asserted that 'justification . . . based upon an equal or superior right in the defendant must clearly be a legal right. Such right may derive from property, real or personal or from contractual rights.'

The Court of Appeal in *Edwin Hill and Partners v First National Finance Corporation*[248] cited the American case of *Winters v University District Building and Loan Association*[249] as an example of an overriding property right. Here the mortgagee bank was justified in discouraging a buyer from purchasing the mortgagor's property: it was entitled to demand better security from this assignee of the mortgagor, even though that led to a breach of contract by the assignee.[250]

Of course the most common example of justifying the tort by reference to an 'equal or superior right' is where there is a collision of contracts. It is clear that this defence protects a defendant who induces breach in order to protect his *pre-existing* contract, with which the second contract is inconsistent.[251]

Indeed, protecting an earlier right may justify a new agreement/variation between the original contracting partners, even though that necessitates a breach of the plaintiff's contract. Thus in *Edwin Hill and Partners v*

---

[246] [1902] 2 KB 88, p. 96.
[247] [1989] 1 WLR 225, p. 233.
[248] [1989] 1 WLR 225.
[249] 268 Ill App 147 (1932).
[250] In *Rogers Cable TV Ltd v 373041 Ontario Ltd* (1994) 22 OR (3d) 25 Epstein J, Ontario Court of Justice the plaintiff had entered into contracts for the provision of cable with tenants in an apartment block and a separate agreement with the building owners for the provision of cable and all the incidental access rights for the installation of equipment. Subsequent owners of the building (not bound by their predecessors' contract with the plaintiff) informed the tenants of a more advantageous contract for cable provision that they had finalized with a different cable provider. Though they thereby induced breaches of the plaintiff's contract with the tenants, they were held to be justified on the basis that they were asserting an equal or superior right to the plaintiff's contract right—otherwise they would lose control over who would be permitted onto their own property.
[251] It would appear that this defence can only be raised where the defendant asserts his own 'equal or superior' right. In *Greig v Insole* [1978] 3 All ER 449 the defendants submitted that, as the governing bodies of cricket, they were entitled to interfere with the contracts between county cricket players and World Series Cricket. However, Slade J felt only the clubs themselves could raise this point.

First National Finance Corporation[252] the defendant, a finance company, had provided a substantial loan to a property developer to enable him to develop a property; this contract contained an express power of sale and power to appoint a receiver. The property developer had engaged the plaintiff as architects for this development. When the developer was unable to repay, the defendant, instead of exercising their power of sale,[253] chose instead to finance the development themselves, making it a condition of this agreement that the contract with the plaintiff should be terminated, thereby reaching an accommodation beneficial to both the contracting parties. This was held to be a justified inducement to breach: the defendant was asserting an 'equal or superior right'. Here the defendant's original contract which predated the plaintiff's contract was still being asserted when the defendant induced the breach.[254] Though the original contract was varied, the overall effect on the plaintiff was the same as if the original contract had been enforced. The right under the original contract was to enforce the charge and bring the contract to an end. It had been agreed by the parties that if the defendant, under the original contract, had appointed a receiver, a new architect could have been appointed.[255] The dismissal of the plaintiff could have been justified under the existing contract. Therefore, the overall effect of the varied deal was the same as asserting the original superior right.[256]

The fact that the defendant's contract pre-existed the plaintiff's was obviously important in *Edwin Hill and Partners v First National Finance Corporation*. But what if the defendant's contract, though innocently entered into, is subsequent to and inconsistent with the claimant's?[257] Would that innocence provide a defence should the defendant exercise his contract rights to the detriment of the claimant? There are *dicta* either way

---

[252] [1989] 1 WLR 225.

[253] This would have been insufficient, as undeveloped land, to cover the loan. Cf. the facts of *Dirassar v Kelly* (1966) 59 DLR 2d 452.

[254] The fact that he was *de facto* enforcing the earlier contract appeared important in the judgments of Stuart-Smith and Nourse LJJ, the latter commenting that the new financing deal was 'intended to support the [original] right', [1989] 1 WLR 225.

[255] O'Dair, above, n. 230, p. 229, however, contends that it was not obvious that the appointment of a receiver should have the effect of terminating the plaintiff's contract, unless the contract of loan contained a special power to this effect.

[256] This result should be compared to the facts of the '*Nadezhda Krupskaya*' [1997] 2 Lloyds LR, 35 Rix J. There the defendants were the owners of a vessel, sub-sub-chartered to their main competitors, the plaintiffs. By their original charter they had no right to object to any subletting and an attempt to vary this, in the defendants' favour, came too late. The plaintiffs had already entered into the relevant sub-charter: the inducement to breach that sub-charter could not be justified. The case itself looks more like an example of indirect than direct inducement.

[257] Unless both parties knew of the earlier contract, the second contract is not invalid: *British Homophone v Kunz* (1935) 152 LT 589. See Lauterpacht, above, n. 117.

on this point, Cohen-Grabelsky[258] acknowledging that the authorities are not easily reconcilable. Yet Gardner notes: 'the superiority of the defendant's contract apparently rests on its temporal priority. There is no case, other than *Swiss Bank Corp v Lloyds Bank*[259] to the effect that innocently entering into a subsequent contract will justify interference with an earlier inconsistent one.'[260]

(ii) Private interest as justification

Here there are greater uncertainties partly because of a dearth of case law, other than American decisions. Such decisions can provide useful illustrations (and for the justification of public interest), though with the *caveat* that justification plays a far more important role in the American version of the tort.[261]

Thus it is likely that a justification for inducing breach of contract based on the protection of health and safety (either the defendant's or his family's) would be accepted by the English courts. Cane notes: 'there is a public interest in the protection of persons from death and bodily injury or illness.'[262] Carpenter examples, from American law, *Legris v Marcotte*[263] where it was held that no liability arose when a mother, whose children attended a private school, induced the principal to break his contract with the parents of children at the school who were suffering from an infectious disease. Indeed, the relationship between the inducer and contract

---

[258] Cohen-Grabelsky, N., 'Interference with Contractual Relations and Equitable Doctrines' 45 MLR (1982) 241; see also Rogers, W. V. H., *Winfield and Jolowicz on Tort*, 15th edn. (London: Sweet & Maxwell, 1998), p. 633. Treitel, G. H., *The Law of Contract*, 9th edn. (London: Sweet & Maxwell, 1999) asserts, p. 565: 'the principle on which it [the defence of justification] is based appears to be equally applicable where C's contract with A was made after B's [with A] but in ignorance of it.'

[259] [1979] Ch 548, pp. 569–73.

[260] Gardner, above, n. 234, p. 291 and note Goff LJ in *Pritchard v Briggs* [1980] Ch 338, 399–405. Of course, it might be argued that such an innocent defendant, in insisting on his contract rights is merely preventing the performance of the claimant's contract rather than inducing breach. Note the position of a secured creditor as against unsecured creditors: in *WA Ellis Services Ltd v Stuart Wood* 1993 2 EG 43 plaintiffs argued unsuccessfully that the tort arose because the defendant had taken a secured charge when the company was in such a parlous financial position that prior unsecured creditors would almost certainly not be paid. Anthony Watson QC (sitting as deputy judge Ch D) asserted (p. 47): 'as a matter of principle it seems to me that taking a debenture which might result in a contract with a third party being broken, in general would be too remote from the breach of contract to amount to the tort of unlawful interference with contract.'

[261] In *Knapp v Penfield* (1932) 256 NYS 41 the defendant was the promoter for a musical show and was not liable when she demanded that the inexperienced plaintiff, who had been contracted to star in the show, was dismissed. The court found that the recovery of the defendant's large financial investment was dependent on the success of the play. However, it is submitted that the courts on this side of the Atlantic would be cautious about such a proposed defence.

[262] Cane, above, n. 207, p. 224.

[263] (1906) 129 Ill App 67.

breaker may provide a wider justification. Lord James in *S Wales Miners' Federation v Glamorgan Coal Co*[264] mentioned the possibility of justification in cases where 'the claims of relationship or guardianship demand an interference amounting to protection'.[265]

(iii) Public interest as justification

Justification based on public interest may relate to the use of public powers or privileges. The *bona fide* actions of a regulatory body in inducing breach of contract might amount to justification (at least where the contract in question is expressly or impliedly subject to that regulatory function). In *Posluns v Toronto*[266] the Toronto Stock Exchange had withdrawn approval for the plaintiff's continued employment (which had been subject to the Exchange's control). They were held to be justified in any consequent breach they induced.[267] However, the court stressed that the Exchange had acted within its bye-laws and complied with the rules of natural justice.[268] Again, a public body may induce a breach of contract and justify that by reference to the concept of statutory privilege. So in *Stott v Gamble*[269] a film was banned by the licensing justices, leading to justified breach of contract between the plaintiff and theatre proprietors.

Obviously any defence of public interest has to be weighty enough to persuade the court that it is a social interest 'of greater public import than is the social interest involved in the protection of the plaintiff's interest'.[270] Thus there would appear to be a clear public interest in the protection of public health and safety. In *Church of Scientology of California v Kaufman*[271] Goff J refused an interlocutory injunction in a case where one of the defendants was alleged to have induced breach of the plaintiffs' contract. The public interest defence succeeded, the defendants having provided clear evidence that the works of the plaintiffs (which were central to the contract alleged to have been breached) might do harm to the physical or mental health of readers.[272]

---

[264] [1905] AC 239, p. 249.

[265] *Crofter Handwoven Harris Tweed v Veitch* [1942] AC 435, pp. 442–3: 'a father may persuade his daughter to break her engagement to marry a scoundrel' without being liable (V. Simon LC); *Gunn v Barr* [1926] 1 DLR 855.

[266] 46 DLR (2d) (1964) 210; 53 DLR (2d) (1966) 193.

[267] Heydon, J. D., 'The Defence of Justification in Cases of Intentionally Inflicted Economic Loss' 20 U Toronto LJ (1970) 140, p. 167 'public interest in reputable financial dealings'.

[268] See also *Shearson Lehman Hutton Inc v Maclaine Watson & Co Ltd* [1989] 2 Lloyd's Law Reports 570, Webster J.   [269] [1916] 2 KB 504.

[270] Carpenter, C., 'Interference with Contract Relations' 41 Har L Rev (1928) 728, p. 745.

[271] [1973] RPC 635.

[272] Goff J noted the views of Lord Denning MR in *Hubbard v Vosper* [1972] 2 QB 84, pp. 95–7 (a case of breach of confidence and copyright) that the defence of public interest could be made out where the material in issue 'indicated medical quackeries of a sort which might be dangerous if practised behind closed doors'.

Though mere advice does not give rise to the tort, there may be situations where that advice is deemed to be persuasion. The Restatement (Second) of Torts grants a 'privilege' that denies liability for such persuasion given in the context of a 'welfare' relationship,[273] i.e. where the defendant is responsible for the welfare of another and in such capacity acts to protect the other by inducing breach of his contract. A spiritual or legal adviser, doctor, parent (or person *in loco parentis*) or teacher may be included in this category. The Restatement requires 'honest' advice and would appear, therefore, to be a qualified defence. It is likely that a similar defence applies in England, largely limited to requested professional advice[274] or welfare advice. Of course, on occasion welfare advice could merge into a public morality defence (see below) and would not then require the presence of a welfare relationship.[275]

Ultimately, this category shades into a justification based on a moral imperative or duty, where case law reveals only one case of clear application. It has been assumed that a defendant can raise 'public morality' as a defence to the tort, an assumption based on the case of *Brimelow v Casson*.[276] Here the defendants were held to owe a duty to their members to take all necessary steps to compel the plaintiff to pay his chorus girls a living wage so that they were not driven to supplement their earnings through prostitution. Their attempt to coerce the plaintiff by inducing theatre proprietors to break their contracts with the plaintiff was held to be justified.[277] No case has applied this principle subsequently. This is perhaps not surprising, as the notion of moral duty raises two problems for a court: how to weigh economic loss against moral concern; conversely how to ensure that the support for that moral concern will be

---

[273] In fact the Restatement (Second) of Torts, ss.770 and 772 contain a range of 'advice' privileges: from professional (and presumably, therefore, disinterested) requested advice to such unrequested advice.

[274] *Brown v Spamberger* (1959) 21 DLR 2d 630: seems to go too far. Here far from disinterested advice was volunteered, where no welfare relationship was involved. The vendor of land was advised by the purchaser that the vendor's commission agreement with the defendant was 'unenforceable' which led to a breach of that contract. It is hard to see that the English courts would follow this.

[275] It may well be that welfare advice would include unsolicited advice on a moral dilemma posed by the contract: a judge may be reluctant to appear to be taking sides in a moral debate. Weir, T., *A Casebook on Tort*, 9th edn. (London: Sweet & Maxwell, 2000), p. 613 notes: 'it is an error to suppose that all contracts are equally binding: it depends very much what interests are involved . . . if a pregnant woman contracts to have a lawful abortion I certainly cannot be sued by the disappointed clinic if I persuade her to break her word and keep the baby.'

[276] [1924] 1 Ch 302.

[277] The basis of the decision is not clear: Simonds J in *Camden Nominees v Forcey* [1940] Ch 352, p. 366 believed the decision to rest on an application of the doctrine of *ex turpi causa non oritur actio*. However, it was approved in *Crofter Hand Woven Harris Tweed v Veitch* [1942] AC 435, p. 495 (Lord Porter).

effective.[278] Thus it has been described as an 'extreme case' by Peter Gibson LJ in *Timeplan Education Group v NUT*.[279]

Finally, it may be that even where a possible justification exists, the courts would require a 'legitimate' reliance on that justification. In *Read v Operative Society of Stonemasons*[280] Collins MR asserted: 'the justification to be of any avail must cover their whole conduct, the means they used as well as the end they had in view.' There are indications, therefore, that there may be a notion of legitimate application, attached to the defence.[281]

Category 2: Causing Breach or Interference with Contract as Unlawful Interference with Trade

Since *Lumley v Gye* the courts have 'actively promoted'[282] the tort, so that a variety of torts appear to have been revealed within that principle. The most frequently cited summary of these torts contained under the umbrella title of 'inducing breach of contract' is to be found in the judgment of Jenkins LJ in *D.C. Thomson & Co Ltd v Deakin*.[283] The forms of the tort, other than the classic form of direct persuasion (as in *Lumley v Gye*), that he identified, *viz*. direct intervention and indirect intervention in the contract have been accepted by courts and commentators alike.

However, as has already been suggested, this process of extending the tort from its classic formulation should be reversed and we should refuse to accept the 'gospel-like quality'[284] attributed to Jenkins LJ's suggested torts. It is clear that both direct and indirect interference are examples of the general tort of unlawful interference with trade. Whereas direct *persuasion* focuses on the claimant's contract rights and protects against a direct inducement to breach those rights, direct and indirect *intervention* focus on the deliberate use of unlawful means by the defendant, i.e. 'the intervener, instead of so acting upon the mind of the contracting party himself, by some other act, tortious in itself, prevents the contracting

---

[278] Thus it is not clear whether the intervention in *Brimelow v Casson* [1924] 1 Ch 302 had the desired effect or whether it may have driven the out-of-work chorus girls into full-time prostitution.

[279] [1996] IRLR 457, p. 460.

[280] [1902] 2 KB 732, p. 737.

[281] Commenting on the American concept of improper interference with contract, Carpenter, above, n. 270, p. 746 noted 'the privilege is conditional or qualified; that is, it is lost if exercised for the wrong purpose. In general, a wrong purpose exists where the act is done other than as a reasonable or bona fide attempt to protect the interests of the defend-ant.' However, it is not necessary to show actual breach of contract to fall within the American tort of interference with contractual relations.

[282] Fleming, J., *The Law of Torts*, 9th edn. (Sydney: LBC Information Services, 1998), p. 756.

[283] [1952] Ch 646.

[284] Weir, above, n. 1.

party from performing the bargain'.[285] Prevention is the key but there must be unlawful means used to bring about that prevention, so that lawful, aggressive competition is allowed.

By locating these 'varieties' within the general tort, it is apparent that the intention required involves a directed, 'aimed at' harm. It is not sufficient that the harm to the claimant simply be an inevitable consequence of the defendant's deliberate actions. An intention to harm the claimant is paramount, 'were it otherwise, the limitations slowly elaborated against unduly wide recovery for economic loss caused by negligent acts would be swept away by somewhat unreal extensions of the "intentional" economic torts'.[286] It also becomes clear that it is no longer contract rights that are the focus of liability. Trade or even 'economic interests' are protected. The 'half-way' tort of unlawful interference with contract performance, often pleaded where it is feared that the ultimate breach of contract may not be established,[287] is therefore an unnecessary addition to the economic torts. The emphasis on contract performance is a red herring. Such cases should be seen for what they are—examples of the general tort. The defendant is liable because he has intentionally used unlawful means in order to harm the claimant's economic interests. *Dimbleby & Sons Ltd v NUJ*[288] provides a good example of the general tort being masked by the half-way tort. In that case the plaintiff's journalists refused, in breach of their contracts of employment, to provide copy, causing the plaintiff problems in his contract with his publishing company. By going to 'extraordinary shifts' the plaintiff was able to produce its newspapers and provide its publisher with copy. Sir John Donaldson found this to be an unlawful interference with the plaintiff's commercial contract. Hindrance—i.e. making the contract more onerous—was sufficient for the tort. But this is not *Lumley v Gye* liability: it is unlawful (inducing breach of the journalists' contracts) interference with trade.[289] The half-way tort does not in fact exist.[290]

Given these varieties have been relied upon in major cases, especially

---

[285] As Lord Evershed MR noted in *Thomson v Deakin* [1952] Ch 646, p. 678.

[286] Wedderburn, above, n. 1, para 24–18.

[287] In fact such fears will often be unfounded. The effect of the particular exclusion clause needs to be analysed. If the effect of such a clause is to limit liability rather than exclude the obligation to perform then the co-contractor will still be in breach of contract and the defendant will still be liable for causing the breach. This follows Lord Diplock's analysis in *Photo Productions v Securicor* [1980] AC 827. In that case he asserted: 'every failure to perform a primary obligation is a breach of contract.'

[288] [1984] 1 WLR 67, at Court of Appeal level. The House of Lords did not consider this point [1984] 1 WLR 427.

[289] It may, of course, be questioned whether the plaintiff as 'piggy in the middle' should have been allowed to sue.

[290] See Carty, H., 'Intentional Violation of Economic Interests: the Limits of Common Law Liability' 104 LQR (1988) 250, pp. 257–8.

involving secondary industrial action, their ingredients have been discussed by the courts. What follows is a definition of these 'varieties' based on that discussion. However, in reality these cases are better seen as involving a short-sighted view as to the true scope of the liability identified. Though contract breach appears important in the ingredients identified below, in fact it is not important. Rather liability is dependent on the use of additional unlawful means to effect economic harm. The modern analysis of liability once described as direct or indirect interference is now to be found in the chapter on unlawful interference with trade.[291]

Direct intervention

There is tort liability for direct intervention[292] where the defendant 'does an act which, if done by one of the parties to it, would have been a breach'. Liability, therefore, would result should the defendant physically prevent the claimant's contractual partner from performing his contract, an example given by both Lord Evershed MR and Jenkins LJ in *Thomson v Deakin*.[293] Liability for direct intervention would also arise, according to Morris LJ in that same case, should the defendant force the partner to break his contract with the plaintiff by depriving the partner of his only possible means of performing the contract: 'as for example, by removing the only available essential tools or by kidnapping a necessary or irreplaceable servant.'[294] Thus in *GWK Ltd v Dunlop Rubber Co*,[295] a car manufacturer had contracted with the plaintiffs to display the plaintiffs' tyres on the cars, when they were exhibited at a motor show. The defendants were held liable for this tort when they removed the plaintiffs' tyres (a trespass to the manufacturer's goods) and replaced them with their own.

The better view is that even with direct intervention cases, unlawful means must be used by the defendant in order to effect the breach.[296] This was the view of Lord Evershed MR in *Thomson v Deakin*. He asserted: 'acts of a third party lawful in themselves do not constitute an actionable interference with contractual rights merely because they bring about a breach of contract, even if they were done with the object and intention of bringing about such a breach.'[297] He instanced a defendant who, knowing of a supply contract for a particular commodity between the plaintiff and his

---

[291] See Ch. 5.   [292] Jenkins LJ [1952] Ch 646, pp. 694–5.
[293] Ibid. 695.   [294] Ibid. 702.
[295] (1926) 42 TLR 376: note the court included compensation for loss of prestige.
[296] Rix J *The Nadezhda Krupskaya* [1997] 2 Lloyd's Law Reports 35, p. 40 'I am far from satisfied that the contractually valid exercise of a right of withdrawal . . . could ever be tortious, even if done with the intention of destroying some sub-charter.' Heydon, J. D., 'The Future of the Economic Torts' 12 UWALR (1975–6) 1, pp. 1–2 would disagree given his view of *Einhorn v Westmont Investments Ltd* (1969) 6 DLR (3d) 71.
[297] [1952] Ch 646, p. 693.

contractual partner and wishing to deprive the defendant of the benefit of the contract, buys up that commodity in the market, rendering it impossible for the partner to perform the contract. In such a case, the defendant would not be acting tortiously.[298]

Indirect intervention

With indirect intervention (often referred to as indirect inducement)[299] the ultimate breach of which the claimant complains[300] must be a necessary[301] consequence of the defendant's unlawful act.

The classic example of the tort in a trade dispute would be an attack on the claimant's commercial contracts by persuading others to participate in a boycott of deliveries to the claimant or a boycott of the production of goods destined for the claimant.[302] In legal terms this might well involve the defendant inducing employees to break their contracts of employment (unlawful means) in order to disable their employer from fulfilling his obligations under the commercial contract he has with the claimant. This, of course, is the context in which Jenkins LJ accepted the principle of indirect intervention. Here there would be indirect intervention in the claimant's contract (indirect because the claimant's contract partner has not been approached directly) and unlawful means would have been used to achieve the desired end result.[303]

With this variety of the tort it is clearly established that the defendant must employ unlawful means in order to cause the ultimate breach of the claimant's contract. In *Thomson v Deakin* the Court of Appeal were asked to accept that indirect intervention did not require this additional element of unlawfulness. It was argued that provided the defendants intentionally caused a breach of the plaintiff's contract, then they should be liable, by analogy with the tort of direct inducement. However, it was held that there must be unlawful means used, prior to the plaintiff's contract being broken. There is thus a clear difference between the direct persuasion to breach of contract and the intentional bringing about of the breach by

---

[298] Cf Heydon, above, n. 1, p. 31; Rogers, above, n. 258, agrees with the author.

[299] This extension was established in *Thomson v Deakin* [1952] Ch 646 and accepted in *Stratford v Lindley* [1965] AC 269.

[300] Note that if the general tort of unlawful interference with trade is alleged, no breach of contract need be shown.

[301] Doubts on how strict this causation requirement is were raised by Hoffmann LJ in *Middlebrook Mushrooms Ltd v TGWU* [1993] ICR 612, pp. 624–5 and see Jenkins LJ in *Thomson v Deakin* [1952] Ch 646, p. 697 'the contract breaker was unable, as a matter of practical possibility, to perform his contract'.

[302] For a case not on these classic lines see *News Group Newspapers v SOGAT 82* [1987] ICR 181, where nuisance was the unlawful means used.

[303] The ultimate breach could be many stages removed see *Merkur Island Shipping Corp v Laughton* [1983] 2 AC 570.

indirect means.[304] As Morris LJ accepted in *Thomson v Deakin*, only if those indirect means involve 'wrongdoing' will the defendant be liable. Thus in *Thomson v Deakin* itself, the plaintiffs (printers and publishers) relied on paper supplied under contract by Bowaters Sales Ltd. When a trade dispute arose between the trade union and the plaintiffs, trade unionists were called upon by the defendants not to handle goods destined for the plaintiffs. Bowaters' drivers informed their employer that they were not prepared to deliver paper to the plaintiffs. Bowaters decided that they would not require their drivers to do so, thereby breaching their supply contract with the plaintiffs. The defendants might have intended this ultimate breach of the commercial contract[305] but the defendants could not be liable because (as luck would have it)[306] no unlawful means had been used to achieve this breach: the drivers were not in breach of their contracts of employment because their employer, Bowaters, had not required the deliveries to be made.

RATIONALE

As has been shown, the umbrella title 'inducing breach of contract' for all the torts discussed above is at best misleading. By separating out the varieties of the tort it is clear that the torts of direct intervention and indirect intervention are swallowed up and thereby expanded by the more recently acknowledged tort of unlawful interference with trade. In essence whether or not a breach of contract results then becomes irrelevant:[307] for Fleming they are examples of the general tort of unlawful interference, the breach of contract being only make-weight. The deliberate use of unlawful means justifies the intervention of the law—as it does throughout the species of the general tort. The doctrine of joint tortfeasance has no relevance to such examples of unlawful interference with trade, for, as Elias and Ewing[308] point out: '[they involve] a change in the

---

[304] Lord Denning was not at first prepared to accept this: see *Daily Mirror Newspapers v Gardner* [1968] 2 B 762, p. 782; however, he accepted the difference as necessary in *Torquay Hotel v Cousins* [1969] 2 Ch D 106, p. 138.

[305] Though the Court of Appeal were not convinced that there was any evidence of any actual knowledge by the defendants of any contract between Bowaters and the plaintiffs.

[306] The focus on certainty and limits on liability are bound to throw up such cases where through luck rather than endeavour the defendant is not liable in the economic torts. Rogers, above, n. 258, comments that: 'despite the arbitrary results capable of being produced by the requirement of illegality' if the requirement were abandoned 'a much greater burden would have to be placed upon the defence of justification if we were to avoid the intolerable situation that A was liable to C whenever and however he knowingly brought about a breach of a contract between B and C' (p. 626).

[307] See Fleming, above, n. 282, p. 759, n. 72.

[308] Elias, P., and Ewing, K., 'Economic Torts and Labour Laws: Old Principles and New Liabilities' 41 CLJ (1982) 321, p. 329 (re *Torquay Hotel v Cousins* [1969] 2 Ch 106).

underlying principle of *Lumley v Gye* for the defendant can no longer be said to be responsible for the unlawful conduct of the third party. He is liable for his own conduct independently of third party liability.'

CONCLUSION

The tort of inducing breach of contract—of which there is only one true variety—needs to be kept within strict bounds to avoid the courts becoming embroiled in a general debate as to what is permissible competitive behaviour. Weir is rightly critical of the tendency to enlarge the tort: he suggests that this has led to room for error and 'baleful consequences'.[309] To avoid such consequences, the tort requires a 'targeted' breach of the claimant's contract and the presence of inducement/procurement of that breach (rather than prevention *per se*). The development of the tort in America is proof of this need.[310] There, interference with contract or prospective contractual relations may lead to liability, with *prima facie* tort liability for intentional harm.[311] Academic dissatisfaction over the scope of the tort led to difficulties in defining the tort for the Restatement (Second) of Torts.[312] In order to meet the objection that liability for intentional interference *per se* would unduly restrict free enterprise and the competitive process, the concept of 'improper' interference was inserted in the ultimate draft.[313] Yet clarity—obviously important in the commercial world—demands that liability be imposed on grounds that are certain and that the defence of justification should be residual. Once the tort is seen to demand intentional procurement of a breach (or indeed of another tort) then its affinity with the doctrine of joint tortfeasance becomes clear.

---

[309] Weir, above, n. 1, p. 41.

[310] [In] Germany, France and the United States a client consulting his lawyer about a proposed course of action can be told no more than he runs the risk of being made to pay if the court finds his conduct immoral, unreasonable or improper' (Weir, above, n. 1, p. 68).

[311] Indeed, in California Danforth, above, n. 6, p. 1505 notes 'the tort protects all advantageous relations' including protection against negligent interference with such relations (at least where the foreseeability and relationship are high) see *J'Aire Corp v Gregory* 598 P. 2d 60. (1979) Calif SC.

[312] Restatement (Second) of Torts ss. 766–74. See Partlett, above, n. 177, p. 786.

[313] The interference could be improper through motive or means, with the relevant factors that need to be balanced listed in the Restatement (Second) of Torts, s.767 (noted in Ch. 10).

4

Intimidation

HISTORY AND MODERN FORM

Prior to 1964, the tort of intimidation was an 'obscure, unfamiliar and peculiar cause of action', having its roots in cases involving physical violence and threats.[1] Thus in *Garret v Taylor*[2] it was held that a quarry-man had a cause of action against the defendant who had caused the plaintiff's customers to discontinue buying the quarried stone by threatening them with 'mayhem'. 'Mayhem' was interpreted by the judges in *Allen v Flood* as violence.[3] In *Tarleton v M'Gawley*[4] the plaintiff was trading with natives from his ship, off the coast of Africa. To dissuade the natives from trading with his rival, the defendant shot and killed natives who approached the plaintiff's ship. Lord Kenyon said that the plaintiff was entitled to recover for the harm done to his trade by the 'improper' conduct of the defendant. There are also *dicta* in *Keeble v Hickeringill*[5] that it would not be lawful for rival schools to take to violence in order to 'persuade' scholars to attend their own establishment.

However, the modern form of this economic tort arose 'out of the circumstances of modern industrial relations'.[6] In *Rookes v Barnard* the plaintiff sought to use this tort where he had been lawfully dismissed by his employer, due to pressure put on that employer by the defendants. That pressure took the form of threatened strike action by the defendants (the plaintiff's colleagues)[7] which constituted a threat to break their

---

[1] The notion of liability in criminal law for 'coercion' was central to the judicial response to the emerging trade unions in the nineteenth century, see e.g. *R v Druitt* (1867) 10 Cox 592, combination to insult and annoy held to be an actionable conspiracy; cited by Lord Macnaghten in *Quinn v Leathem* [1901] AC 495.　　　　　　　[2] (1620) Cro. Jac. 567.

[3] See [1898] AC 1, e.g. Lawrance J, p. 58 and Wright J, p. 104.

[4] (1793) Peake NP 270.

[5] (1706) 11 East 574, p. 575. At times, however, Holt CJ comes close to a *prima facie* tort basis of liability. He is reported as asserting 'he that hinders another in his trade or livelihood is liable to an action for so hindering him', while another report contains the following example in his judgment: 'suppose defendant had shot in his own ground, if he had occasion to shoot it would have been one thing, but to shoot on purpose to damage the plaintiff is another thing and a wrong' (11 Mod 74, p. 75). However, in *Allen v Flood* [1898] AC 1, *Keeble v Hickeringill* was held to be of doubtful authority, with the cases referred to by Holt CJ examples of unlawful means or conspiracy liability.

[6] Lord Evershed [1964] AC 1129, p. 1185.

[7] Rookes had originally belonged to the trade union but later resigned. To ensure 100 per cent membership, all his colleagues passed a resolution that unless Rookes was dismissed there would be a strike.

contracts of employment.[8] Obviously, Rookes could not complain of what his employer had done: they were entitled to dismiss him with notice. Rather, he relied on the threats to break the contracts of employment and sued the defendants for intimidation and conspiracy.[9] In essence, he had to succeed on the intimidation allegation, otherwise the defendants would be protected by the then extensive statutory immunities from economic tort liability for those involved in a trade dispute. His case centred on the argument that the tort of intimidation was not limited to threatened physical harm or nuisance but was wide enough to encompass a threatened breach of contract.

Both the Court of Appeal and the House of Lords accepted that the tort existed. The defendants' counsel had sought to argue that the earlier cases were based on nuisance, rather than the tort the plaintiff alleged. But this was rejected, Lord Hodson[10] noting that *Garrett v Taylor* and *Tarleton v MGawley* could not be explained on the ground of nuisance or some other recognized tort. However, the Court of Appeal refused to accept that the tort of intimidation extended to a threat to break a contract. They held that the tort should be confined to intimidation involving acts of violence, or threats of a tortious or criminal character. The decision of the Court of Appeal appears to have been on 'prudential grounds';[11] the real issue behind the case was whether the court was happy to create a tort that would be central to the lawfulness or otherwise of trade disputes. Thus Donovan LJ expressly took into account 'wider considerations'[12] than simply precedent. The fact that the new tort would drive 'a coach and four'[13] through the then statutory immunities, rendering statutory protection against liability 'largely illusory', and encouraging 'lightning strikes' were important considerations.[14] Moreover, the court pointed to the fact that threats to strike are so common that if the tort existed, it was odd that it had not already been accepted.[15]

---

[8] This was conceded by counsel. Note that Russell LJ in *Morgan v Fry* [1968] 2 QB 710 held that notice of breach should not be regarded as unlawful means.

[9] The defendants were officials of the union and apart from one, also employees of BOAC. The official who was not an employee, Silverthorne, was held liable in conspiracy. He would also be liable as a joint tortfeasor (see Ch. 2). This was doubted by Donovan LJ [1963] 1 QB 627, p. 684 but the House of Lords had little difficulty in holding Silverthorne to be jointly liable.

[10] [1964] AC 1129, p. 1198.

[11] See Hamson, C. J., 'A further note on *Rookes v Barnard*' [1964] CLJ 159, p. 160.

[12] [1963] 1 QB 623, p. 628.

[13] The phrase used by the defendants' counsel.

[14] Donovan LJ [1963] 1 QB 623, p. 683. He continued that if the plaintiff were correct 'the policy which workmen should pursue in order to avoid liability is to strike first and negotiate afterwards'.

[15] Interestingly, coercion was alleged in *Allen v Flood* [1898] AC 1 but it was found as a fact that no compulsion resulted from the advice given.

However, in a decision that surprised many,[16] the House of Lords found in favour of the plaintiff. In a 'bold instance of judicial lawmaking',[17] where the absence of direct authority provided a 'clear hand' according to Lord Evershed,[18] they held that a threat to break a contract constituted sufficient unlawful means for liability.[19] Lord Reid held that: 'threatening a breach of contract may be a much more coercive weapon than threatening a tort . . . and if there is no technical reason requiring a distinction between different kinds of threats, I can see no other ground for making any such distinction.'[20] According to Lord Evershed, logic and reason required this result for, as Lord Devlin asserted: 'the nature of the threat is immaterial . . . all that matters to the plaintiff is that metaphorically speaking a club has been used.' So in *Rookes* the defendants were liable.[21] The acknowledgement of this as the tort of intimidation denied the defendants the immunity then contained in the Trade Disputes Act 1906 and led to the Trade Disputes Act 1965, conferring immunity for the new tort.[22]

INGREDIENTS

Intimidation involves the defendant using an unlawful threat to successfully compel another to obey his wishes in order to harm the claimant.[23]

---

[16] Lord Evershed [1964] AC 1129, p. 1186 noted that the court had all the relevant *dicta* since *Mogul v McGregor* [1892] AC 25 drawn to their attention and he conceded: 'upon the face of them these *dicta* may tend more to support the restriction of the tort than its extension so as to include threats of breach of contract.' The only authority directly in support were two Irish cases: *Cooper v Millea* [1938] IR 749; *Riordan v Butler* [1940] IR 347.

[17] Hoffmann, L., '*Rookes v Barnard*' 81 LQR (1965) 116, p. 116. Wedderburn, K. W., 'Intimidation and the Right to Strike' 27 MLR (1964) 257: 'in *Rookes v Barnard* the House of Lords has invented a new extension of civil liability.'

[18] [1964] AC 1129, p. 1180.

[19] *Rookes*, of course, is also important for its discussion of exemplary damages. Though exemplary damages were not appropriate in the case itself, they were awarded in the intimidation cases, *Messenger Newspapers Group Ltd v NGA (1982)* [1984] IRLR 397, Caulfield J, to teach the defendants that 'tort does not pay'.

[20] [1964] AC 1129, p. 1169.

[21] The case can be squared with the earlier decision in *White v Riley* [1921] 1 Ch 1 on the basis that the strike notice was in effect a sufficient notice of termination, not a breach (see Wedderburn, K. W., 'The Right to Threaten Strikes' 25 (1962) MLR 513, p. 519).

[22] At times, the courts have been uncertain as to the precise effect of a strike notice on the contract of employment see e.g. *White v Riley* [1921], CA. In *Morgan v Fry* [1968] 2 QB 710 Lord Denning found that the strike notice, being equivalent to notice for lawful termination, was not to be deemed unlawful means for the tort of intimidation. However, the suggestion that it could operate to 'suspend' the contract was rejected in *Simmons v Hoover* [1977] QB 284. For Donovan LJ in *Rookes v Barnard* [1963] 1 QB 623 few strikes would not involve breach by the strikers.

[23] See Lord Denning's definition in *Morgan v Fry* [1968] 2 QB 710. Lord Evershed MR, *Rookes v Barnard* [1964] AC 1129, p. 1183 'the intention . . . of the threat was to injure'.

Thus there must be a deliberate threat, that threat must involve an unlawful act and be effective,[24] there must be an intention to harm the claimant, and damage must ensue.[25] Though the threat will most commonly be to someone other than the claimant himself, it would appear that the tort can also take the form of a two-party threat, directly between the defendant and the claimant. It is possible that the tort has a defence of justification: Lord Devlin made such a suggestion in *Rookes*[26] and Lord Denning suggested that intimidation by trade union officials against troublemakers might be justified.[27] However, this defence is best discussed within the context of the general tort of unlawful interference with trade.[28]

This tort should be distinguished from the suggested tort of 'harassment'. Scott J in *Thomas v NUM*,[29] referred to such a tort, which given its width could render a defendant liable for 'intimidatory acts or words' *per se*.[30] Though the existence of such a tort was doubted by Stuart-Smith J in *News Group Newspapers Ltd v SOGAT (82)*,[31] uncertainty still remained, as liability for 'harassment' was debated by the courts, within the context of the tort of nuisance. Given the classic view of private nuisance is that only those with a legal interest in land can sue, the courts were asked to consider who could sue in an action for 'harassment', akin to private nuisance. Plaintiffs sought to extend protection in this way beyond those with an interest in land. So the concept of harassment and the tort of nuisance led to liability in *Khorasandjian v Bush*,[32] based on harassing phone calls to the child of the houseowner. The House of Lords in *Hunter v Canary Wharf Ltd*,[33] overturned this attempt to deflect the tort of nuisance from its role as a tort protecting property, but did not categorically deny the existence of the tort of harassment.[34] However, for Lord

---

[24] i.e. the person threatened acts or refrains from acting, as coerced by the defendant.

[25] Stuart-Smith J in *Newsgroup Newspapers Ltd v SOGAT (82)* [1987] ICR 181, p. 204: 'the tort of intimidation is committed when A delivers a threat to B that he will commit an act or use means unlawful against B, as a result of which B does or refrains from doing some act which he is entitled to do, thereby causing damage either to himself or C.'

[26] [1964] AC 1129, p. 1209.

[27] *Morgan v Fry* [1968] 2 QB 710, p. 729 and *Cory Lighterage v TGWU* [1973] ICR 339, pp. 356–7.

[28] Where the threat is that of breach of contract it might be that a wider justification, akin to that applying in the tort of inducing breach, might apply. This defence is discussed in Ch. 3.

[29] [1986] Ch 20.

[30] Harassment causing intended injury to health would appear to fall within *Wilkinson v Downton* 1897 2 QB 57.

[31] [1987] ICR 181, p. 206.

[32] [1993] QB 727, CA.

[33] [1997] 2 WLR 684; see Cane, P., 'What a Nuisance' 113 LQR (1997) 513.

[34] Thus Lord Hoffmann, ibid. 707: 'I do not ... say that *Khorasandjian* was wrongly decided. But it must be seen as a case of intentional harassment, not nuisance' (the perceived gap in tort liability being 'protection against intentional harassment causing distress without actual bodily or psychiatric illness'); Lord Goff, p. 692, 'the tort of harassment has now received statutory recognition'.

Hoffmann the possible development of this area of the common law has been overtaken by the passage of the Protection from Harassment Act 1997. This was passed because of a growing public unease about the apparent lack of liability (or at least easily established liability) for 'stalkers' and other 'harassers'. The Act creates criminal liability for activities that a 'reasonable person' ought to know amounts to harassment (not otherwise defined) and builds civil liability onto the crime so established. How this new offence (worrying in its potential breadth and uncertainty), with its possibility of civil redress will relate to the tort of intimidation is unclear. Certainly the Act allows for damages not only for the anxiety caused but also 'for any financial loss'.[35] However, as such the offence and statutory tort would appear to involve only a two-party scenario and as such would not prove useful in the trade competition setting.[36]

Intentional harm

There must be an intention to compel a particular course of action[37] and the claimant 'must be a person whom [the defendant] intended to injure'.[38] Malice of course is not necessary.[39] For the sake of logic, the definition of the requisite intention must be the same as for the tort of unlawful interference with trade and will be discussed in Chapter 5.

Threat

Threat was defined by Peterson J in *Hodges v Webb*[40] as: 'an intimation by one to another that unless the latter does or does not do something the former will do something which the latter does not like.' Threats obviously involve an element of coercion: what must be present, according to Lord Denning,[41] is an intention to compel another to obey the defendant's wishes. So the threat must be of the 'or else' kind, causing the person threatened to act in a desired manner, 'with the result that loss ensues'.[42]

Case law distinguishes 'idle abuse', which is not to be taken seriously, from threats.[43] Again, in theory there is a distinction to be made between

---

[35] s. 3(1)(2).

[36] It might have more worrying implications for picket lines, however, resurrecting nineteenth-century criminal liability for 'black looks'.

[37] *Huljich v Hall* [1973] 2 NZLR 279, p. 285, McCarthy J.

[38] Stuart-Smith J *Newsgroup Newspapers Ltd v SOGAT (82)* [1987] ICR 181, p. 204.

[39] Atkin LJ in *Ware & De Freville v MTA* [1921] 3 KB 40, p. 82 'does not necessarily involve any feeling of hostility or ill will'.

[40] [1920] 2 Ch 70, p. 89.

[41] *Morgan v Fry* [1968] 2 QB 710, p. 724.

[42] Turner P in *Huljich v Hall* 2 NZLR 279, p. 288.

[43] See e.g. Stuart-Smith J in *Newsgroup Newspapers Ltd v SOGAT (82)* [1987] ICR 181, p. 204.

threats and mere warnings[44] although McCardie J acknowledged that 'the distinction may indeed sometimes be subtle'.[45] Similarly, there is a difference between threats and advice,[46] Hart and Honoré commenting: 'it seems that to avoid liability advice must be disinterested and unaccompanied by pressure.'[47]

Whether the communication involves a threat is, of course, a matter of fact, depending on the circumstances of the case. A threat may not necessarily be violent: Vaughan Williams LJ in *Santen v Busnach*[48] stated that a man may give a notice, the wording of which is not offensive, but in such a manner and under such circumstances as to constitute a threat. The threat may be implied: in a case involving a hostile picket line,[49] the phrase 'scab, we will get you' was interpreted as meaning 'we will get you if you do not stop working for the plaintiffs', given the obvious intention of the pickets to dissuade people from continuing to work.[50] However, a threat of 'union trouble' was held to be too vague in *Pete's Towing Services Ltd v NIUW*[51] as it could involve either lawful or unlawful conduct.

Moreover, the threat must be effective. As Lord Denning noted in *Morgan v Fry*:[52] 'the person so threatened must comply with the demand rather than risk the threat being carried into execution.' Unless the person threatened 'succumbs' to the threat, 'the tort is not complete'.[53] However, where the threats are serious and there is a real risk that they will be effective, the court might grant injunctive relief.[54] Heydon contends that as there is no objective standard of a 'reasonable response' liability could still ensue, though the person threatened acceded to a 'ludicrously weak' threat.[55]

[44] See Lord Loreburn LC in *Conway v Wade* [1909] AC 506, p. 510.

[45] *Pratt v BMA* [1919] 1 KB 114, p. 261.

[46] Lord Donovan in *Stratford v Lindley* [1965] AC 269, p. 340 'I should take much convincing that the mere notification of an existing state of affairs [here, the embargo] was itself a "threat" which could form a claim for intimidation.'

[47] Hart, H. L. A. and Honoré, T., *Causation in the Law*, 2nd edn. (Oxford: Clarendon Press, 1985), p. 190.

[48] (1913) 29 TLR 214.

[49] *Newsgroup Newspapers Ltd v SOGAT (82)* [1987] ICR 181, p. 204.

[50] For Wedderburn, above, n. 17, p. 267 in industrial action 'the possibilities of "implied intimidation" are . . . endless'.

[51] [1970] NZLR 32.

[52] [1968] 2 QB 710.

[53] Stuart-Smith J in *Newsgroup Newspapers Ltd v SOGAT (82)* [1987] ICR 181, p. 204.

[54] Ibid. 205.

[55] Heydon, J. D., *Economic Torts*, 2nd edn. (London: Sweet & Maxwell, 1978), p. 64. Though he notes that a weak threat may be evidence of the lack of an intention to injure.

Unlawful act

Although the ingredient of threats gives the tort its name, the essence of
the tort is the use of unlawful means. The threat must be an unlawful one.
It is the unlawful element that is important: the use of a threat, in itself, is
neutral.[56] As Lord Reid noted: 'so long as the defendant only threatens to
do what he has a legal right to do he is on safe ground . . . but I agree with
Lord Herschell that there is a chasm between doing what you have a legal
right to do and threatening to do what you have no legal right to do.'[57]
Thus there is no tort of coercion *per se*.[58] 'There is nothing unlawful in
giving a warning or intimation that if the party addressed pursues a
certain line of conduct, others may act in a manner which he will not like
and which will be prejudicial to his interests, so long as nothing unlawful
is threatened or done.'[59] This distinguished *Rookes* from *Allen v Flood*
where no unlawful acts were held to be involved.

Obviously it is critical to determine what is included in this concept of
unlawfulness. Lord Denning noted that unlawful means included
'violence, tort and breach of contract'[60] but did not imply that this was an
exhaustive list.[61] The concept must be the same for all the economic torts
that focus on the defendant's unlawful means[62] if these torts are ever to
achieve a rational development. It is logical, therefore, to explore the
nature of unlawfulness in the context of the general tort of unlawful interference, later.[63]

Damage

The claimant must prove that the damage to him was caused by the
defendant's threat, for it is 'the person damnified by the compliance' who
can sue in intimidation.[64] All intended losses would be recoverable as

---

[56] Though a threat could give rise to an action for inducing breach of contract: see Ch. 3.

[57] [1964] AC 1129, p. 1168.

[58] Holmes J (dissenting) remarked in *Vegelahn v Guntner* 167 Mass 92, p. 107, that the
unlawfulness of 'threats' depends on what you threaten. In *Hardie & Lane Ltd v Chilton* [1928]
2 KB 306 (approved by the House of Lords in *Thorne v MTA* [1937] AC 797) the threat by the
defendant (a trade association) to place the plaintiff on a stop list unless he paid a fine for
breaking the rules of the association was held not to be tortious.

[59] Lord Wright *Crofter v Veitch* [1942] AC 435, p. 467.

[60] Russell LJ in *Morgan v Fry* [1968] 2 QB 710 suggested that not every threat to breach a
contract would be sufficient. However, this has not been explored in case law. Such a proposition, however, would appear to run counter to the established view that any breach of
contract is sufficient for the tort of inducing breach of contract. See Ch. 3.

[61] *Morgan v Fry* [1968] 2 QB 710.

[62] The torts of intimidation, direct intervention in contract, and indirect inducement of
contract breach. Unlawful conspiracy is probably better seen as secondary liability. See Chs.
2 and 10.   [63] See Ch. 5.

[64] Lord Denning *Morgan v Fry* [1968] 2 QB 710, p. 724.

would all consequences that were not too remote. Widgery J in *Morgan v Fry*[65] awarded damages to the plaintiff on the basis of the weeks of unemployment following his dismissal (due to intimidation of his employer) and the subsequent drop in wages in his new job.[66] Presumably compensation for injury to feelings (on a par with inducing breach of contract)[67] would be arguable.[68]

Two-[69] and three-party liability

As the facts of *Rookes v Barnard* demonstrate, intimidation usually arises in a three-party situation. The middleman is threatened with an unlawful act in order to harm the claimant.[70] The middleman must give in to the threat in order for harm to the claimant to result.[71] However, it would appear that intimidation can also arise in a two-party setting, i.e. where the defendant makes the unlawful threat directly to the claimant[72] in order to injure him (by causing him to act[73] to his detriment). It would appear that this version of the tort exists: Wedderburn suggests that the *dicta* could hardly be stronger.[74] Lord Devlin, in *Rookes*, accepted the two-part version of this tort, propounded in the then current edition of Salmond on Torts. This gave as an example of the tort of intimidation 'a trader who has been compelled to discontinue his business by means of

[65] [1968] 1 QB 521, pp. 548–9 (the actual decision was overturned by the Court of Appeal).

[66] However, the judge took into account an estimation of how long, but for the defendants' interference, he was likely to have stayed in his former job.

[67] Though not apparently available for the tort of conspiracy see Ch. 2.

[68] See Ch. 1 and Giliker, P., 'A "new" head of damages: damages for mental distress in the English law of Torts', 20 LS (2000) 19.

[69] Note that the Court of Appeal in *Welton v N. Cornwall DC* [1997] 1 WLR 570 accepted that *Hedley Byrne* liability (in negligence) could result from coercion/compulsion and not simply advice/information: see Mullender, R., 'Negligent Misstatement, Threats and the Scope of the *Hedley Byrne* Principle' 62 MLR (1999) 425.

[70] Lord Devlin, *Rookes v Barnard* [1964] AC 1129, p. 1208: 'it must be A's object was to injure C through he instrumentality of B.' McGregor, H., *McGregor on Damages*, 16th edn. (London: Sweet & Maxwell,1997) notes, para. 1940 that the tort 'has been pressed into use largely in the area of interference with contractual relations existing between the plaintiff and the person intimidated'.

[71] Lord Denning in *Stratford v Lindley* [1965] AC 269, p. 284; *Huljich v Hall* [1973] 2 NZLR 279, p. 286.

[72] Rogers, W. V. H., *Winfield and Jolowicz on Tort*, 15th edn. (London: Sweet & Maxwell, 1998) is surely right when he suggests (p. 638, n. 65) that a threat issued to the plaintiff would still constitute the tort, though the threat relate to a third party, rather than the plaintiff himself.

[73] Or, indeed, refrain from acting.

[74] In *Clerk and Lindsell on Torts*, 18th edn. (London: Sweet & Maxwell, 2000), paras. 24–85. See *Allen v Flood* [1898] AC 1, 17; *Stratford v Lindley* [1965] AC 269, p. 285 (Lord Denning); p. 302 (Salmon LJ); p. 336 (Pearce LJ). A decision based on two-party intimidation can be found in *Newsgroup Newspapers Ltd v SOGAT 82* [1987] ICR 181, against the 7th defendant. As with deceit, it is clear that a two-party economic tort is unlikely to be a prime weapon against excessive competitive practices.

threats of personal violence made against him by the defendant, with that intention'. Lord Evershed was also in favour of the recognition of two-party intimidation, in that same case. Its existence was strongly argued for by Lord Denning in *D & C Builders v Rees*[75] and accepted by McCarthy J in *Huljich v Hall*.[76] However, the possibility of liability in tort for two-party intimidation raises difficult policy issues where the threat involved is a breach of contract.

INTIMIDATION AND CONTRACT

In *Rookes* the plaintiff was allowed to complain about a threat to breach a contract—the contract between the defendants and their employer—to which he was not a party.[77] This has led to criticism that privity of contract can be circumvented by this tort (a similar criticism, of course, is levelled by some against *Lumley v Gye* liability).[78] Lord Wedderburn is particularly critical of *Rookes* on this basis, noting: 'never before in English law has a third party been allowed to rely for his cause of action on a breach of civil obligations existing between two other persons or on any threat of such breach. This novel manoeuvre may be said to deny the most basic distinctions between tort and contract.'[79] Indeed, this was the worry of Pearson LJ in the Court of Appeal in *Rookes* itself. He saw the action as an attempt by the plaintiff to enforce the contract between the defendants and the employer and rejected such an attempt as '[the plaintiff] is not entitled to require the parties to perform it nor to recover damages from either of them for not performing it'.[80]

However, it is not so obvious that *three*-party intimidation offends the doctrine of privity. For Lord Reid in *Rookes*, the privity objection was a 'red herring'.[81] With intimidation, the claimant's claim is not based on breach of contract, though that is the heart of the threat. Rather, it is an action brought against a defendant who has used unlawful means as a deliberate weapon against the claimant.[82] It is the use of an unlawful

[75] [1966] 2 QB 617.   [76] [1973] 2 NZLR 279, p. 285.
[77] Cf. *Lumley v Gye* where the plaintiff was attempting to protect his own contract rights.
[78] With intimidation, the fact that the claimant seems to 'benefit' from the contract is the concern; with inducing breach of contract, it is the fact that the defendant appears to bear the 'burden' of the contract to which he is not a party that is the major objection. Lord Pearce in *Rookes* asserted ([1964] AC 1129, p. 1234) 'to draw a line at this point, viz. between contract and tort, seems to me inconsistent with the principle that underlies *Lumley v Gye*'. However, intimidation is in fact based on a different principle. See Ch. 10.
[79] Above, n. 17.   [80] [1963] 1 QB 623, p. 695.
[81] Hoffmann, above, n. 17, p. 125.
[82] Heydon, above, n. 55, p. 61: 'the extension is not inconsistent with the privity of contract doctrine, for the plaintiff is not suing on the contract, he is suing in respect of the unlawful means of threatening breach' and see Elias, P., and Ewing, K., 'Economic Torts and

weapon that renders the action tortious: Lord Watson in *Allen v Flood* defined 'illegal' as 'means which in themselves are in the nature of civil wrongs'.[83] This concept of an unlawful attack on the claimant's economic interests has been the method the common law has devised to distinguish between aggressive and excessive competitive behaviour. As Hoffmann notes of cases such as *Tarleton v M'Gawley*: 'their importance is to show that the means used by A to cause loss to C can be unlawful because they involve acts which are unlawful to B . . . [so] . . . in deciding what means A can be allowed to use in order to cause loss to C, the law draws the line at conduct which is unlawful towards B.'[84] With *Rookes*, breach of contract is added to torts as possible 'civil wrongs' for liability in this area.[85]

However, does a threatened breach of contract also constitute unlawful means for the *two*-party version of the tort? If it does, then every threat to break a contract would also be the tort of intimidation, and, given this tort is but a species of unlawful interference with trade, every intentional breach of contract would also be the tort of unlawful interference with trade.[86] Is the tort–contract divide, therefore, to be abandoned in this area?

The two leading commentators on the economic torts, Wedderburn and Weir, argue for an all-or-nothing approach on this point. Either breach of contract is unlawful means for both two- and three-party intimida-tion—and for the tort of unlawful interference with trade—or it is not unlawful for any. Interestingly, the two commentators decide on opposite solutions. Weir maintains that it is tortious intentionally to hurt a plaintiff by breaking your contract with him. As he points out 'contracts are almost inevitably involved in the economic torts because people arrange their affairs that way'.[87] Wedderburn argues that to accept breach of contract as unlawful means is to 'contravene the logic of the law'.

Labour Law: Old Principles and New Liabilities' 41 CLJ (1982) 321, p. 334: 'this is nothing illogical or unreasonable in terms of general legal principles. The essence of the tort is the threat of unlawful coercion and the particular unlawful threat which produces the coercion should be irrelevant.'

[83] [1898] AC 1, pp. 97–8.   [84] Above, n. 17, p. 118.

[85] Whether equitable wrongs and breaches of trust/fiduciary duty are also included is discussed in Chs. 5 and 10.

[86] Sales, P., and Stilitz, D., 'Intentional Infliction of Harm by Unlawful Means' 115 LQR (1999) 411, p. 424 argue that a threat to break the contract may give rise to liability, though the actual breach should not. Where breach is concerned, 'the invocation of the intentional tort [i.e. unlawful interference with trade] would not supplement the existing rules of [contractual] liability, but would subvert them' for in contract recoverable loss is governed by what was in the contemplation of the parties at the time of contracting. However, with threatened breach, 'the threat of a breach of contract is used by D as an instrument to an end (to cause harm to P) which is not contemplated by the consensual distribution of risk under the contract itself'.

[87] Weir, T., 'Chaos or Cosmos: *Rookes, Stratford* and the Economic Torts' [1964] CLJ 225, p. 229. However, in *Economic Torts* (Oxford: Clarendon Press, 1997), p. 67 he appears to have rejected this view. Elias and Ewing, above, n. 82, p. 334 accept breach of contract as tortious.

However, it would appear that a middle route can be steered. On this analysis, a threatened breach of contract would be sufficient where there are three parties involved (the claimant unable to sue on the contract at the heart of the threat) but not sufficient in two-party intimidation. It is likely that this is the 'solution' the courts would take.[88] Lord Reid in *Stratford v Lindley*[89] stressed that 'a case where a defendant presents to the plaintiff the alternative of doing what the defendant wants him to do or suffering loss which the defendant can cause him to incur is not necessarily *in pari casu* and may involve questions which cannot arise where there is intimidation of a third person'. In a three-party situation, no privity problem arises, according to Lord Reid, because the plaintiff's cause of action is independent of the middleman's, i.e. the fact that the unlawful act is a breach of contract is irrelevant: once an act is classified as unlawful the form that act takes ceases to be important. In effect the breach of contract is simply a means to an end.[90] However in two-party intimidation, where the threat is of breach of contract, there is no way that the form the unlawful means takes could be termed 'irrelevant'. Unlike threatening violence to your contract partner, the threat to break your contract involves no separate tort (e.g. assault, battery).

In liability based on *Lumley v Gye*, the tort being a form of secondary civil liability, the defendant is in effect joined to the contractor's breach. However, there is no need in two-party intimidation, involving a threatened breach of contract,[91] to allow an additional tort claim. The claimant has sufficient protection and remedies. As Burns comments[92] in the light of the plaintiff's relatively protected position, there seems 'no compelling reason' why the tort of intimidation should be made available to him.[93] Thus he has his contract rights—including the right to sue for anticipatory breach—when the threat to break the contract is made by the defendant. He also has protection from economic duress, a doctrine that has only emerged since the 1970s and is still in need of 'clarification and systemization'.[94] In effect it fills the gap where two-party threats of breach of

---

[88] See Hoffmann, above, n. 17 and Maitland J in *Central Canada Potash Co Ltd v Govt of Saskatchewan* (1978) 88 DLR 609, p. 640.

[89] [1965] AC 269, p. 325.

[90] Cf. Lord Wedderburn, above, n. 17, pp. 263–7: 'to sustain his action in tort, the plaintiff has to prove the breach (actual, or as in *Rookes*, threatened) of that extraneous contract. No semantic stratagem can obscure this infringement of the rules of privity of contract.'

[91] Cf. two-party intimidation where the tort may be necessary where the claimant has acceded to the threat. Again, the tort provides a useful 'gloss' on established tort liability.

[92] Burns, P., 'Tort Injury to Economic Interests: Some Facets of Legal Response' 58 Can Bar Rev (1980) 134, pp. 135–6.

[93] Heydon, however, doubts whether the situation is so clear-cut, above, n. 55, pp. 64–5.

[94] Phang, A., 'Whither Economic Duress? Reflections on 2 Recent Cases' 53 MLR (1990) 107, p. 107. See also Carty, H., and Evans, A., 'Economic Duress' [1983] JBL 218.

contract are involved.[95] According to Lord Diplock and Lord Scarman in *The Universe Sentinel*,[96] economic duress involves coercion/compulsion, induced by pressure which the law does not regard as legitimate. The two fundamental ingredients are, therefore, 'illegitimate coercion'.[97] To threaten to break your contract 'unless . . .' is certainly illegitimate pressure (indeed, that is the classic example of economic duress),[98] but such a threat may not be sufficiently coercive. With economic duress the court has to decide when commercial pressure becomes coercion: the remedies are restitution or avoidance of the 'new' contract. Indeed, the right to avoid the contract may be lost through affirmation.[99] Tort compensation is not the issue as economic duress *per se* is not tortious.[100]

It would appear, therefore, that a threat to break your own contract gives rise to contractual or restitutionary remedies only. In such a case tort protection is not necessary.[101]

RATIONALE AND RELEVANCE

The tort of inducing breach of contract supports the claimant's contract rights by making the defendant inducer a joint tortfeasor in all but name. However, the tort of intimidation does not as such protect contract rights (though it might have that effect) and is not a tort involving secondary liability. It is the deliberate use by the defendant of unlawful means in order to harm the claimant that leads to liability. As such, it is clear that intimidation, unlike inducing breach of contract, is a tort imposing primary liability. It is part of the tort of unlawful interference with trade and shares the same rationale as that tort. It is the use of an unlawful

---

[95] It may also protect the middleman in three-party intimidation.

[96] *Universe Tankships Inc v ITWF* [1982] ICR 262. The twist in *Dimskal Shipping Co SA v ITWF* [1992] 2 AC 152 was that the pressure applied by the international trade union was legitimate under Swedish law (the coercion occurring in Sweden), though the proper law of contract involved English law. As the duress attached to the contract, the doctrine applied. See also *Huyton SA v Peter Cremer GmbH & Co* [1999] 1 Lloyd's Rep 620.

[97] Both Atiyah, P., 'Economic Duress and the "Overborne Will"' 98 LQR (1982) 197 and Birks, P., 'The Travails of Duress' [1990] LMCLQ 342 are critical of the phrase 'coercion of the will' used by Lord Scarman in *Pao On v Lau Yin Long* [1980] AC 614, p. 635. They argue that duress does not operate by overbearing the will.

[98] See *The Siboen and the Sibotre* [1976] 1 Lloyd's Rep 293; *The Atlantic Baron* [1979] QB 705; *Atlas Express Ltd v Kafco Ltd* [1989] 1 All ER 641.

[99] *North Ocean Shipping Co Ltd v Hyundai Construction Co Ltd* [1979] QB 705.

[100] Of course, the form the pressure takes may involve an independent economic tort.

[101] The decision of the House of Lords in *Dimbleby v NUJ* [1984] 1 WLR 427 would appear surprising. There the middleman in a secondary boycott was allowed to sue not for the direct inducement of his employees' contracts of employment (that was covered by statutory immunity) but for the intended hindrance that caused in his contracts with the boycotted company. In effect the middleman was allowed to sue for the breach of his contracts and as such would presumably be allowed to sue for threatened breaches.

weapon deliberately to hurt the economic interests of the claimant which is the reason for the general tort. This of course is Lord Reid's rationale for the tort of intimidation in *Rookes* and it is for this reason that his explanation of the tort is to be preferred to that of Lords Evershed and Devlin. They focused on liability for threats to breach, rather than breach itself[102] and hence felt that the doctrine of privity was not attacked by the tort. However, their reasoning creates an illogical distinction between a threat to breach and the breach itself. On the other hand, Lord Reid's reasoning breaks down any such distinction and sees intimidation for what it really is: intentionally causing loss by unlawful means.

Indeed, the plaintiff's counsel in *Rookes* urged the House to create a general principle of liability.[103] Such a general principle had been lurking in case law throughout the development of the economic torts. Thus in *Allen v Flood*, Lord Watson referred to an innominate tort of 'causing loss by means in themselves illegal',[104] while Lord Dunedin in the 1925 case, *Sorrel v Smith*[105] summarized the famous trilogy of cases (*Mogul Steamship, Allen v Flood,* and *Quinn v Leathem*) as 'you are not entitled to interfere with another man's method of gaining his living by illegal means'. However, the reaction of the House of Lords in *Rookes* was to focus instead on the specific tort of intimidation. In part this was due to Salmond in the first edition of his text on torts. In 1907 he had ascribed the name 'intimidation' to the various authorities such as *Tarleton v M'Gawley*, at a time when threats were regarded as the basis of the decision in *Quinn v Leathem*.[106] Having found a tort recognized by one of the leading commentators[107] the House of Lords preferred to develop this rather than become involved in a general analysis of economic tort liability.[108] So, against a background of confused and confusing conflicting judicial

---

[102] [1964] AC 1129, p. 1208, Lord Devlin asserted: 'it is said that to give a cause of action offends against the rule that one man cannot sue on another's contract. The cause of action arises not because B's contract is broken; it arises because of the action which B has taken to avert a breach.'

[103] He sought to gain their approval for the tort suggested by McCardie J in *Pratt v BMA* [1918–19] All ER 104, viz. p. 111 '[the infliction of] actual pecuniary damage upon another by the intentional employment of unlawful means to injure that person's business'. Controversially McCardie J asserted that those unlawful means 'may not comprise any specific act which is *per se* actionable'.

[104] [1898] AC 1, p. 107.

[105] [1925] AC 700.

[106] It was for a while believed that liability in *Quinn v Leathem* [1901] AC 495 was based on the coercive threats to call a strike. However, this was condemned as 'the leading heresy' by Lord Dunedin in *Sorell v Smith* [1925] AC 719.

[107] Though that recognition seemed to ignore the fact that the real unlawfulness of *Tarleton* itself was the murder of the natives, rather than mere threats.

[108] Interestingly, Heydon, above, n. 55, pp. 63–4 believes the House of Lords was constrained by *Allen v Flood* and would have preferred to base liability on intentionally caused economic loss.

perceptions of the role of the common law in this area the court looked for some form of comparative certainty.

Hoffmann is critical of this caution:[109] '[intimidation] should have been treated as a variant form of a wider tort of causing loss by unlawful means.' No distinction would then be made between threatened unlawful acts and the unlawful acts themselves. Weir agrees that the case raised the opportunity for a rationalization of economic tort liability but believes that arguably it sowed the seeds of this development. He accepts that if all *Rookes* achieved was 'the christening of a new nutshell tort of "intimidation", then legal science would have no reason to be very grateful'. But at the time of the decision itself Weir contended that the discussion in *Rookes* promised to create order out of chaos, that order being the creation of a general tort with an emphasis on intentional harm and unlawful means.

However, almost forty years on, the general tort of unlawful interference is still in need of final definition and rationalization. Whether the tort has a wider role to play—extending tort liability rather than simply rationalizing it—is a matter to be resolved in the next chapter. What needs to be underlined is the fact that the tort of intimidation does add an important gloss to the general tort. Threatened unlawful acts are equated to the unlawful acts themselves, even though as Turner P noted in *Huljich v Hall*[110] 'a threat to commit a tort does not generally give rise to an action in damages unless the tort is committed and then the damages arise not from the threat but from the tort itself'.

CONCLUSION

Intimidation is part of the wider general tort and its ingredients of unlawful means, intention, and justification should be defined as in the wider tort. However, the tort of intimidation is not limited to the protection of economic interests. In *Godwin v Uzoigwe*[111] the tort was successfully relied upon where a teenager had been brought from her home in Nigeria and kept in the defendants' home as a virtual slave, working excessive hours for no pay, kept short of food, physically beaten, and forbidden to leave the home. The Court of Appeal found threats of unlawful conduct, deliberately aimed at the plaintiff to coerce her to obey the defendants' orders. The tort of intimidation applied. In such cases of physical threats and harm, of course, trespass to the person torts would frequently be available.[112]

---

[109] Above, n. 17, p. 121.   [110] [1973] 2 NZLR 279, p. 288.

[111] [1993] Fam Law 65. And see *Gumpo v Church of Scientology* [2000] CP Rep 38.

[112] Lord Herschell in *Allen v Flood* [1898] AC 1, pp. 136–7 noted that the tort in *Garrett v Taylor* (1620) Cro. Jac. 567 is not dependent on trade: a houseowner 'similarly affected prejudicially in the occupation and enjoyment of his property by acts in themselves wrongful' could use the tort.

5

Unlawful Interference with Trade

Though some reference to this tort can be found in *Rookes v Barnard*[1] and *Stratford v Lindley*[2] the *modern* emergence of a tort nominated 'unlawful interference with trade' can be ascribed to Lord Denning. Having laid the seeds for this tort in *Daily Mirror Newspapers Ltd v Gardner*,[3] he felt emboldened to assert in *Torquay Hotel Co Ltd v Cousins*[4] 'I have always understood that if one person deliberately interferes with the trade or business of another, and does so by unlawful means . . . then he is acting unlawfully, even though he does not procure or induce any actual breach of contract.'[5] Although in the parliamentary debate over what became the Employment Act 1980, Lord Hailsham stated[6] that no such tort existed, by 1983[7] it was accepted by Lord Diplock in *Merkur Island Shipping Corporation v Laughton*.[8]

---

[1] [1964] AC 1129, p. 1178 where Lord Reid seemed to believe that the tort existed.

[2] [1965] AC 269, pp. 324–5 (the defendant 'threatened to use unlawful means to interfere with the plaintiff's business'), again Lord Reid, though he was joined in his opinion by Viscount Radcliffe (p. 328, the defendants 'have inflicted injury on the plaintiffs in the conduct of their business and have resorted to unlawful means to bring this about') and Lord Upjohn (p. 337, *Rookes v Barnard*, a case 'where the defendants caused loss to the plaintiff by using unlawful means to induce a third party to inflict loss upon him'). Mason J in *Kitano v Commonwealth* (1973) 129 CLR 151, pp. 173–4 saw the development of the general tort as arising from these two cases. However, it is hard not to agree with the assertion of the defendants' counsel in *Hadmor Productions Ltd v Hamilton* [1981] ICR 690 (at Court of Appeal level) that the tort 'crept' into *Stratford obiter* and *ex concessu*.

[3] [1968] 2 QB 762, p. 782. Indeed, he even considered the possibility of liability where the means employed were lawful but in *Torquay Hotel v Cousins* [1969] 2 Ch 106 confirmed that unlawful means were necessary.

[4] [1969] 2 Ch 106, p. 139.

[5] Subsequently he mapped its genealogy in *Hadmor Productions Ltd v Hamilton* [1981] ICR 690.

[6] Hansard HL Debs Vol. 410, col. 681, 12 June 1980. Lord Wedderburn replied that 'a student of today must be affected by legal myopia if he did not understand the existence of this tort', ibid., col. 686.

[7] *Merkur Island Shipping Corporation v Laughton* [1983] 2 AC 570, p. 609 'the common law tort . . . of interfering with the trade or business of another person by doing unlawful acts'. There was, however, no real discussion of this 'genus of torts' in the judgment: Lord Diplock simply agreeing with the plaintiff's concession that the then statutory immunities covered this tort. Rather, Lord Diplock appeared to focus on an acceptance of Lord Denning's other suggestion in *Torquay Hotel*, viz. that there is a half-way economic tort of interference with contract (discussed in Ch. 3).

[8] [1983] 2 AC 570, p. 609. However, he did little more than acknowledge its existence, deciding the case on the 'half-way' tort of unlawful interference with contract performance.

However, it is noteworthy that, as Lord Denning acknowledged,[9] the 'first recognizable formulation' of the tort[10] was as early as 1898, in *Allen v Flood* itself. Of course in that era the common law was attempting to formulate the proper scope of liability for intentionally inflicted economic loss and *Allen* itself rejected the notion that liability could ensue for an 'unjustified' or badly motivated 'interference with trade'. In so doing, the majority members of the House of Lords reviewed earlier cases to underline the importance of unlawfulness.[11] Indeed, Lord Watson came close to a general formulation of an unlawful interference tort when he discussed the grounds on which a person can be made legally responsible to the plaintiff for procuring the act of another by the use of illegal means.[12] Subsequently, in *Quinn v Leathem*,[13] Lord Lindley asserted that the underlying principle[14] was 'wrongful acts done intentionally to damage a particular individual and actually damaging him'.

Yet the tort remains obscure, described by one commentator recently as 'embryonic'.[15] In part this must be due to the lack of consensus that has dogged the development of all the economic torts. So even in the landmark decision of *Allen v Flood* there is a lack of real agreement in the various judgments. While Lord Watson did attempt a broad analysis of the tortious liability involved, Lords Herschell, Shand, and Davey did not even go so far as to give *Lumley v Gye* wholehearted support.[16] Subsequently, Lord Halsbury (who, of course, had dissented in *Allen*) capitalized on this uncertainty to reject the wider implication of *Allen*. In *Quinn*

In *Hadmor Productions Ltd v Hamilton* [1983] 1 AC 191, pp. 202–3, he asserted 'it is important to recognize that we now have a separate and distinct tort of interference with the business of another by unlawful means'.

[9] In *Hadmor Productions v Hamilton* [1981] ICR 690, p. 708. He drew authority for this assertion from Lord Herschell ([1898] AC 1, p. 138) and Lord James (p. 180).

[10] Sales, P., and Stilitz, D., 'Intentional Infliction of Harm by Unlawful Means', 115 LQR (1999) 411, p. 411.

[11] Bagshaw, R., 'Can the Economic Torts be Unified', 18 OJLS (1998) 729, p. 730 [the majority view] 'is the foundation of the general economic tort of causing economic harm by unlawful means'.

[12] [1898] AC 1, p. 96. He asserted that there are only two grounds on which a person who procures the act of another may be liable—either as inducer of the other's unlawful act or as procurer of that other's act (which may itself be lawful) where the procurement has been by unlawful means and the harm thereby caused to the plaintiff was intentional (the use of unlawful means 'directed against' the plaintiff).

[13] [1901] AC 495, p. 535.

[14] He was referring in fact to *Lumley v Gye*.

[15] Mullany, N., 'Beaudesert Buried', 111 LQR (1995) 586 notes the 'embryonic tort of unlawful interference with trade'.

[16] Lord Herschell, *Allen v Flood* [1898] AC 1, p. 123 'I am not concerned now to inquire whether the decision in *Lumley v Gye* was right . . . there are . . . arguments the other way and I must not be understood as expressing an opinion one way or the other, whether such an action can be maintained.' Perhaps more understandably he also appeared unhappy with the tort of simple conspiracy, given his interpretation ([1898] AC 1, p. 140) of *Mogul Steamship Co v McGregor* [1892] AC 25.

v Leathem he avoided extending *Allen* to its logical conclusion (that would have heralded the creation of a tort of unlawful interference) by high-lighting the additional factors in that case of combination[17] and threats. Yet, as Elias and Ewing point out 'many statements in *Quinn v Leathem* are simply irreconcilable with *Allen v Flood* and do support the view that it is a tort deliberately to harm another without justification'.[18] Indeed, the report of the Royal Commission on Trade Disputes and Trade Combina-tions in 1906[19] noted that the coexistence of *Allen* and *Quinn* had created a situation 'which is bound to produce contradiction and uncertainty'. So in 1903, in the case of *Giblan v NALUGBI*,[20] the Court of Appeal were still debating whether the violation of the right to trade was a pos-sible tort (such a proposition had indeed found favour with the majority of the judges called in to advise the House of Lords in *Allen*)[21] and even in 1964 not all members of the House of Lords were convinced that the matter had been resolved. Lord Devlin stated in *Rookes v Barnard*: 'I do not think it is necessary for the House to decide whether or not malicious interfer-ence by a single person with trade, business or employment is or is not a tort known to law ... I mean *Quinn v Leathem* without the conspiracy.'[22] Before Lord Denning, therefore, the possibility of the tort was lurking in the cases (and indeed its application was suggested by the appellants' counsel in *Rookes v Barnard*) but its existence was obscured by the oppos-ing judicial perceptions of the role of common law, particularly in control-ling trade union action. Even today, in many cases, the tort of unlawful interference is tagged on to other economic torts, pleaded as a safety net, rather than a firm tort in its own right.[23]

In *Merkur Island Shipping Corporation v Laughton*, Lord Diplock claimed that unlawful interference with trade was the genus economic tort, other varieties of the 'general' economic torts being but species of it.[24] Certainly,

---

[17] Which is now the orthodox way of distinguishing the two cases see e.g. Lord Dunedin in *Sorrel v Smith* [1925] AC 700, p. 723.

[18] Elias, P., and Ewing, K., 'Economic Torts and Labour Law: Old Principles and New Liabilities' 41 CLJ (1982) 321, p. 324.

[19] 1906, Cmnd. 2825, Sir Geoffrey Lushington.   [20] [1903] 2 KB 600.

[21] And echoes of such a doctrine can be found in Lord Denning's judgments: see espe-cially *Ex parte Island Records* [1978] Ch 122.   [22] [1964] AC 1129, pp. 1215–16.

[23] Often it is discussed in addition to an existing economic tort, as in *Hadmor Productions v Hamilton* [1981] ICR 690 where though the Court of Appeal based its decision on unlawful interference, Lord Diplock, delivering the decision of the House of Lords, based the decision on the tort of intimidation. Or it is muddled with the 'half-way tort' of interference with contract performance (as in *Marina Shipping Ltd v Laughton* [1982] QB 1187 and *Merkur Island Shipping Corp v Laughton* [1983] 2 AC 570) but not relied upon in any of these cases.

[24] Including inducing breach of contract. As has been argued in Ch. 3, this must be wrong (and see discussion in Ch. 10). This of course means that Weir is also wrong. He contends in *Economic Torts* (Oxford: Clarendon Press, 1997), p. 28: 'I believe that the tort of inducing breach of contract has now been absorbed into the general tort of causing harm by unlawful means.'

liability for direct and indirect interference with contract (i.e. causing rather than directly procuring the breach) can be neatly squared with this wider tort,[25] while Rogers[26] notes that the tort is an 'irresistible inference from the acceptance of the tort of intimidation'. However, Lord Diplock's assertion is, in fact, wrong. It is obviously the case that simple conspiracy is not covered by this tort. But more importantly, as has already been suggested, inducing breach of contract and unlawful conspiracy are torts which create, in effect, secondary liability.[27] It is more than arguable that the liability they create mirrors the liability which flows from the doctrine of joint tortfeasance.[28] These torts provide the claimant with *additional* defendants to sue. Unlawful interference with trade, on the other hand, creates new protection for the claimant by imposing primary liability on the interferer, whose wrong resides in his own unlawful act, rather than in his participation in someone else's wrongful act.[29] The 'magic' of unlawful interference is to allow the claimant, though indirectly attacked via a third party, to sue on his own behalf.

As such, therefore, the tort does not encompass all the 'general' economic torts. That said, however, it does offer the frame for those that extend the defendant's liability from middleman to claimant. And, tantalizingly, it has the potential to provide a more general framework for intentional tort liability, to encompass the tort of three-party deceit, much of the tort of malicious falsehood (where lies are involved)[30] and perhaps beyond.[31]

Thus the need for its elucidation (and in particular the definition of intention and unlawful means)[32] is ever more pressing, though the diffi-

---

[25] See more detailed discussion in Chs. 3 and 10.

[26] Rogers, W. V. H., *Winfield and Jolowicz on Tort*, 15th edn. (London: Sweet & Maxwell, 1998), p. 650.

[27] See Sales and Stilitz, above, n. 10.

[28] See Carty, H., 'Joint Tortfeasance and Assistance Liability' 19 LS (1999) 489. This is also discussed in Ch. 10.

[29] Sales and Stilitz, above, n. 10, p. 412 'the intentional tort constitutes a free-standing, independent species of primary liability, founded on the central concept of the intentional infliction of harm upon another by unlawful means'.

[30] The tort can in theory give rise to liability for untruths, believed to be true by the defendant, which are published 'maliciously'. This version of the tort would not fall within the tort of unlawful interference. Sales and Stilitz, above, n. 10, p. 432 note that malicious falsehood, having as it does a number of features 'which reveal a strong influence from the law of defamation' is a tort 'which, although in its essentials founded on the same elements as the intentional harm tort, has developed somewhat different principles of liability by virtue of the influence of another proximate area of tort law'. This is discussed further in Ch. 10.

[31] See in particular Sales and Stilitz, above, n. 10, p. 436 'the intentional harm tort presents the courts with the opportunity to develop general and coherent principles of tort liability ... offering scope for development of general principles of liability in respect of harm inflicted intentionally as a counterpart to the generalization of the reasonable care or reasonable behaviour standard in the non-intentional sphere'.

[32] Would these have to be consistent with the other economic torts? See discussion in Ch. 10.

culties that have bedevilled the economic torts since their first appearance in the nineteenth century are still liable to undermine this process. No doubt the problem is compounded by the fact that Lord Denning revived the tort at a time when he seemed eager to extend economic tort liability generally.[33] So he was prepared to employ the tort of unlawful interference in controversial applications such as *Acrow (Automation) Ltd v Rex Chainbelt Inc* (creating a tort out of contempt).[34] Again, imprecision[35] in the tort is likely given that the majority of cases where the tort is pleaded are interlocutory, a stage at which, according to Neill LJ in *Associated British Ports v TGWU*,[36] 'the courts should not attempt finally to resolve difficult questions of law'. Thus it is not perhaps so surprising that in *Lonrho v Fayed*[37] (where its existence was conceded) it was described in the Court of Appeal[38] as a comparatively new tort, of 'uncertain ambit',[39] the precise boundaries of which have to be established 'from case to case'.[40] Indeed, in the same case, Butler-Sloss LJ described this as a difficult 'not to say obscure' branch of the law of tort.

INGREDIENTS

However, though its detailed limits have yet to be refined,[41] the outline of the tort is now established. Henry J, in *Barretts & Baird (Wholesale) Ltd v IPCS*,[42] stated that it involved 'interference with the plaintiffs' trade or business ... [by] unlawful means ... with the intention to injure the plaintiffs'. There is also a need to prove actual harm: 'the action should in fact injure [the plaintiffs]'. Of course, apart from the need to show intention, unlawful means and harm to trade, the possibility of a defence

---

[33] The result in part of his crusade in the 1960s and 1970s to protect the little man against the 'battalions' of the trade unions and to protect the record industry against 'bootleggers' and 'pirates'. See *Ex parte Island Records* [1978] Ch 122; *Carlin Music Corp v Collins* [1979] FSR 548; *Re M's Application* (1979) 123 SJ 142. In all of these cases the harm looks foreseeable rather than targeted.

[34] Discussed below. And see *Ex parte Island Records* [1978] Ch 122 (tort liability for harm consequent on criminal activity). The general rule he proposed was summarized and criticized by Lord Diplock in *Lonrho v Shell* [1982] AC 173.

[35] Neill LJ in *Associated British Ports v TGWU* [1989] ICR 557, p. 573 'the precise limits and characteristics of this tort are uncertain'.

[36] Ibid. 570.

[37] [1995] 2 QB 479.

[38] Reference is made throughout this chapter to the decision of the Court of Appeal in *Lonrho v Fayed* [1990] 2 QB 479. In fact the decision was affirmed by the House of Lords [1992] 1 AC 448, but the House of Lords focused not on the tort of unlawful interference but on the tort of unlawful conspiracy, taking the opportunity to overrule the Court of Appeal in *Metall und Rohstoff AG v Donaldson Lufkin & Jenrette* [1990] 1 QB 391 (see Ch. 2).

[39] Woolf LJ, [1990] 2 QB 479, p. 493.   [40] Ibid., Ralph Gibson LJ, p. 492.

[41] Ibid., Dillon LJ, p. 492.   [42] [1987] IRLR 3, p. 6.

of justification needs to be assessed, given *dicta* favour the existence of such a defence for some of the economic torts involving unlawful means.[43]

To assess the limits of the tort it will be necessary to draw on cases concerning intimidation[44] and direct and indirect interference with contract. In the discussion that follows it will be seen that the relevant case law is complex and contradictory. A range of responses is discernible. The nature of these responses will be analysed later, against an assessment of the rationale of the tort.

Intention

Intentional harm is at the heart of the tort of unlawful interference with trade (as it is for all the important economic torts, bar passing off). Though judicial discussion of the intention required can sometimes involve a worrying reference to the motivation of the defendant,[45] it is clear that motive is not important, as such. So Dillon LJ in *Lonrho v Fayed* rejected the assertion that for this tort the predominant purpose of the defendant must be to injure the plaintiff rather than to pursue own advantage (as it is in simple conspiracy).[46]

Once motive is discarded, the problem still remains that there are 'competing views' on the proper definition of intention for this tort. As Rogers notes[47] the first of these views favours a wide definition of intentional harm to include foresight of inevitable[48] or even probable[49]

---

[43] See Chs. 3 and 4.

[44] Lord Reid in *Rookes v Barnard* [1964] AC 1129, p. 1167 asserted that it would be absurd to make the defendant liable for threatening but not for doing.

[45] Even while a narrow view of intention is being advocated. So in *Barretts & Baird (Wholesalers) Ltd v IPCS* [1987] IRLR 3 though the judge (Henry J) rejects inevitable victims as within the scope of liability, he at times 'inconsistently advocates a predominant purpose test' Sales and Stilitz, above, n. 10, p. 427. This has increased the imprecision surrounding the tort: in *Pinky's Pizza Ribs Pty Ltd v Pinky's Seymour Pizza & Pasta Pty Ltd*, SC Victoria, CA June 30, 1999, Tadgell JA commented that the exact nature of the element of intention has not been definitely settled, citing *Barretts* for the proposition 'the defendant must be proved to have a predominant intention to injure rather than advance his own interests'. Similarly in *Van Camp Chocolates Ltd v Aulsebrooks Ltd* [1984] 1 NZLR 354 there is a confusion in the discussion between the concepts of intent and predominant purpose.

[46] [1990] 2 QB 472, p. 488: 'No predominant purpose to injure is required where the tortious act relied on is injury by wrongful interference with a third-party's contract with the victim, nor should it in my view be required where the wrongful interference has been by the practice of fraud on a third party, aimed specifically at the plaintiff.' The need for such a predominant purpose 'would be inconsistent with the way that Lord Diplock treated this tort and the tort of conspiracy differently in his speech in *Lonrho v Shell* (no. 2) and in *Hadmor v Hamilton*'.   [47] Above, n. 26, p. 654.

[48] Note the Restatement (Second) of Torts, s.8A states that the word 'intent' is used throughout the Restatement 'to denote that the actor desires to cause consequences of his act, or that he believes that the consequences are substantially certain to result from it'.

[49] *Dicta* of Lord Alverstone in *National Phonograph Co v Edison-Bell* [1908] 1 Ch 335.

consequences. The second view favours a narrow definition that requires deliberate harm, with the defendant 'targeting' the claimant.

In *Lonrho v Fayed* Woolf LJ favoured the first view.[50] He believed that the plaintiff should be compensated 'if the defendant has deliberately embarked on a course of conduct, the probable consequence of which on the plaintiff he appreciated'.[51] However, the majority of judicial opinion would seem to favour the need for targeted harm, rather than simply inevitable harm. Lord Watson in *Allen v Flood*[52] noted that liability would ensue where the defendant had used illegal means 'directed against' the plaintiff. This was applied by the majority of the Court of Appeal in *National Phonographic Ltd v Edison-Bell*.[53] In *Quinn v Leathem*[54] Lord Lindley spoke of liability where the plaintiff is wrongfully and intentionally 'struck at through others'. In *Rookes v Barnard*,[55] Lord Devlin, referring to three-party intimidation, contended: 'it must be proved that [the defendant's] object is to injure [the plaintiff] through the instrumentality of [the middleman]', Lord Evershed echoing this view.[56] Lord Denning himself appeared at times[57] to favour targeted harm as the requisite intention. So, in *Torquay Hotel v Cousins*[58] he referred to the need for 'deliberate interference with the plaintiff's trade'.[59] More recently, in *Lonrho v Fayed*, Dillon LJ asserted[60] that liability could arise where fraud on a third party was 'aimed specifically at the plaintiff', it having been conceded by the plaintiff that he must prove that the unlawful act 'was in some sense directed against' him or intended to harm him. Ralph Gibson LJ in the same case supported the narrower view of intention, alluding[61] to the requirement that the conduct be 'directed against' the plaintiffs. Again, for Stuart-Smith LJ in *Associated British Ports v TGWU* the essence of unlawful interference

---

[50] [1995] 2 QB 479, p. 494.

[51] In *Millar v Bassey* [1994] EMLR 44, a case where the plaintiff caused rather than induced a breach of contract between the third party and the plaintiff. Beldam LJ adopted a similar view of intention but that case contained a powerful dissenting opinion from Peter Gibson LJ. See discussion in Ch. 10 on intention and the economic torts.

[52] [1898] AC 1, p. 96.

[53] [1908] 1 Ch 335, Buckley LJ, p. 361, liability based on the use of illegal means 'directed against the plaintiffs'.

[54] [1901] AC 495.

[55] [1964] AC 1129, p. 1208.

[56] Ibid. 1183 'where the intention and effect of the threat is to injure such third party'.

[57] Though cf. for example *Ex parte Island Records* [1978] Ch 122.

[58] [1969] 2 Ch 106, 139.

[59] [1969] 2 Ch 106, p. 139. Interestingly, Lord Denning in *Lonrho v Shell* at CA level stated 'it is sufficient if the . . . conspiracy is aimed at or directed at the plaintiff', *The Times*, 7 March 1981. Upjohn J in *DC Thomson v Deakin* [1952] Ch 646, p. 663 stated: 'the fact that the natural and probable consequence of that act is that Bowaters may be compelled to break their contracts with the plaintiffs is not sufficient to constitute the tort alleged.'

[60] [1990] 2 QB 479, p. 488.

[61] Ibid. 492.

with trade 'is deliberate and intended damage',[62] Butler-Sloss LJ agreeing that the 'object and intention' of the defendant must be to injure.[63]

It is perhaps not surprising, therefore, that Henry J in *Barretts & Baird v IPCS*[64] decided that those inevitably harmed by strike action would be unable to show the necessary intentional harm. In *Indata Equipment Supplies Ltd v ACL Ltd*, Otton LJ defined the tort as 'one person using unlawful means with the object and effect of causing damage to another'.[65] This view would also seem to reject 'recklessness' as sufficient for liability.[66] Overall, paraphrasing Ralph Gibson LJ in *Lonrho v Fayed*,[67] the intention provides the sufficient 'nexus' between the means employed and the harm caused to the claimant.[68] The fact that the claimant is the defendant's target (for whatever reason) is important: as Lord Lindley noted in *Quinn v Leathem*[69] 'the intention to injure the plaintiff . . . disposes of any question of remoteness of damage'.[70]

Indeed, Commonwealth decisions mirror this narrow view of intention: Cooke J in the New Zealand Court of Appeal decision in *Van Camp Chocolates Ltd v Aulsebrooks Ltd*[71] asserted that this tort required deliberate interference, so that interference that was no more than an 'incidental consequence', though 'foreseen and gratifying to the defendant' was not sufficient. He stressed that to impose liability in such a case would be 'to stretch the tort too far'. In *Cheticamp Fisheries Co-operative v Canada*[72] the Court of Appeal of Nova Scotia asserted that the harm must be 'directed at the plaintiff'. In Australia, McLelland J asserted in *Copyright Agency Ltd*

---

[62] [1989] ICR 557, p. 586. He of course contrasted this with his view of the lesser intention required in the tort of inducing breach (see discussion in Ch. 3). He used this as an argument for a wide definition of unlawful means.

[63] Ibid. 579. Despite *dicta* to that effect by Lord Alverstone CJ in *Edison-Bell* [1908] 1 Ch 335.

[64] [1987] IRLR 3.

[65] [1998] FSR 248, p. 259.

[66] *Three Rivers DC v Bank of England* [1996] 3 All ER 558, 579–83, Clarke J compared the tort of misfeasance in a public office with the economic torts based on an intention to injure and justified a tighter definition of intention for the latter torts on the basis that 'these are torts which can be and ordinarily are committed by private individuals or entities'. However, as misfeasance 'consists in the purported exercise of a power otherwise than in an honest attempt to perform the relevant duty', recklessness may be sufficient for this tort (p. 581). The Court of Appeal dismissed the appeal, as did the House of Lords [2000] 2 WLR 1220. Reckless indifference is sufficient to establish liability in the tort of misfeasance in public office.

[67] [1990] 2 QB 479, p. 492.

[68] Note also Sales and Stilitz contend (above, n. 10, p. 412) 'it is the defendant's intention to cause harm to the plaintiff that establishes [the] nexus'.

[69] [1901] AC 495, p. 537.

[70] And see discussion in Ch. 10.

[71] [1984] 1 NZLR 354, p. 360. The case involved the misuse of the plaintiff's confidential information by a trade rival, enabling the defendant to create an inferior rival product.

[72] 123 DLR (1995) 121, p. 132 (Nova Scotia CA).

v Haines[73] that for the general tort 'one essential criteria for its application must be the existence in the mind of the wrongdoer of a purpose or intention of inflicting injury on the plaintiff'. Furthermore, the imposition of tort liability by the High Court of Australia in *Beaudesert Shire Council v Smith*[74] for inevitable harm, consequent on an intended and unlawful act, having been disapproved of by the House of Lords in *Lonrho v Shell*,[75] has now been overruled.[76]

Most commentators[77] agree with the need for targeted, directed harm. Heydon[78] contends that those who inflict inevitable loss will not be liable as 'the tort is so strongly one of intention' while for Weir[79] 'the plaintiff always has to show that the defendant was aiming at him'. Again, Sales and Stilitz support a narrow definition of intention, given it represents a form of proximity mechanism to keep liability within bounds.[80] They reject a formulation like Woolf LJ's which would catch a wide range of competitive commercial activity, rendering particularly onerous action taken in the context of a complex network of contractual relationships[81] and which would prove a major problem for those who take industrial action. There, though the *target* of such action is likely to be the trade dispute employer,[82] such action has an inevitable impact on third parties, the customers and commercial partners of the claimant under attack.[83]

---

[73] [1982] 1 NSWLR 182, p. 194.   [74] (1966) 120 CLR 145.

[75] [1982] AC 173, p. 463.   [76] *Northern Territory v Mengel* (1995) 129 ALR 1.

[77] Payne, D. J., 'Inducing Breach of Contract' 7 Current Legal Problems (1954) 94; Elias and Ewing, above, n. 18, p. 327 'there appears to have been no case in English law where the plaintiff has not been the deliberate target of the defendants' [this of course predates the judgment of Woolf LJ in *Lonrho v Fayed*] cf. Smith, R. J., 'The Economic Torts: their Impact on Real Property', 41 Conv (1977) 318, p. 327 who contends that knowledge of inevitable loss is sufficient.

[78] Above, n. 24, pp. 65–6.

[79] Weir, T., 'Chaos or Cosmos: *Rookes, Stratford* and the Economic Torts' [1964] CLJ 230.

[80] Of course they use this argument to support their view that the unlawful means mechanism is not so critical in establishing liability for unlawful interference with trade.

[81] This orthodox view would seem to perceive the majority suggestion in *Millar v Bassey* as wrong. As Weir asserts (*Economic Torts*, above, n. 24, p. 43) once it is accepted that you have to be targeted in order to sue 'Miss Bassey could not be pursued in the law courts by the by-blows of her decision not to sing'.

[82] It is for this reason that it is submitted that *Barretts and Baird v IPCS* [1987] IRLR 3 is to be preferred to the approach in *Falconer v ASLEF* [1986] IRLR 331 though Rogers, above, n. 26, p. 629 is right to point out that the plaintiffs were not 'ricochet' victims as they were in *Millar v Bassey*. The targeting of the employer was to pressurize him as the supplier of services in both *Barretts* and *Falconer* (though Sales and Stilitz, above, n. 10, pp. 428–9 support the latter decision, distinguishing between 'necessary and deliberate' harm in the latter and 'inevitable' harm in the former).

[83] As has already been noted, liability for such inevitable consequences was denied by Henry J in *Barretts and Baird v IPCS* [1987] IRLR 6, p. 8 where he pointed out that such extensive third-party liability would severely limit the right to take action and in the commercial field 'would make large inroads into the doctrine of privity of contract'.

Unlawful means

By requiring unlawful means, English law rejected a tort of unjustifiable interference or any *'prima facie* tort theory', as arose in America.[84] Moreover, in the typical three-party scenario that is the setting for this tort, the requirement for unlawful means reveals the 'magic' of the tort. The claimant can gain protection based on unlawful means, though he is not directly a victim of the wrong effected by the defendant. The tort of unlawful interference 'is parasitic on means that are defined as unlawful otherwise than because they amount to torts to the plaintiff'.[85]

However, though a crucial issue[86] in determining the scope of the tort, Rogers[87] notes that the definition of this concept 'has tended to be passed over in the cases with little analysis', while Fleming[88] is critical of an approach '[that] has been casuistic, without any evident rationale related to policy ends and suffering from some inexplicable inconsistencies'.[89] Indeed, Hughes rightly comments that 'the complexity of this branch of the law stems largely from the fact that there is no simple or uniform concept of unlawful means'.[90] The following is a summary of the (conflicting) case law to date. At the end of the chapter is an attempt to offer policy choices for formulating a coherent rationale.

(i) Torts and breach of contract as unlawful means

Case law reveals that all torts constitute unlawful means.[91] This, of course, would include statutory torts but importantly also the other economic torts.[92] The tort of intimidation means that threats of unlawful acts as well as unlawful acts are included, adding an important new dimension to economic tort liability.[93]

---

[84] *Tuttle v Buck* 119 NW 949 (1909). Weir, above, n. 24, p. 73 notes that the doctrine however has limited application. [85] Bagshaw, above, n. 11, p. 730.

[86] Elias and Ewing, above, n. 18, p. 336; Hughes, A. D., 'Liability for Loss Caused by Industrial Action' 86 LQR (1970) 181, p. 182. Note Sales and Stilitz are critical of this 'preoccupation' (above, n. 10, p. 411), arguing that a more helpful approach to understanding the tort is to focus more closely upon the element of intention.

[87] Above, n. 26, p. 651. [88] Ibid. 700.

[89] In *Merkur Island Shipping Corporation v Laughton* [1983] 2AC 579 Lord Diplock stated that to fall within this 'genus' of torts the unlawful act 'need not involve procuring another person to break a subsisting contract or to interfere with the performance of a subsisting contract'. No other clues were offered. [90] Hughes, above, n. 86, p. 182.

[91] Including e.g. trespass *(Plessey v Wilson* [1982] IRLR 198) and illegal distraint *(Huljich v Hall* [1973] 2 NZLR 279).

[92] Including, of course, inducing breach of contract. This was the basis of liability in *Dimbleby v NUJ* [1984] 1 WLR 67, though rather surprisingly there the 'piggy in the middle' was the plaintiff himself.

[93] See discussion in Chs. 4 and 10. In *Lonrho v Fayed* [1990] 2 QB 479, Ralph Gibson LJ p. 492 sees the existence of the tort of intimidation as evidence that the unlawful means do not have to be actionable *per se*.

Once the torts of inducing breach of contract, inducing breach of statutory duty and unlawful conspiracy, are identified as forms of secondary action, it is clear (and has been accepted by the courts) that the unlawful acts at the heart of these torts must be actionable by the claimant. The effect of the economic tort here is to extend the range of defendants, often to bring in the real instigator of the harm, of which the claimant complains. The participation of the defendant in the third party's *actionable* wrong is at the heart of liability. With the unlawful interference tort, however, the claimant gains the advantage of a new cause of action, with primary liability on the part of the defendant, emanating from his use of the unlawful means against a third party.

However, it would appear that the unlawful means, though they must be capable of giving rise to liability in tort,[94] need not be actionable by the third party.[95] So in *National Phonograph Co v Edison-Bell*[96] lies told to third parties in order to gain an economic advantage at the expense of the plaintiff were held to be unlawful means, though no action in deceit could have been brought by the third parties, who themselves were not harmed. *National Phonograph* has been accepted by the Court of Appeal in *Lonrho v Fayed*: Dillon LJ asserting that liability did not depend on 'a complete tort'[97] as he could see 'no valid reason why the tort should need, as against the third party, to have been complete to the extent that the third party had himself suffered damage'. This was echoed in the judgment of Ralph Gibson LJ who did not accept that the alleged fraudulent misrepresentations used to deceive a public official 'cease to be unlawful means for the purposes of the tort of unlawful interference with business because there is no identifiable financial loss caused in addition to the fact that a public official has been caused to do by the fraud what otherwise he would not have done, or not to do what otherwise he would have done'.[98]

---

[94] This is, of course, consistent with 'mere' crimes and breaches of statutory provisions not being sufficient to constitute unlawful means in the tort, though the argument that if inchoate torts were sufficient, so must non-actionable statutory breaches was relied upon by the plaintiffs in *Associated British Ports* (see Neill LJ [1989] ICR 557, p. 573). The fact that the unlawful means used must be capable of constituting torts leads to a rejection of the statement by McCardie J in *Pratt v BMA* [1919] 1 KB 244, p. 260 that the intentional employment of unlawful means to injure another's business would lead to liability 'even though such unlawful means do not comprise any specific act which is *per se* actionable'. McCardie J's *dicta* were criticized by Scrutton LJ in *Ware & De Freville v Motor Trade Association* [1921] 3 KB 40, p. 69, to the effect that it was hardly useful to describe something as unlawful, though no act composing the means be unlawful.

[95] Lord Wedderburn terms this an 'inchoate cause of action' in *Clerk and Lindsell on Torts*, 18th edn. (London: Sweet & Maxwell, 2000), para 24–76. Wedderburn notes (para 24–70) 'where the plaintiff relies upon a threat of unlawful means which is tortious against a third party, there is of course no need for him to prove that the tort was complete as against the third party (for example by way of damage being suffered by that party)'.

[96] [1908] 1 Ch 335.   [97] [1990] 2 QB 479, p. 489.

[98] Ibid. 492.

This is in line with the 'magic' of the tort: the claimant is able to sue because the means used are within the ambit of tort law already.[99] So Eekelaar notes that as the tort allows the transfer of the unlawfulness of acts to the benefit of the plaintiff, it is not necessary for the tort to be 'completed' by the infliction of harm on the third party, the damage being suffered by the claimant.[100]

Controversially, contract breach is also capable of constituting unlawful means for the tort of unlawful interference with trade. This follows the decision of the House of Lords in *Rookes v Barnard*.[101] Once this established that a threatened breach of contract is unlawful means, *in the three-party scenario*,[102] an actual breach of contract (in order to harm the claimant) must also lead to liability. Indeed, Lord Reid asserted in *Rookes*: 'it would be absurd to make [a defendant] liable for threatening to do [an act] but not for doing it.'[103] Thus it is submitted that the tort of unlawful interference with trade includes the situation where the defendant deliberately harms the claimant by breaking his (the defendant's) contract with the third party, on whom the defendant knows the claimant is relying.[104] Of course in such a situation the claimant may decide to use the more established tort of indirect interference with contract. But the existence of the tort of unlawful interference means that the claimant is protected even where there is no contract between the claimant and the third party.[105] As with intimidation, the real difficulty in accepting breach of contract as unlawful means arises in the two-party version of the tort.[106] The issue here is whether every intentional breach of contract should also constitute the tort of unlawful interference.[107]

---

[99] For this reason Elias and Ewing (above, n. 18) are wrong to suggest that such a definition of unlawful means comes close to a concept of 'improper' rather than *unlawful* tools (p. 338).

[100] Eekelaar, J., 'The Conspiracy Tangle' (1990) 106 LQR 225, p. 226.

[101] [1964] AC 1129, discussed in Ch. 4.

[102] Where only two parties are involved, the tort may not apply: see discussion in Ch. 4.

[103] [1964] AC 1129, p. 1168.

[104] Despite *Rookes v Barnard* [1964] AC 1129, however, this is not uncontroversial. In *Barretts & Baird v IPCS* [1987] IRLR 6 Henry J commented: 'it does not seem to me necessarily to follow that the fact that a breach of contract is "unlawful means" for the purposes of establishing the tort of intimidation, means that it necessarily is in the tort of unlawful interference with a trade or business' (p. 9). However, he was prepared to accept it as arguable.

[105] The tort would apply even where there was no contract between the third party and the claimant but the claimant had reasonable expectations of continued supplies. Again, there may be a contract but no breach as between the third party and the claimant—as would be the case, for example, where the third party, because of the defendant's unlawful act, lawfully terminated his contract with the claimant.

[106] See Ch. 4.

[107] Sales and Stilitz, above, n. 10, p. 424 are prepared to accept that though a breach of the defendant's contract with the claimant will not constitute the unlawful interference tort, a threat to do so will. This is because the threat of a breach is used by the defendant 'as an instrument to an end (to cause harm to [the plaintiff]) which is not contemplated by the

(ii) Breach of fiduciary duties and equitable obligations as unlawful means

It may be arguable that breach of trust, fiduciary duty or equitable obligation constitute unlawful means for this tort. However, the effect of this
argument would be to 'tortify' these wrongs.[108] Such an effect would
certainly disturb some judges:[109] in *Metall und Rohstoff AG v Donaldson
Lufkin & Jenrette*,[110] as we have already seen,[111] the Court of Appeal
refused to accept a tort of inducing a breach of trust, on a par with the
principle of *Lumley v Gye*. More specifically, Cooke J, in the New Zealand
Court of Appeal was concerned that to view breach of confidence as
unlawful means was to pre-empt a decision to create a tort of breach of
confidence (*Van Camp Chocolates Ltd v Aulsebrooks Ltd*).[112] However, the
Court of Appeal in *Jarman & Platt Ltd v Barget Ltd*[113] did not discount the
possibility that breach of confidence could constitute unlawful means and
that proposition was accepted by Otton LJ in *Indata Equipment Supplies Ltd
v ACL Ltd*,[114] though Simon Brown LJ asserted that this was 'a difficult
issue'.[115]

This issue of course raises a wider debate on the continued division of

consensual distribution of risk under the contract itself. It follows that the policy considerations which apply to limit the damages recoverable as a result of a breach of contract do not
apply to what may be recovered in respect of loss suffered in consequence of a threatened
breach.'

[108] Though the equitable wrong could also be a breach of contract, as in *Prudential v Lorenz*
(1971) 11KIR 78.

[109] Note also in *Stein v Blake* [1998] 1 All ER 724, p. 727 and *Yukong Line of Korea v Rends-
berg Investments Corp (no. 2)* [1998] 1 WLR 294 third parties were not permitted to enforce
fiduciary duties.

[110] [1990] 1 QB 391, p. 481 (Slade LJ). Hoffmann LJ in *Law Debenture Trust v Ural* suggested
this was 'only because the ground was already covered by the equitable doctrine of knowing assistance' [1993] 1 WLR 138, p. 151 (reversed on other grounds, [1995] Ch 152). That
said, in *Crawley BC v Ure* [1996] QB 13 the court appeared more sympathetic to this possibility.

[111] See Ch. 3.

[112] [1984] 1 NZLR 354, p. 360. Whether breach of confidence does constitute a tort in its
own right is still unclear. Rogers, above, n. 26, p. 468, n. 16 notes the 'tort-based' language of
Lords Bridge and Lowry in *X Ltd v Morgan-Grampian (Publishers) Ltd* [1991] 1 AC 1 though
this has to be compared with the views of Evans LJ in *Kitechnology BV v Uncor Gmbh* [1995]
FSR 765, p. 777 who stated that it was clear such claims do not arise in tort. The Supreme
Court of Canada in *Cadbury Schweppes Inc v FBI Foods Ltd* [2000] FSR 491 seemed to accept
that it was a *sui generis* action. See also Ch. 10.

[113] [1977] FSR 260, p. 278.

[114] [1998] FSR 248. He admitted that there were uncertainties surrounding the tort but 'on
the particular circumstances of this case ... would hold that the breach of confidence
coupled with the ruthless conduct [of the defendant] would amount to unlawful means'.
Does that mean that only 'ruthless' breaches of confidences are relevant to the tort?

[115] Ibid. 264. Owen J remarked that had it been necessary 'I would have been prepared to
say that the tort of unlawful interference had been established' (p. 263). See discussion in
Ch. 10.

civil wrongs,[116] Berg[117] contending that *Metall und Rohstoff AG v Donaldson Lufkin & Jenrette Inc*[118] shows that the courts are not yet willing to break down the divide wholesale.

(iii) Crimes[119] and breach of statutory provisions as unlawful means

There are cases which accept crimes and breaches of statutory provisions, not civilly actionable in themselves, as sufficient unlawful means.[120] Lord Devlin in *Rookes v Barnard*[121] stated that it was not disputed that a threatened crime would 'of course' constitute unlawful means, while Lord Denning in *ex p Island Records*[122] saw a statutory crime as sufficient, though not necessarily giving rise to tort liability in its own right. He argued that such an approach permitted the court to avoid engaging in what he termed the game of chance to discern the intention of Parliament behind the statutory crime. He also held that criminal contempt was sufficient unlawful means in *Acrow (Automation) Ltd v Rex Chainbelt Inc.*[123] There a dispute between the plaintiffs and an American company led to an injunction restraining that company from impeding the plaintiffs in their manufacture of equipment that incorporated the defendants' (essential) components. The American company had sufficient control over the defendants to enable them to direct the defendants as to whom they could supply. Despite the injunction, the defendants were directed not to supply the plaintiffs, causing them to refuse to enter into new contracts of supply with the plaintiffs.[124] In so doing, they were clearly in contempt. For Lord

---

[116] See Ch. 10. That this divide is under attack cannot be doubted see e.g. Smith, L., 'Constructive Trust for Breach of Fiduciary Obligation' 114 LQR (1998) 14, p. 17 who questions why breaches of common law duties cannot amount to wrongful means to enable a court to impose a constructive trust (to recoup wrongful gains), in the light of the acceptance by the SC of Canada that breach of confidence would support a constructive trust in *LAC Minerals Ltd v Corona Resource Ltd* [1989] 2 SCR 574 61 DLR (4th).

[117] Berg, A., 'Accessory Liability for Breach of Trust' 59 MLR (1996) 443.

[118] [1990] 1 QB 391.

[119] Note also the *Springhead Spinning* principle, discussed in the conclusion to this chapter.

[120] Note Lord Wright in *Crofter v Veitch* [1942] AC 435, p. 462 asserted that unlawful acts were involved where a strike was conducted 'by means of conduct prohibited by [the Conspiracy and protection of Property Act 1875]', although Scott J in *Thomas v NUM* [1986] 1 Ch 20, p. 56 commented '[the plaintiffs] can complain in a civil action of picketing which is a tort but not of picketing which is criminal'.

[121] [1964] AC 1129.

[122] [1978] Ch 122.

[123] [1971] 3 All ER 1175, Phillimore J. Rogers, above, n. 26, p. 654 notes that though the American company committed a civil contempt by disobeying the injunction, the defendant committed a criminal contempt, interfering with the course of justice: see *AG v Times Newspapers Ltd* [1992] 1 AC 91. Sales and Stilitz argue that the case involved a civil contempt only (above, n. 10, p. 421).

[124] There was no inducement to breach as the supply company were simply refusing to enter into new contracts and there was no unlawful threat alleged to support an allegation of intimidation.

Denning, abetting the breach of a High Court injunction was unlawful means for the tort of unlawful interference with trade.

But there are clearly decisions that cast doubt on the correctness of this approach. *Hargreaves v Bretherton*[125] establishes that the crime of perjury is not capable of constituting unlawful means for the tort. Again, in *Chapman v Honig*[126] (approved by Lord Hoffmann in *Harrow LBC v Johnstone*)[127] the majority of the Court of Appeal held that the victimization by a landlord of a tenant who had been subpoenaed to give evidence in an action brought against the landlord was not actionable in tort, even if it were a contempt of court. *Chapman*, in which Lord Denning had dissented,[128] was not referred to in *Acrow* and arguably, therefore, *Acrow* was decided *per incuriam*.[129] Further, in *Acrow* itself, Megaw LJ denied tort liability, granting an injunction instead on the basis of the fact that the defendants were aiding and abetting a defiance of an injunction. So for Howarth[130] 'it is doubtful whether crimes which are not otherwise actionable in tort should count' as unlawful means.

As for statutory obligations or provisions, Lord Diplock in *Lonrho v Shell*[131] (though a case on foreseeable rather than intended harm) was obviously opposed to a doctrine which would circumvent the need to establish statutory torts by reference to Parliament's intention. He stressed the general principle that a breach of statutory duty is only actionable in tort if the plaintiff can show that the duty or obligation is imposed for the protection of a class of which the plaintiff is one or that it is imposed for the benefit of the public at large and the plaintiff can show he has suffered some special damage. So he took the opportunity to attack the earlier judgment of Lord Denning in *ex parte Island Records* where recording companies had sought civil redress against bootleggers who,

---

[125] [1959] 1 QB 45.   [126] [1963] 2 QB 502.   [127] [1997] 1 WLR 459, p. 477.

[128] Indeed, earlier in *AG v Butterworth* [1963] 1 QB 696 Lord Denning had suggested *obiter dicta* 'if the witness has been damnified [by the contempt] he may well have redress in the civil courts'.

[129] Again, the Court of Appeal in *Acrow* did not grant sufficient discussion to the High Court decision in *Elliot v Klinger* [1967] 1 WLR 1165. In that case, Stamp J refused an injunction in a similar situation because the plaintiff already had a remedy against those who were aiding and abetting the breach of an injunction: by bringing proceedings for contempt of court. In such an action it is the court who decides whether to grant an injunction in lieu of committal. Lord Denning simply stated that as Acrow had applied for an injunction by a separate writ, *Elliot v Klinger* proved no obstacle. Sales and Stilitz (above, n. 10, p. 421) contend that *Chapman* is not a difficulty for *Acrow* as the intentional tort was not as such raised and of course no business interest was in issue.

[130] Howarth, D., *Textbook on Tort* (London: Butterworths, 1995), p. 491.

[131] [1982] AC 173. The plaintiff alleged that the defendant had contravened the Sanctions Order passed pursuant to the Southern Rhodesia Act 1965. This made the supply of oil to Rhodesia a criminal offence. As a result Lonrho was unable to profit from its oil pipeline in Rhodesia until sanctions were lifted. It claimed that the alleged breaches of the Order by the defendants prolonged the life of the illegal regime in Rhodesia and in so doing prolonged Lonrho's loss of profits.

though liable for criminal offences, were not as such liable under the relevant statutory provisions. It would appear legitimate, therefore, to interpret *Lonrho v Shell*, as Elias and Ewing suggest,[132] as a bar to the use of the unlawful interference tort to outflank the rules of construction for establishing statutory torts.[133] Indeed, the Court of Appeal in *RCA v Pollard*[134] held that *ex parte Island Records* had been overruled by *Lonrho v Shell*.

That said, there are more recent pronouncements from the Court of Appeal that favour accepting non-actionable transgressions as unlawful means. So in *Associated British Ports v TGWU*,[135] statutory wrongs that did not amount to a statutory tort were asserted to be capable of amounting to unlawful means for the tort by Butler-Sloss LJ.[136] She stressed that *Lonrho v Shell* was a decision 'not based on specific intention but on foreseeable damage'.[137] And Stuart Smith LJ relied on *Acrow* to support his assertion that *Lonrho v Shell* did not affect the tort of unlawful interference with trade.[138] Indeed, Beldam LJ in *Law Debenture Trust Corpn v Ural Caspian Oil Corpn*[139] went further than *Acrow* (a case of procuring a breach of the injunction), asserting that where the defendant took action which

---

[132] They assert that 'though his judgment is not free from ambiguity', Lord Diplock appeared to be saying 'no civil action in tort can lie unless the statutory contravention is independently actionable' (above, n. 86, p. 337). They go on to say, of course, that this cannot finally determine the matter.

[133] That on the true construction of the Act it is apparent that the statutory obligation or prohibition was imposed for the benefit or protection of a particular class of individuals or that the statute creates a public right.

[134] [1983] Ch 135 (a case of intended harm).

[135] [1989] ICR 557.

[136] As Cane, P., *Tort Law and Economic Interests*, 2nd edn. (Oxford: Clarendon Press, 1996) comments on the view of Butler-Sloss and Stuart-Smith LJJ in *Associated British Ports v TGWU* [1989] ICR 557—that a plaintiff can rely on inducement of breach of statutory duty as unlawful means 'even if the actions of neither the inducer nor the induced were independently unlawful'—this 'renders the tort of inducement of breach of statutory duty superfluous' (p. 197).

[137] Butler-Sloss and Stuart-Smith LJJ also asserted that cases such as *RCA v Pollard* [1982] Ch 135, *CBS v Amstrad* [1988] Ch 61 (at Court of Appeal level) and *Rickless v United Artists Corp* [1988] QB 40 were not relevant as 'none involved intention to injure' ([1989] ICR 557, p. 579; p. 585 respectively). However, *Rickless v United Artists Corp* did involve intentional harm, with inducing breach of contract established.

[138] Neill LJ, the third member of the court, however, noted that he saw 'great force' in the defendants' argument that 'a breach of statutory duty cannot be relied on as unlawful means . . . unless it is actionable'. But he felt that it would be wrong to try to resolve the matter at interlocutory level. With respect, Stuart Smith LJ's argument that the statutory breach need not be actionable since breach of contract can be unlawful means and yet is not actionable by the plaintiff, cannot be accepted. The point about unlawful interference with trade is the issue whether the unlawful act must be actionable *by someone* rather than necessarily by the claimant.

[139] [1994] 3 WLR 1221, p. 1235 'if [because of *Acrow*] it is to be regarded as unlawful to do an act which amounts to contempt of court because it interferes with the rights of a party who has obtained an injunction, it is difficult to see why it should not similarly be regarded as unlawful to do acts which might prevent or hinder the obtaining of an injunction'. Would this include perjury?

prevented or impeded the party subject to the injunction from complying with its terms, that would be actionable by the plaintiff 'under the principle in *Acrow's* case'. While in *Department of Transport v Williams*[140] the Court of Appeal granted an injunction to restrain the defendants from preventing or interfering with the plaintiffs' construction of a motorway, pursuant to statutory authority. Wilful obstruction of the plaintiffs in the exercise of their statutory powers was held to amount to the tort, at least for the purposes of an interlocutory appeal.[141] Dillon LJ found the requisite unlawful act in the contravention of s.303 of the Highways Act 1980, creating criminal liability for wilful interference with motorway building. He asserted 'by virtue of s.303 any wilful interference is unlawful and, in my judgment, constitutes unlawful means for the purposes of this tort . . . anything which is illegal under any statute provides the unlawful means'.[142]

(iv) Beyond legal wrongs

Some courts have gone so far as to suggest that unlawful means include acts that the defendant is not at liberty to commit, even though no civil wrong or illegality is involved. Contempt, a form of quasi-crime, would clearly fall within this analysis. But this concept would clearly go wider than that. So in *Daily Mirror v Gardner*, Lord Denning contended that an agreement presumed void as contrary to the public interest under the restrictive trade practices legislation would be unlawful means.[143] This would appear to be contrary to the House of Lords pivotal decision in *Mogul* to the effect that (in a case concerning the common law doctrine of restraint of trade) agreements may be void and unenforceable, without being unlawful.[144] Given that the common law restraint doctrine and the

---

[140] (1993) 138 Sol L J LB5, *The Times*, 7 December 1993 CA.

[141] Dillon LJ did make it clear that he was not prepared to decide the issue of law 'of such potential importance' on an interlocutory appeal. In the case, the injunction granted on the basis of the trespass of the defendants was not challenged. It was the injunction based on 'wrongful interference with business' that was the subject of the appeal: this related to possible future obstruction of the work. The case centred on the issue of unlawful means, defendants' counsel having conceded that the injunction could be granted for the tort of wrongful interference with business if the defendants had interfered with the plaintiff's activities by unlawful means.

[142] Lexis transcript. He relied on *dicta* of Templeman LJ in *R v CC Devon and Cornwall ex p CEGB* [1982] QB 458, p. 478. In *Emms v Brad Lovett Ltd* [1973] 1 NZLR 82, a breach of a byelaw was held to be unlawful means for the tort.

[143] *Daily Mirror Newspapers Ltd v Gardner* [1968] 2 QB 762. See also *Brekkes v Cattel* [1972] Ch 105. In *Hadmor Productions v Hamilton* [1981] ICR 690 plaintiff's counsel invited the Court of Appeal to introduce a new tort of unjustifiable interference in restraint of trade: Lord Denning commented that he would leave this point to another day.

[144] Guest, A. G., and Hoffmann, L. H., 'When is a Boycott Unlawful?' 84 LQR (1968) 310. They comment (p. 316) 'there is no more ground for saying that an agreement which is contrary to the public interest constitutes unlawful means for the purposes of common law torts than a contract in restraint of trade, which is contrary to public policy'.

statutory provisions on restrictive trade practices had similar aims and effects, it would appear odd that the rationale of *Mogul* should not be mirrored in *Gardner*. Indeed, Heydon notes 'it is odd that the careful structure set up by Parliament for investigating cartels involving slow and detailed proceedings before a specialist tribunal should be undercut by allowing interlocutory proceedings in tort before a single Chancery judge'.[145] However, the decision in *Daily Mirror v Gardner*, though widely disapproved of by commentators, was accepted by Butler-Sloss and Stuart Smith LJJ in *Associated British Ports v TGWU*.[146] If potential unenforceability can amount to unlawful means, then it would be hard not to accept that economic duress amounts to unlawful means. And if the concept of 'unlawful means' in this tort is based on the public interest in attacking certain conduct then Heydon might be right to suggest that acts in breach of natural justice could suffice.[147]

Of course the wider the definition of 'impermissible', the closer the courts may be pushed into *de facto* accepting 'improper' means as the test for 'unlawful' means. Indeed, Lord Denning, though suggesting a test of 'acts the defendant is not at liberty to commit' at one point suggested that unlawful means could include 'interference with the freedom of the press'.[148]

What this survey of judicial reaction to the concept of 'unlawful means' reveals is that there is a real need to address the role of unlawful interference with trade, rather than this haphazard approach which has only given rise to contradiction and complexity.

Trade

The tort requires that the claimant be harmed.[149] In fact, it is commonly pleaded as a catch-all where the claimant's contract rights are breached or interfered with. So litigation where the tort has been pleaded has tended to focus on contract performance or expectation. *Dimbley v NUJ*[150] is a clear example of this process.

---

[145] Heydon, J. D., *Economic Torts*, 2nd edn. (London: Sweet & Maxwell, 1978), p. 67. Sales and Stilitz, above, n. 10, p. 419 agree that the decision in *Gardner* is 'very hard to justify'.

[146] [1989] ICR 551, Stuart Smith LJ noting that the decision was not referred to in *Lonrho v Shell* 'because the House was not then considering this tort'.

[147] He cites *Posluns v Toronto Stock Exchange* (1964) 46 DLR (2d) 210, pp. 290–333 and *Orchard v Tunney* SC of Canada 1957 where the union official falsely told the plaintiff's employer that the plaintiff had been suspended from membership, leading (intentionally) to the lawful dismissal of the plaintiff. However, such could be seen as an example of the unlawful interference tort, with deceit as the unlawful means.

[148] *Associated Newspapers v Wade* [1979] ICR 664, pp. 708–9.

[149] Cane, above, n. 136, p. 157.

[150] [1984] 1 WLR 67 (CA); the House of Lords did not consider the half-way tort of unlawful interference with contract performance.

But such a cautious use does not necessarily represent the scope of the interest being protected by the tort of unlawful interference. 'Business' or 'livelihood' are sometimes used as co-terminous with the concept of trade[151] and, as Cane notes, in competitive contexts trade 'consists most importantly of the making of advantageous contracts'.[152] This was highlighted in *Stratford v Lindley*[153] where Lord Upjohn[154] asserted that protection was required 'so as to enable [the plaintiffs] to carry on business in the usual way by entering into new contracts from time to time with their customers', while Lord Reid stressed that the interference with the supply of barges 'in addition to interfering with existing contracts . . . made it impossible to do any new business with the barge hirers. It was not disputed that such interference with business is tortious, if any unlawful means are employed'.[155] Again, in *Dimbleby v NUJ* the plaintiff, though he was able to produce his newspaper, succeeded in the tort, the unlawful interference having rendered that activity more onerous and therefore less profitable. At its widest, of course, 'trade' could be synonymous with 'economic interests'—a possibility accepted by Fleming[156] and Rogers, who comments that 'if trade or business is to be regarded as a requirement of the tort there is a danger that the genus may be narrower than the species'.[157] Though obviously most cases arise in the context of business he believes 'it is not apparent why liability should be confined to cases where those activities are interfered with'. For Elias and Ewing an important feature of the tort is that it should protect 'not merely the plaintiff's legal rights but also his wider interests'.[158] It might well be that the title unlawful interference with *trade*, therefore, is a misnomer.[159]

---

[151] Of course, conversely, the House of Lords in *Allen v Flood* [1898] AC 1 were at pains to note that 'trade' *per se* has no special protection, refuting *Keeble v Hickeringill* (1707) 11 East 574. Lord Herschell noted that this argument 'found most favour with the learned judges who think the plaintiffs entitled to judgment'.

[152] Above, n. 136, p. 151.

[153] [1965] AC 269.

[154] Ibid. 339.

[155] Ibid. 324.

[156] Fleming, J., *The Law of Torts*, 9th edn. (Sydney: LBC, 1998), p. 771 ' "trade or business" appears to be merely a synonym for economic interests'.

[157] Above, n. 26, p. 650. Certainly a wide view of the interest being protected has been taken in the tort of 'simple conspiracy': see Ch. 2.

[158] Above, n. 18, p. 336. Mann LJ in *Department of Transport v Williams* (1993) 138 Sol LJ LB5 'a business can encompass the construction of a special road'—though it should be noted that the defendants did not suggest to the contrary, the interlocutory appeal being concerned with the issue of unlawful means.

[159] Weir, above, n. 24, p. 71: 'It is an undesirable novelty, doubtless associated with the misnomer of the tort, that the nature of the economic interest adversely affected by unlawful activity should be regarded as being of any importance.' Indeed, there is an argument—forcefully put by Sales and Stilitz, above, n. 10—that liability for intentional and unlawful harm is not restricted even to the vague concept of economic interests—certainly with intimidation, physical well-being is clearly covered.

Much of this, of course, is speculation as there has been little judicial discussion on the nature of the interest being protected. And certainly, some courts are concerned about accepting an indeterminate concept of harm. It is not established that 'all cases of interference with advantageous business opportunities' are covered.[160] So in *Lonrho v Fayed* Woolf LJ expressed his reservation[161] 'whether the business asset which allegedly has been damaged [the freedom to bid] is in fact capable of being a business interest for the purposes of the tort of unlawful interference'. Again, the Court of Appeal in *RCA v Pollard* were unwilling to focus on trade interests other than the interest in contract performance. In the case itself, this meant that though interference with the recording contract would merit protection, interference with the economic advantages to be obtained from that contract (the potential profits from the exclusive recording contracts being reduced by the bootlegging activity) would not. This, however, would appear to unduly limit the concept to contract expectations.[162]

This reluctance to accept a wide definition of the interest being protected may result from a concern lest speculative losses be recoverable.[163] However, given that unlawful means are required and provided the normal rules on remoteness and a narrow view on intention are accepted, such fears would appear to be unfounded.

Two- and three-party interference

The unlawful interference tort is most important and useful in its three-party version: such being 'the paradigm case of the intentional harm tort envisaged in Lord Watson's speech in *Allen v Flood*'.[164] However, there may be a two-party version of the tort, a possibility accepted in the Canadian case of *Cellular Rental Systems v Bell Mobility* by Montgomery J.[165] And the possibility of two-party liability shadows the discussion of Lord Diplock in *Dimbleby v NUJ*.[166] There the plaintiff had entered into a print-

---

[160] Cane, above, n. 136, p. 151, n. 4.

[161] [1990] 2 QB 479, p. 493. Ralph Gibson LJ p. 492 noted (without resolving) that the point had been raised as to 'the nature of the business by reference to which the plaintiff must prove he has been damaged'.

[162] In the case itself, though, the bootleggers were not aiming at the plaintiff, rather they were 'misappropriating' the performance.

[163] Sales and Stilitz, above, n. 10, suggest that the tort has been dogged by the 'ghost' of *Keeble v Hickeringill* and that the tort should now no longer depend on the nature of the interest which is invaded (p. 430).

[164] Sales and Stilitz, above, n. 10, p. 420. Weir, above, n. 79, p. 227 'one can bloody one's neighbour's nose unaided, but to ruin him usually requires assistance'.

[165] (1994) 116 DLR (4th) 514.

[166] Where the inducing breach of contract claim was transformed into a claim for unlawful interference, to avoid the statutory immunities afforded at the time to those engaged in industrial action.

ing contract with a 'blacked' company, causing the defendant union to induce their journalist members not to supply the plaintiff with copy. The plaintiff alleged, *inter alia*, that he had been harmed by unlawful means (the inducement of the journalists to break their contracts) and he succeeded even though he had managed (with difficulty) to produce his newspaper.

Where the unlawful means in a two-party context constitute an actionable tort, the fact that the tort of unlawful interference with trade might also be available would add little to the claim.[167] So in *The Tubantia*[168] the defendants' deliberate interference with the plaintiffs' salvage operation gave rise to a claim in trespass and intentional injury to business. This should be contrasted with the two-party version of the tort of intimidation which does appear to provide a useful 'add-on' liability to existing tort law, rendering the defendant liable for threatened torts, where the claimant accedes to that threat.[169]

Most agree, however, that the possibility of a two-party version of the tort of unlawful interference with trade does raise controversial issues. This is most obviously the case where the unlawful means are a breach of contract.[170] As a contract claim, the normal contract measure of damages applies even in the case of deliberate breach.[171] Thus it would appear wrong to allow the claimant to 'sidestep' this rule by allowing him to rely on the tort of unlawful interference with trade.[172] However, it may be that more generally[173] the tort is best limited to the three-party setting,

---

[167] Though note that in the 1980s there was a worrying tendency for some judges to develop nuisance as a quasi-economic tort, particularly in the case of picket lines, as an obvious way for plaintiff to circumvent the then statutory trade dispute immunities.

[168] [1924] P 78.

[169] But presumably not where the claimant resists the threat.

[170] As Sales and Stilitz note 'there may be policy considerations in play which have influenced the common law to limit the scope of the liability imposed between the parties when one acts unlawfully towards the other' (above, n. 10, p. 420). They suggest that there should be no tort liability for breach of contract between the parties themselves and that breach of the duty of good faith by an insurer should only give a right to the insured to terminate the contract and recover the premium (as decided by the Court of Appeal in *Banque Keyser Ullmann SA v Skandia (UK) Insurance Co Ltd* [1990] 1 QB 665—that limit should not be sidestepped by use of the tort of unlawful interference with trade. See also Eekelaar, J, above, n. 100, p. 226: outside the three-party setting, 'cases demand a different analysis'.

[171] Sales and Stilitz, above, n. 10, p. 423.

[172] Interestingly, they argue that a *threatened* breach should constitute unlawful means even in the two-party version of the tort: the policy bar on contract breach as tort does not apply. As 'the threat of the breach of contract is used by D as an instrument to an end (to cause harm to P) which is not contemplated by the consensual distribution of risk under the contract itself' (above, n. 10, p. 424). Though Weir appeared happy to accept two-party breach of contract as a tort in 1964 (above, n. 79, p. 232), he appears now to doubt the wisdom of this (see *Economic Torts*, above, n. 24, p. 67).

[173] Though Sales and Stilitz argue otherwise (above, n. 10, p. 421): 'the use of unlawful means with the intention to harm another may . . . be actionable, notwithstanding that only

demanding 'an extraneous unlawful element'.[174] This can only be resolved by establishing the rationale of the tort (see below).

Justification

Payne argued that actions unlawful in themselves could not be justified,[175] and there are *dicta* to support this view. So, Lord Lindley noted in *Quinn v Leathem*[176] 'the intention to injure the plaintiff negatives all excuses' while Collins MR *Read v Friendly Society of Stonemasons*[177] thought it desirable to guard against the notion that though the act be unlawful, 'just cause' could be used to avoid liability. More recently, Webster J in *Shearson Lehman Hutton Inc v Maclaine Watson & Co* stated 'there can be no justification for a civil wrong'.[178] However, as with all other aspects of this tort, there is uncertainty on this point. Cornish asserts that part of the general characteristics of the economic torts is that they will not apply if some ground of justification is open to the defendant. As has been seen, there are *dicta* supporting the possibility of the defence in intimidation[179] and indirect inducement to breach of contract.[180] Lord Denning in *Acrow* applied the concept of justification to the tort of unlawful interference with trade, while this defence was accepted in principle in *Canada Volkswagen Canada Ltd v Spicer.*[181]

Of course, this issue is intimately bound up with the nature of the unlawful acts, sufficient for liability in the tort. As Fleming notes[182] 'the more diluted the concept [of unlawful means], the greater the pressure to recognize conflicting public policy as justification'. Such a view has caused Heydon to comment that if unlawful means were not a necessary ingredient in these torts, justification would be far more important and the balancing of competing interests would become an 'open and acknowledged task for the courts'.[183] However, if such a defence exists, it

two parties are involved. D's intention to harm P renders actionable that which would not otherwise be actionable' (they example the use of crime or statutory breach to deliberately harm).

[174] Fleming, above, n. 156, p. 768. The fact that there is a two-party version of intimidation would not conflict with such a view—the tort of intimidation adding a necessary protection where the claimant accedes to the unlawful threat.

[175] Above, n. 77, p. 111. Cf. Weir, above, n. 79, p. 230 who suggests that the courts should not be misled by the phrase 'you can't justify a wrongful act'.

[176] [1901] AC 495, p. 537.

[177] [1902] 2 KB 732.

[178] [1989] 2 Lloyd's Rep 570, p. 633.

[179] *Morgan v Fry* [1968] 2 QB 710, p. 729; *Cory Lighterage v TGWU* [1973] ICR 339, pp. 356–7.

[180] Ch. 3. [181] (1979) 91 DLR (3d) 43, pp. 60–1.

[182] Above, n. 156, p. 771.

[183] Heydon, J. D., 'Justification in the Intentional Economic Torts', 20 U of Toronto LJ (1970) 139, p. 182.

is inconceivable that it would be on a par with the defence of justification which applies to the tort of inducing breach of contract.[184] At best, therefore, it would be very residual.

Some commentators accept that the defence could be raised where the unlawful means used are 'incidental' or 'trivial'. Thus Weir suggests that 'the defendant may perfectly well be able to justify hurting the plaintiff' by means of a wrongful act against a third party where e.g. that involves what he terms 'the white lie' or 'trivial breach of contract'.[185] Again, Elias and Ewing are concerned that incidental illegalities would lead to arbitrary liability.[186] They can point to *dicta* such as that of Russell LJ in *Morgan v Fry* who noted 'in *Rookes v Barnard* it did not arise for decision whether in this branch of tort any and every breach of contract was a sufficient unlawful means'.[187] However, it is difficult to see that such a defence would work, given there has to be an effective targeting of the claimant for liability to arise and effective pressure or indirect harm.

RATIONALE

There are a range of possible responses to the scope of liability encompassed by the tort of unlawful interference with trade—each response having different implications for tort liability. There is an obvious need to address these responses, in order to deliver the courts from the mess of this area of tort law, a mess resulting from the present *ad hoc* approach.[188] At the heart of this debate is the role of the common law in regulating competition and economic activity. What is revealed in such an exercise is that it is the concept of unlawful means that is the key to order and coherence in this tort, it being generally acknowledged that targeted harm is necessary.[189]

---

[184] Sales and Stilitz, above, n. 10, p. 418.

[185] Above, n. 79, p. 230.

[186] Above, n. 18. For Fleming, above, n. 156 (re intimidation) 'the doctrine would become intolerably oppressive if it were not restricted to situations where the threat to commit the unlawful act, or its actual commission, is not only part of the design . . . but also the very intimidating factor that proved decisive in coercing submission' (p. 768).

[187] [1968] 2 QB 710, p. 737. Indeed, in *Rookes v Barnard* Lord Devlin referred to 'technical illegality' [1964] AC 1129, p. 1218.

[188] Fleming, above, n. 156, p. 768. Elias and Ewing, above, n. 18, p. 336 identify the problem as 'the tendency is for judges to decide whether particular means are unlawful without considering the underlying principles which should determine this question'.

[189] Cf. Sales and Stilitz, above, n. 10, who argue that the 'preoccupation' with the ambit of unlawful means has been unhelpful and that a better way forward lies in focusing upon the element of intention.

Policy 1: Liability arising from intended harm

For Heydon,[190] to create liability parasitic on illegalities 'created for quite other than the regulation of trade competition' is inherently unsatisfactory. He is critical of the arbitrary mechanism of unlawful means (however defined), arguing that the courts should rationalize the position by basing liability on the presence of intentionally caused loss rather than on the theoretically more restrictive notion of causing loss by unlawful means. So for Heydon, if *Allen v Flood* were ignored and a tort of 'intentionally and unjustifiably causing economic loss' established, the law would be provided with a sounder theoretical basis, better able to attack 'an abuse of the right to compete'.[191] In such a tort, a dynamic role would be ascribed to the judges, with the focus on justification. Moreover, given the potential width of such a tort, it is likely that the concept of trade would be given a narrow meaning.

However, acceptance of Lord Herschell's 'chasm'[192] still directs the development of the economic torts. Burns rightly points out that no better opportunity could have presented itself for rejecting the principle of *Allen v Flood* than *Rookes v Barnard*. As he notes: 'the difficulties in deciding that a threatened breach of contract was unlawful were manifest . . . the direction for the House of Lords was open. They, instead of endorsing a shift of emphasis to some concept other than unlawful means, chose to follow the path of *Allen v Flood*'[193] and Sales and Stilitz, though arguing for a general tort of intentional harm, accept that 'the requirement of unlawful means delimits what conduct by [the defendant] will be regarded as illegitimate'.[194] Thus the American *prima facie* tort theory, as applied in *Tuttle v Buck*,[195] has no place in the English economic torts (apart from the anomalous tort of simple conspiracy). As Fleming notes: 'our courts, unlike the American, may have felt uneasy about adopting an amorphous principle of intentional interference with economic relations, which would have entailed controversial judgments about "justification"; instead they preferred the safer criterion of "unlawful means".'[196] There will be no resurrection of the 'right to trade' principle espoused by Holt CJ in *Keeble v Hickeringill* and tort law will be the better for that.

That being so, it is important that the concept of 'unlawful means' should not be so defined as to amount to 'improper means'. Obviously,

---

[190] Above, n. 145, p. 124.
[191] See also the views of Fleming (concerned about 'capricious results', above, n. 156).
[192] [1898] AC 1, p. 121.
[193] Burns, P., 'Tort injury to economic interests: some facets of legal response' 58 Can Bar Rev (1980) 103, p. 154.
[194] Above, n. 10, p. 414.
[195] 119 NW 949 (1909).
[196] Above, n. 156, p. 699.

the vaguer the concept of 'unlawful', the more chance that this process could occur. This was a process Lord Denning appeared to be embracing in *Associated Newspapers Group Ltd v Wade* [197] when he asserted that liability could result from deliberate interference with press freedom. As Elias and Ewing note, this is, in effect, simply dubbing what the judge considers unacceptable to be unlawful, 'which is precisely what *Allen v Flood* forbids the judges to do'.[198]

Policy 2: Unlawful means as means the defendant 'is not at liberty to commit'

Policy 2 involves as wide a protection that can be achieved (given the harm has been inflicted intentionally) while accepting the legitimacy of *Allen v Flood*. The need for 'unlawful means' is seen as a mechanism to allow the courts in. Bagshaw contends that 'unlawful means' can only be accepted as a satisfactory factor if it is identical with or in some way approximates to 'behaviour that is unacceptable between competitors and should give rise to liability in tort'.[199] The attraction of policy 2 would seem to be that it allows the concept of 'unlawful means' to be manipulated to reflect this approximation. Sales and Stilitz also seek a definition that would render the issue of what is unlawful means 'less acute',[200] contending that certain definitions are 'unnaturally restrictive or arbitrary'.[201] They accept that this would entail 'an expansive feature'.[202]

It is clear that policy 2 would create new liability in tort: the policy does not require actionable civil wrongs for liability.[203] Elias and Ewing argue that this does not run counter to *Allen v Flood* and *Lonrho v Shell*. This is because intention alone does not establish liability;[204] nor does simply the commission of an unlawful act.[205] Rather it is the combination of the two that 'creates a sufficient nexus between the plaintiff and defendant for the creation of legal liability'.[206] So the intention to harm would 'tortify' the

---

[197] [1979] ICR 664, p. 691 'interference with the freedom of the press is so contrary to the public interest that it is to be regarded as the employment of unlawful means'.

[198] Above, n. 18, p. 338. They point out 'this would appear to be an idiosyncratic view and was rightly not relied upon by either of the other two judges in that case'. Fleming, above, n. 153, p. 768 comments that the development of the 'genus' tort could lead to *Allen* being 'outflanked' due to the ambiguity and wide scope of 'unlawfulness'.

[199] Above, n. 11, p. 732.   [200] Above, n. 10, p. 414.

[201] Above, n. 10, p. 15. At p. 417 they note 'the difficulty in seeking to circumscribe the ambit of the intentional tort by arbitrary categorization of means as lawful or unlawful'.

[202] Above, n. 10, p. 415. For Weir there is no need to show a duty owed, the requisite proximity being established by the fact of targeting the plaintiff (above, n. 79, p. 232).

[203] For Sales and Stilitz 'this strict test of intention justifies imposing liability . . . where none otherwise would be recognized by law' (above, n. 10, p. 430).

[204] So complying with *Allen v Flood* [1898] AC 1.

[205] So complying with *Lonrho v Shell* [1982] AC 173.

[206] Above, n. 18, p. 338.

use of crimes, quasi-crimes such as contempt[207] and breaches of statute. Given that the tort would demand some element of unlawful means, the concept of trade could be given a wide meaning, with Sales and Stiltiz arguing that any harm could be covered.

It would of course be helpful to have a definition of 'unlawful means' to guide the courts. However, those who support this policy have in fact suggested a number of different definitions. Weir, Sales, and Stiltiz,[208] and Lord Denning (the modern architect of the tort) suggest acts 'which the actor was not at liberty to commit'.[209] Weir also suggests 'impermissible'[210] as a useful definition, while Sales and Stiltiz further suggest 'doing what you have no legal right to do'[211] and 'illegitimate'.[212]

Bagshaw argues that 'clarity is ... not in itself a sufficient reason for accepting a particular factor as a determinant of tort liability',[213] and Weir asserts that some imprecision is still better than the total uncertainty of 'improper' as the test of unlawful means.[214] However, the problem with imprecision—which lies at the heart of policy 2—is that it may allow the court to apply a general test of 'unacceptable' behaviour, which blurs the distinction between policies 1 and 2.[215] The imprecision at the heart of policy 2 becomes apparent when the supporters of this policy cannot agree on its full scope. So though Lord Denning in *Daily Mirror Newspapers Ltd v Gardner* was happy to find that an agreement presumed void under the restrictive trade practices legislation was sufficient unlawful means (presumably on the basis that the defendants were 'not at liberty' to use such an agreement to harm another) and Elias and Ewing appear content with this decision,[216] Sales and Stiltiz reject this view. For them (citing *Mogul* in support) using a void boycott agreement to harm the claimant was not something the defendants were 'forbidden by law from doing'.[217] Again, it is not clear whether policy 2 would include breach of

---

[207] Weir, above, n. 79 and Sales and Stiltiz (above, n. 10) argue that *Chapman v Honig* [1963] 2 QB 502, CA is wrong, the latter suggesting (p. 421) 'it may be that the relevance of the intentional harm tort was passed over ... because no business interest of the plaintiff was interfered with'.

[208] Above, n. 10, p. 414 employing means 'which D is not, according to law, at liberty to employ', citing Lord Reid in *Rookes* [1964] AC 1129, pp. 1168-9.

[209] Above, n. 79, p. 226. As do Elias and Ewing, provided certain provisos are added (above, n. 18, p. 339).

[210] Weir, above, n. 79, p. 226 'inflicting intentional damage by impermissible means'—though he goes on to define these as 'methods reprobated by the law of crime, tort and contract'.

[211] Above, n. 10.   [212] Above, n. 10, p. 419, the use of an 'illegitimate' club.

[213] Above, n. 11, p. 732.   [214] *Economic Torts*, above, n. 24, p. 74.

[215] Though Sales and Stiltiz argue that the focus on unlawful means rather than 'improper means' provides 'a clear guide for the D to know what he may and may not do' (above, n. 10, p. 414, n. 13).   [216] Above, n. 18, p. 338.

[217] Though note that at one point they suggest (above, n. 10, p. 418) 'if it is the D's object to harm P, then it is incumbent upon D to act scrupulously lawfully in seeking to achieve that object'.

confidence[218] or breach of fiduciary duty as sufficient to constitute 'unlawful means', though they appear to be 'illegitimate' acts the defendant would not be 'at liberty to commit'.[219]

Further, though Sales and Stilitz and Weir accept a two-party version of the tort, the former are far more cautious in this area. They reject Weir's view that every intentional breach of contract is also a tort,[220] contending that 'this version of the tort is of more limited application' given 'where only two parties are involved, numerous categories of civil liability have long been established and the balance between the interests of the [plaintiff] and [the defendant] has been carefully worked out'.[221]

Nor can commentators agree whether the defence of justification would apply, should policy 2 be accepted. Weir argues that there is more scope for such a defence where other than torts constitute the unlawful means,[222] while Sales and Stiltiz reject the defence altogether.[223] Furthermore, though Elias and Ewing and Sales and Stiltiz accept that there must be exceptions to liability for the use of 'impermissible' means—and in particular highlight the lack of civil liability for intentional harm caused by perjury—Weir contends that *Hargreaves v Bretherton* was wrongly decided.[224]

Policy 3: Unlawful means as civil wrongs including equitable wrongs

This is linked to policy 4, below. However, though not allowing crimes *per se* or breaches of statutory provisions to constitute unlawful means, it

---

[218] Sales and Stiltiz (above, n. 10, p. 417) contend that breach of confidence will suffice, citing *Jarman & Platt v Bargett* [1977] FSR 260, CA and *Indata Equipment Supplies Ltd v ACL Ltd* [1998] FSR 248, CA. Weir, however, above, n. 79, p. 226 only expressly includes 'crime, tort and contract'.

[219] Nor is it clear whether some of these commentators would be happy to find economic duress as sufficient 'unlawful means'. For economic duress, the coercion or compulsion must have been induced by pressure which the law does not regard as legitimate. Sales and Stiltiz (above, n. 10) are content to envisage liability for two-party threatened breach of contract.

[220] Above, n. 79, p. 229 (though his views appear to be changing: see *Economic Torts*, above, n. 24, p. 67).

[221] Above, n. 10, p. 420. They also instance the lack of tort liability where there is a breach of the duty of utmost good faith between the insurer and the assured: *Banque Keyser Ullmann SA v Skandia (UK) Insurance Co Ltd* [1990] 1 QB 665.

[222] Above, n. 79, p. 230.

[223] Above, n. 10, p. 418.

[224] Above, n. 79, p. 225. Again though Elias and Ewing and Weir would hold that 'technical illegality' was not sufficient for liability, Sales and Stiltiz would reject this view (above, n. 10, p. 418) 'even when trivial'. Elias, P., and Tettenborn, A., 'Crime, Tort and Compensation in Private and Public Law' [1981] CLJ 230, p. 232, suggest (re statutory crimes) 'a more creative solution might be to decide that a criminal provision should grant liability in tort for causing loss by unlawful means unless there are clear reasons of policy or in its interpretation why it should not'.

would allow all civil wrongs, not just torts and breaches of contract, to constitute unlawful means in the tort of unlawful interference. In effect it would 'tortify' breaches of equitable obligation or trust where intentional harm is involved. There are *dicta* to support such an approach;[225] other *dicta* indicate that it would be preferable that an overall reconsideration of the law of obligations be undertaken, rather than an indirect, back-door attack on the division of civil wrongs.[226]

Policy 4: Unlawful means as torts and breaches of contract

For policy 4, unlawful means would have to amount to wrongs, capable of being civilly actionable with a right to damages.[227] This would include all torts, breaches of contract (though not in the two-party version),[228] and most common law crimes since 'they usually also constitute torts'.[229] But a breach of statutory duty would only involve the necessary unlawful means where a statutory tort arose.[230] Breaches of equitable obligation and fiduciary duty would not be unlawful means (though breach of confidence may one day amount to a tort). Such a policy is probably closest to the philosophy of *Allen v Flood*, Lord Watson remarking in that case that illegal means are 'means which in themselves are in the nature of civil wrongs'.[231] Since the claimant is taking the benefit of the unlawfulness of the act, Eekelaar suggests 'it would seem to follow that [the unlawful act] must constitute the fundamental ingredients of some tort or . . . breach of contract'. He concludes that if this were not the case civil liability could be imposed on the defendant outside the normal scope of tortious liability 'simply because he reached his victim through an agent rather than directly'.[232]

Obviously, this policy ascribes a limited role to the tort—but a role that may still be important. In the three-party scenario, the rationale of the tort would appear to be that where tort law or contract law is prepared to impose liability, that can be extended to the intended victim of such unlawfulness. If so, then this policy choice limits the scope of the tort by reference to unlawful means, capable of being actionable wrongs at common law. The tort involves the 'the magic of transfer of liability', no more, no less.[233]

---

[225] See *Prudential Assurance v Lorenz* (1971) KIR 78.
[226] See discussion above.   [227] Rogers, above, n. 26 , p. 652.
[228] See more detailed discussion in Ch. 4.   [229] Elias and Ewing, above, n. 18, p. 336.
[230] Fredman, S. is critical of the fact that this policy appears to treat breach of contract 'more seriously' than breach of a penal statute ('The Right to Strike: Policy and Principle' 103 LQR (1987) 176, p. 180: 'there is little logic in such a hierarchy of values').
[231] [1898] AC 1, pp. 97–8.   [232] Above, n. 100, p. 226.
[233] Eekelaar, above, n. 100, p. 226 'the unlawfulness of his acts towards the intermediary are transferred to the benefit of the plaintiff'.

This is a policy that would lead to greater certainty[234] and ensure that the inner logic of other areas of tort law would not be 'casually cast to one side'.[235] Moreover, private wrongs would not be created out of public wrongs[236] and the courts would have to consider the division of the law of obligations as a whole, rather than tampering with it in an indirect way (by holding breach of equitable obligation or fiduciary duty to be unlawful means). The tort would simply transfer private liability, rather than readjust the scope of tort law.

The adoption of such a policy would indicate that there is no reason to have a two-party version of the tort.[237] If the unlawful means have to be actionable anyway the tort adds nothing in the two-party setting.[238] A claimant unable to support an allegation based on another tort, would not be able to use the tort of unlawful interference with trade to attack the defendant.[239] Moreover, policy 4 means that the tort of intimidation, though clearly framed on unlawful interference, adds an important new dimension to economic tort liability, to include threatened unlawful acts.[240] More generally, the defence of justification would appear to be unnecessary and trade could be widely defined, with an obvious argument in favour of all harm being covered.

Policy 4 looks to Parliament for any rigorous control of competitive or harmful economic practices, denying a dynamic role to the economic torts.

CONCLUSION

Until the issue of unlawful means is resolved the tort of unlawful interference will remain unclear and its application extended on an *ad hoc* basis by the interlocutory process. The sounder its conceptual basis, the nearer we are to establishing cosmos from chaos.[241]

---

[234] And has a similar frame to the imposition of secondary liability.

[235] Buckley, R. A., 'Liability in Tort for Breach of Statutory Duty' 100 LQR (1984) 204 is critical of any move to rationalize the economic torts by illegalities drawn from other branches of the law.

[236] Bagshaw, above, n. 11, p. 730 notes that *DoT v Williams* was a 'controversial' decision.

[237] Indeed, Rogers, above, n. 26, p. 651 suggests that in the two-party setting 'it would be a travesty of history' to unify such 'disparate' wrongs as e.g. false imprisonment (causing business problems) and breach of contract (as unlawful interference with trade) under one heading of tort.

[238] And as has already been argued intentional breach of contract is not a tort in its own right.

[239] The defamation case *Marrinan v Vibart* [1963] 1 QB 234 supports this view.

[240] It would appear to follow that if policy 4 is accepted for the tort of unlawful interference, then the unlawful acts that must be threatened for the tort of intimidation must also involve actionable civil wrongs.

[241] See Weir, above, n. 79.

As part of this clarification process, the tort needs to be distinguished from an obscure principle of equity. This doctrine would appear to accept that trading activities and the commercial exploitation of the contracts that lie behind such activities constitute 'property' that will be protected against criminal activity by injunction, even where no separate cause of action has been established. In *Springhead Spinning Co v Riley*[242] the defendants (trade union officials) had by placards and advertisements notified workmen not to contract with the plaintiff. The plaintiff relied on 'an old-established jurisdiction of the Court of Equity, although applied to a new subject', to prevent a reduction in their profits, as a result of the defendants' action. Though there is little discussion of legal principle, Malins V-C commented on the 'misguided' acts of the defendants which tended to 'the destruction of that property which is the source of their own support and comfort in life'. No tort liability was established, but the injunction was granted in order to protect the plaintiff's property, his business interests.[243] In *Ex parte Island Records*[244] Waller LJ granted the injunction on the grounds of the equity principle alone. He was willing to define property for this principle as including the economic advantages of the plaintiff's exclusive recording contracts.

However, the scope and legitimacy of the principle is still unclear. Though in *Gouriet v UPOW*,[245] Viscount Dilhorne and Lord Edmund-Davies cited the *Springhead Spinning* case with approval, they did so without any real discussion.[246] Vinelott J in *RCA v Pollard* (at High Court level) noted that statements in cases before the Judicature Acts concerning the Court of Chancery's jurisdiction to grant injunctions to restrain interference with rights of property 'must be read with some caution',[247] while Nicholls LJ was opposed to such a doctrine in *CBS v Amstrad*.[248] Again,

---

[242] (1868) LR 6 Eq 551.

[243] In *Emperor of Austria v Day and Kossuth* (1861) 3 De GF&J 217 the term 'property' appears to cover the interest Hungarian citizens had in the stability of their currency, when an injunction was granted to protect their 'property', threatened by the defendant's alternative Hungarian banknotes. This principle, however, was controversial even in this era. Lord Cairns in *Prudential Assurance Co v Knott* (1875) 10 Ch App 142 dissented from it, asserting that an injunction would only lie where enforcing a legal right was involved. However, support for the principle can be found in the speech of Lindley LJ in *J. Lyons & Sons v Wilkins* [1896] 1 Ch 811, p. 826 (a picketing case, like *Springhead Spinning* itself).

[244] [1978] 1 Ch 122, p. 144. In *RCA v Pollard* [1983] Ch 135, CA, Oliver LJ referred to the principle but found it unnecessary to decide whether it still existed. It is also worth remembering that where persons suffer special damage as a result of a breach of a penal statute, the Attorney-General may seek an injunction if the public interest is affected (either of his own motion or at the instance of a member of the public).

[245] [1978] AC 435.

[246] Ibid. 492 and 506 respectively.

[247] [1982] 1 WLR 979.

[248] [1988] Ch 61, p. 69. The decision was affirmed by the House of Lords: [1988] AC 1013. However, cf. Lawton LJ in *RCA v Pollard* [1983] Ch 135, p. 149 who did not seek to 'question in any way the underlying principles enunciated in those cases'.

the authority of the *Springhead Spinning* principle was asserted by Neill LJ in *Associated British Ports v TGWU*[249] to be 'at the very least reduced'. Markesinis and Deakin point out that if such a doctrine still exists 'the odd situation arises of an injunction being made available to an individual damaged by an unlawful act, but damages nevertheless being unavailable in respect of the same wrong'.[250] Wedderburn goes further and suggests that this is 'a doctrine which probably cannot now be supported'.[251]

---

[249] [1989] ICR 573, p. 581. Butler-Sloss LJ thought it unlikely to be a doctrine separate from unlawful interference with trade 'but it may retain a flicker of life for nursing on some future occasion and it is not necessary to consider it further'.

[250] Markesinis, B., and Deakin, S., *Tort Law*, 4th edn. (Oxford: Clarendon Press, 1999). Was this, however, behind the decision in *DoT v Williams* ?

[251] Above, n. 95, para 24–77.

6

Deceit

Originally, most actions for deceit involved misconduct associated with legal procedures. The tort developed from these thirteenth-century roots 'as part of the legal control of trickery', so that cases couched in deceit existed as early as the fourteenth century.[1] Indeed, the action for deceit 'played a modest part in developing the incipient law of contract'[2] being used by the courts to extend their jurisdiction to actions for breach of warranty, accessory to contracts for the sale of goods.[3] The only feature in common between the original actions for deceit and the warranty actions was the fraud involved. However, alongside the development of the action for deceit (an action on the case), the courts were developing the action for assumpsit so that by the late eighteenth century the separation of tort and contract had emerged. Thus assumpsit was used for false warranty[4] and the action for deceit was ready to be clearly separated from contract law in the case of *Pasley v Freeman*:[5] the basis of the modern law of deceit.

In *Pasley v Freeman* the defendant falsely represented that a third party to whom the plaintiff was proposing to sell goods, was creditworthy. When the plaintiff suffered loss through relying on the representation it was held that the defendant was liable in deceit.[6] The fact that there was

---

[1] Hepple, B., and Matthews, P., *Tort: Cases and Materials*, 4th edn. (London: Butterworths, 1991), p. 149. See Baker, J. H., and Milsom, S. F. C., *Sources of English Legal History* (London : Butterworths, 1986), ch. 20. Bragg, R., *Trade Descriptions* (London: Clarendon Press, 1991) notes that the majority of these early cases relates to horses and comments (p. 1) 'it is often said that yesterday's horse dealer and today's car dealer have much in common'.

[2] Fleming, J., *The Law of Torts*, 9th edn. (Sydney: LBC, 1998), p. 694.

[3] Neither debt nor detinue being extensive enough. Thus actions for breach of warranty (as to the quality and fitness of goods sold) made by the seller at the time of sale were treated as deceit. See Holdsworth, W. S., *A History of English Law* (London: Methuen & Co. Ltd, 1923), vol. 3, pp. 428–34.

[4] *Williamson v Allison* (1802) 2 East 446, p. 451: 'because it was found more convenient to declare in assumpsit for the sake of adding the money counts.' The idea of being misled was replaced by the concern with the agreement or undertaking.

[5] (1789) 3 Term Rep 51. Allen, D., *Misrepresentation* (London: Sweet & Maxwell, 1988), p. 39 'the extension of liability for deceit to a non-contractual situation, in which the defendant did not benefit from the fraud, was novel, and, in founding liability upon the knowledge of falsity, the case laid the basis for the modern law of deceit'.

[6] Atiyah, P., *The Rise and Fall of Freedom of Contract* (Oxford: Clarendon Press, 1979) notes, p. 469 that in the more robust judicial climate of the mid-nineteenth century such a decision

no contract between the parties was irrelevant. What was emphasized was the dishonesty element: the essence of the action was the deception of the plaintiff (even though the defendant himself did not gain from that deception). 'This innovation put renewed emphasis on the scienter in fraud, since actual knowledge of the falsity seemed the only justifiable basis of liability if the misrepresentation was to be actionable even in the absence of personal gain.'[7] The tort of deceit was subsequently summed up by Parke B[8] as requiring 'a falsehood told with an intention that it should be acted upon by the party injured' which causes damage to him.

However, at this stage equity was prepared to help in the case of careless misrepresentations by providing for rescission outside the common law limits of fraud or total failure of consideration. And by the middle of the nineteenth century, the chancery courts, by focusing on the need to honour trust, were 'approaching a compensatory remedy for failing to make representations good'.[9] The major issue by the end of the nineteenth century in this area therefore was whether damages were available beyond actions for fraud.

The answer to this was provided by the 'uncompromising decision'[10] of the House of Lords in *Derry v Peek*, embodying into English law 'the strongest form of nineteenth-century laissez-faire individualism'.[11] The plaintiff had invested in the defendant tramway company on the strength of its prospectus which indicated that the trams would run on steam or mechanical power (rather than being horse-drawn). Board of Trade consent was necessary for this and though the defendants had believed that such consent would be forthcoming, in fact it was ultimately denied.[12] The result was that the company was wound up and the plaintiff's investment was lost. The plaintiff sued for deceit but, overruling the Court of Appeal,[13] the House of Lords held that negligence was

---

might have gone the other way, self-reliance being stressed (and in fact there was a dissenting judgment on this point). However, in the era of *Pasley v Freeman* false character references appear to have been perceived as a particular problem.

[7] Stoljar, S. J., *Mistake and Misrepresentation* (London: Sweet & Maxwell, 1968), p. 133. Note Ashurst J (1789) 3 Term Rep 51, p. 62: 'the malice is more diabolical if he had not the temptation of gain.'

[8] *Langridge v Levy* (1837) 2 M&W 519.

[9] Cornish, W. R., and Clark, G. de N., *Law and Society in England 1750–1950* (London: Sweet & Maxwell, 1989), p. 217. They note that it is striking that this development in equity occurred just as the common law idea of consideration and privity were in 'converse movement'. [10] Ibid. 221.

[11] Stevens, R., 'Hedley Byrne v Heller: Judicial Creativity and Doctrinal Possibilities' 27 MLR (1964)121, p. 121.

[12] The House of Lords' decision was based on the trial judge's finding that the defendants believed the statements to be true.

[13] Cotton LJ had stated that to make a statement 'without any reasonable ground for believing it to be true' would constitute deceit: cited by Lord Herschell (1889) 14 App Cas 337, p. 360.

not sufficient for such liability. The chancery view that negligent misstatement could give rise to compensation was rejected by Lord Bramwell as something that would cause 'mercantile men . . . to cry out'.[14] Damages would result only from fraud or contract breach.[15]

As Fleming comments[16] 'no one could quarrel with this refusal to equate credulity with dishonesty'. The real problem with the decision was that it indicated that no tort other than deceit could result from misstatements.[17] This block on the development of the law on liability for statements was only finally removed in 1963 by the House of Lords in *Hedley Byrne & Co v Heller & Partners Ltd*[18] which established common law liability for negligent misrepresentation causing financial loss beyond deceit, contract, and equitable relationships.

IMPORTANCE AND THE POSSIBILITY OF THREE-PARTY DECEIT

The fact that the tort is likely to arise from bargaining transactions 'has mentally coloured the elements of the action [for deceit] which largely reflect the ethical and moral standards of the market place'.[19] The presence of deceit may affect a contractual claim[20] by denying equitable relief[21] or by providing a defence to an action for breach of contract[22] or

---

[14] (1889) 14 App Cas 337, p. 349, echoing the trial judge, Stirling J, Cornish and Clark, above, n. 9, comment that 'one resonance of *Derry v Peek* sounded against any broad scope of equitable fraud'.

[15] Though soon afterwards, in a House of Lords dominated by chancery judges, an exception was created for liability in negligence where there was a special fiduciary or quasi-fiduciary relationship between the parties. Thus the process that would lead to *Hedley Byrne* had begun in *Nocton v Ashburton (Lord)* in [1914] 2 AC 932.   [16] Above, n. 2, p. 704.

[17] Lord Bramwell (1889) 14 App Cas 337, p. 347 'to found an action for damages there must be a contract and a breach or fraud'.

[18] [1964] AC 465.   [19] Fleming, above, n. 2, p. 695.

[20] There is a useful discussion of the effect of deceit on a contract by Cane, P., *Tort Law and Economic Interests*, 2nd edn. (Oxford: Clarendon Press, 1996), pp. 167–72.

[21] *Re Banister* (1879) 12 Ch D 131, CA: 'The considerations which induce a court to rescind any contract and the considerations which induce a court of equity to decline to enforce specific enforcement are by no means the same' (Jessel MR, p. 142). Turner, A., *Spencer, Bower and Turner: the Law of Actionable Misrepresentation*, 3rd edn. (London: Butterworths, 1974): 'misrepresentation operates as . . . an invalidating cause, no less than a cause of action' p. 330.

[22] Of course, fraud, as an example of illegality, may also provide a defence in a tort action. In applying this defence the rather vague test of 'the public conscience' appeared to be favoured in cases such as *Saunders v Edwards* [1987] 1 WLR 1116. This was rejected for contract and property claims by the House of Lords in *Tinsley v Milligan* [1994] AC 340, though Lord Goff (dissenting, but not on this point) found the actual decision in *Saunders v Edwards* 'unassailable'. It would appear that the defendant has to establish that the claimant's conduct is reprehensible enough and forms so much part of the claim against the defendant as to justify refusing the claimant any remedy (see *Standard Chartered Bank v Pakistan National Shipping Corp* [2000] 1 Lloyd's Rep 218, CA).

by allowing the claimant to rescind the contract.[23] However as a tort, it also provides a right to damages—an important factor in the era prior to *Hedley Byrne v Heller*[24] and the Misrepresentation Act 1967 when, in the absence of deceit, the plaintiff would have to prove breach of warranty to obtain damages under the contract itself.[25]

Deceit has a limited role as a remedy against commercial misrepresentation. A difficult tort to succeed in given 'charges of fraud should not be lightly made or considered',[26] it does not provide protection against general allegations of fraud.[27] Moreover, it is the person intentionally deceived by the defendant who alone can sue in the classic two-party form of the tort. Should the defendant lie about his own goods to gain a competitive advantage no liability in the two-party version of the tort will arise.[28] This explains the tort's limited importance in the area of trade competition. Heydon:[29] 'it is of little use to a competitor of the liar; he has not acted to his detriment on a false statement, but rather has been injured because others acted upon it.' The tort is largely overshadowed in importance by liability for negligent misstatement and by state regulation of trade misdescriptions.

However, despite this classic view it is clear that the tort may have a role to play in a three-party scenario.

First, where bribery is the issue[30] the tort, or rather a version of it, may protect the claimant. To bribe an agent[31] is a fraud on the principal, the briber and agent being joint tortfeasors.[32] In *Salford v Lever*,[33] the cause of action against the briber was stated by Lord Esher MR and Lopes LJ to be fraud. Hence 'since the agent was necessarily party to the bribery, it follows that the tort was a joint tort of briber and agent'. The claimant can

---

[23] It should be noted that rescission in contract operates from the date of the rescission, whereas in tort the rescission is *ab initio*. Under s. 2(2) Misrepresentation Act 1967 the court has a discretion to award damages in lieu of rescission.

[24] [1964] AC 465.

[25] Unlike damages for contract breach, compensating for failure to perform, deceit compensates for the consequences of the misrepresentation.

[26] *Mason v Clarke* [1955] AC 778, p. 794.

[27] There is no general liability for 'fraud' i.e. dishonesty see *Amalgamated Metal Trading v DTI, The Times*, 21 March 1989.

[28] Though the tort of passing off might provide some help.

[29] Heydon, J. D., *Economic Torts*, 2nd edn. (London: Sweet & Maxwell, 1978), p. 87.

[30] Tettenborn, A., 'Bribery, Corruption and Restitution—the Strange Case of Mr Mahesan' 95 LQR (1979) 68; Needham, C., 'Recovering the Profits of Bribery' 95 LQR (1979) 536; *Armstrong v Strain* [1951] 1 TLR 856; *Grant v Gold* [1900] 1QB 233; *Hovenden v Millhof* (1900) 83 LT 41.

[31] Agent or other fiduciary is a concept which appears to have a wide definition in this area: see *Reading v AG* [1951] AC 507, HL.

[32] As with deceit generally, there is no defence of contributory negligence in an action based on bribery: *Corporacion National del Cobre de Chile v Sogemin Metals Ltd* [1997] 2 All ER 917.

[33] [1891] 1 QB 168.

recover either the bribe[34] (as money had and received by the agent to the use of his principal)[35] or tort damages based on the loss due to the bribed transaction. He cannot recover both.[36] Where the tort is relied upon, the claimant must prove actual loss. The application of the tort in this context is, of course, hard to reconcile with the basic ingredients of the tort. Evans J in *Arab Monetary Fund v Hashim* termed it a hybrid form of legal wrong which does not accord easily with the tort of deceit[37] and there is a possibility that what we have here is in fact a *sui generis* tort of bribery.[38]

More importantly, for the purposes of economic tort analysis, there may be a three-party version of the tort of deceit. Classic deceit involves lies intended to be relied upon by the claimant. No intention to harm as such is required. However, in *National Phonograph Co Ltd v Edison-Bell Consolidated Phonograph Co Ltd*[39] lies told to third parties in order to gain an economic advantage at the expense of the plaintiff[40] were held by the

[34] Indeed, in *AG for HK v Reid* [1994] 1 AC 324, the Privy Council held that the agent is accountable for the bribe or property representing the bribe, holding the bribe in trust for the person to whom the duty was owed. A proprietary interest, therefore, exists in the bribe (*Lister v Stubbs* (1890) 45 Ch.D 1 was overruled as not being consistent with the principle that a fiduciary must not be allowed to benefit from his own breach of duty).

[35] On this basis there is no need for loss to have been incurred by the principal: *Boston Deep Sea Fishing v Ansell* [1888] 39 Ch Div 339 CA, though Evans J in *AMF v Hashim* [1993] 1 Lloyd's Rep 543 noted that the judgment in *Hovenden v Millhof* (1900) 83 LT 41 demonstrated that the basis of the restitutionary claim is the bribe-giver's receipt of money from the principal equivalent to the amount of the bribe. In fact equity had already developed a principle that an agent who received any secret advantage for himself from the other party to the transaction when he was representing his principal had to account for that profit to the principal: *Fawcett v Whitehouse* (1829) 1 R&M 132 Any contract obtained by such bribes could of course be rescinded. The briber of the agent can be required to account for profits: *Fyffes Group Ltd v Templeman, The Times*, 14 June 2000, Toulson J.

[36] This was established by the Privy Council in *Mahesan s/o Thambiah v Malaysia Government Officers' Co-operative Housing Society Ltd* [1979] AC 374. There land was bought on behalf of the principal by the agent at a vastly inflated price due to a bribe from vendor to the agent. The bribe is recoverable as money had and received. By deciding that these are alternative not cumulative remedies, the Privy Council applied the House of Lords's decision in *United Australia Ltd v Barclays Bank Ltd* [1941] AC 1 and rejected *dicta* to opposite effect in *Salford Corp v Lever* [1891] 1 QB 168. In *Clef Aquitaine SARL v Laporte Materials (Barrow) Ltd* [2000] 3 All ER 493, CA, the claimant recovered damages on the basis that he would have entered into a more profitable contract but for the bribery

[37] [1993] 1 Lloyd's Rep 543, p. 565. Tettenborn, above, n. 30, p. 69 'rather delphically, this cause of action is sometimes termed "fraud" '.

[38] *AMF v Hashim* [1993] 1 Lloyd's Rep 543, p. 564. Lord Diplock in *Mahesan s/o Thambiah v Malaysia Government Officers' Co-operative Housing Society Ltd* [1979] AC 374, p. 381 found the liability of the briber to the principal to be a 'rational development' from the principal's right in equity to rescind the contract with the briber. As Evans J pointed out in *AMF v Hashim* the judgment is mainly concerned to trace the development of the principal's right to recover the bribe from the bribe-giver as well as from the agent, rather than damages for deceit.

[39] [1908] 1 Ch 335.

[40] The plaintiffs, fearful of competition from the defendants, had agreements with their wholesale and retail dealers, whereby these dealers would not sell to the defendants. Through fraud, the defendants obtained the plaintiffs' goods, contrary to these agreements.

Court of Appeal to render the defendant liable in tort. This was so though no action in deceit could have been brought by the third parties, who were not themselves harmed. Here, the reliance and harm were separated—the third parties relied on the deceit and the plaintiff was harmed. But importantly there is an added ingredient for liability. The defendant intended to cause economic harm to the plaintiff. The 'nexus' between the lies and the plaintiff was this intended harm. Both Buckley LJ and Kennedy LJ relied on the speech of Lord Watson in *Allen v Flood* [41] where he notes that the defendant may be liable for the actions of another should he have 'procured his object' by unlawful means. For Buckley LJ, the deceit which the defendants used brought them 'exactly within these words'. [42] That liability in *National Phonograph* required intentional harm was stressed subsequently by Oliver LJ in *RCA v Pollard* [43] and Dillon LJ in *Lonrho v Fayed*. [44] What emerges from this—and is seen more clearly in the discussion of the Court of Appeal in *Lonrho v Fayed* [45]—is that deceit can give rise to liability in a three-party setting where it constitutes the unlawful means for the wider tort of unlawful interference with trade. [46] This is discussed further in Chapter 5.

INGREDIENTS OF CLASSIC DECEIT

There are five essential ingredients in the classic two-party version of the tort of deceit: a false representation made by the defendant; knowledge of its falsity by the defendant; an intention by the defendant that the claimant should act in reliance on that representation; action by the claimant in such reliance; and damage thereby caused to the claimant. Maugham J in *Bradford Building Society v Borders* [47] did not in fact list all five, omitting damage. However, this fifth ingredient was stated to be 'the gist of the action' by Lord Blackburn in *Smith v Chadwick*. [48] Where the representation is as to a third-party's credit, however, there is the added requirement contained in s.6 of the Statute of Frauds Amendment Act

---

[41] [1898] AC 1, p. 96. [42] [1908] 1 Ch 335, p. 361.

[43] [1983] Ch 135, p. 151: 'the case was . . . one of fraudulent conduct aimed specifically at the plaintiffs and those with whom they had contracts.'

[44] [1990] 2 QB 479, p.489: '[in *National Phonograph*] the fraud was clearly directed against the plaintiff.'

[45] [1990] 2 QB 479 (the case went on appeal to the House of Lords but on the issue of conspiracy only: [1992] 1 AC 448).

[46] *Lonrho v Fayed* [1990] 2 QB 479 was an appeal on a striking out application. It was accepted that telling lies about yourself, in order to deny the plaintiff a commercial advantage could constitute the tort of unlawful interference with trade, though the majority accepted the plaintiff's concession that the defendant must be shown to have 'aimed' at the plaintiff. See Chs 5 and 10.

[47] [1941] 2 All ER 205, p. 211. [48] (1884) 9 App Cas 187, p. 190.

1828 that the representation should be in writing. This provision was introduced to reinforce the need for contract guarantees to be in writing (as required by the Statute of Frauds) by preventing the use of the tort of deceit to circumvent this requirement.[49]

These ingredients of the tort (and the fact that to prove fraud requires a high degree of probability)[50] keep its scope narrow. They also limit the classic version of the tort to a two-party situation (though bribery liability is somewhat different). It is necessary to explore these ingredients more fully.

False representation

The misrepresentation must be one of a past or existing fact: though that includes a statement of opinion[51] or intention[52] (or law)[53] not honestly believed in. It may be expressed or implied. Conduct may be sufficient: Campbell LC in *Walters v Morgan*[54] noted that 'a nod or a wink or a shake of the head or a smile from the purchaser intended to induce the vendor to believe in the existence of a non-existent fact, which might influence the price of the subject to be sold' would be sufficient. A statement may be implicit in conduct which creates a misleading impression[55] or otherwise amounts to an assertion or is a deliberate concealment of a defect. In *Gordon v Selico*[56] the defendant was liable for fraudulently concealing the presence of dry rot, prior to letting the property to the plaintiff. Goulding J found the concealment amounted to a false representation that the flat

---

[49] The section does not apply to contract claims re negligent advice (*Banbury v Bank of Montreal* [1918] AC 626) nor to the tort of negligence (*W. B. Anderson & Sons Ltd v Rhodes (Liverpool) Ltd* [1967] 2 All ER 850. However, it does apply to s.2(1) Misrepresentation Act 1967 (*UBAF Ltd v European American Banking Corp* [1984] QB 713—which held that the signature of the company's authorized agent is the signature of the company for the Act).

[50] *Hornal v Neuberger Products Ltd* [1957] 1QB 247. 'Charges of fraud should not be lightly made or considered': *Mason v Clarke* [1955] AC 778, p. 794.

[51] At least where the parties are not both equally acquainted with the facts.

[52] *Edgington v Fitzmaurice* (1885) 29 Ch D 459, p. 483 : 'it is true that it is very difficult to prove what the state of a man's mind at a particular time is, but if it can be ascertained it is as much a fact as anything else', Bowen LJ.

[53] There is no direct authority on this, though the commentators are unanimous. As Fleming, above, n. 2, comments: 'the argument that all men know the law and therefore cannot be misled about it is a threadbare fiction which was never intended to shield swindlers' (p. 698).

[54] (1861) 3 D F&J 718.

[55] The classic example always given is *R v Barnard* (1837) 7C.& P. 784: purchaser in university town wore college cap and gown to falsely give the impression that he was a member of a college and therefore creditworthy. A more modern instance (in a claim brought under section 2(1) of the Misrepresentation Act 1967) is *Spice Girls Ltd v Aprilla World Service BV*, *The Times*, 5 April 2000, where by participating in the filming of advertisements for the claimant, the defendant pop group represented that they would not break up during the term of the advertising contract.

[56] (1984) 275 EG 899.

did not suffer from dry rot and the defendants did not challenge this finding in the Court of Appeal.[57]

Indeed, deliberate obscurity may amount to a misrepresentation. In
Whife v Cullen & Partners[58] the plaintiffs were induced to accept a form of
business lease that was obscurely worded but which was in fact so grossly
unfavourable as to render the rent ultimately payable uneconomic, with
surrender an inevitability. The Court of Appeal refused to strike out the
plaintiffs' claim in deceit (or rather, unlawful conspiracy, based on deceit),
as the lease was 'a wolf in sheep's clothing', represented to be a genuine
lease for a period of time when in fact it was nothing of the sort. Of course
partial disclosure could also amount to deceit if 'the witholding of that
which is not stated makes that which is stated absolutely false'.[59] Failing
to disclose a material change or subsequently discovered inaccuracies
amounts to deceit, given that the tort is only complete when the representation is acted upon.[60]

However, the general rule is that non-disclosure of the truth does not
amount to the tort of deceit. 'Mere silence, however morally wrong, does
not support an action of deceit.'[61] Though there are limited circumstances
that give rise to a duty to disclose (mainly contracts *uberrimae fidei* or fiduciary relationships[62] or dealings with a dangerous chattel)[63] there is no
equivalent of the provision in the Restatement (Second) of Torts[64] that a
duty can arise in a business transaction where the facts are basic to the
transaction and the representee would reasonably expect a disclosure of
those facts. Fleming[65] notes that the common law position: 'reflects generally accepted ethics for parties dealing at arm's length . . . the individual-
istic attitude of the common law to bargaining transactions has, in
general, encouraged distrust of others in the marketplace and the
discounting of sales talk as unworthy of justifiable reliance.'[66] It is thus
the fact of inaccurate information that activates the tort, not the lack of
sufficient information.

---

[57] See Gleeson, L., and McKendrick, E., 'The Rotting Away of Caveat Emptor' 1987 Conv
121.
[58] *The Times*, 15 November 1993, CA.
[59] Lord Cairns *Peek v Gurney* (1873) LR 6 HL 377, p. 403.
[60] *Northern Bank Finance v Charlton* [1979] IR 149, p. 166.
[61] Viscount Maugham, *Bradford Building Society v Borders* [1941] 2 All ER 204, p. 211.
[62] e.g. principal/agent; trustee/beneficiary.
[63] In *Hamble Fisheries Ltd v L. Gardner & Sons Ltd* (the Rebecca Elaine) [1999] 2 Lloyd's Rep
1, p. 9 Nourse LJ stated 'knowledge of a dangerous defect in a product may provide a foundation for a case of fraud against a person who makes or circulates a dangerous product
without warning of the danger of physical damage known to him'. He further noted 'there
is a great gulf in law . . . between the duty not to be dishonest which is almost universal and
the more circumscribed duty not to be careless'.
[64] Restatement (Second) of Torts s. 551(2)(e).   [65] Above, n. 2, p. 696.
[66] Above, n. 2, p. 690, 'the harshness of this view is somewhat mitigated by the dominant
role that implied warranties have come to play in ensuring consumer protection'.

In line with the other economic torts involving misrepresentations, 'mere puffs' or exaggerated self-commendation are not actionable, presumably on the basis that they are not material.[67] In addition, in deceit there is a rule based on *Vernon v Keys*[68] that a misstatement by a vendor of the lowest price he is prepared to accept or by a purchaser of the highest price he is prepared to pay, will not amount to deceit. However, it would appear that this exception is limited to these propositions only.[69]

Knowledge of falsity

The state of a defendant's mind, necessary for an action in deceit was authoritatively discussed by the House of Lords in *Derry v Peek*.[70] The false representation has to be made: 'knowingly . . . without belief in its truth . . . or recklessly, careless[71] whether it be true or false.'[72] At the very least there must be an indifference to the truth. Carelessness is not sufficient for this tort: it took some seventy years to establish negligent liability for careless misstatements. Lord Herschell went on to make clear that an honest belief in the truth of the statement will defeat any action in deceit. As the Privy Council noted in *Akerheim v De Mare*:[73] 'the question is not whether the defendant in any given case honestly believed the representation to be true in the sense assigned to it by the court on an objective consideration of its truth or falsity, but whether he honestly believed the representation to be true in the sense in which he understood it albeit erroneously when it was made.' Even if the defendant had previously had knowledge of facts contrary to his current representation, if at the time of making that representation he has honestly forgotten that prior knowledge, he is not liable.

Conversely, where the claimant has yet to act upon the representation, the defendant will be liable should it become untrue *ex post facto* or should he learn of its falsity subsequently—or indeed should he change his mind as to his intention. Representations may, of course, have a continuing effect, as in *Slough Estates plc v Welwyn Hatfield DC*[74] where the defendant council secretly changed its mind about restricting a rival trading development, thereby inducing the plaintiffs to continue with their trading complex. In the case of an ambiguous statement the court will assess what

---

[67] For criticism of this view see Wolff, J., 'Unlawful Competition by Truthful Disparagement' 47 Yale LJ (1937–8) 1304.

[68] (1810) 12 East 632.

[69] *Haygarth v Wearing* (1871) LR 12 Eq 320.

[70] (1889) 14 App Cas 337.

[71] In the sense of not caring.

[72] Lord Herschell (1889) 14 App Cas 337, p. 376.

[73] [1959] AC 789, p. 804, PC.

[74] [1996] 2 PLR 50.

the defendant intended the statement to convey: he will be liable if he intended to convey the fraudulent impression or was willing that the recipient should get that impression.[75]

Intention that the claimant should act in reliance

Foreseeable reliance is not sufficient for this tort: there must be an intention that the claimant should rely on the representation.[76] Lord Maugham underlined this in *Bradford Third Equitable Benefit BS v Borders*,[77] noting that the plaintiff must prove that the defendant made the statement 'with the intention that it should be acted upon by the plaintiff or by a class of persons which will include the plaintiff'.[78] The defendant need not have singled out the claimant in particular: 'it is not necessary that the representation should be made to the plaintiff directly; it is sufficient if the representation is made to a third person to be communicated to the plaintiff'.[79] Indeed, it is sufficient if the misrepresentation is communicated to a class of persons of whom the claimant is one, or even is made to the public generally, with a view to its being acted on, and the claimant as one of the public acts on it and suffers damage as a result.[80] A public advertisement for the lease of a farm which involved fraudulent statements and caused loss to the plaintiff who took a lease rendered the defendant liable to the plaintiff[81]—the plaintiff on the facts being one of a class of persons against whom the advert was directed. Indeed, the required intention can be present where there has been a 'transfer' of the fraudulent representation. In *Pilmore v Hood*[82] the defendant was liable when he made a false statement concerning his business to a third party and failed to correct it though he knew the third party had communicated the representation to the plaintiff, to whom the defendant sold the business.

In essence, of course, the issue is the defendant's intention:[83] to whom

---

[75] Cross LJ in *Gross v Lewis Hillman Ltd* [1970] Ch 445, p. 459. See also *Henry Ansbacher & Coln v Diamond* [1996] 2 All ER 774.

[76] This was lacking in *Tackey v McBain* [1912] AC 186.

[77] [1941] 2 All ER 205, p. 211.

[78] Lord Denning MR thought it likely that a representation expressed to be 'without responsibility' would not render the defendant liable, see *Diamond v Bank of London & Montreal Ltd* [1979] QB 333 at 347 CA; however, note *Commonwealth Commercial Banking v Brown* 126 CLR (1972) 337.

[79] It does not have to be a specifically identified person: *Commonwealth Commercial Banking v Brown* 126 CLR (1972) 337.

[80] Quain J in *Swift v Winterbottom* (1873) LR 8 QB 244, p. 253; cited with approval by Blackburn J in *Richardson v Silvester* (1873) LR 9 QB 34, p. 36.

[81] *Richardson v Silvester* (1873) LR 9 QB 34.   [82] (1838) 5 Bing NC 97.

[83] *Commonwealth Commercial Banking v Brown* (1972) 126 CLR 337, the defendant is liable to 'the person whom it is intended should act upon it' Menzies J. The Restatement (Second) of Torts, s.533 examples an architect who gives a fraudulent certificate as to the amount of work done by a builder for use in obtaining an advance from a bank.

was the representation addressed? In *Peek v Gurney*,[84] e.g., the false statements in a prospectus were held to be directed to shareholders and not to the plaintiff purchasers on the stock market. There is, therefore, no liability under this tort for a 'reasonable expectation' that the misrepresentation will be repeated to another, 'a reminder of the law's pervasive concern lest liability for misrepresentation entail an excessive burden out of all proportion to the fault intended'.[85] This obviously limits the tort and is a limit not found in the Restatement (Second) of Torts[86] which extends liability to persons 'whom [the defendant] intends or has reason to expect to act' on the representation.

However, motive is immaterial: 'if fraud be established it is immaterial that there was no intention to cheat or injure the person to whom the false statement was made.'[87]

Reliance by claimant: 'materiality'

The representation must have been relied upon by the claimant: he must have been influenced by it. It need not be the sole reason for the subsequent actions as long as it 'materially contributed to his so acting'.[88] The tort will arise even though the victim is aware to some extent of the untruth of the statement, provided he is not aware of the full extent of the untruth.[89] Indeed, the reliance may even be careless and yet sufficient for the tort,[90] nor is contributory negligence a defence to an action for deceit[91] and the Law Reform (Contributory Negligence) Act 1945 does not apply.[92] To say I lied but you should not have believed me is obviously objectionable on policy grounds: 'the liar can hardly complain that his dupe was

---

[84] (1873) LR 6 HL 377, applied in *Al Nakib Investments v Longcroft* [1990] 1 WLR 1320.
[85] Above, n. 2, p. 710.
[86] Restatement (Second) of Torts, s.531.
[87] V Maugham *Bradford Building Society v Borders* [1941] 2 All ER 205 at 211; *Polhill v Walter* (1832) 3 B and Ad 114.
[88] *Edgington v Fitzmaurice* (1885) 29 Ch D 459.
[89] *Gipps v Gipps* [1978] 1 NSWLR 454.
[90] *Dobell v Stevens* (1825) 3 B&C 623; *Pilmore v Hood* (1838) 5 Bing NC 97; *Redgrave v Hurd* (1881) 20 Ch D 1. In *Whife v Cullen & Partners* CA, *The Times*, 15 November 1993 the carelessness of the plaintiffs' agent (their solicitor) was held to be no defence. Provided the claimant was influenced by the defendant's misrepresentation, the defendant will be liable even though the claimant was also partly influenced by a mistake of his own, Bowen LJ in *Edgington v Fitzmaurice* (1885) 29 Ch 459, p. 483.
[91] *Alliance & Leicester Building Society v. Edgestop Ltd* [1993] 1 WLR 1462, Mummery J.
[92] *Nationwide Building Society v Thimbleby & Co, Independent*, 15 March 1999, Blackburne J. The Court of Appeal in *Standard Chartered Bank v Pakistan National Shipping Corp (Reduction of Damages)* [2000] 2 Lloyd's Rep 511, held that there is no defence of contributory deceit as it has always been the law that a defendant who has been found liable in deceit cannot establish a defence based upon the contributory fault of the plaintiff (Sir Anthony Evans dissention). In the case itself the claimant's own deceitful conduct towards a third party was in part responsible for its loss.

gullible.'[93] It is, therefore, no defence to claim that the representation is not material in the sense that it would not have induced a reasonable person to act. The question is simply whether the representation was relied upon by the claimant.

The need to show reliance by the claimant himself[94] is a severe limitation on the scope of deceit. Indeed, even the more modern tort of negligence appears to render success less likely where the misstatement is not relied upon by the claimant but a third party.[95] A *Wilkinson v Downton* scenario is not within the tort, given in such a case that there is no reliance but rather harmful effects result from the lies told.[96]

Damage[97]

The claimant must prove damage as a consequence of acting on the misrepresentation. The defendant will be liable whether he intended the harm or not.[98] Although predominantly financial harm will be the damage alleged in this tort, physical harm (including personal injury, mental distress,[99] and even inconvenience)[100] is covered,[101] as is damage to property.

As far as financial harm is concerned, the claimant is to be put into the

[93] Weir, T., *Casebook on Torts* 9th edn. (London: Sweet & Maxwell, 2000), p. 573, commenting on *Alliance & Leicester BS v Edgestop* [1994] 2 All ER 38.

[94] Whether there is reliance should the plaintiff's agent have knowledge of the truth depends on the facts: in *Strover v Harrington* [1988] 2 WLR 572 the purchaser's solicitor had authority to receive the relevant information so that the plaintiff was 'estopped' from denying that he had received the information that negated the earlier untruth, cf. *Wells v Smith* [1914] 3 KB 722 where the agent was party to the fraud.

[95] See discussion in Ch. 9.

[96] *Wilkinson v Downton* [1897] 2 QB 57. So Wright J in that case was prepared to award damages in deceit for the train fare necessitated by the lie ('a misrepresentation intended to be acted upon by the plaintiff') but not for the illness and suffering experienced. He created a wide liability for intentional infliction of physical harm instead. Sales, P., and Stilitz, D., 'Intentional Infliction of Harm by Unlawful Means' 115 LQR (1999) 411 suggest that *Wilkinson v Downton* should properly be understood as a specific instance of a wider principle of liability based on intentional harm (encompassing physical as well as economic harm).

[97] See generally McGregor, H., *McGregor on Damages*, 16th edn. (London: Sweet & Maxwell, 1997), ch. 39.

[98] *Edgington v Fitzmaurice* (1885) 29 Ch D 459.

[99] *Shelley v Paddock* [1980] QB 348. The possibility of damages for anxiety and distress was raised by Winn LJ in *Doyle v Olby* [1969] 2QB 158. Though the damages for distress were termed 'aggravated damages' in *Archer v Brown* [1985] QB 408, McGregor (above, n. 97) disputes this, para. 1993: 'the true position is that the plaintiff should be entitled to compensation for any mental distress he has suffered; such damages will become aggravated only if they fail to be increased because the heinousness of the defendant's conduct is considered to have added to the plaintiff's suffering.'

[100] *Mafo v Adams* [1970] 1 QB 548 CA. Here the defendant tricked the plaintiff into leaving a protected tenancy. His damages included compensation for physical inconvenience and discomfort.

[101] See *Langridge v Levy* (1937) 2 M&W 519.

position he would have been in had the representation not been acted upon,[102] based on 'the actual damage directly flowing from the fraudulent inducement'.[103]

Where a contract ensues from the deceit, the normal assessment will be the difference between the price paid and the market value of the goods or property concerned, at the time of the transaction. However, this is not an inflexible rule, as Lords Browne-Wilkinson and Steyn noted in *Smith New Court Securities Ltd v Scrimgeour Vickers (Asset Management) Ltd*.[104] So the court can take into account continuing representations and the fact that the claimant may be 'locked into' the property. The 'date of transaction' rule was not applied, for example, in *Doyle v Olby*[105] or in *East v Maurer*.[106] There has always been an exception to the rule where the open market at the transaction date was a false market, the price inflated because of a misrepresentation made by the defendant to the market generally. In such a case the 'true' value as at the transaction date has to be ascertained, with the benefit of hindsight.[107] But there was an added twist in *Smith New Court Securities* itself. There the defendant's agent had induced the purchase of Ferranti shares by deceit.[108] However, prior to this transaction,[109] there had been a wholly unrelated fraud on Ferranti, by a third party. This led to a vastly overvalued market price and, on its disclosure, to a massive decline in the value of the Ferranti shares. In assessing the loss to the plaintiffs, who sold their shares for a fraction of the price they had paid for them, the false market price of the shares at the time of the transaction was disregarded. Rather, damages were assessed by deducting the price of eventual resale of the shares by the plaintiff from the price paid. Due to the prior fraud, the shares were 'already pregnant with disaster' and the result of the transaction induced by the defendant's fraud was that the plaintiff had become 'locked into' the property.

Given deceit is subject to the normal tort measure of damages, loss of expected profits on the contract, undermined by the fraud, are irrecoverable.[110] However, the court may award loss of likely profits (rather than

---

[102] *Barley v Walford* (1846) 9 QB 197, a false representation by the defendant to the plaintiff that his product was a copy of a registered design. The plaintiff was entitled to lost profits when he terminated his production of those goods, as a result.

[103] Lord Atkin *Clark v Urquhart* [1930] AC 28, p. 68.

[104] [1997] AC 254.   [105] [1969] 2 QB 158.

[106] [1991] 1 WLR 461.   [107] *McConnel v Wright* [1903] 1 Ch 546.

[108] A false statement that others were interested in purchasing the shares.

[109] Cf. if this had occurred subsequently: Lord Steyn *Smith New Court Securities Ltd v Scrimgeour Vickers Ltd* [1997] AC 254, p. 285 'the position would have been different if the loss suffered by Smith arose from a subsequent fraud'.

[110] Cf. Restatement (Second) of Torts, s.549(2): 'the recipient of a fraudulent misrepresentation in a business transaction is also entitled to recover additional damages sufficient to give him the benefit of his contract with the maker, if these damages are proved with reasonable certainty.'

loss of bargain profits) where the case so demands. In *East v Maurer*[111] there was a false representation by the defendant vendor of a hairdressing business that he was not intending to compete in his neighbouring salon. The plaintiffs were compensated not for the profits of the business as represented but rather for the profits they would have had, had they not relied on the misrepresentation, on the purchase of a similar hairdressing business for a similar sum—the hypothetical profitable business they would have become involved with, but for the deceit.

Unlike negligence and its protection of only those losses that are reasonably foreseeable, directness is the test for remoteness in deceit. Following *Doyle v Olby*[112] any consequential loss that is direct,[113] even though not reasonably foreseeable, is recoverable, given 'it does not lie in the mouth of the fraudulent person to say that [the damage] could not reasonably have been foreseen'.[114] This means that, as Lord Denning noted, 'the defendant is bound to make reparation for all the actual damage directly flowing from the fraudulent inducement'.[115] This was accepted by the House of Lords in *Smith New Court Securities Ltd v Scrimgeour Vickers (Asset Management) Ltd*, Lord Steyn commenting that 'it is a rational and defensible strategy to impose wider liability on an intentional wrongdoer'.[116] He contended that such a policy served two purposes: as a deterrent in discouraging fraud (civil remedies playing a 'useful and beneficial role' in the battle against fraud) and as an indicator of moral behaviour given 'the law and morality are inextricably interwoven'. In cases where reliance on the misrepresentation has led to a lost alternative benefit or opportunity, reliance loss may be the appropriate measure. In *Archer v Brown*[117] the plaintiff recovered expenses reasonably and properly incurred, including bank interest on money borrowed as a result of the deceit. The better view is that exemplary damages, not having been available for deceit prior to *Rookes v Barnard*,[118] are still not available.

---

[111] 1991] 1 WLR 461, CA.

[112] [1969] 2QB 158. McGregor, above, n. 97, para. 1963 notes that most cases dealing with the measure of damages in deceit involve contracts for the sale of shares to the plaintiff, while with consequential losses the 'preponderance of authority' lies with actions where the contract into which the plaintiff has been induced is other than for the purchase of shares (para. 1983).

[113] It is not always easy to assess what losses are direct, however. Note the difference of judicial opinion in *Gould v Vaggelas* (1985) 56 ALR 31.

[114] [1969] 2 QB 158, p. 167.

[115] [1969] 2 QB 158, p. 167. Lord Steyn in *Smith New Court Securities Ltd v Scrimgeour Vickers Ltd* [1997] AC 254, p. 281 termed this a 'negative interest' to be put back in the position he would have been had no false representation been made.

[116] *Smith New Court Securities* [1997] AC 254, p. 279.

[117] [1985] QB 401, p. 407.

[118] The Court of Appeal in *A.B. v. South-West Water* [1993] Q.B. 507 suggested that Lord

Of course, claimants are obliged to take reasonable steps to mitigate their loss, once they are aware of the fraud. As Lord Browne-Wilkinson noted in *Smith New Court Securities Ltd v Scrimgeour Vickers (Asset Management) Ltd*, 'once the fraud has been discovered, if the plaintiff is not locked into the asset and the fraud has ceased to operate on his mind, a failure to take reasonable steps to sell the property may constitute a failure to mitigate his loss, requiring him to bring the value of the property into account at the date when he discovered the fraud or shortly thereafter'.[119]

DECEIT AND VICARIOUS LIABILITY

A special approach has developed in determining vicarious liability where the employee or agent is liable for deceit. Unlike torts where the borderline between vicarious liability and freedom from such liability can be drawn by reference to the concept of 'course of employment', with fraud the courts look to the reliance of the claimant on the authority given to the employee/agent by the principal.[120] As Lord Greene MR commented in *Uxbridge Permanent Benefit Building Society v Pickard*[121] the imposition of vicarious liability in deceit focuses on the 'actual or ostensible authority upon the faith of which some third person is going to change his position'. This was reaffirmed by the House of Lords in *The Ocean Frost*.[122] Lord Keith asserted: 'the essential feature for creating liability in the employer is that the party contracting with the fraudulent servant should have altered his position to his detriment in reliance on the belief that the servant's activities were within his authority, or, to put it another way, were part of his job.'[123] For the employer or principal to be liable, therefore, the employee or agent has to be acting within the scope of his authority—once this is so the employer/principal will be liable even though the employee/agent intended simply to benefit himself.[124] The employee cannot of course confer such authority upon himself simply by alleging he has it: the employer must have induced the belief that such authority exists.

Though the employee may be part of a fraud on a client that *in itself*

Devlin's speech in *Rookes v. Barnard* did not extend the range of torts in which awards of exemplary damages may be made. In *Kuddus v Chief Constable of Leicestershire, The Times,* 16 March 2000, CA the 'causes of action' test suggested in *AB v South-West Water* was followed (to deny exemplary damages for misfeasance in public office).

[119] [1997] AC 254, p. 266.
[120] Lord Keith *The Ocean Frost* [1986] 1 AC 717, p. 780: 'dishonest conduct is of a different character from blundering attempts to promote the employer's business interests.'
[121] [1939] 2 KB 248.   [122] [1986] 1 AC 717.
[123] [1986] 1 AC 717, p. 781.
[124] *Lloyd v Grace, Smith & Co* [1912] AC 716.

will not render the employer vicariously liable. In *Credit Lyonnais v ECGD*[125] there was a fraud on the plaintiff bank by a third party.[126] To make this scam work, the third party corrupted a senior employee of the Export Credit Guarantee Department who dealt with the underwriting of guarantees. Though the employee was clearly involved in the third party's fraud as a conspirator and joint tortfeasor, these fraudulent activities (e.g. signing letters on the defendant's notepaper, indicating that the transactions were acceptable to the bank) were held not to be within his authority. The acts that were performed within his normal employment duties (issuing routine guarantees), though they set the scene for the fraud, were not themselves unlawful and had no adverse consequences on the plaintiffs.[127] The deceit to which the employee was a party was not within the course of his employment. The ECGD, therefore, were not vicariously liable.[128]

RATIONALE

The closeness of the classic version of the tort of deceit to contract liability shaped judicial attitudes to its development. The tort developed in an era where the common law courts were keen on the notion of self-reliance and *laissez-faire* and were hostile to attempts to undermine the sanctity of contract (which was also the reason for the slow development of liability for careless misstatements, seemingly an attack on the doctrine of consideration).[129] It was the common law insistence on certainty that culminated in *Derry v Peek* (with not one chancery Law Lord included in that court)[130] and left equity's concern with good faith to be developed elsewhere. Thus

---

[125] [1998] 1 Lloyd's Reps 19, CA; [1999] 2 WLR 540, HL.

[126] This involved the third party posing as a considerable exporter of commercial goods and inducing the bank to purchase (fraudulent) bills of exchange, drawn by him on what were in fact fictitious buyers. The banker's guarantees for these were issued by the Export Credit Guarantee Department.

[127] He did nothing unlawful in issuing the guarantees as such and as Lord Woolf noted: 'indeed, if the Bank had taken the action which it should have done to protect itself, it was ECGD who would have suffered the loss ... since ECGD would have had to honour the agreements.'

[128] Interestingly, the plaintiff tried to avoid the problems of an orthodox approach to vicarious liability by pressing both the Court of Appeal and House of Lords to consider extending the doctrine of joint tortfeasance (to include assistance liability) and/or to establish a new tort of assisting in the violation of another's right. Neither court seemed impressed by these arguments.

[129] See Lord Devlin in *Hedley Byrne v Heller* [1964] AC 465, pp. 525–8. Atiyah, above, n. 6, p. 468: 'apart from the case of express warranty, the only protection accorded to contracting parties in derogation of the principle of *caveat emptor* was the case of actual fraud.'

[130] As was pointed out by Atiyah, above, n. 6, p. 673 who comments that it is therefore hardly surprising that Pollock noted all Lincoln's Inn thought the decision wrong. However, the end of the nineteenth century saw some movement away from Victorian individualism into acceptance of a 'new morality', see e.g. *Redgrave v Hurd* (1881) 20 Ch D 1.

Derry v Peek[131] severely restricted the tort in keeping with the spirit of the period, when courts refused to interfere with the activities of a business-man 'whether he was abusing his rights . . . or driving his competitors out of business'.[132] As Stoljar noted: '[Derry v Peek] . . . in actual result, if not in its reasoning, displays a pronounced bias in favour of *caveat emptor* which also explains its strong insistence on the seller's moral fraud.'[133] The classic form of deceit is not part of the real framework of the economic torts. Rather the important role that the economic torts play is in three-party settings, extending the protection of the claimant from the immediate cause of the economic harm to the 'real' cause of that harm.

Given this development of deceit 'the element of public confusion and, therefore, of the protection of the general interest of society at large, is quite irrelevant'.[134] Deceit focuses on the representee rather than the damaging effects as such. Moreover, it seeks to protect in only the most extreme cases given 'a charge of fraud is such a terrible thing to bring against a man that it cannot be maintained in any court unless it is shown that he had a wicked mind'.[135]

The common law, therefore, does not play a central role in consumer protection.[136] It was Parliament that took the lead in protecting consumers against commercial misdescription, though the first examples of state control over the misdescription of products in the Merchandise Marks Acts from 1887 onwards[137] were motivated from a desire to protect traders from their dishonest competitors rather than as a means of consumer protection.[138] With the dawning of 'the age of the consumer' such protection was deemed inadequate, leading to the Trade Descriptions Act 1968[139] which seeks to deter trading abuses in the interests of consumers.[140]

---

[131] (1889) 14 App Cas 337.

[132] Stevens, above, n. 11, p. 133, n. 46. The first reference is to *Bradford v Pickles* [1895] AC 587; the second to *Mogul Steamships v McGregor* [1892] AC 25.

[133] Stoljar, above, n. 7, p. 142, n. 91. For Atiyah, above, n. 6, 'the decision in *Derry v Peek* was not only the final triumph of common law over equity; it was the final triumph of market principles in the law of contract' (p. 673).

[134] Phillips, J., and Coleman, A., 'Passing off and the Common Field of Activity' 101 LQR (1985) 242, p. 243.

[135] *Le Lievre v Gould* [1893] 1 QB 491, p. 498, Lord Esher.

[136] Of course, contract law as a control mechanism has been 'enhanced' by the Sale of Goods Act 1979, as amended by the Sale and Supply of Goods Act 1994.

[137] Merchandise Marks Acts 1887–1953. Criticized as obscure and inadequate by the Molony Committee (Committee on Consumer Protection) 1962 Cmnd. 1781.

[138] Oughton, D., and Lowry, J., *Textbook on Consumer Law* (London: Blackstone Press, 1997), p. 11.

[139] This put the interests of the consumer centre-stage. It is concerned with false or misleading descriptions of goods and services. Prices are now dealt with in Part III of the Consumer Protection Act 1987.   [140] It has strict liability as the norm.

CONCLUSION

The real regulation of 'trading abuse which operates to the detriment of consumers'[141] is via specific legislation (such as the Financial Services Act 1986 and the Companies Act 1985),[142] the criminal law (Trades Descriptions Act 1968), codes of practice and self-regulation. What is perhaps most interesting is that Parliament has not provided a civil action for consumers *per se*[143] (and indeed the courts have declined to create one out of the Trade Descriptions Act 1968). This should be contrasted with the approach in America[144] and Australia.[145]

---

[141] Oughton and Lowry, above, n. 138, p. 360—some of these provisions are based on health and safety grounds, rather than economic protection e.g. Food (Safety) Act 1990 (s.14 an offence to serve an article 'not of the quality demanded by the purchaser'); Medicine Act 1968 (s.93 offence to issue a false or misleading advertisement for a medicine).

[142] Indeed, the immediate effect of *Derry v Peek* was to cause Parliament to enact the Directors' Liability Act 1890 which imposed a statutory obligation on those who issue a prospectus.

[143] No provision was made in the Act itself for civil liability, the Consumers' Association citing their lack of lobbying power (compared to the CBI and National Chamber of Commerce) as the main reason for this: see Ramsay, I., *Consumer Protection* (London: Weidenfeld & Nicolson, 1989), p. 203.

[144] The Lanham Trade Mark Act 1946, s.43(a).

[145] The Trade Practices Act 1974, s.52. This provides protection against commercial conduct that is misleading or deceptive. Though part of a consumer protection statute, however, the vast majority of actions are brought by competitors rather than consumers.

7

Malicious Falsehood

HISTORY AND NOMENCLATURE[1]

An action for slander of title was available from at least the end of the sixteenth century[2] so that an oral denial of the plaintiff's title to land, preventing him from leasing or selling it, was actionable. Despite its name, this action was not derived or descended from the defamation torts of libel and slander.[3] Rather, it was an action on the case for special damage resulting from a falsehood.[4] It protected against falsehoods denigrating the plaintiff's title to land. The fact that falsehoods were proved and that they were 'calculated' to harm in the way described[5] was sufficient—lies as such were not central to the tort. In effect such disparagements were at your peril. Though the courts quickly established that a party should not be deterred from putting forward *bona fide*[6] claims to the land at issue and that any such claims of right were 'privileged',[7] this privilege was destroyed on proof of 'malice'.[8]

The action then fell out of favour for 150 years. Plaintiffs were hampered in their attempts to extend liability beyond land title concerns by the courts' adherence to the concept of *caveat emptor*[9] and their reluctance to extend

---

[1] See Newark, F. H., 'Malice in Actions on the Case' 60 LQR (1944) 366; Morison, W., 'The New Law of Verbal Injury' 3 Syd LR (1959–61) 4; Prosser, W., 'Injurious Falsehood: the Basis of Liability' 59 Col L Rev (1959) 425; and Heydon, J. D., *Economic Torts*, 2nd edn. (London; Sweet & Maxwell, 1978), pp. 81–8.

[2] Recognized in *Booth v Trafford* (1573) Dalison 102 and see e.g. *Gerard v Dickenson* (1590) Cro Eliz 196. Newark (above, n. 1) asserts that the first case in which any principle was laid down was *Banister v Banister* 1583, not reported, but cited by Coke 4 Co Rep 17a.

[3] Stuart Smith LJ is wrong to assert in *Khodaparast v Shad* [2000] 1 All ER 545, p. 556 that 'malicious falsehood is a species of defamation' Bowen LJ in *Ratcliffe v Evans* [1892] 2 QB 525 asserted 'such an action is not one of libel or slander' (p. 527). Clearly, however, as Sales, P., and Stilitz, D. note there are a number of features of the tort 'which reveal a strong influence from the law of defamation' ('Intentional Infliction of Harm by Unlawful Means' 115 LQR (1999) 411, p. 432)—in particular the need for untruths published to a third party and the test of malice.

[4] Prosser, above, n. 1, p. 431 'nothing is better settled, since *Malachy v Soper* 132 ER 453 (1836)' than this.

[5] It was necessary for the plaintiff to show that the words in some way referred to the plaintiff's title—a common area of dispute see e.g. *Elborow v Allen* 1623 Cro Jac 642.

[6] So in *Gerrard v Dickenson* 4 Co Rep 18 (a) (1590), the defendant knew that the lease she relied upon was forged.

[7] Or giving professional legal advice to that effect: *Johnson v Smith* Moore 187 (1584).

[8] Malice as such was not an element of liability, therefore, at this time.

[9] See e.g. *London v Eastgate* (1618) 2 Rolle Rep 72.

liability for words beyond those affecting reputation (especially under the influence of Holt CJ in the eighteenth century).[10] When the tort was revived the issue of 'malice' came increasingly to the fore in the allegations[11] so that by 1870, in *Steward v Young*[12] the court held malice to be necessary for liability.

Thus malice had become central to the tort by the time it was extended to cover a wider variety of falsehoods as in the closing decade of the nineteenth century[13] 'matters sorted themselves out in a rush'.[14] Having come to include falsehoods, whether written or oral,[15] tort liability was initially extended in *Wren v Weild*[16] from slander of title to land, to include impugning the plaintiff's title to goods ('slander of goods'). Within five years disparagement as to quality (involving no denial of title) was recognized, in *Western Counties Manure Co v Laws Chemical Manure Co.*[17] Here the defendant alleged that the plaintiff's manure was 'of low quality' and Bramwell B asserted: 'it seems to me that where a plaintiff says you have without lawful excuse made a false statement about my goods to their

[10] There were some seventeenth-century cases that indicated liability for false statements that injured another in their trade or profession (even though not defamatory): e.g. *Watson v Vanderlesh* (1627) Het 69 (allegation that the plague had been at the plaintiff's inn). However, these did not extend to false statements as to the quality of goods. There were also cases were liability hinged on injury to a man's trade through accusations against the trader's spouse: *Bodingley's Case* (1662) cited Anon (1680) 1 Vent 348 ('scold'); *Browne v Gibbons* (1703) 1 Salk 206 ('whore'), and see *Riding v Smith* (1876) 1 Ex D 91 which had an important part to play in developing the nineteenth century extended version of the tort. In the eighteenth century overall, however, 'little attempt appears to have been made to induce the courts to recognize an action by a trader in respect of words which did not impute misconduct or incompetence' (Morison, above, n. 1, p. 7).

[11] Newark, above, n. 1, p. 370, 'the popularity of this type of action seems to have abated after the first decade of the seventeenth century and in the eighteenth century it all but dies away'. It was revived in *Hargrave v Le Breton* (1769) Burr 2422. According to Newark there was much 'wild talk' on the issue of malice in *Hargrave v Le Breton* (1769) Burr 2422. 'The tragedy is that the discussion on malice resulted in the inaccurate headnote [that the action required the plaintiff to prove malice] which . . . is the cause of most of the subsequent misunderstanding' (p. 372).

[12] (1870) LR 5 CP 122.

[13] Morison, above, n. 1, asserts that *Sheperd v Wakeman* (1662) 1 Sid 79 should not be seen as the origin of the tort of malicious falsehood. For Morison this case is one of defamation, involving an imputation that the plaintiff was endeavouring to negotiate a bigamous marriage. Slander of title cases were discussed because the defendant set up the excuse that he used the words complained of in bona fide assertion of a claim that the plaintiff was his own wife and the courts' only experience of the defence of a bona fide claim of title was in slander of title actions.

[14] Morison, above, n. 1, p. 10.

[15] See *Malachy v Soper* (1836) 3 Bing NC 386

[16] (1869) LR 4QB 730, though *Malachy v Soper* 132 ER 453 (1836) appeared to accept this at an earlier date.

[17] (1874) LR 9 Ex 218—though Lord Herschell still doubted the correctness of this decision in *White v Mellin* [1895] AC 154.

comparative disparagement, which false statement has caused me to lose customers, an action is maintainable.'[18] By 1892, the general principle of the emergent tort was summarized thus by Bowen LJ in *Ratcliffe v Evans*:[19] 'an action will lie for written or oral falsehoods, not actionable *per se*, or even defamatory, where they are maliciously published, where they are calculated in the ordinary course of things to produce and where they do produce, actual damage.'

In view of the incremental development of the tort, it has attracted different names. Thus the tort can be labelled: slander of title/slander of goods; injurious falsehood;[20] trade libel;[21] disparagement[22] of goods or malicious falsehood. Given the action is not dependent on the principles of defamation, is not limited to disparagement, and focuses on the presence of malice, it is submitted that the term malicious falsehood best suits the tort[23]—indeed, this term was used by Bowen LJ in *Ratcliffe v Evans* and has been used in all recent cases.[24]

IMPORTANCE

Prosser notes that 'the tort is broader in scope than any of the specific names conferred upon it would indicate'.[25] Case law reveals that on the whole it protects against a particular form of intentional interference with economic relations and is not limited to situations only involving slander of title or disparagement of goods. *Ratcliffe v Evans*[26] was a successful claim based on the false statement that the plaintiff had ceased to carry on business, while in *Riding v Smith*[27] the tort was used where the defendant published false accusations against the plaintiff trader's wife, calculated to deter customers. A lie[28] that the plaintiff did not deal in certain goods

---

[18] (1874) LR 9 Ex 218, p. 222.   [19] [1892] 2 QB 524, p. 532.

[20] Coined by Sir John Salmond and used in the USA see e.g. Restatement (Second) of Torts, s.623A.

[21] Though Morison, above, n. 1, is particularly hostile to this, given it erroneously ties the tort to defamation.

[22] Lord Watson in *White v Mellin* [1895] 154, p. 167: 'in order to constitute disparagement . . . it must be shewn that the defendant's representations were made of and concerning the plaintiff's goods; that they were in disparagement of his goods and untrue; and that they had occasioned special damage to the plaintiff.'

[23] S.3 Defamation Act 1952 describes this wrong by the formula 'action for slander of title, slander of goods or other malicious falsehood'.

[24] See e.g. *Compaq Computer Corp v Dell Computer Corp Ltd* [1992] FSR 93 (Aldous J); *Vodafone Group plc v Orange Personal Communications Services Ltd* [1997] FSR 34 (Jacob J); *Macmillan Magazines Ltd v RCN Publishing Co Ltd* [1998] FSR 9 (Neuberger J).

[25] Above, n. 1, p. 425.   [26] [1892] 2 QB 524.

[27] (1876) 1 Ex D 91, p. 94.

[28] Note that lies as such are not necessary for liability in this tort: see the discussion below, comparing 'deceit malice' with 'motive malice'.

was actionable in *Jarradale Timber Co v Temperley & Co*[29] while a false statement that the plaintiff was employed by the defendant (calculated and
actually causing lost sales and commission) was held to be within the tort
in *Balden v Shorter*.[30] In *Customglass Boats v Salthouse*[31] a false statement
that the defendant had designed a successful boat (when it fact the plaintiff had been the designer) was actionable, as was a false claim that the
defendant's newspaper had a circulation some twenty times greater than
the plaintiff's rival newspaper in *Lyne v Nicholls*.[32] False representations
that the plaintiff tenant had gone away and ceased to trade (to force him
to leave) rendered the defendant landlord liable in *Joyce v Motor Services*.[33]
A system of 'switch selling' in *Rima Electric Ltd v Rolls Razor*[34] though not
passing off (as there was no confusion) was held to be a malicious falsehood on the facts. The defendant had indicated that they were obtaining
the plaintiff's goods at below the prices charged to ordinary stockists
which was likely to cause those legitimate dealers in the plaintiff's goods
to feel aggrieved and look elsewhere for the products in question.[35] Nor
does the tort only protect the claimant's trade: in *Kaye v Robertson*[36] and
Joyce v Sengupta[37] prospective financial loss was recovered by non-
traders. Indeed, in *Khodaparast v Shad*[38] it was accepted by the Court of
Appeal that aggravated damages could be awarded, to include compensation for anxiety, distress, and injury to feelings.

Such cases reveal the tort as protecting against falsehoods that are calculated to cause economic harm to the claimant: 'it may cover any false statements about a person (other than one concerned solely with personal
reputation) which causes a third party to act to that person's financial
detriment.'[39] It would appear, therefore, that the tort, though developed
from a group of related torts, should now be viewed as unified in principle and application. *Ratcliffe v Evans* accepted a wider principle of which
the specific cases were but examples,[40] while more recently Nicholls V-C

---

[29] 11 TLR 119 (QBD 1894).   [30] [1933] Ch 427.
[31] [1976] RPC 589. However, it is submitted that the better view should be that this
involves the general tort of unlawful interference, rather than malicious falsehood, given
that no reference is made to the plaintiff as such. This is further argued in Ch. 10.
[32] (1906) 23 TLR 86.
[33] [1948] Ch 252
[34] [1965] RPC 4 Wilberforce J—where alternative goods were offered to customers in
response to their request for the plaintiff's goods.
[35] Cf. *Ajello v Worsley* [1898] 1 Ch 274, Sterling J.
[36] [1991] FSR 62, CA.
[37] [1993] 1 WLR 337.
[38] [2000] 1 All ER 545, CA
[39] Cane, P., *Tort Law and Economic Interests*, 2nd edn. (Oxford: Clarendon Press, 1996),
p. 100, n. 459.
[40] Though it was still debated whether there are two separate actions in *Sungravure Pty v
Middle East Airlines Airliban SAL* (1975) 134 CLR 1, 21; *Swimsure (Laboratories) v McDonald* 79
2 NSWLR.

in *Joyce v Sengupta* commented: 'this cause of action embraces particular types of malicious falsehood such as slander of title and slander of goods, but is not confined to those headings.'[41]

However, it would be wrong to view the tort as of major importance. In the past the ability to succeed under the tort was limited by two factors: the need to prove special damage[42] and the need to prove malice. Though the former limit no longer applies to the majority of actions brought under the tort (due to s.3 Defamation Act 1952) the usefulness of the tort is still severely limited by the need to prove malice. The policy of the courts at the end of the nineteenth century was to rein in the developing tort: Cornish notes that 'at an early stage of both the modern tort and modern advertising, the courts showed particular reluctance to allow such actions to succeed'.[43] Doubtless, this is the reason that it has been subjected to little academic analysis, Wolff terming it 'an orphan among legal actions' and commenting that it had been neglected by the jurists and misunderstood by the courts.[44]

This lack of easy protection led to the intervention of Parliament in one important area. One of the most frequent allegations of the tort in the nineteenth century involved the 'common law threats action'[45] used against a defendant where unjustified allegations were raised that the plaintiff was selling goods in infringement of a patent or copyright. Here, the difficulty in succeeding in the tort appeared to undermine the legitimate concerns of the rightful owner of the intellectual property right concerned. Given 'intellectual property is protectable by litigation alone, and not also by possession, the ability to assert rights is crucial'.[46] Hence the introduction of special statutory rights against 'threats', not limited by the need to show malice or the need to prove their falsity and damage. This process continued throughout the twentieth century, so that statutory torts arise where the defendant threatens proceedings and is unable to prove infringement of a patent,[47] registered design,[48] registered trade

---

[41] [1993] 1 WLR 337, p. 341.

[42] In *White v Mellin* [1895] AC 154 the House of Lords underlined the fact that unlike defamatory words, injurious words were not actionable *per se*, even though they were calculated to injure a man in his trade.

[43] Cornish, W., *Intellectual Property*, 4th edn. (London: Sweet & Maxwell, 1999), p. 656.

[44] Wolff, J., 'Disparagement of Title and Quality' 20 Can B Rev 430 (1942), p. 446.

[45] See Morison, above, n. 1, p. 12.

[46] See Cornish, W., above, n. 43, p. 655.

[47] Patents Act 1977 s.70. Where any person by circulars, advertisements or otherwise threatens any other person with proceedings for infringement of a patent, any person aggrieved thereby (who need not be the person to whom the threats were made, so long as he is hampered in his trade by the threats) may bring an action for a declaration that the threats are unjustifiable and for an injunction and damages.

[48] Registered Designs Act s.26.

mark[49] or design right.[50] Copyright has never been accorded this statutory protection, so only the tort of malicious falsehood is available in such a case.[51]

The tort of malicious falsehood, therefore, has a minor part to play in the regulation of competition. It is clearly overshadowed by the tort of passing off, freed as that tort has been from its origins in fraud. In recent years the tort of malicious falsehood has typically been pleaded where the claimant takes offence at the defendant's comparative advertising. Due to changes in registered trade mark law, it is now possible under s.10(6) Trade Marks Act 1994 to use a trade rival's trade mark in such advertising, a practice that had been forbidden under the Trade Marks Act 1938.[52] This has led to a surge in comparative advertising and a series of cases where both malicious falsehood and infringement of the registered mark have been claimed, notably: *Compaq Computer Corp v Dell Computer Corp Ltd;*[53] *Vodafone Group plc v Orange Personal Communications Services Ltd;*[54] *Cable & Wireless plc v BT plc;*[55] and *Macmillan Magazines Ltd v RCN Publishing Co Ltd.*[56] In reality the real focus of these claims is whether the advertisement complies with the concept of 'fair' comparative advertising as defined in s.10(6).[57] Indeed, Jacob J in *Cable & Wireless plc v BT plc*[58] considered that the tort claim often added nothing (though it increased costs)[59] given it is difficult to imagine a case where the tort would provide wider protection (provided of course, the trade mark involved had been

[49] Trade Marks Act 1994 s.21.   [50] Copyright Designs and Patents Act 1988 s.253.

[51] *Dicks v Brooks* (1880) 15 ChD 22. See also *Mentmore Manufacturing Co Ltd v Fomento* (1955) 72 RPC 157 where the defendant, relying on a successful claim for patent validity in the Court of Appeal, but with an appeal pending to the House of Lords, falsely threatened customers of the plaintiff that their stock could as a result be seized and they could be sued.

[52] Though as Jacob J notes in *Vodafone Group plc v Orange Personal Communications Services Ltd* [1997] FSR 34, p. 39, a number of trades tended not to use this provision.

[53] [1992] FSR 93. Misleading comparisons between different models produced by the parties.

[54] [1997] FSR 34 Jacob J: claim that the defendant's mobile phone service would save customers an average of £20 per month, compared to plaintiff's system.

[55] [1998] FSR 383 Jacob J 'another battle in the telephone wars' (p. 384) where price comparisons were objected to as misleading.

[56] [1998] FSR 9, Neuberger J. The case involved assertions that the defendant's rival nursing recruitment magazine was more successful in a number of ways than the plaintiff's.

[57] Comparative advertising which makes use of the trade rival's registered trade mark (which is likely) will not infringe that mark unless it is not in accordance with 'honest practices in industrial or commercial matters' and takes 'unfair advantage of, or is detrimental to, the distinctive character or reputation of the Trade Mark'. Of course there is still self-regulation in this area: see the Advertising Standards Authority's Code. See also the Comparative Advertising Directive 97/55/EC

[58] [1998] FSR 383 Jacob J (p. 385) and see *British Airways plc v Ryanair Ltd*, unreported, 5 December 2000, Ch. D.

[59] Hence he considered it 'wasteful' to have included the malicious falsehood claim in *Vodafone Group plc v Orange Personal Communications Services Ltd* [1997] FSR 34, given the difficulties in applying the 'one meaning' rule (on which see text).

registered). To knowingly put forward a false statement would not be honest practice.[60] The modern importance of the tort, therefore, is minimal, though recently there have been indications that it has a potential for development (at least as far as the interest it protects is concerned).[61]

'The essentials of this tort are that the defendant has published about the plaintiff words which are false, that they are published maliciously and that special damage has followed as the direct and natural result of their publication.'[62] Though cases often involve denigration or disparagement, neither are necessary for the tort to be established. However, though any falsehood is encompassed, it must be economic harm that is caused, which requirement has limited the tort usually to 'falsehoods about property, profession, trade or business'.[63]

In analysing the tort, its relationship to the torts of defamation and passing off needs be explored.

False statement concerning the claimant or his property

There must be a false statement of some sort. 'If the statement is true, however malicious the defendant's intention might be, no action will lie.'[64] As in deceit, the statement may be oral, written, implied,[65] or emanate from conduct.[66] In deceit, a statement of opinion that is false may be actionable and though the point is undecided for malicious falsehood, Rogers[67] argues the same should apply to the tort of malicious falsehood. It is for the claimant to prove that the allegations are false.[68]

The meaning of the words may be in issue: if so, the proper meaning must be established, before their truth or falsity can be tested. The meaning

---

[60] Conversely in *Emaco Ltd v Dyson Appliances Ltd* [1999] ETMR 903, Parker J a comparative advert was not malicious but failed the 'honest practice' test of s.10(6) Trade Marks Act 1994.

[61] *Khodaparast v Shad* [2000] 1 All ER 545, CA: damages awarded for injury to feelings. The potential of the tort to develop, following *Khodaparast v Shad* was noted by Lord Steyn in *Gregory v Portsmouth CC* [2000] 1 All ER 560.

[62] Glidewell LJ, *Kaye v Robertson* [1991] FSR 62, CA.

[63] Cornish, above, n. 43, p. 652. Though note *Khodaparast v Shad* [2000] 1 All ER 545, CA, aggravated damages may include damages for anxiety, distress, and injury to feelings.

[64] Maule J *Pater v Baker* (1847) 3 CB 831, p. 868.

[65] The false disparagement could be either direct or 'by innuendo' per Whitford J in *McDonalds v Burgerking* [1986] FSR 45, p. 59 (reversed by CA, [1987] FSR 112).

[66] Conduct may amount to a statement: see *Wilts United Dairies v Robinson* [1958] RPC 94, CA; *Royal Baking Powder Co v Wright, Crossley & Co* (1901) 18 RPC 95.

[67] Rogers, W. V. H., in *Gatley on Libel and Slander*, 9th edn. (London: Sweet & Maxwell,1998), para. 20.5.

[68] *Burnett v Tak* (1882) 42 LT 743 cf. defamation.

is for the court to determine and evidence of the meaning to others is inadmissible.[69] The principle would appear to be the same for malicious falsehood and libel, namely 'what is the meaning to the ordinary man?' (though Jacob J was unhappy with this in *Vodafone Group plc v Orange Personal Communications Services Ltd*).[70] This 'one meaning rule' means that a 'right' meaning has to be established and was considered (in the context of a libel claim) by the House of Lords in *Rubber Improvements Ltd v Daily Telegraph Ltd*.[71] The ordinary man 'can and does read between the lines in the light of his general knowledge and experience of worldly affairs'. Part of this process of establishing the meaning of the words objected to, is to consider what inference might be drawn by the ordinary man. Neuberger J in *Macmillan Magazines Ltd v RCN Publishing Co Ltd*[72] noted that where a specialist magazine is concerned, so that the advertising objected to is directed to a specialist group of people (in that case advertisers and recruiters) 'there must be a respectable argument for saying that one should judge the advertisement by the effect that it would have on such advertisers and not by the effect that it would have on the general public'.

The false statement must concern the claimant or his property. Lord Watson in *White v Mellin* (a slander of goods claim) stressed 'it must be shown that the defendant's representations were made of and concerning the plaintiff's goods'.[73] The concern may be indirect as in *Riding v Smith* (where false allegations were made of the trader's wife who assisted in his business) but for the defendant to tell lies about himself is not the tort,[74] unless that in some way implicates the claimant.[75] However, Cornish notes that the courts have held that an untrue claim to a title of any kind or to be an inventor or designer is a falsehood that may be actionable by the legitimate owner of the title in question.[76] So in *Customglass v Salt-*

---

[69] Jacob J *Vodafone Group plc v Orange Personal Communications Services* [1997] FSR 34, p. 37.

[70] [1997] FSR 34, pp. 37–9. It is obviously difficult to establish a single, natural, and ordinary meaning, given different people may react in different ways to a statement. He would prefer the approach taken in the tort of passing off: false to a substantial number of people.

[71] [1964] AC 234, p. 258.

[72] [1998] FSR 9, Neuberger J.

[73] [1895] AC 154, p. 167.

[74] Rogers suggests (above, n. 67, para. 20.1, n. 1) that where the defendant tells lies to another about himself in order to induce that other to deal with him rather than with the claimant, that may be the tort of unlawful interference with trade—the lies being the unlawful means. See *National Phonograph Co Ltd v Edison-Bell Consolidated Phonograph Co Ltd* [1908] 1 Ch 335. This is discussed further in Chs. 6 and 10.

[75] Thus the statement in *Cambridge University Press v University Tutorial Press* [1928] 45 RPC 335 (involving a claim that the defendant produced a prescribed school text, when in fact the plaintiff did) would not be actionable as a malicious falsehood.

[76] Above, n. 43, pp. 652–3. However, it is argued below and in Ch. 10 that these are better seen as examples of unlawful interference with trade, not involving statements 'about' the claimant.

house[77] the false statement that the defendant had designed the plaintiff's boat was malicious falsehood, as was the defendant's false claim to be the only authorized importer of certain machinery in *Danish Mercantile Co Ltd v Beaumont*,[78] when it was the plaintiff who was in fact the sole distributor of these items. In *Serville v Constance*[79] the defendant's false claim to a boxing title in fact held by the plaintiff was held capable of amounting to malicious falsehood. Here, the indirect attack on the plaintiff's title will be prevented. As in defamation, the claimant does not have to be named as such.[80]

A special approach has arisen in cases which involve allegations of malicious falsehood through comparative advertising of any sort. With malicious falsehood, there is an obvious danger that the courts may become too involved in arbitrating on the competitive process, given that 'comparison lies at the root of modern advertising'.[81] Thus the courts are concerned that they should not be turned 'into a machinery for advertising rival productions by obtaining a judicial determination which of the two was the better'[82] (interestingly, a similar concern was raised in a modern passing off case, *Parma Ham*, involving an alleged quality misrepresentation).[83] In effect in this area, the courts allow a limited form of disparagement, so that a mere misleading comparison of the defendant's goods to the claimant's is not actionable. Rather, as Heydon points out 'there must be some real harshness of criticism or some false factual allegation' to prevent the action from 'breeding actions about the relative merits of rival products'.[84]

Of course, 'mere puffs' are not actionable in any of the 'misrepresentation' torts.[85] But this policy has gone one step further in malicious falsehood: an allegation of superiority over the particular claimant's product (or specific attributes of the product) may not be covered by the tort.[86] The argument is that the assertion 'my goods are better than the claimant's' is

---

[77] [1976] 1 NZLR 36.   [78] (1950) 67 RPC 111, Roxburgh J.

[79] [1954] 1 All ER 662, p. 665, Harman J.

[80] In *Lyne v Nicholls* (1906) 23 TLR 86, Swinfen Eady J, a false assertion that the defendant's newspaper had a circulation twenty times any other weekly paper in the district (there being only one such newspaper, the plaintiff's) was actionable (though the action failed as no damage was proved).

[81] Cornish, above, n. 43, p. 655.

[82] Lord Herschell, *White v Mellin* [1895] AC 154 'consider what a door would be opened if this were permitted. That this sort of puffing advertisement is in use is notorious . . . the Court would be bound to inquire in an action brought, whether this ointment or this pill better cured the disease which it was alleged to cure; whether a particular article of food was in this respect or that better than another.'

[83] See Ch. 8.   [84] Above, n. 1, p. 85.

[85] The idea appears to be that 'mere sales talk' will not affect the consumer unduly.

[86] Note the Restatement (Second) of Torts, s.649 provides for a 'conditional privilege' allowing competitors to make an unduly favourable comparison in which they do not believe 'if the comparison does not contain false assertions of specific unfavourable facts'.

only a more dramatic presentation of what is implicit in the statement 'my goods are the best in the world'.[87] The fact that the defendant is aware that his statement is false, in such a case, will not amount to malice. So in *White v Mellin*,[88] the defendant sold infant food manufactured by the plaintiff, to which he affixed a label commending his own infant food as 'being far more nutritious and healthful than any other preparation'. Lord Herschell was keen not to be drawn into the competitive process and indicated that latitude must be given to trade rivals: there was no direct disparagement of the plaintiff's product and no liability, therefore. This approach was readily taken up subsequently by the Court of Appeal in *Hubbuck v Wilkinson*.[89] There, the defendant published reports of experiments comparing his and the plaintiff's paints. He claimed that the tests were slightly to the defendant's advantage, but that for all practical purposes the parties' products could be regarded as equal. The plaintiff claimed that the report was untrue and that his paint was, in fact, superior. Despite the technical data the defendant had purported to provide in support of his untrue statements, there was held to be no malicious falsehood.[90] Given that to allege that your own goods are better than other people's would not render the defendant liable, it made no difference whether such a statement was made in general terms or used specific allegations.

Exactly where the line is drawn between 'self-commendation' and unacceptable disparagement is not always readily discernible from earlier case law. In part this is due to the issue of disparagement often being a matter of construction and implication. However, where the language of the disparagement is clear and strong, the court will be willing to act. So in *Thorleys Cattle Food v Alassam*[91] an allegation that the plaintiff had foisted a fictitious article on the public, different to that represented was malicious falsehood. It was the strength of the language used by the defendant ('foist', 'caution') that was important for this decision, at least one of the judges being undecided initially whether this was simply a case of the defendant commending his own wares. Again in *Linotype Co Ltd v British Empire*[92] the parties were rival manufacturers of type-setting machines. The defendant sought to publish allegations about the plaintiff's machines. Though mere criticism of the machine was permissible,

---

[87] Wolff, J challenges this, given the important part which advertising and sales persuasion play in shaping consumer reaction, 'Unfair Competition by Truthful Disparagement' 47 Yale LJ (1937–8), p. 1304.

[88] Decided some twenty years after *Western Counties v Lawes*, it is hard not to perceive a reluctance to accept the tort, or at least its extensions as to quality disparagement.

[89] [1898] 1 QB 86 CA.

[90] Interestingly, *Allen v Flood* was used to support the decision: competition *per se* was lawful.

[91] (1886) 14 Ch D 763, CA.   [92] (1899) 81 LT 331, HL.

the statements were held to be malicious falsehoods because they imputed that the plaintiff supplied worthless machines. In *London Ferro-Concrete Co Ltd v Justicz*[93] the defendant went beyond merely saying that his methods were better than the plaintiff's when he asserted that the plaintiff's methods were inadequate. It is the untrue statement about the claimant's goods which attracts liability, taking the case out of mere comparison into disparagement.[94] So Lord Shand commented in *White v Mellin*[95] that if the defendant had stated that the plaintiff's food was 'positively injurious' or contained 'deleterious ingredients' there would have been good grounds of action.[96]

A coherent, modern test for distinguishing between self-commendation and disparagement is that contained in the judgment of Walton J in *De Beers v International General Electric*.[97] The defendant circulated a pamphlet which purported to be the report of laboratory experiments, comparing the plaintiff's and defendant's rival products. The defendant argued that the pamphlet was in effect no more than a glorified statement that the defendant's product was better than the plaintiff's.[98] Walton J accepted that the case required him to draw the line between what is and what is not permissible when denigrating a rival. Walton J suggested the following test: 'whether a reasonable man would take the claim being made as being a serious claim or not.' In the alternative, it may be useful to ask whether the defendant has pointed to a specific allegation of some defect or demerit in the plaintiff's goods. But Walton J himself noted that this might not be of universal application, given the allegation might still not be taken seriously by the reasonable man if delivered in a light-hearted or extremely vituperative manner. In the case itself, specific reference to scientific tests meant that the allegations would be taken seriously.

It might be questioned whether some of the earlier decisions in this area would be decided in the same way in a modern action, in an era where *caveat emptor* is no longer the guiding rule. However, it would appear that the tort is no easier to establish now, in an age where the judiciary assume a sophisticated consumer, well aware of advertisers' techniques and tricks. So Whitford J in *McDonalds v Burgerking*[99] warned that

---

[93] 68 RPC (1951) 261, CA.

[94] Hodson LJ in *Cellactite v Robertson* CA [1957] CLY 1989: the general proposition of the law is: comparison—yes; but disparagement—no. [95] [1895] AC 154, p. 171.

[96] See also *Alcott v Millers* [1904] 91 LT 722 allegation that the plaintiff's wood paving-blocks were 'in a rotten condition'. According to Walton J in *De Beers v International General Electric* [1975] 2 All ER 599, p. 606 : 'this is a statement which is obviously intended to be taken and would be taken seriously by a reasonable man.'

[97] [1975] 2 All ER 599.

[98] The plaintiff also alleged unfair competition and unlawful interference with trade.

[99] [1986] FSR 45, p. 46. In fact, the case involved an example of a poor effort at comparative advertising, as given the obscure wording 'nobody appears to have recognized the fact that it was a comparative advert at all' (p. 54).

'advertisements are not to be read as if they were some testamentary provision in a will or a clause in some agreement with every word being carefully considered and the words as a whole being compared.'[100] Indeed, Jacob J noted in *Vodafone Group plc v Orange Personal Communications Services Ltd*[101] that the public are used to the ways of advertisers and are aware that they will stress the good points of a product and ignore others. The more precise the claim, he suggested, the more likely the reasonable man would take it seriously; the more general or 'fuzzy', the less so. So in *Vodafone* itself, the public would have realized that a generalized comparison[102] between prices for the parties' competing telecommunications services would involve the inclusion of different tariffs (based on personal or business use).

Calculated to cause harm

As well as being false, the statement must be calculated to cause actual economic harm.[103] The statement must be likely to produce this result.[104] Though often mingled with the discussion of malice in the tort,[105] it is a separate ingredient in the tort.[106] Stable J in *Wilts United Dairy v Robinson*[107] discussed the necessary fault element in the tort, concluding that where this was present the defendant would be liable: 'provided it is clear from the nature of the falsehood that it is intrinsically injurious.' By this he meant 'being inherent in the statement itself'. This requirement stems from the fact that the original action for slander of title involved false-

---

[100] Sentiments echoed by Michael Crystal QC (sitting as a deputy High Court judge) in *BT v AT&T Communications*, unreported 18 December 1996 where he noted that the court should not encourage a microscopic approach to the construction of a comparative advert and should remember that the public expect hyperbole.

[101] [1997] FSR 34.

[102] Cf. *Compaq Computer Corp v Dell Computer Corp Ltd* [1992] FSR 93, Aldous J, the defendant was liable for the tort where he made direct comparisons in price between his and the plaintiff's computer systems, where the systems being compared were materially different (re storage capacity and access time).

[103] Glidewell LJ *Kaye v Robertson* [1991] FSR 62, p. 67, necessary for the plaintiff to prove that the words were calculated to produce damage.

[104] This is the paraphrase offered for the statutory concept of 'calculated to cause pecuniary damage' offered by Mahon J in *Customglass Boats v Salthouse Boats* [1976] RPC 589, p. 602.

[105] *Kaye v Robertson* [1991] FSR 62, p. 67, Glidewell LJ: 'malice will be inferred if it be proved that the words were calculated to produce damage and that the defendant knew when he published the words that they were false or was reckless as to whether they were false or not.'

[106] The issue of the distinction between malice and 'calculated to cause harm' was raised in the litigation between the former MP Rupert Allason and the *Daily Mirror* and its then political journalist Alastair Campbell In *Allason v Campbell* 9 February 1995, CA (unreported, Lexis transcript) Balcombe LJ stated that it would be open to the plaintiff at trial to argue that 'calculated' contained an element of intention.

[107] 57 RPC 220, p. 237.

hoods uttered at peril. No intention to harm had to be shown, but the falsehoods had to be inherently harmful.

Publication

Malicious falsehood, like passing off, is a three-party tort: the falsehood must be uttered to a third party (or indeed the world at large). Whether a negligent or accidental publication is sufficient is undecided[108] but it would appear that republication that is the natural and probable consequence of the initial deliberate publication will render the defendant liable. Thus in *Cellactite & British Uralite v HH Robertson Co*[109] the defendant's sales manual advised their salesman how to denigrate the plaintiff's rival product. The defendant banned the republication of this manual but a sub-agent provided a copy to an architect who, as a result, did not use the plaintiff's product or thereafter recommend its use. The Court of Appeal held the defendant liable, on the basis that the republication to the architect was the natural and probable result of the original publication.

Malice[110]

Whitford J observed in *McDonalds v Burgerking*[111] that 'passing off lies close very often to trade libel, but whereas in passing off motive may be quite immaterial, to succeed in trade libel . . . malice must be established'.

Whenever it arises the word 'malice' causes problems of interpretation[112] and no more so than with the tort of malicious falsehood. At one stage in the tort's development, it would appear that the requirement to show malice was parallel to the requirement in defamation, where malice is used to rebut the defence of privilege. In effect, once the defendant had uttered a falsehood, inherently likely to harm the plaintiff's title, he would be liable unless he could raise a privilege. And that privilege could then be defeated by the plaintiff's proof of malice. However, it is clear now that 'malice' is a key feature of the tort and must be proved by the

---

[108] Brazier, M., and Murphy, J., *Street on Torts*, 10th edn. (London: Butterworths, 1999), p. 139. Rogers, above, n. 67, para. 20.4 believes it is not sufficient, though cf. Restatement (Second) of Torts, s.630.

[109] [1957] CLY 1989.

[110] Note in the absence of malice the court might be persuaded to grant a declaration, *Loudon v Ryder (no 2)* [1953] 1 CH 423. This was a wrongful claim that property belonged to the estate of the intestate, not the plaintiff. There was no malice, but a declaration was granted as to the plaintiff's title.

[111] [1986] FSR 45, p. 60. Reversed by Court of Appeal, [1987] FSR 112.

[112] Scrutton LJ in *Shapiro v La Morta* 40 TLR (1923) 201, p. 203, 'the terms "malice" and "malicious" have caused more confusion in English law than any judge can hope to dispel'.

claimant in all cases of malicious falsehood. The need to prove malice confined this tort 'to those circumstances which were most incontrovertibly unjustifiable'.[113]

The real issue has become to pinpoint the definition of malice applied by the courts. A review of case law reveals that malice can be proved in various ways, summarized by Heydon[114] as either personal spite, or an intention to injure the plaintiff without just cause or excuse or knowledge of the falsity of the statement. However, it is difficult to separate personal spite from the related concepts of improper motive and intention to injure without lawful excuse.[115] It is simpler and consistent with leading modern case law to define malice as either[116] 'motive' malice (*mala fides* means that an honest belief will not negate liability)[117] or 'deceit' malice (lies where indifference as to the effect on the claimant will not negate liability). The absence of good faith is, therefore, due to either the knowledge of falsity or the malicious intention. So, 'if you publish a defamatory statement about a man's goods which is injurious to him, honestly believing that it is true, your object being your own advantage and no detriment to him, you obviously are not liable'.[118]

(i) Malice as lies: 'deceit malice'

Knowledge of the falsity of a statement, calculated to harm the claimant is sufficient to constitute malice.[119] It would appear that recklessness as to the falsity of the allegations is sufficient, on a par with deceit: in *Cellactite & British Uralite v HH Robertson Co*[120] inaccuracies in a sales manual concerning the plaintiff's rival product were 'reckless statements',

---

[113] Cornish, above, n. 43, p. 652. Guidance on the timing of a submission of no case to answer on the issue of malice was given by the Court of Appeal in *Barker v Statesmen and National Publishing Co Ltd, The Times,* 8 January 1997.

[114] Heydon, above, n. 1, p. 83.

[115] See the formula in *Customglass Boats v Salthouse* [1976] 1 NZLR 36, p. 49 'an intention to injure the true owner of the property or alternatively, publishing with an indirect or dishonest motive', Mahon J. In the case itself, the defendant knew the statements in question were untrue. McCardie J in *BRT v CRC* [1922] 2 KB 260, p. 269 'the mere absence of just cause or excuse is not of itself malice ... malice in its proper and accurate sense is a question of motive, intention or state of mind'.

[116] Thus Lord Herschell LC in *White v Mellin* [1895] AC 154, p. 160 said that by the word maliciously: 'it may be intended to indicate that the object of the publication must be to injure another person and that the advertisement is not published bona fide merely to sell the advertiser's own goods or at all events that he published it with a knowledge of its falsity.'

[117] Aiming to injure, rather than to further legitimate concerns will render the motive impermissible

[118] Stable J in *Wilts United Dairies v Robinson* 57 RPC 220, p. 237.

[119] Knowledge may be 'imposed' on the defendant by the claimant alerting him to the untruth of the statement: *Customglass Boats* [1976] 1 NZLR 36, p. 49. The issue of knowledge is resolved not by recourse to 'the reasonable man' but an assessment of whether the defendant did or did not believe what he alleged: *Pitt v Donovan* (1813) 1 M&S 639, p. 649.

[120] 1957 CLY 1989, CA.

amounting to malice. And in *Spring v Guardian Assurance* Glidewell LJ in the Court of Appeal adopted Lord Diplock's definition of malice from the defamation case, *Horrocks v Lowe*.[121] Here recklessness, whether the statement be true or not was held to constitute malice.[122] In *Joyce v Sengupta*[123] the Court of Appeal reinstated the plaintiff's claim for malicious falsehood where she sought to prove malice on the 'calculated, reckless indifference to the truth or falsity of the allegations'. There she alleged that the defendant journalist had published the police suspicions as though they were fact and without taking any steps to check or verify them. This 'cavalier way' of work was reckless.

Once 'deceit malice' is established,[124] there is no need to prove an intention to harm the claimant. This was underlined by Stable J in *Wilts United Dairies v Robinson*.[125] 'If a man says something that he knows to be untrue, it is malicious *ipso facto*, because he has said something that is false and something that he knows to be false.' Here the defendants were selling old second-hand stock of the plaintiff's condensed milk as their current product. Stable J was satisfied that there was no intention to harm the plaintiff: 'I do not think the defendants cared a row of pins whether it was the plaintiff's milk or whether it was one of their competitors' milk. They were not there to harm the plaintiff, what they were out for was making a profit, to advantage themselves.' The malice consists in the fact that what the defendant published he knew to be false,[126] 'albeit that your only object is your own advantage and with no intent or desire to injure the person in relation to whose goods the falsehood is published'.[127] For Prosser:[128] 'the deliberate liar must take the risk that his statement will prove to be economically damaging to others if a reasonable man would have foreseen the possibility.'

---

[121] [1975] AC 135, p. 150.

[122] Atkin LJ in *Shapiro v La Morta* 40 TLR (1923) 201, CA, was willing to go no further than this: 'I shall assume that a statement made by a man who knows that it is likely to injure and knows that it is false is made maliciously, and I shall make the same assumption if he knows that it is likely to injure and has no belief whether it is true or false and makes it recklessly, not caring whether it is true or false.'

[123] [1993] 1 WLR 337.

[124] This may be difficult, though note Jacob J in *Vodafone Group plc v Orange Personal Communications Services Ltd* [1997] FSR 34, p. 45 'there may be cases where a man makes a statement which is so self-evidently false that if he says he believed it, one does not believe him'. An example of this was surely *Kaye v Robertson* [1991] FSR 62 where the inability to consent was apparent.

[125] 57 RPC 220.

[126] 57 RPC 220, p. 237.

[127] 'I say "intrinsically", meaning not deliberately with the intention to injure but as being inherent in the statement itself.' It is submitted, therefore, that the apparent view of Maugham J in *Balden v Shorter* [1933] Ch 427 that knowledge of the falsity is no more than evidence of improper motive and, therefore, malice is too restricted. This was, indeed, the conclusion of Stable J in *Wilts United Dairies v Robinson* 57 RPC 220.

[128] Above, n. 1, p. 438.

The fact that liability can rest on knowledge of falsity underlines the importance of the additional need to show that the falsehood was 'calculated to harm the plaintiff'. This was underlined by Glidewell LJ in *Kaye v Robertson*:[129] 'malice will be inferred if it be proved that the words were calculated to produce damage and that the defendant knew when he published the words that they were false or was reckless as to whether they were false or not.' In the case itself the defendants were malicious because they knew (either at the time or subsequently) that the plaintiff was in no condition to give informed consent.[130]

(ii) Malice as mala fides: 'motive malice'

The majority of claims for malicious falsehood will involve allegations that the defendant knew of the falsity of his statements. However, it is also in theory possible to bring a successful claim for malicious falsehood where though the defendant believes the statement to be true, the defendant has impermissible motives in making his statements, calculated to injure the claimant.[131] Various phrases are used in the case law to cover this concept of fault in the tort: *mala fides*;[132] dishonest object;[133] indirect object;[134] improper motive.[135] In addition some cases look for an intention to harm the claimant,[136] without just cause or excuse.[137] The issue appears to be the motivation of the defendant, in which case this method of proving fault must be fairly limited; self-interest being the motivation for most

---

[129] [1991] FSR 62, p. 67.

[130] In theory that was the issue in the case: whether he consented to the interview or not.

[131] This was contended by plaintiff's counsel in *Spring v Guardian Assurance*, [1993] 2 All ER 273, p. 288 (at Court of Appeal level) and appeared to be accepted by Glidewell LJ, who referred to the speech of Lord Diplock in *Horrocks v Lowe* [1975] AC 135.

[132] *Halsey v Brotherhood* (1881) 19 Ch D 386 Lord Coleridge LCJ asserted that the disparagement must be untrue *and mala fide*, for the purpose of injuring the plaintiff and not in the bona fide defence of the defendant's own property.

[133] e.g. *Greers Ltd v Pearman & Carder Ltd* (1922) 39 RPC 406 Scrutton LJ: 'maliciously . . . in the sense of being made with some indirect or dishonest motive.'

[134] e.g. *Greers Ltd v Pearman & Carder Ltd* (1922) 39 RPC 406 for Bankes LJ the question is whether the defendant knew the facts to be untrue 'maliciously, for this purpose means with some indirect object'—here the lack of belief meant malice was present.

[135] *Halsey v Brotherhood* (1881) 19 Ch D 386, p. 389 per Lord Coleridge CJ requires a 'distinct intention to injure, apart from the honest defence of the defendants' own property'. *Balden v Shorter* [1933] Ch 427, p. 430: 'malice in the law of slander of title and other forms of injurious falsehood means some dishonest or otherwise improper motive', Maughan J.

[136] Montague Smith J in *Steward v Young* (1870) LR 5CP 122, p. 127: 'it is essential also that it should be malicious . . . [not] in the worst sense, but with intent to injure the plaintiff.'

[137] *Ratcliffe v Evans* [1892] 2 QB 524 focuses on 'damage wilfully and intentionally done without just cause or excuse'. Maliciously was defined as 'without just cause or excuse' by Lord Davey in *Royal Baking Powder Co v Wright, Crossley & Co* (1901) 18 RPC 95, p. 99 (and this was quoted by McCardie J in *British Railway Traffic v CRC Co* [1922] 2 KB 260, p. 268). The same phrase was used in *Joyce v Motor Surveys Ltd* [1948] Ch 252.

competitors. Collins MR asserted in *Dunlop v Maison Talbot*:[138] 'it [is] not malice if the object of the interference was to push his own business . . . To make the act malicious it must be done with the direct object of injuring that other person's business.'

This area has perhaps caused the most uncertainty in the tort. In part this is due to the failure to distinguish 'deceit malice' from 'motive malice'. In some of the leading cases where motivation is referred to, the defendant in fact clearly had the requisite knowledge to be liable anyway. So in *Joyce v Motor Services Ltd*[139] the defendant was liable for deliberately lying to others that the plaintiff had moved address and ceased trading. Again in *London Ferro-Concrete Co Ltd v Justicz*[140] though it was clear that the court believed that the defendant wanted the contract that had gone to the plaintiff for himself, the defendant did not believe in the truth of the statements made about the plaintiff's building methods. Such cases are less than helpful in attempting to define the requisite intention in the tort.

Case law is consistent with the view that for this tort intention (in the absence of the knowledge of falsity) has a restricted meaning. To seek to undermine the plaintiff's trading position by honest means, in order to gain a competitive advantage is the nub of successful and permissible competition: this was accepted in *Allen v Flood*.[141] Rather 'motive malice' involves both intentional infliction of harm and impermissible motivation.[142] As in simple conspiracy, it is the motivation that leads to liability in the absence of any unlawful act. *Mala fides* is the key to this form of fault in the tort, making it difficult to use motive malice to succeed. Moreover, such insistence on malice serves to protect free speech, a point that has surfaced in some of the case law (see discussion of the tort's rationale, below).

So deliberately harming for no good reason will lead to liability as 'one who speaks for such a malevolent purpose takes the risk that what he says will prove to be false'.[143] As Stable J noted in *Wilts United Dairy v Robinson*: 'if you publish a statement which turns out to be false but which you honestly believe to be true, but you publish that statement not for the

---

[138] (1904) 20 TLR 579, p. 581, CA. Collins MR, p. 579 '[the threat to sue] must be shown to have been made for the purpose of injuring the plaintiffs and not for the bona fide protection of the defendant's rights and without any real intention of following up by action or other legal proceedings'.

[139] [1948] Ch 252.   [140] 68 RPC (1951) 261, CA.

[141] [1898] AC 1.

[142] Though *dicta* might lead to any intentional infliction of harm being sufficient as in *Dunlop Co Ltd v Maison Talbot* (1904) 20 TLR 579, p. 581: 'it was not malice if the object of the writer was to push his own business, though at the same time it might incidentally injure another person's business', other *dicta* (especially in that case) indicate that motivation is the key to this form of malice.

[143] Prosser, above, n. 1, p. 437.

purpose of protecting your own interests and achieving some advantage to yourself but for the purpose of doing him some harm' you will be liable because the object that you had in mind was to injure the plaintiff and not to advantage yourself. Conversely, an intention to promote yourself, though at the expense of the plaintiff is lawful. 'A statement . . . does not give a ground for action merely because it is untrue and injurious to the plaintiff; there must be also the element of *mala fides* and a distinct intention to injure the plaintiff apart from the honest defence of the defendant's own property.'[144]

The issue is probably best encapsulated in *Spring v Guardian Assurance*, where the Court of Appeal accepted that the test of what constitutes malice in the tort of malicious falsehood is the same as the test in relation to the torts of libel and slander.[145] The idea appears to be that where falsehoods concerning the claimant's economic interests are concerned, an honest belief in the truth of the disparagement (or whatever shape the falsehood takes) is sufficient to negate liability unless the freedom to speak the truth is being misused.[146]

Damage: economic harm[147]

Derived from an action on the case, the tort is not actionable *per se*.[148] Damage has to be proved and must arise 'naturally and reasonably' from the false statement.[149] Though where commercial loss was inevitable the courts were prepared to accept proof of general business loss, rather than

---

[144] Lord Coleridge CJ, *Halsey v Brotherhood* (1881) 19 ChD 386, p. 389 basing his judgment on *Wren v Weild* (1969) LR 4QB 730. See also *White v Mellin* [1895] AC 154 per Lord Herschell, p. 160: 'by [malice] it may be intended to indicate that the object of the publication must be to injure another person, and that the advertisement is not published bona fide merely to sell the advertiser's own goods, or at all events, that he published it with a knowledge of its falsity.'

[145] See [1993] 2 All ER 273, p. 288 per Glidewell LJ, agreeing with the trial judge. The plaintiff appealed on the issue of negligence and breach of contract ([1995] 2 AC 296).

[146] To cite Lord Diplock from *Horrocks v Lowe* [1975] AC 135: 'for some purpose other than that for which the privilege is accorded by law, e.g. venting personal spite or ill will . . . idea of improper motive . . . dominant motive to get private advantage unconnected with the duty/interest which constitutes the reason for the privilege.'

[147] Brazier and Murphy, above, n. 108, p. 140, n. 16 note that when the damage complained of is physical injury, this tort is presumably not applicable but *Wilkinson v Downton* [1897] 2 QB 57 must be relied on.

[148] *Malachy v Soper* 1836 3 Bing NC 371, p. 383 Tindal CJ: there must be 'an express allegation of some particular damage resulting to the plaintiff'. Bowen LJ in *Ratcliffe v Evans* [1892] 2 QB 524, CA, p. 532: 'in all actions . . . on the case where the damage actually done is the gist of the action, the character of the actions themselves which produce the damage and the circumstances under which these acts are done must regulate the degree of certainty and particularity with which the damage done ought to be stated and proved.'

[149] *Hadden v Lott* (1854) 15 CB 411.

loss of particular customers (as in *Ratcliffe v Evans*),[150] this requirement proved to be a severe limit on the tort. Indeed, it rendered the action 'rare in the extreme' according to the Porter Committee.[151] Unlike deceit, where harm to the claimant may be readily quantifiable, in cases of malicious falsehood, the harm will often be the failure to obtain an expected benefit.

However, this situation has largely been remedied by s.3 of the Defamation Act 1952. This relieves the claimant from the requirement to prove damage where the words complained of are calculated to cause the claimant pecuniary damage in respect of any trade or business.[152] As Cane notes: 'since the tort is most often used in commercial contexts, in practice the typical plaintiff will not have to prove pecuniary loss—it will be presumed from the making of the statement.'[153] Sir Donald Nicholls V-C noted in *Joyce v Sengupta*[154] that s.3 was not limited to nominal damages as : 'the whole purpose of s.3 was to give the plaintiff a remedy in malicious falsehood despite the difficulty of proving loss. A plaintiff is seldom able to call witnesses to say they ceased to deal with him because of some slander that had come to their ears . . . s.3 was enacted to right this injustice. The section would fail in its purpose if, whenever relied on it could lead only to an award of nominal damages.'

The concept of damage has been expanded recently to include economic harm rather than commercial interests *per se*. So in *Kay v Robertson*[155] Glidewell LJ stated the relevant damage to be the harm to the plaintiff's 'potentially valuable right to sell the story of his accident and his recovery when he is fit enough to tell it'. This would obviously be seriously prejudiced by the defendant's publication, falsely claimed to be based on an interview to which the plaintiff had freely consented.[156] In

---

[150] A question of good sense according to Bowen LJ in *Ratcliffe v Evans* [1892] 2 QB 524, p. 533: 'in an action for falsehood producing damage to a man's trade, which in its very nature is intended or reasonably likely to produce, a general loss of business, as distinct from the loss of this or that known customer, evidence of such general decline of business is admissible.' In *Ratcliffe v Evans* the plaintiff's business was stated to have ceased by the defendant's weekly newspaper. The plaintiff proved a general loss of business since the publication; but he gave no specific evidence of the loss of any particular customer or orders, by reason of such publication. Court of Appeal held the general loss of business was sufficient.
[151] (1948) Cmnd. 7536.
[152] 'That regrettable tradesmen's charter' per Weir, T., *A Casebook on Tort*, 9th edn. (London: Sweet & Maxwell, 2000), p. 578. If the words complained of are not in respect of 'any office, profession, calling, trade or business' they must be published in writing or 'other permanent form' (which includes broadcasting).
[153] Cane, above, n. 39, p. 99.   [154] Ibid. 96.   [155] [1991] FSR 62, p. 68.
[156] Though obviously the Court of Appeal were anxious to provide some sort of *ad hoc* privacy right, the tort of malicious falsehood meant that the remedy provided for Kaye was limited to the newspaper withdrawing its allegation that their story had been obtained with consent. After *Douglas v Hello! Ltd*, The Times, 16 Jan 2001, CA it would appear that privacy is protected by the action for breach of confidence.

Joyce v Sengupta,[157] the Court of Appeal accepted that the false allegation that the plaintiff had been forced to leave her job with the Princess Royal because of acts in breach of confidence was likely to cause her pecuniary loss by seriously prejudicing her opportunity to obtain other employment, requiring trust and confidence. It is clear, therefore, that the tort is not limited to traders (as is passing off)[158] and can protect against[159] interference with prospective economic advantage, even of a non-commercial nature.

Thus the focus of the tort is on economic loss. There is no recovery for injury to reputation.[160] Lord Denning in *Fielding v Variety Incorporated*[161] asserted that damages for injured feelings were also not available in a claim for malicious falsehood. This latter assertion, however, was questioned by the Court of Appeal in *Joyce v Sengupta*, Sir David Nicholls V-C finding it 'manifestly unsatisfactory'[162] that damages for distress should not be available. This view has found favour with the Court of Appeal in *Khodaparast v Shad*.[163] There, aggravated damages were awarded where the defendant had circulated material falsely indicating that the claimant had been involved in telephone sex services. She obtained damages not only for the consequent loss of her job as a teacher, but also for the anxiety and distress caused.[164] However, it is still clear that injury to reputation is not covered by this tort.[165]

Defences

It is difficult to see what defences of justification could apply to this tort, given genuine disputes as to title or comparative quality are not actionable anyway. As such there are no defences of qualified privilege or fair comment as in defamation.[166] However, commentators agree[167] that should the occasion of the malicious falsehood be one which would attract the defence of absolute privilege in the tort of defamation (e.g. statements in judicial proceedings), then there would also be a defence in

---

[157] [1993] 1 AER 897.

[158] So in *Kaye v Robertson* [1991] FSR 62, the plaintiff could not succeed in passing off because he was not in the position of a trader in relation to his interest in the story about his accident and recovery.

[159] Fleming, J., *The Law of Torts*, 9th edn. (Sydney: LBC Information Services, 1998), p. 716.

[160] This is only protected by the tort of defamation.

[161] [1967] 2 QB 841, p. 850.

[162] [1993] 1 All ER 897, p. 907, CA.

[163] [2000] 1 All ER 545, CA

[164] Both before and after the issue of proceedings.

[165] See e.g. Otton LJ in *Khodaparast v Shad* [2000] 1 All ER 545, pp. 557–8.

[166] See Mummery J in *CHC Software v Hopkins and Wood* [1993] FSR 241.

[167] See e.g. Brazier and Murphy, above, n. 108, p. 141 and Rogers, *Gatley on Libel and Slander*, above, n. 67, para. 20.9.

the tort of malicious falsehood.[168] So in *Samuels v Coole & Haddock*[169] the defendants were a firm of solicitors who had successfully supported their application to strike out the plaintiff's third-party proceedings against their clients by an affidavit, sworn by one of their partners. The plaintiff sought to sue the defendants for malicious falsehood, on the basis of allegations made against him in that affidavit. There was held to be no cause of action as the affidavit came within the absolute privilege of witness immunity.

RELATIONSHIP TO DEFAMATION AND PASSING OFF

To attempt a comprehensive consideration of the tort of malicious falsehood, it is necessary to compare it with the other torts that protect against published falsehoods: passing off and defamation. With recent cases the distinction between malicious falsehood and these torts has become less clear.

Defamation

Malicious falsehood and defamation have different origins. Thus their focal points are different: malicious falsehood involves a complaint about damage to purely financial interests, whereas defamation concerns aspersions on the reputation and good name of the claimant himself.[170] As Weir pithily comments, malicious falsehood 'guards not honour but wealth',[171] leading him to complain that 'it would perhaps have been better if corporations had not been allowed to sue in defamation but limited to malicious falsehood'.[172]

Thus the difference is said to be between 'attacking a man personally and merely injuring him in his trade by attacking his goods or professional technique'. But commercial attacks may often reflect on the trader personally so that there may be a fine line between libelling the goods only and libelling the claimant's conduct of his business.[173] Indeed, the

---

[168] The Restatement (Second) of Torts, s.635 accepts this but s. 646A also applies the defence of qualified privilege (or 'conditional privilege') However, the examples given are based on facts where the defendant acts bona fide and has an honest belief. It is not clear how the tort in America is affected by the free speech provisions of the First Amendment. This does apply to commercial free speech, because it disseminates information: *Virginia State Board of Pharmacy v Virginia Citizens Consumer Council Inc* (1976) 425 US 748.

[169] [1997] 9 CL 591

[170] To paraphrase Mummery J in *CHC Software v Hopkins and Wood* [1993] FSR 241, p. 247.

[171] Above, n. 152, p. 579.   [172] Ibid., p. 579.

[173] 'One of the grey areas of the common law', per Cooke P in *Bell-Booth Group v AG* [1989] 3 NZLR 148, p. 153. The line between an imputation against a company's product and an

point that the same facts can give rise to both actions[174] was successfully used by the plaintiff in *Joyce v Sengupta*. The defendant alleged that the plaintiff, as the Princess Royal's maid, had stolen her employer's letters and handed them to a national newspaper, as a result of which she was about to be dismissed. She sued in malicious falsehood rather than defamation, in order to obtain legal aid to pursue her claim. In the lower court, the judge had struck out her claim as he found it was in essence a case of libel for which no legal aid was available (and which would entitle the defendant to jury trial).[175] However, the Court of Appeal found that she had a choice of action where defamatory allegations could damage her financial prospects as well as her reputation and in making that choice there was no abuse of the process of the court. The effect on her future employment prospects could constitute the relevant economic harm for the tort.[176]

Passing off

The torts of passing off and malicious falsehood have some similarities. Both protect claimants against misrepresentations published to others and both are limited to deserving claimants: either because the passing off must be likely to harm the claimant's own goodwill or because the disparagement must concern the claimant. In neither tort, therefore, are mere false representations published in the course of trade sufficient, though such representations might affect the claimant's trade. This point was most recently (and strongly) made by Jacob J in *Schulke & Mayr UK Ltd v Alkapharm UK Ltd*,[177] denying liability for 'false representations in the air'.

---

imputation reflecting in a defamatory way on the company can be a fine one: see the speech of Lord Halsbury LC in *Linotype Co Ltd v British Empire Type-Setters Machine Co Ltd* (1899) 81 LT 331.

[174] See e.g. *Griffiths v Benn* (1911) 27 TLR 346, p. 350, Cozens-Hardy MR : 'words used, though directly disparaging the goods, may also impute such carelessness, misconduct or want of skill in the conduct of his business by the trader as to justify an action of libel.'

[175] It should be noted, however, that now the Community Legal Service, does not fund either malicious falsehood or defamation litigation. A malicious falsehood action survives the death of either party. However, the limitation period for both defamation and malicious falsehood is now the same (1 year) by reason of Defamation Act 1996 which substituted s.4A Limitation Act 1980.

[176] They also alleged that the damages for malicious falsehood would be insignificant compared to the costs involved. In *Khodaparast v Shad* [2000] 1 All ER 545, the allegations (that the claimant was involved in the telephone sex industry) were also clearly defamatory but she relied on malicious falsehood. Though damages for injury to reputation were not available, the Court of Appeal awarded damages for anxiety and distress (as well as damages for the pecuniary harm, consequent on the loss of her job).

[177] [1999] FSR 161, p. 166 where the court rejected the assertion that mere false statements about the defendant's own product could amount to malicious falsehood as 'a far-reaching and bold submission It would mean that many aspects of the law of passing off would become unnecessary . . . it would involve a very considerable extension by the common law into a field mainly regulated by statute.'

However, though Salmond, who coined the term 'injurious falsehood', listed passing off as one variety of that tort, important differences in the necessary ingredients of the two torts have emerged as they developed. Passing off (clearly the more important of the two) involves the defendant misrepresenting something about *his* trade that affects the claimant's goodwill; malicious falsehood concerns an attack on the claimant's economic interests pure and simple. So typical claims of passing off involve the defendant attempting to use the success of the claimant's product or business rather than denigrate it, as in the typical malicious falsehood claim.[178] It is possible to broadly distinguish between these torts on the ground that passing off protects against misappropriation (protecting the claimant's goodwill against diversion), while malicious falsehood protects trading reputation (against lies or spiteful falsehoods).[179] However, such a stark distinction of course fails to reveal the possible scope of either tort (and in particular the modern, subtle versions of passing off).

Yet it is important to realize that the boundaries between the two torts have never been sharply drawn and it has always been apparent that the same facts might give rise to both torts, especially where there is a misrepresentation concerning the quality of the plaintiff's goods being sold by the defendant. This was the case in *Wilts United Dairies v Robinson*.[180] Here the plaintiff's inferior stock was sold as fresh stock. The plaintiff established both passing off and malicious falsehood—malice being based on knowledge that the stock was out of date.[181] However, for malicious falsehood there must be sufficient reference to the claimant,[182] rather than simply assertions concerning the defendant (one of the reasons the claim for malicious falsehood, pleaded in the lower court, failed in *Bristol Conservatories*).[183]

---

[178] Fleming, above, n. 159, p. 783.

[179] Heydon, above, n. 1, distinguishes them as theft (passing off) and the destruction of business reputation (malicious falsehood), p. 85.

[180] [1958] RPC 94, CA.

[181] Again, falsely to claim your inferior goods are the claimant's would threaten the claimant's economic interests, so that if malice were involved it would amount to both passing off and malicious falsehood

[182] Which is why it is argued (in Ch. 10) that cases such as *Customglass Boats v Salthouse Bros* [1976] 1 NZLR 36 (false statement that the defendant had designed the plaintiff's boat) are better categorized as examples of the tort of unlawful interference with trade Indeed, cases such as this (and *Danish Mercantile Co Ltd v Beaumont* (1950) 57 RPC 111, Roxburgh J., defendant's false claim to be the only authorized importer of certain machinery, when this was in fact the plaintiff) might now also involve the tort of passing off.

[183] So there was insufficient reference in *Bullivant v Wright* (1897) 13 TLR 201 where the defendant falsely claimed to have designed and manufactured the cable way in fact designed and manufactured by the plaintiff. The court felt this was closer to a passing off claim. In *Copydex Ltd v Noso Products Ltd* [1952] 69 RPC 38, Vaisey J was not certain whether the defendant alleging that his product was 'as seen on television' (when in fact it was the

RATIONALE AND POTENTIAL

In line with the economic torts generally, competition is not unduly hampered by this tort. As Cane notes: 'although the tort can be committed in non-competitive situations, the main justification for the requirement of malice is probably the preservation of competition.'[184] Trade rivalry is viewed as healthy and a reason to limit the scope of disparagement actions. So the need to show malice indicates the common law's unwillingness to become immersed in the disputes of trade rivals. Excessive competition of a particular kind is prevented, but in line with judicial caution as to the role the courts (and claimants) should play in policing competitive practice. The tort is based on the 'peril factor'.[185] Though the tort has obvious affinities with the tort of unlawful interference with trade, it focuses not on unlawful acts but on falsehoods uttered at peril.[186] The fact that they are intrinsically likely to harm the claimant and are either known to be lies (deceit malice) or uttered *mala fides* (motive malice) justifies the imposition of liability.

The claimant must show that he was the focus of the falsehood and that it was calculated to harm him (as well as being malicious) in order to succeed. False statements about the defendant's own goods *per se* are not actionable as malicious falsehoods. Only deserving claimants can complain, therefore, and this again provides a serious brake on the tort's development. This was recognized by Jacob J in *Schulke & Mayr UK Ltd v Alkapharm UK Ltd*,[187] where the plaintiff sought to argue that a false advertisement extolling the virtues of the defendant's rival product but not naming the plaintiff's product was capable of amounting to malicious falsehood, on the basis that there would be diversion of sales and trade loss. For Jacob J this was 'a far reaching and bold submission' that would mean that many aspects of the law of passing off would become unnecessary. He felt, in line with the traditional caution of the common law in such matters, that any such extension would be better decided by Parliament.

Thus lies *per se* are not tortious, nor can the claimant claim on the basis that the defendant has gained an unfair competitive advantage by such lies. As Cornish comments: 'in contrast with passing off at the end of the

plaintiffs', though anonymously) was passing off, slander of title or malicious falsehood. However, in *Customglass Boats v Salthouse Bros* [1976] 1 NZLR 36 there was no direct or indirect reference to the plaintiff.

[184] Above, n. 39, p. 99.

[185] Which factor overrides the normal approach to liability contained in the general tort of unlawful interference with trade: see Ch. 5.

[186] See discussion in Ch. 10.

[187] [1999] FSR 161.

nineteenth century, the courts deliberately confined this tort to those circumstances which were most incontrovertibly unjustifiable.[188] Their caution stands as one of the chief barriers to the adoption of any broad conception of unfair competition.'[189]

Unlike passing off, the public interest in preventing consumer misinformation is not debated in cases involving the tort—presumably because it is so severely limited. However, another public interest does have a role in shaping the tort and in its application. The need to prove malice also underlines the concern of the common law to preserve commercial free speech, where there is a bona fide basis for making the statements, though they may be damaging to the claimant. In a competitive economic system it is desirable to facilitate the discussion of the merits of products. Misinformation causes inefficient market choices (which is a key reason for the expansion of the tort of passing off). However, if it becomes too easy to use the tort of malicious falsehood, then discussion might be stifled. Of course, this point is even stronger where the statements emanate from a consumer group[190] or investigative journalists.

This seemed to be acknowledged by Lord Denning in *Drummond-Jackson v BMA*.[191] Here the defendants published a scientific paper attacking the plaintiff's dental technique. The plaintiff succeeded in defamation but there was a strong dissent from Lord Denning who felt that such criticism might be in the public interest and as such the plaintiff should have been allowed only the protection of malicious falsehood, with the need to show malice and that it was untrue. He noted: 'it would be a sorry day if scientists were to be deterred from publishing their findings for fear of libel actions. So long as they refrain from publishing personal attacks, they should be free to criticize the systems and techniques of others. It is in the interests of truth itself. Were it otherwise, no scientific journal would be safe.'[192] In effect the tort would appear to be in line with the European Convention on Human Rights at least as it relates to freedom of speech. Of course, if malicious falsehood becomes detached from commercial interests pure and simple and meanders into the area of privacy protec-

---

[188] As the major expansion of the tort of malicious falsehood took place right at the end of the nineteenth century, it did not develop parallel equitable protection, as the tort of passing off had done.

[189] Above, n. 43, p. 652.

[190] There has been a worrying trend in the USA for individual states to create Food Libel statutory wrongs to protect against agricultural disparagement—where that food is produced in the state concerned and therefore obviously economically important. One of these statutes was used (unsuccessfully) by Texas cattlemen in 1996 against Oprah Winfrey, the television personality who, on a syndicated TV show, allowed an unedited claim by one of her guests that a large portion of American herds was infected by BSE to be broadcast, together with her reaction.

[191] [1970] 1 WLR 688.

[192] Ibid. 695.

tion (as it appeared to do in *Kaye v Robertson*),[193] then the courts may need to reassess this attitude.

The concern to protect free speech is also reflected in the approach to interim injunctions in claims of malicious falsehood.[194] Where the words are not manifestly false (as they were in *Kaye v Robertson*) and the defendant intends to justify a statement, the defamation rule contained in *Bonnard v Perryman*[195] is applied and no interim injunction will be awarded. This was confirmed by Oliver J in *Bestobell Paints Ltd v Bigg*.[196] Here the alleged falsehood was the defendant's allegation that the plaintiff's paint was of poor quality, to put pressure on the plaintiff to settle a claim arising from its purchase and use. The court would not restrain the publication of this statement, the reason for such a policy being 'that an interlocutory restraint in any case that is not obvious would operate as an unjust fetter on the right of free speech and the defendant's liberty (if he is right) to speak the truth'.[197] Such a view is of course strengthened by Article 10 of the European Convention on Human Rights. Its protection of freedom of expression includes the protection of information of a commercial nature.[198]

CONCLUSION

The tort is little used and has largely been superseded by more effective, specific statutory provisions covering 'threats' actions and comparative advertising. It is therefore no more than a safety net for the most extreme forms of falsehood that directly affect the claimant's economic interests and has no greater role to play than that in the competitive process. However, whether the courts will develop the scope of malicious falsehood, working towards a publicity or privacy right, might prove interesting in the future.

---

[193] [1991] FSR 62, CA. Although the CA in *Douglas v Hello! Ltd*, The Times, 16 Jan 2001, saw privacy as protected by the action for breach of confidence.

[194] *Microdata v Rivendale Ltd* [1991] FSR 681, p. 689; *Macmillan Magazines Ltd v RCN Publishing Co Ltd* [1998] FSR 9

[195] [1891] 2 Ch 269, applied earlier to malicious falsehood in *Coulson v Coulson* (1887) 3 TLR 846.   [196] [1975] FSR 421 Oliver J.

[197] Oliver J contended that in such a case the principle in *American Cyanamid* did not apply: Aldous J in *Compaq Computer Corp v Dell Computer Corp* [1992] FSR 93 disagreed (though in a case where the defendant could not justify his statements). However, the essence of the claim must relate to free speech: cf. *Microdata v Rivendale*, [1991] FSR 681, where the claim was essentially one for interference with contractual performance.

[198] Freedom of expression is of course subject to such formalities 'necessary in a democratic society . . . for the protection of the reputation or rights of others'. As far as the granting of injunctions is concerned, the test of necessity would appear to be less strict in relation to speech connected with commercial competition: *Markt Intern Verlag GmbH and Klaus Beerman v Germany* (1990) 12 EHRR 161, ECHR.

8

Passing Off

Though the origins of passing off are 'doubtful',[2] by the nineteenth century the tort was seen as originating in the tort of deceit. However, unlike deceit, it gives the trade rival, rather than the deceived customers, the right to sue. The classic case involves a trader, innocently or otherwise, 'passing off' his goods as the goods of the claimant.[3] Lord Diplock noted in *Erven Warnink BV v Townend (J.) & Sons (Hull) (Advocaat)*[4] that the particular setting for the development of the tort was the defendant's improper use of trade marks or their equivalent 'so as to produce in potential purchasers the belief that his goods were those of a rival trader'. However, the tort has been the subject of continued development 'to meet changing conditions and practices in trade',[5] a development fuelled 'by modern market research which uncovers buyers' patterns providing alternative stratagems to simple counterfeit'.[6]

Given deceit was the key to the tort, fraud had been a necessary ingredient at common law. Had this restriction proved permanent 'the tort might well have been reduced to impotence as a means of economic regulation in the public interest'.[7] However, equity was prepared to focus on

[1] For a detailed discussion of the tort see Wadlow, C., *The Law of Passing-off*, 2nd edn. (London: Sweet & Maxwell, 1995). Also Cornish, W. R., *Intellectual Property*, 4th edn. (London: Sweet & Maxwell, 1999), ch. 16 and Morison, W., 'Unfair Competition and Passing Off', 2 Syd L Rev (1956) 50.

[2] Per Harman J in *Serville v Constance* (1954) 71 RPC 146, pp. 148–9. The Elizabethan case alleged subsequently to be its origin may not have involved passing off at all (it is unclear whether its essence was deceit or defamation). For detail see Morison, above, n. 1, p. 54 and generally, Schechter, F., 'The Historical Foundation of the Law Relating to Trade-Marks' 40 Har L Rev (1927) 813; Wadlow, above, n. 1, pp. 9–31. The term 'passing off' was first used in *Parry v Truefitt* (1842) 49 ER 749 (although only in the headnote).

[3] Though Morison, above, n. 1, p. 56 notes that: 'the earlier definitions of passing off . . . indicate that it is essential that there should be this composite act of selling together with a misrepresentation before the tort is made out.' In *Spalding v Gamage*, it was accepted by the House of Lords that it is the misrepresentation that creates liability even without actual passing off. Lord Parker expressly preferred the proposition 'nobody has any right to represent his goods as the goods of somebody else' to the proposition 'nobody has the right to pass off his goods as the goods of somebody else'.

[4] [1979] AC 731, p. 740.

[5] Falconer J in *Lego System Atkieselskab v Lego M Lemelstrich* [1983] FSR 155.

[6] *Comitie Interprofessional du Vin de Champagne v Wineworths Group Ltd* [1991] 2 NZLR 432, Jeffries J.

[7] Morison, above, n. 1, p. 54.

the effect of the misrepresentation, rather than the defendant's intention[8] so an injunction might be awarded to restrain a misrepresentation that was calculated to deceive, even though there was no proof of an intention to deceive. The merger of the two strands of development after the Judicature Acts 1873 left the tort one of strict liability, based on misrepresentation.[9] Judicial debate as to the nature of the interest that the tort protected culminated in the speech of Lord Parker in *Spalding v Gamage*,[10] the case which provided the twentieth-century framework for the tort. He identified 'goodwill'[11] or customer connection as the property right which will be protected against certain sorts of misrepresentation. In doing so, he expressly rejected any property in the trade mark or name in itself.[12]

Decisions such as *Spalding*, with their emphasis on the protection of customer connection meant that the tort was now no longer 'anchored . . . to the name or trade mark of a product or business'.[13] Passing off became a tort of misrepresentation, to protect 'those indicators in the process of commercial competition by which one rival distinguishes his products or services from those of another'.[14]

However, though fraud is no longer a necessary ingredient in the tort,[15]

---

[8] See *Millington v Fox* (1838) 3 My & Co 338.

[9] Registered trade mark protection was the result of pressure for surer protection (without having to prove a trade reputation) and for reciprocal international protection against foreign imitation of British marks: see Cornish, above, n. 1, pp. 598–601. See also Carty, H., 'The Development of Passing Off in the Twentieth Century', in Dawson, N., and Firth, A. (eds.), *Trade Marks Retrospective*, vol. 7, *Perspectives on Intellectual Property* (London: Sweet & Maxwell, 2000).

[10] (1915) 32 RPC 273, HL. Lord Diplock in *Advocaat* [1979] AC 731, p. 740 pointed out that the House of Lords in *Reddaway v Banham* did not identify the legal nature of the right being protected by a passing off action so that it remained 'an action *sui generis* which lay for damage sustained or threatened in consequence of a misrepresentation of a particular kind'.

[11] The concept of goodwill is a broad one. According to Lord Diplock in *Advocaat* [1979] AC 731, p. 741 it is 'perhaps best expressed in words used by Lord Macnaghten in *IRC v Muller & Co's Margarine Ltd* [1901] AC 217, pp. 223–4 "the attractive force that brings in custom"'.

[12] As had Lord Herschell in *Reddaway v Banham* [1896] AC 199, HL, which in fact provides the classic discussion of the tort at the end of the nineteenth century. And see also the *dicta* of Lord Kingsdown in *Leather Cloth Co Ltd v American Leather Cloth Co Ltd* (1865) 11 ER 1435, p. 1438 that the defendant should not be allowed to use 'names, marks, letters or other indicia by which he may induce purchasers to believe that the goods which he is selling are the manufacture of another person' (the *dicta* is in fact based on the view of Lord Langdale in *Perry v Truefitt* (1845) 49 ER 749, p. 752).

[13] Lord Scarman, *Cadbury Schweppes v Pub Squash Co* (*Pub Squash*) [1981] RPC 429 PC.

[14] Cornish, W. R., 'The International Relations of Intellectual Property' 52 CLJ (1993) 46, p. 52.

[15] Though there is the doctrine of 'instruments of deception' discussed by Wadlow above, n. 1, p. 230: 'primary liability for passing-off attaches to the business actually responsible for goods which are inherently likely to deceive ultimate purchasers or consumers.' It was thought that this version of the tort was complete when the defendant disposed of the goods complained of. However, the doctrine appears to have been widened in the Court of Appeal decision in *British Telecommunications plc and others v One In A Million*, [1999] FSR 1. There the defendants by registering the plaintiffs' company names as their domain names ('cyber-

the presence of fraud is significant. If the object of the defendant is to deceive, the court is ready to infer that deception has occurred or is likely to do so: 'why should we be astute to say that [the defendant] cannot succeed in doing that which he is straining every nerve to do.'[16] Thus the presence of fraud may lead the court to apply the tort even where it is not clear that all elements of the tort have been proved. The most recent examples of this approach are the series of cases involving 'scams'[17] to gain financial advantage by registering a famous name and demanding that the 'legitimate' owner pay for its return. Attempts to extort[18] money by registering famous names as company names or domain names were held in the late 1990s to constitute passing off.[19] Unfortunately this loosening of the strict requirements of the tort is sometimes also applied where the court disapproves of the trading methods of a defendant, in the absence of fraud as such. This process is aided by the fact that the majority of passing off cases are at interlocutory level only.

The classic case of passing off involves a misrepresentation as to the source of the goods.[20] However, case law throughout the twentieth century revealed the elastic nature of this action.[21] Each expansion has

---

squatting') as part of a scam to gain money from the legitimate owners, were held liable for passing off, threatened passing off and instruments of deception. Aldous LJ discerned a jurisdiction to grant injunctive relief where the defendant is equipped with or intending to equip another with an instrument of deception. That included the registration of a name, even one that is not inherently deceptive.

[16] Lindley LJ *Slazenger v Feltham* (1889) 6 RPC 531, p. 538.

[17] The term was used by Laddie J in *Direct Line Group Ltd v Direct Line Estate Agency Ltd* [1997] FSR 374, p. 376.

[18] The term was used by Lightman J in *Glaxo plc v Glaxo-Wellcome Ltd* [1996] FSR 388, p. 390: 'the price for not damaging the goodwill.' The 'scam' is dependent on an implied threat that otherwise the claimant's goodwill will be exploited (either by the defendant's trading under that name or 'equipping' others so to do).

[19] Given the defendant in such a case does not usually make use of the company or domain name himself but rather offers it for sale, there would appear to be some difficulty in showing either a misrepresentation or harm to goodwill (the names were not being used nor were there threats to use them in a manner that would constitute passing off). However, the courts in these cases get round the problem by not alluding to it(!), by finding evidence of a threatened passing off, sufficient for an interlocutory injunction or by extending the concept of 'instrument of deception' to include liability where a defendant is equipped with or intends to equip another with an instrument of fraud. See *Direct Line Group Ltd v Direct Line Estate Agency Ltd* [1997] FSR 374 Laddie J (the defendants had a reputation for incorporating famous trade marks as company names); *Glaxo plc v Glaxo-Wellcome Ltd* [1996] FSR 388, Lightman J; *British Telecommunications plc v One in a Million* [1999] FSR 1, CA. Morcom, C., 'Leading Cases in Passing Off' in *Trade Marks Retrospective*, above, n. 9, p. 19 notes the similarities in the earlier case of *Panhard et Levassor v Panhard-Levassor Motor Co Ltd* [1901] 2 Ch 513.

[20] This was acknowledged to be so even at the end of the twentieth century: Lord Oliver in *Reckitt & Colman Products v Borden Inc* [1990] RPC 340, HL summarized the general proposition contained in the tort as 'no one may pass off his goods as those of another'.

[21] 'This most protean of torts', Lord Diplock in *Advocaat* [1979] AC 731, p. 740. And see Carty, above, n. 9.

fuelled the hopes of those who seek to refashion the tort into an action for misappropriation or unfair competition, particularly those involved in the character merchandising industry and those involved with prestige products or names.

This process has been aided by the lack of sufficient judicial and academic analysis of the tort, arguably because it is perceived to be a 'minor' tort.[22] Yet the high number of reported cases on passing off provide evidence of its continued importance in the commercial world. Obviously part of its importance is as a parallel action to the statutory protection of trade marks.[23] Where registrable marks are concerned, the addition of the tort to what is a claim under the registered system sometimes adds little. Yet, the tort—and its fluid nature—may be vitally important when the aggrieved party has failed to register or believes that the technical requirements of the registered system may defeat his claim.[24] However, the tort has an importance of its own, separate from its protection of trade marks as such.[25] Passing off is a misrepresentation tort and there may be various possible settings for the relevant confusion concerned, not just trade names or product 'get up'.[26] Lord Scarman in *Cadbury Schweppes Pty Ltd v Pub Squash Co Pty Ltd*[27] (*Pub Squash*), acknowledged that the misrepresentation could involve other descriptive material 'such as slogans or visual images, which radio, television or newspaper advertising campaigns can lead the market to associate with the plaintiff's product, provided always that such descriptive material has become part of the goodwill of the product'.[28] So advertising or promotional campaigns could give rise to misrepresentations as to source or quality. In *Elida-Gibbs*

---

[22] 'As a so-called minor tort it has merited generally no more than superficial attention and analysis by legal scholars. The legacy of this neglect is the growth of a tort of which the legal rules and the factual limitations of their application are unclear and in respect of which the policy underlining the development of it has remained sadly obscure', Phillips, J., and Coleman, A., 'Passing off and the "common field of activity"' 101 LQR (1985) 242, p. 242.

[23] Now contained in the Trade Marks Act 1994.

[24] Combinations of features may not be a sign under the Trade Marks Act 1994. Moreover, with registered trade marks, ss.10 and 11 contain specific defences. Overall Wadlow concludes, above, n. 1, p. 2: 'Passing-off and the law of registered trade marks deal with some overlapping factual situations, but deal with them in different ways and from different standpoints.'

[25] The Trade Marks Act 1994 does not affect the law relating to passing off: TMA 1994, s.2(2).

[26] There are hints of this even in the nineteenth-century cases see e.g. James LJ in *Singer Manufacturing Co v Loog* (1880) 18 ChD 395, p. 412, false representation by use of 'any mark, sign or symbol, device *or other means* . . .' [emphasis added].

[27] [1981] RPC 429, p. 490.

[28] The test for this is whether 'the product has derived from the advertising a distinctive character which the market recognizes'.

v Colgate-Palmolive,[29] an expensive new promotional campaign for the plaintiffs' product was protected against the defendants' use of a similar theme. Again in *United Biscuits v Asda*, the promotion of the defendants' rival product (marked as their own product) by a cuddly sea-bird character was restrained in view of the plaintiffs' distinctive use of a cuddly sea-bird for their product.[30]

It is in this area of advertising and promotional activities generally that pressure is growing for expansions in the tort. Claimants increasingly use allegations of connection misrepresentation to prevent 'free-riders' on their success. Their pressure has been intensified given the judicial acceptance of public awareness of merchandising, licensing, and diversification. Similarly, allegations of product misrepresentation have led to attempts to push the tort towards a more general protection against 'unfair trading'. Given there is such pressure on the tort at the start of the twenty-first century it is regrettable (though hardly surprising), that 'far from unfolding in a consistent and purposeful manner, passing off has largely developed through *ad hoc* decisions which were often motivated primarily by a desire not to let an unmeritorious defendant escape liability'.[31] It is apparent that the time is ripe for a review of its present scope, against an assessment of its rationale. Only by such a process can the legitimacy or otherwise of any extensions be judged.[32]

INGREDIENTS: THE CLASSIC TRINITY

The modern definition of the tort was considered by Lord Diplock in *Warnink (Erven) BV v Townend and Sons Ltd*, the '*Advocaat*' decision.[33] He presented his definition as part of an analysis of the English law on unfair trading and certainly on the facts of the case itself sought thereby to expand the scope of the tort. For Lord Diplock five characteristics[34] provide the essence of the tort: a misrepresentation; made by a trader in the course of trade; to his prospective customers; calculated to injure the

---

[29] [1983] FSR 95.

[30] An ambience or image may be protected: see the Canadian cases referred to by Wadlow, above, n. 1, pp. 448–9. In the lower court in *My Kinda Town v Soll* [1983] RPC 407 the plaintiffs had alleged that passing off could result from the defendants' use of a similar style in their restaurants, but this issue was not before the Court of Appeal.

[31] Wadlow, above, n. 1, p. 11.

[32] Naresh, S., 'Passing-off, Goodwill and False Advertising: New Wine in Old Bottles', 45 CLJ 97 (1986), p. 97 complains that the 'judicial extensions of liability . . . owe more to the manipulation of verbal formulae than to clarification of its foundations'.

[33] [1979] AC 731, HL.

[34] Derived from the so-called 'drinks' cases (see below, n. 178) and *Spalding v Gamage* (1915) 84 LJ Ch 449.

business or goodwill of another; and which does so injure or probably will do so. The reformulation has been followed in some leading cases, sometimes amalgamated with aspects of Lord Fraser's case-based test in *Advocaat*, which emphasized the need for goodwill in the jurisdiction.[35]

This redefinition has underlined the fact that the classic case is not a good rule-of-thumb test and that the varieties of passing off are species that have to be accommodated within the single genus tort. However, the danger of this formulation is that it appears to loosen the tort from its strict requirement that goodwill—actual customer connection—must be harmed (harm to 'business' is a wider concept). Moreover, Lord Diplock's speech implicitly allows for wide extensions of the tort, with policy factors providing the necessary limits to such extensions. So, Lord Diplock accepted that not all factual situations that presented the five characteristics of his test would give rise to a cause of action in passing off.[36] The court could decide that there was present some 'exceptional feature which justifies, on grounds of public policy withholding from a person who has suffered injury in consequence of the deception practised on prospective customers or consumers of his product a remedy in law against the deceiver'. This uncertainty has no doubt fuelled attempts to restructure the tort. Following *Advocaat* it was forecast by some that the tort of passing off had all but been enlarged into a general unfair trading tort.[37]

However, given the complexity of this definition and the uncertainty that it contains within itself it is perhaps not surprising that subsequently the courts have usually applied a simpler formula for the tort: the so-called 'classic trinity'.[38] This defines the tort by reference to three concepts: misrepresentation, goodwill, and damage. In *Consorzio del Prosciutto di Parma v Marks and Spencer plc*[39] (*Parma Ham*) Nourse LJ commented 'although these speeches [of Lord Diplock and Lord Fraser]

---

[35] For Megarry VC in *BBC v Talbot* [1981] FSR 228 and the Court of Appeal in *Budweiser* [1984] FSR 413 both statements are to be taken as a composite, while Kerr J in *Nishika Corp v Goodchild* [1990] FSR 371 stated 'these two statements of principle complement one another, Lord Diplock emphasizing what has been done by the defendant to give rise to the complaint and Lord Fraser what the plaintiff has to show as a prerequisite of complaining'. However, the Court of Appeal in *Bristol Conservatories* disapproved of this [1989] RPC 455, p. 460.

[36] The use of policy to limit the tort was noted by Browne-Wilkinson VC in *Mirage v Counter Feat Clothing* [1991] FSR 145, p. 156.

[37] Dworkin, G., 'Unfair Competition: Is the Common Law developing a new Tort?' [1979] EIPR 241, p. 241 comments on the 'widespread speculation as to whether the courts are at last developing a general common law doctrine of unfair competition'.

[38] Lord Oliver in *Reckitt & Colman Products v Borden Inc* [1990] 341, HL; *Consorzio del Prosciutto di Parma v Marks and Spencer plc* [1991] RPC 351, CA; *Harrods Ltd v The Harrodian School Ltd* [1996] RPC 697. That said, Lord Diplock's 'test' was used by Laddie J and the Court of Appeal in *Chocosuisse Union des Fabricants de Chocolat v Cadbury Ltd* [1999] RPC 866.

[39] [1991] RPC 351, CA.

in *Advocaat* are of the highest authority, it has been my experience . . . that they do not give the same degree of assistance in analysis and decision as the classical trinity'. He went on to note the 'welcome return' to the classic approach to the elements of a passing off action.[40] All three concepts of the classic trinity link together and shape each other: none are freestanding. The misrepresentation must be 'calculated to injure' the claimant's goodwill and must cause or be probable to cause such damage.[41] It is customer reliance on the misrepresentation which is the cement between the three elements of this trinity.[42] Adherence to the classic trinity has meant thus far that the tort does not present the courts with the unenviable (and commercially suspect) task of determining what is 'unfair' trading practice or commercial 'misappropriation'.

Without a precise application of all elements of the trinity the focus of the tort changes (as will be discussed below). Although 'confusion' and 'reputation' are sometimes referred to as equivalents of the key ingredients, the use of such alternatives can mask the rationale and obscure the basis of the tort. So, the concept of misrepresentation is not synonymous with the notion of confusion,[43] a point stressed by Lord Scarman in *Pub Squash*[44] and reiterated by Robert Walker J in *Barnsley Brewery Co Ltd v RBNB*[45] where he noted: 'there must be deception, whether intentional or unintentional. If there is no deception, mere confusion or the likelihood of confusion is not sufficient to give a cause of action.' Indeed, the Court of Appeal in *Bristol Conservatories Ltd v Conservatories Custom Built Ltd*[46] noted that there may be passing off without confusion.[47] Nor is reputation alone sufficient: goodwill means actual customer connection or experience. So in *Anheuser-Busch Inc v Budejovicky Budvar PN*[48] (the Budweiser case) the plaintiffs were unable to succeed in their claim of passing off because, though their product's name was well known by a substantial number of people in England, it was not at that time available in the English market. More recently, Walker J in *Nice and Safe Attitude Ltd v Piers*

---

[40] [1991] RPC 351, p. 369.

[41] See Lord Diplock in *Advocaat* [1979] AC 731 and Lord Oliver in *Reckitt & Coleman Products v Borden Inc* [1990] RPC 340, HL.

[42] Laddie J in *Elvis Presley Trade Marks* [1997] RPC 543, p. 554 underlined the importance in the tort of reliance on the misrepresentation, in the context of a character merchandising case. The appeal was dismissed by the Court of Appeal: [1999] RPC 567.

[43] Despite the lapse by Nourse LJ in *Consorzio del Prosciutto di Parma v Marks and Spencer plc* [1991] RPC 351, CA.

[44] [1981] RPC 429, pp. 490–1. [45] [1997] FSR 462, p. 467.

[46] [1989] RPC 455.

[47] Wadlow, above, n. 1, p. 9: 'the concept of confusion was irrelevant when the misrepresentation was such as to leave no room for confusion.' See also Lord Greene MR in *Marengo v Daily Sketch & Daily Graphic Ltd* [1992] FSR 1 (decided in 1946) CA: 'no one is entitled to be protected against confusion as such . . . the protection against which a man is entitled is protection against passing off which is quite a different thing from mere confusion.'

[48] [1984] FSR 413.

Flook[49] pointed out that reputation, devoid of commercial goodwill, was insufficient.

The three areas that require elucidation are therefore: misrepresentation; goodwill; and damage. The main extensions in the tort in this century have centred on the misrepresentations that are actionable in passing off. However, both goodwill and the related concept of damage have been subjected to pressure (both direct and indirect) to expand.

(A) MISREPRESENTATION

Establishing likely deception

The importance of misrepresentation in the tort was reaffirmed by the Privy Council in *Pub Squash*. They held that there must be a misrepresentation, not merely misappropriation of a trade value. So when the plaintiffs opened up the market for a 'macho' soft drink,[50] they could not allege passing off against the defendants using the same idea and advertising theme. Lord Scarman also noted that any deception must be more than momentary and inconsequential. Of course, as *Spalding* acknowledged, the misrepresentation must relate to the claimant's goodwill, discussed in detail below.

The proper approach in establishing deception is to ask the question: 'is the defendant's use of such mark, name or get up calculated to deceive?' For the Court of Appeal in *Neutrogena Corp v Golden Ltd*[51] the correct legal test on the issue of deception was whether on the balance of probabilities a substantial number of members of the public would be misled into purchasing[52] the defendants' product in the belief it was the plaintiffs' product.[53] It is the overall impact of the evidence that is important. The assessment of likely deception may not present the court with too taxing a problem. In *Miss World (Jersey) Ltd v James ST Productions Ltd*[54] the plaintiffs, the proprietors of the goodwill in the title 'Miss World'

---

[49] [1997] FSR 18.

[50] It was to be presented as a man's drink, fit for, and a favourite with, rugged masculine adventurers', Lord Scarman [1981] RPC 429, p. 486.

[51] [1996] RPC 473.

[52] In theory post-sale confusion (after any disclaimers or distinguishing labels at the point of sale had been removed) could lead to liability, provided there was clearly a continuing representation. However, thus far courts in this country have rejected such claims as improbable: see *Bostick Ltd v Sellotape GB Ltd* [1994] RPC 556 Blackburne J and the views of Jacob J in *Hodgkinson & Corby Ltd v Wards Mobility Ltd* [1995] FSR 175, p. 182. An allegation of post-sale confusion has led to a successful claim for passing off in New Zealand: *Levi Strauss & Co v Kimbyr Investments Ltd* [1994] FSR 335 but the claim seemed to focus on 'dilution'.

[53] See also *Mont Blanc Simplo GmbH v Philip Morris, The Times*, 2 February 2000.

[54] [1981] FSR 309, CA.

objected to the release of the defendants' film, 'Miss Alternative World'. This was a grotesque take-off of the original. The plaintiffs had sought to argue that the public might believe that the plaintiffs had gone into the business of making 'adult' films. However, the Court of Appeal found there to be no danger of confusion. Similarly in *Morning Star Co-Operative v Express*[55] the plaintiffs, who published the *Morning Star* newspaper, objected to the proposed title *Daily Star*, for the defendants' new newspaper. However, given the difference in the name, get-up, content, sales technique, and readership, the two papers were so different in every way that 'only a moron in a hurry would be misled'.[56]

When assessing likely deception, the court will consider the likely customers[57] of the goods/services (provided that such persons use ordinary care and attention).[58] The particular expertise or lack of it of such persons will be taken into account. In *Bollinger v Costa Brava Wine Co Ltd* (*Spanish Champagne*), for example, Danckwerts J noted: 'there is . . . a considerable body of evidence that persons whose life or education has not taught them much about the nature and production of wine but who from time to time want to purchase "champagne", as the wine with the great reputation, are likely to be misled by the description "Spanish Champagne".'[59] Conversely, in *Guccio Gucci SpA v Paolo Gucci* the evidence of likely customers was gained by a survey that involved filter questions to identify likely customers of 'upmarket' products.[60]

Moreover, the setting for the purchasing transaction will be taken into consideration. How the goods will be displayed and purchased are important considerations.[61] So in *Kimberley-Clark Ltd v Fort Sterling Ltd*, a case involving supermarket purchases, the UK Marketing Director for the plaintiffs asserted (without challenge) that a typical weekly family shopping trip among the 25,000 different items ranged in a typical supermarket takes forty minutes and that items such as toilet paper (the subject of

[55] [1979] FSR 113, p. 117, Foster J.

[56] And see *United Biscuits (UK) Ltd v Burton Biscuits* [1992] FSR 14. Here there were similar products with similar get-up; however, Vinelott J found no 'appreciable risk that an ordinarily prudent shopper would be likely to confuse the two' (p. 27).

[57] The customers do not have to be paying customers: see *Illustrated Newspapers Ltd v Publicity Services Ltd* [1938] Ch 414 where the defendants inserted advertisements into the plaintiff's magazines, provided free in hotels. Both the public and advertisers were held to be the misrepresentees. And on a similar point see *Mail Newspapers v Insert Media* [1987] RPC 521.

[58] Danckwerts J in *Bollinger v Costa Brava Wine* [1961] 1 All ER 561.

[59] [1961] 1 All ER 561, p. 567.

[60] [1991] FSR 89.

[61] See *HFC Bank plc v Midland Bank plc* [2000] FSR 176: 'potential customers wishing to borrow what, for them, may be quite large sums of money from a bank can reasonably be expected to pay rather more attention to the details of the entity with whom they are doing or seeking to do business', Lloyd J.

the case) were subject to rapid purchasing decisions.[62] The case, therefore, had to be judged on the basis of the reaction of normal but busy shoppers.

Obviously it is ultimately a matter for the judge whether such deception is likely,[63] and forming his own opinion he is not confined to the evidence of witnesses called at the trial.[64] Yet it is commonplace for the parties in a passing off action to present expert evidence and survey evidence, particularly on the likelihood of deception and the issue of sufficient goodwill or trade reputation.[65] Expert evidence may be particularly useful where a specialist product or market is involved.[66] However, the experience a judge possesses as an ordinary shopper or customer would enable him to assess the likelihood of confusion as well as any other in a typical claim. So Blackburne J in *Dalgetty Spillars Food Ltd v Food Brokers Ltd*[67] found the evidence of marketing experts inadmissible, given the case concerned a straightforward food product. As for survey evidence,[68] it is often the case that the methodology of such surveys will be open to attack and certainly pure questionnaire evidence will seldom be helpful. Jacob J in *Neutrogena Corp v Golden Ltd*[69] noted that oral evidence of those alleged to have been deceived or confused was to be preferred.

In *Advocaat*, Lord Diplock singled out the *defendant's* customers as the targets of the deception. Wadlow comments that this analysis highlights the fact that the defendant in a passing off case is always concerned to benefit himself: 'so that misrepresentations to the plaintiff's customers are only made because they are potentially customers of his.' In the typical case,[70] however, whether it is the claimant's or the defendant's customers who are to be considered is largely an academic question, given that the misrepresentation is normally broadcast 'to the world at large'.[71] Nor,

---

[62] In another supermarket purchase case, *Jif Lemon* [1990] 1 WLR 491 it was held to be no defence that the customers would not have been misled if they were more literate, careful, perspicacious, wary or prudent.

[63] A point stressed by Lord Parker in *Spalding v Gamage* (1915) 32 RPC 273, p. 286.

[64] Indeed, even if there is no evidence of confusion, the court could still conclude that passing off has been established: Sir Raymond Evershed MR *Electrolux Ltd v Electrix Ltd* (1954) 71 RPC 23, CA.

[65] For a full discussion see Wadlow, above, n. 1, pp. 564–78. Such evidence, effectively presented, may decide the case at interlocutory level by tipping the balance beyond the *de minimis* level—Inglis, A., and Stevens, P., 'Passing Off—Charities, Descriptive Names and Nicknames' 18 3 EIPR (1996) 166, p. 167.

[66] Accepted by Blackburne J in *Dalgetty Spillars Food Ltd v Food Brokers Ltd* [1994] FSR 504 and Ferris J in *NAD Electronics Inc v NAD Computer Systems Ltd* [1997] FSR 380.

[67] [1994] FSR 504.

[68] Laddie J in *Kimberley-Clark Ltd v Fort Sterling Ltd* [1997] FSR 877 found the survey of limited quantitive value but of some qualitative value as to the attractiveness of the plaintiff's name and the extent to which it overwhelmed the defendant's name.

[69] [1996] R.P.C. 473.

[70] However, when cases on character merchandising are examined, we will see that this is an important consideration.

[71] Wadlow, above, n. 1, p. 221.

indeed, are the recipients of the misrepresentation necessarily customers at all. Passing off may involve misrepresentations made only to suppliers. In *Woolworth (FW) & Co v Woolworths (Australasia) Ltd*[72] the defendants were buying agents for an Australian company that had a similar name to the plaintiffs. Suppliers were confused by the similarity in names and an injunction was granted.[73] In *Waterford Wedgewood plc v David Nagli Ltd*[74] there were no misrepresentations made directly to the public by the defendants, but they were liable for the misrepresentations made by them to the representatives of companies to whom they had supplied counterfeit goods.

Obviously an association or perceived association between the field of activity of the claimant and that of the defendant is always a relevant factor to be taken into account.[75] The closer the parties' lines of business, the easier it is to establish likely confusion. But there is no requirement that the parties should be in competition. In one area of trading, character merchandising, a rule appeared to be emerging demanding a 'common field of activity' before a connection misrepresentation could be alleged.[76] This would rule out passing off protection for this industry, precisely because the parties—a character merchandiser (who is likely to be involved in the entertainment industry) and a defendant trader—are involved in totally different businesses. However, as the requirement of a 'common field of activity' was not evident in passing off cases outside character merchandising[77] and was not a characteristic identified by Lord Diplock in the *Advocaat* case,[78] judges in character merchandising cases began to rely less on the doctrine of 'common field of activity' and focus more on the real issue: was there a misrepresentation? Once there was judicial acknowledgement of public awareness of licensing and character

---

[72] (1930) 47 RPC 337.

[73] See also *Chelsea Man Menswear Ltd v Chelsea Girl Ltd* [1987] RPC 189.

[74] [1998] FSR 92.

[75] Millett LJ in *Harrods v Harrodian School* [1996] RPC 697, p. 714 and see Stephenson LJ in *Stringfellow v McCain Foods (GB) Ltd* [1984] RPC 501, p. 541.

[76] See Phillips and Coleman, above, n. 22, p. 242. This approach was initiated by Wynn-Parry J in *McCulloch v Lewis A May* [1947] 65 RPC 58, where a radio presenter alleged that his professional name was being used to sell a breakfast cereal. Wynn-Parry J held that as the parties were not in the same business, 'the plaintiff is not engaged in any degree in producing or marketing puffed wheat', passing off was not available. This analysis was followed by Walton J both in *Wombles v Wombles Skips* [1977] RPC 99 and in *Taverner Rutledge v Trexapalm Ltd* [1977] RPC 275.

[77] See *News Group Newspapers Ltd v Rocket Record Co Ltd* [1981] FSR 89. Slade J (p. 104): 'the very diversity of the consumer goods which the plaintiffs already market under the catchword "Page 3" might make some readers of the *Sun* newspaper to be more inclined to think that a record in this guise was connected with the plaintiffs.' See also *Alfred Dunhill Ltd v Sunoptic SA* [1979] FSR 337.

[78] Lord Diplock in *Advocaat* 'although the plaintiff and defendant were not competing traders in the same line of business'.

merchandising,[79] there was no problem in identifying possible connection misrepresentations in this field. In *Mirage Studios* v *Counter Feat Clothing Co Ltd*,[80]the court awarded an injunction for the first time in a character merchandising case on the basis of an arguable connection misrepresentation.[81]

Where confusion does arise, it may be a defence that the defendant is making honest concurrent use of the same name or of his own name. With honest concurrent use (which may arise, e.g., where there has been a break up of a company structure)[82] there is no liability as any goodwill is shared between the parties.[83] As far as use of the defendant's confusingly similar personal name is concerned, though a man 'must be allowed to trade in his own name',[84] even honest use may be limited to use as a business name (rather than trading in the name as a mark on goods).[85] Indeed, Ferris J in *NAD Electronics Inc v NAD Computer Systems Ltd* noted that whatever rights there may be in respect of the use of a surname do not extend to the use of a first name, still less a nickname.[86]

---

[79] In *IPC Mags v Black and White Music* [1983] FSR 348, p. 350 Goulding J acknowledged the 'arrival' of character merchandising, for judicial purposes. And see Lord Brightman in the *Holly Hobbie* case [1984] RPC 329, p. 356: 'I am quite prepared to accept that character merchandising, in the sense of the exploitation of the reputation of famous names by making them available to a wide variety of products, has become a widespread trading practice on both sides of the Atlantic.'

[80] In *Mirage Studios v Counter Feat Clothing* [1991] FSR 145 Sir Nicholas Browne-Wilkinson V-C. The plaintiffs were copyright owners of popular cartoon characters, the Teenage Mutant Ninja Turtles. The plaintiffs did not manufacture or market any goods themselves. Rather, a major part of the plaintiffs' business income arose from royalties received from such licensing of the character. The defendant, obviously to cash in on the craze, produced his own humanoid Turtle characters—sporting rather than martial arts turtles—and licensed their use to various clothing manufacturers.

[81] However, reliance on that misrepresentation still has to be shown, despite the views of Browne-Wilkinson V-C in that decision. This may prove difficult: see discussion below. Where a defendant appears bent on fraud the court may not be prepared to listen to arguments about lack of reliance. So, in *Pearson Bros v Valentine & Co* [1917] RPC 267 Peterson J, the defendants supplied their own goods without explanation in response to orders for the plaintiffs' goods. Their defence was that the goods were clearly labelled and the customers ought, therefore, to examine the goods and not be deceived. Rejecting this defence, Peterson J remarked: 'a man makes a representation at his own risk and the person to whom it is made is entitled to rely upon the representation made.'

[82] See e.g. *Habib Bank Ltd v Habib Bank AG Zurich* [1981] 1 WLR 1264 at 1278–9 (Oliver LJ); *Scandecor Development AB v Scandecor Marketing AB* [1998] FSR 500.

[83] For detailed consideration see Wadlow, above, n. 1, pp. 493–500.

[84] Lord Simonds *Marengo v Daily Sketch* (1948) 65 RPC 242, p. 251. Wadlow, above, n. 1, pp. 482–1 casts doubt on this 'defence'.

[85] This distinction is drawn by Lord Simonds *Marengo v Daily Sketch* (1948) 65 RPC 242, p. 251 and see *Parker Knoll Ltd v Knoll International* [1962] RPC 265. In *William Grant & Sons v Glen Catrine Bonded Warehouse, The Times*, 1 May 1999, it was noted that 'provided that the necessary element of confusion was satisfied, even the bona fide use on goods of a genuine personal or geographic name by another trader might be restrained' (Lord Cameron, OH).

[86] [1997] FSR 380 p. 392. See also *Biba Group Ltd v Biba Boutique* [1980] RPC 413, p. 420.

THE CATEGORIES OF MISREPRESENTATION THAT ARE RELEVANT
TO PASSING OFF

After *Spalding,* passing off became 'a tort dealing with certain kinds of commercial misrepresentations'.[87] Cases of express misrepresentation are rare[88]—more commonly the representation in passing off is implied.[89] As Goulding J remarked in *Morny Ltd v Ball & Rogers*:[90] 'the passing off action goes beyond simple representation into a field of greater refinement and subtlety.' The expansion in the number of misrepresentations relevant to the tort reflects this fact. It is useful to separate out the acknowledged categories of misrepresentation that may give rise to an action in passing off, especially as it has been argued that the claimant's claim can be won or lost on the type of misrepresentation they allege.[91] An obvious question is whether this is an exhaustive list.[92] Arguably it is, given that to date only source or quality misrepresentations have qualified for inclusion in the tort, reflecting the classic functions of trade marks generally.[93]

Though it would be neat if a precise chronological development of these extensions could be pinpointed, this is not the case. Rather, extensions have emerged over a period of time, sometimes not acknowledged as an advance in the tort for some years. So though it is always the Court of Appeal's decision in *Spalding v Gamage* that is cited as authority for misdescription of the claimant's product being a relevant misrepresentation in the tort, in fact that decision was pre-empted by the judgment of Swinfen-Eady J in *Teacher v Levy.* There the plaintiff distillers of Scotch

---

[87] Morison, above, n. 1, p. 57.

[88] *Wheeler & Wilson Manufacturing v Shakespear* (1869) 39 LJ Ch 36.

[89] It is sometimes difficult to predict whether the court will accept the claimant's construction of an alleged implied representation. Thus in *Mornay Ltd v Ball & Rogers* (1975) Ltd [1978] FSR 91 Goulding J the defendants marketed a gift package containing the plaintiffs' bathfoam and an unidentified scent, not of the plaintiffs' manufacture. The court accepted that there was arguably a representation that as the two articles were packaged together the plaintiffs had authorized the (inferior) scent to be sold in conjunction with their product.

[90] [1978] FSR 91, p. 92.

[91] Thus Walton, A., 'A Pervasive but often not Explicitly Characterized Aspect of Passing Off' vol. 19 [1987] EIPR 159 points out (p. 163): 'in *Combe v Scholl* . . . the defendants plainly recognized that if they could only get the case running on the normal "get-up" lines they would undoubtedly succeeded and this is the Aunt Sally that they skilfully set up.' This was rejected by the judge, the plaintiffs did not allege that the get up was distinctive of the plaintiffs, but rather that the public would believe that the product was the same as the plaintiffs'. What the plaintiffs did was to allege a 'product misrepresentation' rather than a 'source misrepresentation'.

[92] Lord Parker in *Spalding v Gamage* (1915) 32 RPC 273 'it would be impossible to enumerate or classify all the possible ways in which a man may make the false representation relied on'.

[93] See discussion, below.

whisky sold a whisky of a special quality and brought an action against the defendant pub owners, alleging that they had sold the plaintiff's inferior whisky as their superior product. The judgment highlights the fraud of the defendant and contains no discussion of the tort, apart from the conclusion that the plaintiff had established that inferior whisky had been 'passed off' by the defendant as the superior article.[94] The reason for this often unacknowledged growth appears to be twofold: passing off cases are mainly dealt with at the interlocutory stage, without rigorous examination of the legal principles involved and in some of the more surprising decisions there is an underlying judicial disapproval of the defendants' activities (as was indeed the case in *Teacher v Levy*).

Source misrepresentation

(i) Pure source misrepresentation

This is the typical or 'classic' case[95] of passing off: the defendant representing his goods as those of the claimant. This is 'source' misrepresentation because the customers believe the claimant to be the 'source' of the product. However, the source does not have to be an identified manufacturer or supplier: rather it is necessary to show that the public associate the product with a single commercial source. As Schechter explained,[96] the function of the trade mark is to indicate not necessarily a known source, but that the goods come from the same source as others.[97] So, in *Powell v Birmingham Vinegar*, at Court of Appeal level, Lindley LJ commented: 'a person whose name is not known but whose mark is imitated, is just as much injured in his trade as if his name was known as well as his mark. His mark, as used by him, has given a reputation to his goods. His trade depends greatly on such reputation. His mark sells his goods.'[98] Nor is there any need for actual experience of claimant's product: it is sufficient that it is the claimant's product that the customers want.[99]

---

[94] Wadlow, above, n. 1, p. 266 notes that in Ireland a similar result had been reached earlier still (*Jameson v Clarke* (1902) 12 RPC 255) and in Australia as early as 1869.

[95] The typical case, summarized by Lord Halsbury as 'no man has any right to represent that his goods are the goods of somebody else', *Reddaway v Banham* (1896) AC 199, 204; accepted as the general principle by Lord Parker in *Spalding v Gamage* (1915) 32 RPC 273, p. 283. The 'classic' case according to Lord Diplock in *Advocaat* [1979] FSR 397, p. 400 and see Harman LJ in *Hoffman La Roche v DDSA* [1969] FSR 410, p. 419.

[96] Above, n. 2, p. 816.

[97] Ibid.

[98] 13 RPC 235, p. 250 (1896); affirmed by House of Lords [1897] AC 710.

[99] *Copydex Ltd v Noso Products Ltd* (1952) 69 RPC 38; see also *Sales Affiliates Ltd v Le Jean* [1947] 1 Ch 295 Evershed J: plaintiffs marketed perms under the name 'Jamal'. The defendants were using other perms in treating hair of customers who had asked for a Jamal perm.

For source misrepresentation, the claimant must show it is a 'distinctive' source. As Wadlow points out,[100] 'distinctive' is a term of art in passing off: 'matter such as the name, mark or get up is said to be distinctive if it denotes the goods of the plaintiff to the exclusion of other traders . . . the significance which the relevant public attaches to the supposed mark . . . is all-important.' Given the need to show distinctiveness, a descriptive name will normally not attract protection.[101] Should the claimant's trade name incorporate descriptive words, quite small differences in a competitor's trade name will render the latter immune from action, the policy of the common law being that 'no trader will be allowed to fence in the common of the English language'.[102] The courts are also aware of the unfair advantage protection of descriptive terms would afford the claimant 'trying to monopolize descriptions which others in the art are likely to want to use, without illicit motive, to describe their goods or services'.[103] In *Office Cleaning Services Ltd v Westminster Window and General Cleaners Ltd*[104] both parties carried on office-cleaning businesses, the plaintiff trading under the name 'Office Cleaning Services Ltd', the defendant trading as 'Office Cleaning Association'. Despite the obvious risk of confusion, there was held to be no passing off. In effect in such a case the risk of confusion has to be accepted.[105] However, it has been acknowledged that a descriptive term may become distinctive of the claimant's goods or services alone. In *Reddaway v Banham*[106] the descriptive term 'camel hair belting' had become associated exclusively with the plaintiffs. It was passing off to describe the defendants' product with this phrase, even though it was literally true. The phrase had attracted a 'secondary meaning'.[107]

Distinctiveness may, of course, result from the get-up of the goods.[108] Get-up has been defined as 'those non-verbal features of a product and its

---

[100] Wadlow, above, n. 1, p. 348.

[101] In *eFax.com Inc v Oglesby*, *The Times*, 16 March 2000, the use of the word 'efax' was held to be descriptive by Parker J, as it was in common use in the relevant market. However, with product misrepresentation, descriptive names are protected: see in particular the discussion by Laddie J in *Chocosuisse Union des Fabricants Suisses de Chocolat v Cadbury Ltd* [1998] RPC 117 (appeal dismissed by the Court of Appeal, [1999] RPC 567).

[102] Laddie J in *Antec International Ltd v South Western Chicks Ltd* [1997] FSR 278, p. 284. (On appeal, [1998] FSR 738, CA.)

[103] Laddie J in *Antec International Ltd v South Western Chicks Ltd* [1997] FSR 278, p. 285.

[104] (1946) 63 RPC 35, p. 42; and see *Furnitureland Ltd v Harris* [1989] FSR 536 (Furnitureland/Furniturecity).

[105] Laddie J in *Antec International Ltd v South Western Chicks Ltd* [1997] FSR 278 ([1998] FSR 738, CA).

[106] [1896] AC 199.

[107] The term was first used by Lord Westbury in *Wotherspoon v Currie* (1872) LR 5 HL 508, HL. Cf. the result in *Cellular Clothing Co v Moxton & Murray* [1899] AC 326 where significantly there was no allegation of fraud.

[108] *White Hudson & Co Ltd v Asian Organisations Ltd* [1964] 1 WLR 1466.

presentation which are relied upon by traders to distinguish their products from those of their competitors'.[109] Packaging—e.g., the distinctive 'Jif Lemon'[110]—and even colour combinations on drugs may be 'distinctive' of the claimant's produce. However, this area is not without its controversies. With prescription pharmaceuticals the get-up may be distinctive of the claimant because they had the original patent protection and monopoly rights in the drug. For professionals and patient alike the get-up identifies the drug, while also linking the drug to the original monopoly manufacturer. Claimants may seek to use the tort, when their patent protection expires, to prevent easy generic competition, thereby maintaining the monopoly. Indeed, the Court of Appeal in *Hoffmann-La Roche v DDSA Pharmaceuticals*[111] protected the get-up of the plaintiffs' drug[112] so that it could not be used by compulsory licensees. As Cornish notes this is a 'substantial barrier against a policy of encouraging generic substitution for original proprietary drugs'. Not surprisingly, perhaps, he detects a readiness to distinguish it.[113]

At a more basic level, the protection of get-up or shape has led some courts to fear possible protection of functional aspects of a product, providing claimants with a monopoly in the product itself.[114] Hence in some cases the courts have distinguished between 'functional' get-up[115] and 'capricious get-up,[116] with only the latter (a clear addition to the article rather than the article itself) capable of being protected by passing off.[117] The validity of this distinction was addressed by the House of

---

[109] Fisher J *Tots Toys v Mitchell* [1993] 1 NZLR 325, p. 335.

[110] *Reckitt & Colman Products Ltd v Borden Inc* [1990] 1 WLR 491, HL The defendants had tried to argue that the Jif Lemon was descriptive, saying in effect 'this is lemon juice'.

[111] [1972] RPC 1.

[112] Its size and colour.

[113] Cornish, above, n. 1; see Llewellyn, D., 'Legal Protection for the Coloured Get-up of Ethical Pharmaceuticals' 12 IIC (1981) 185. Rather surprisingly the court found patient confusion even though the goods were not sold over the counter and patients had little or no choice, having no power of selection over which drug was prescribed. However, end-user confusion has also been accepted in Canada: see Gaikis, G., and Sheldon Hamilton, J., 'Prozac Trade Dress Reputation', 20 3 EIPR (1998) 115.

[114] Evans, J., 'Passing Off and the Problem of Product Simulation' 31 MLR (1968) 642. The explanation for the courts' sensitivity in this area is explained by Evans: 'it falls between the protection which merely deprives competitors of the use of confusingly similar names where the dangers of monopoly are least obvious and protection which prevents competitors from putting out an identical product where the dangers of monopoly are most obvious.' His thesis is, however, challenged by Fisher J in the New Zealand case of *Tots Toys v Mitchell* [1993] 1 NZLR 325. He comments (p. 341) that the rationales for passing off and IP design protection are different: '[passing off] protection is not a reward . . . but preservation of the means of distinguishing between goods from different origins.'

[115] Utilitarian features of the product, including features that form part of the product itself.

[116] Arbitrary features, not driven by considerations of utility.

[117] The classic formula for this distinction is contained in the speech of Fletcher Moulton LJ in *J.B. Williams Co v H. Bronnley & Co* (1909) 26 RPC 765, p. 773.

Lords in *Jif Lemon*, where the plaintiffs alleged that the defendants were liable for copying their distinctive lemon-shaped container for lemon juice. Lord Oliver appeared to consider that policy considerations could limit the scope of passing off protection in this area, so that whether the object itself could be protected (rather than any distinctive feature 'conjoined' with it) was 'at least open to doubt'. Lord Jauncey, however, saw no reason to deny the protection of the tort, given other appropriate means for distinguishing the product can be found.[118] Jacob J has argued cogently in *Hodgkinson & Corby Ltd v Wards Mobility Ltd*[119] that Lord Jauncey's view is to be preferred, as it is consistent with the House of Lords' decision in *Edge & Sons Ltd v William Nicholls & Sons Ltd*[120] (*Dolly Blue*). There the plaintiffs supplied laundry blue without their name or other identification, except for a distinctive wooden stick, used to lower the laundry bleach into the water. There was passing off when this was copied by the defendant. On the facts of the case the get-up of the plaintiffs' product provided source motivation based on appearance, where the customers were 'persons of humble station in life'. In such a case, as elsewhere in the tort: 'the defendant must always do enough to avoid deception to escape liability.' The alternative view of the law according to Jacob J would allow a defendant, who is in fact deceiving the public, to continue to do so.

Of course, as Jacob J went on to point out, it is difficult to succeed in product simulation cases: with product simulation cases there may be difficulty in proving confusion and/or reliance[121] as 'people are likely to buy the article because of what it is, not in reliance on any belief of any particular trade origin'. As the difficulties of proof are so great, successful cases of passing off based on the shape of goods are rare.

(ii) Misdescription of the claimant's product

Spalding v Gamage[122] revealed that misrepresentation as to the quality of the plaintiff's goods would be a relevant misrepresentation for the tort. In that case, Lord Parker restated the standard definition of passing of thus: 'A cannot, without infringing the rights of B, represent goods which are not B's or B's goods of a particular class or quality to be B's goods or B's goods of that particular class or quality.'[123] The plaintiffs, who manufactured, *inter*

---

[118] Leading Fisher J in the New Zealand case of *Tots Toys v Mitchell* [1993] 1 NZLR 325 to conclude (p. 340) 'if both the presence of the feature and the particular way in which it has been expressed have been dictated solely by utilitarian considerations, it should not qualify for passing off protection'. In *Jif Lemon*, Lords Bridge, Brandon, and Goff agreed with both speeches.

[119] [1995] FSR 175.   [120] [1911] AC 693.

[121] It would be difficult, therefore, to claim that a particular 'style' of goods has become distinctive of the claimant alone.

[122] (1915) RPC 273, HL.   [123] (1915) RPC 273, p. 284.

alia, footballs, sued the defendants for advertising the plaintiffs' discarded stock of substandard footballs (the 'Orb') as the plaintiffs' new, improved product. As such it was not a straightforward allegation of a misrepresentation as to source: the plaintiffs objected to the misrepresentation as to the quality of these products. Obviously to sell the plaintiffs' inferior products as their superior output could be damaging.

The ability to use passing off to protect against misdescription as well as source misrepresentation involved a major extension of the tort. It became apparent that there was more than one species of wrong included in the wider genus. However, it is clear that such quality misrepresentations are linked to source misrepresentations, as it is the quality of the claimant's product that is being called into question. As Naresh explains, of *Spalding v Gamage* : 'failure to stop the defendant would have damaged the plaintiff's reputation as a supplier of footballs in exactly the same way as this reputation would have been damaged if the defendant had misrepresented its own inferior footballs as coming from the plaintiff . . . source-goodwill can be threatened even by a misrepresentation purely as to quality.'[124]

In cases of product misdescription (of the claimant's product) it is necessary for the claimant to separate the different categories of his products, at least where the representation as to a particular category/quality is implied. The plaintiff succeeded in doing this in *Wilts Utd Dairies Ltd v Thomas Robinson Sons and Co Ltd*[125] where the defendant was selling out-of-date stock (the indication of age would only have been obvious to those in the trade) of the plaintiff's product. The court held they were selling old goods as new and that the plaintiff's goodwill was in fresh milk.[126] However, the plaintiff failed to convince the court of separate categories in *Harris v Warren and Phillips*.[127] The defendants, copyright owners of the plaintiff composer's early work republished the earlier work when the plaintiff's later compositions became popular. She alleged that the defendant wished to deceive the public into believing that this was a recent composition. However, she failed to show the court that there existed two classes of product (early, inferior compositions; new, superior compositions) of differing quality.

As a weapon against sharp practice, therefore, this form of actionable misrepresentation is useful to combat black market circulation of

---

[124] Naresh, above, n. 32, p. 117.

[125] (1958) RPC 94, CA.

[126] It was argued by the defendant that the decision would mean that any retailer who sold a tinned product which unknown to him had gone stale would be guilty of passing off. However, Donovan LJ rejected this: 'in an isolated case of that kind the retailer can fairly be said to be making no representation as to quality.'

[127] (1918) 35 RPC 217.

discarded goods. It may also apply to the grey market and parallel imports, though obviously here the ability to show a misdescription may be harder. In *Colgate-Palmolive Ltd v Markwell Finance Ltd*[128] the plaintiffs were able to show a misrepresentation as to quality where the defendants' parallel imports from Brazil of the plaintiffs' subsidiary company's toothpaste were of inferior standard to the UK products of the parent company. However, there was no such misdescription in *Revlon Inc v Cripps & Lee Ltd*.[129] Where the confusion is largely of the claimant's own making, the parallel importer will probably avoid liability in the tort.[130]

(iii) Connection misrepresentation

This is a variation on source misrepresentation: an allegation by the defendant that his and the claimant's business or goods are in some way connected. The allegation does not necessarily involve the representation that the claimant is the source of the goods concerned but customers/consumers may believe that he has sanctioned the standard of the product concerned or authorized the activities of the defendant in some way. It was accepted by Lord Diplock in *Advocaat* when he noted: '*Spalding v Gamage* led the way to recognition by judges of other species of the same genus, as where . . . a false suggestion by the defendants that their businesses were connected with one another would damage the reputation and thus the goodwill of the plaintiffs' business.'[131]

Thus in *International Scientific v Pattison*,[132] the defendant was a former agent of the plaintiff publishers. He launched a publication in the plaintiff's field, the advertisements for which suggested it was published by or

---

[128] [1989] RPC 497.

[129] [1980] FSR 85, Dillon J. The defendants had bought up the plaintiffs' discarded stock of a discontinued US anti-dandruff shampoo and distributed it in the UK market. No misrepresentation was involved as there was no evidence that this product was of inferior quality to the UK products. As for EC law, and the possibility of a 'Euro-defence' to an action for passing off, though Articles 28 and 30 mean that registered trade mark protection cannot as such be used to prevent parallel imports from within the EC, the fairness of commercial transactions and the defence of the consumer are 'mandatory requirements' giving rise to a derogation from Article 30. See Cohen, L., and Schmit, K., 'Is the English Law of Passing Off Discriminatory to Continental European Trade Mark Owners?', vol. 21 [1999] 2 EIPR 88. Interestingly, in *Mantruck Services Ltd v Ballinloupe Electrical Refrigeration Ltd* [1992] 1 IR a parallel importer successfully argued that the sole distributor of the 'genuine articles' was operating under a scheme that was in breach of Article 85 (now Article 81). With parallel imports originating from outside the EC, the ECJ in *Silhouette International Schmied GmbH & Co KG v Hartlauer Handelsgesellschaft mbH* [1998] FSR 474 held that the exhaustion of rights principle did not apply.

[130] *Heidsieck v Buxton* [1930] 1 Ch 330.

[131] *Harrods Ltd v Harrod* (1924) 41 RPC 74, cited by Lord Diplock in *Advocaat*. Where there has been a previous connection the defendant may truthfully so advertise: *Harrods Ltd v Schwartz-Sackin* [1986] FSR 490 (decided against the defendant on contract grounds).

[132] [1979] FSR 429.

connected with the plaintiff.[133] An injunction was granted. In *Sony v Saray*,[134] the plaintiffs sold their consumer electronic goods through a network of carefully chosen authorized dealers, trained in the maintenance and repair of Sony equipment. The plaintiffs' advertising stressed this fact. The defendants dealt in Sony goods but were not authorized dealers (and there was evidence of a bad reputation). The Court of Appeal found there to be an implied misrepresentation that the defendants were authorized dealers, leading the public to expect that they were entitled to the full back up of the manufacturers.[135]

The exact nature of the misconnection that must be shown by the claimant is not clear. In *Harrods v Harrodian School*[136] Millett LJ held that the relevant connection, to constitute a misrepresentation, must be one by which the plaintiff would be taken by the public to have made themselves responsible for the quality of the defendant's goods or services. So to create a false impression that the plaintiff had sponsored or given financial support to the defendant would not ordinarily be sufficient as 'it is generally recognized that those who provide financial support [to institutions such as schools or football clubs] do not expect to have any control over or to be held responsible for the organisations or institutions they sponsor'.[137] He rejected the plaintiff's contention that it would be sufficient that it was believed that the plaintiff was 'behind' the defendant in some way. Sir Michael Kerr, however, took a much wider view: though the public may wonder what the connection was, provided they assumed that the plaintiff was somehow 'mixed up' with the defendant's business or goods, that would be sufficient.[138] For him a false representation of sponsorship would be within the tort. It is more than arguable that the precise nature of the link does not need defining.[139] Whatever the alleged connection and its nature, it must be such that reliance on it in some way is likely, as is consequent damage to goodwill.

Of course, the court may not agree on the facts that there is an implied representation of connection. Obviously the claimant's case will be strongest where there is actual competition between the parties. However,

---

[133] The defendant argued that any commercial advertisers would identify the publisher before they contracted. However, there was evidence of some confusion at the start.

[134] [1983] FSR 30, CA and see *Nishika Corp v Goodchild* [1990] FSR 371.

[135] Although the court denied it, what looked very like a mandatory injunction was granted: if they wished to continue selling Sony there had to be disclaiming labels attached to the goods. A similar injunction was awarded in *Nishika Corp v Goodchild* [1990] FSR 371.

[136] (1996) RPC 697, Beldam LJ concurring.

[137] (1996) RPC 697, p. 713.

[138] *Ewing v Buttercup Margarine* (1917) 34 RPC 232, p. 237.

[139] Earlier cases provide support for either view in *Harrods* and indeed both Millett LJ and Sir Michael Kerr rely on different *dicta* from Farwell J in *British Legion v British Legion Club (Street) Ltd* (1931) 48 RPC 555.

clearly a connection misrepresentation might be alleged successfully even in the absence of a common field of activity.[140] The question ultimately is whether there is likely to be confusion and with licensing, franchising, and diversification now commonplace, such an allegation may not be difficult to make out (at least for interlocutory purposes). So in *Lego System A/S v Lego M Lemelstrick Ltd*,[141] Falconer J accepted that the mark Lego had become distinctive of the plaintiffs and extended beyond the actual field of their activity in toys and construction kits. The defendants were restrained from using the mark on garden equipment. Of course, the claimant must be able to show reliance on that connection.[142]

Product misrepresentation

It is in this area that we have the most radical extensions of the tort, thus far. Of course, product misdescriptions may be involved in the previous categories of misrepresentation: the *Yorkshire Relish* case shows that source is often important because it is a guarantee of the requisite quality[143] and it is self evident that to misdescribe the plaintiff's product, as in *Spalding v Gamage*, is also a product misrepresentation. However, in this area of 'product misrepresentation' the focus is on the product itself and how it is misdescribed (though obviously the claimant's goodwill has in some way to be attacked by that misdescription).

As with source misrepresentation, there are categories within this heading. But all have *caveats* and limits attached to them, as in moving away from classic passing off, the courts are mindful (or at least on occasion are mindful) of the dangers of overextension. Without a clear concept of product goodwill and product misdescription the tort could be shifted into the unknown territory of protection of a product itself against 'unfair trading'. Indeed, for this reason Naresh is critical of any movement towards passing off being applied to product misdescriptions and believes that *Advocaat* (discussed below) was a wrong turning for the tort. However, in reality the extension into protection against product misrepresentation can be reconciled with the classic perception of the tort, provided the classic trinity is adhered to.

(i) Inverse passing off

Here the claimant's complaint is that the defendant is asserting that the claimant's goods are his goods or that the claimant's quality (as evidenced

---

[140] See earlier discussion. [141] [1983] FSR 155.

[142] Though note the discussion of 'confusion dilution', below.

[143] Indeed, some members of the House of Lords in this case also held this to be passing off because the product actually being obtained was not made from the same ingredients as 'Yorkshire Relish': *Powell v Birmingham Vinegar* [1897] AC 710.

by examples, commendations, or testimonials) is his quality.[144] Various
titles have been given to this situation, perceived in the past as separate
from the main tort of passing off and not worthy of relief. So it has been
termed 'upside down passing off',[145] 'reverse passing off' or 'inverse
passing off'.[146] By claiming the claimant's quality as his own, the defendant clearly seeks to divert sales from the 'real' producer or source of the
quality claimed.[147]

Given the situation in this sort of case is the opposite of a classic passing off action, English[148] courts have traditionally been reluctant to accept
inverse passing off as within the tort. So in *Cambridge University Press v
University Tutorial Press*[149] the defendants advertised their edition of a text
as 'the prescribed edition', though in fact it was the plaintiffs who had
been given permission to supply the prescribed edition. The judge,
though critical of the defendants, held that they were not liable as they
were not representing that their product was the plaintiffs'.[150] Again, in
Tallerman v Dowsing Radiant Heat Ltd[151] the defendants falsely claimed the
testimonials which in fact referred to the plaintiffs' product. The claim
failed, as there was no representation that the product was the plaintiffs'.

Yet a more basic reason for refusing this category of passing off appears
to be that fact that, according to Fleming:[152] 'to grant protection against
such practices would be to elevate the plaintiff's claim to a protected right
of property in the product in question: such monopolies in intangibles are
not granted as a matter of legal policy except upon the terms defined by
legislation relating to copyright, industrial design or patent.' In effect, the
courts have been fearful that inverse passing off as a concept could be
used to promote a misappropriation action, on a par with the decision of
the US Supreme Court in *International News Service v Associated Press*.[153]
There the defendants duplicated the plaintiffs' newscopy and transmitted
it to their own subscribers, without attribution. Holmes J was willing to
stretch passing off to cover this;[154] Pitney J went even further and
accepted the concept of misappropriation.

---

[144] Laddie J in *Matthew Gloag & Son Ltd v Welsh Distilleries Ltd* [1998] FSR 718, p. 724.

[145] Chafee, Z., 'Unfair Competition' 53 Har LR (1940) 1289, pp. 1310–11.

[146] Wadlow, above, n. 1, p. 330.

[147] For a more detailed consideration of this topic see Carty, H., 'Inverse Passing Off: A
Suitable Addition to Passing Off?' 15 10 EIPR (1993) 370.

[148] Cf. the Court of Session in *Henderson v Munroe* (1905) 13 SLT 57.

[149] (1928) 45 RPC 335, Maugham J.

[150] Though no costs were awarded to the defendant.

[151] (1900) 1 Ch 1.

[152] Fleming, J., *The Law of Torts*, 7th edn. (Sydney: LBC, 1987). This passage does not appear
in subsequent editions.

[153] (1918) 248 US 215.

[154] Though he accepted that 'the falsehood is a little more subtle, the injury is a little more
indirect, than in ordinary cases of unfair trade'.

However, these fears are unfounded, provided such cases adhere to the classic trinity. This appears to have been accepted by some courts in the past. In *Copydex Ltd v Noso Products Ltd*[155] the defendant wrongly advertised his product as having been the one 'shown on television', whereas it was in fact the plaintiff's that had been so advertised (though anonymously). An interlocutory injunction was granted by Vaisey J, even though he was not convinced that the tort was made out. In *Plomien Fuel Economiser Co Ltd v National School of Salesmanship Ltd*,[156] the defendant wrongly claimed the results of tests on the plaintiff's product for his own product and this was held to be passing off.[157] And in *Bullivant v Wright*[158] 'converse' passing off was deemed to be sufficiently analogous to 'ordinary' passing off, though relief was denied on other grounds.

Whatever the doubts of the past, however, the arrival of inverse passing off as a part of the tort is implicit in the decision of the Court of Appeal in *Bristol Conservatories Ltd v Conservatories Custom Built Ltd*.[159] The defendants' salesmen showed their prospective customers a portfolio of photographs of conservatories built by the plaintiffs, as if they were samples of their own work. The Court of Appeal refused the defendants' action to strike out the plaintiffs' claim in passing off. Though they would not determine the precise limits of the tort in such an action, they held that the cases cited by the defendants, including *Tallerman v Dowsing Radiant Heat Ltd*,[160] were not authority binding on the court. Thus it is not surprising that the Court of Appeal of the Republic of Singapore in *John Robert Powers School Inc v Denyse Bernadette Tessensohn*[161] saw *Bristol Conservatories* as an example of inverse passing off. Indeed, Laddie J in *Matthew Gloag & Son Ltd v Welsh Distilleries Ltd*[162] accepted the legitimacy of an allegation of inverse passing off.

After *Bristol Conservatories*, however, it is clear that the facts of the *INS* case would still not amount to the tort of passing off here. Morison[163] felt that it could and should be seen as actionable under English law: 'the argument would be that the customer who buys the newspaper from the defendant thinks that it came from a business which is identified in his mind as the business which collected and collated the news. This business

---

[155] (1952) 69 RPC 38.
[156] (1943) 60 RPC 209.
[157] It was deemed to be source misrepresentation by a rather strained analysis—customers wanted goods from a particular source, viz. the one that produced the satisfactory tests. However, Cornish points out that the only issue for the Court of Appeal was as to damages: Cornish, W. R., 'Unfair Competition: a Progress Report' 12 JSPTL (1972) 126, p. 137.
[158] (1897) 13 TLR 201 (the plaintiff could not establish goodwill).
[159] [1989] RPC 455.
[160] (1900) 1 Ch 1.
[161] [1995] FSR 947 and see *Matthew Gloag v Welsh Distilleries* [1998] FSR 719
[162] [1998] FSR 718, p. 724.
[163] Morison, W. L., 'Unfair Competition and Passing-off' 2 Syd Law Rev (1956) 50, p. 65.

is in fact that of the plaintiff.' However, the better view is still that expressed by Brandeis J in his dissenting judgment in *INS*, where he characterized what the defendant had done as 'merely using the plaintiff's product without compensation'. He rejected the view that there had been any misrepresentation: the defendant had merely omitted to mention the source of the information.[164]

However, to avoid turning the tort into one that protects products *per se*, it must be clear that the claimant's goodwill is threatened and—given the possible width of these claims—that threat must be substantial. Unless this is accepted, the tort may be led into wide and uncertain areas, at least in the interlocutory stage. A recent example of this danger is *Matthew Gloag & Son Ltd v Welsh Distilleries Ltd*.[165] There the defendants bought Scotch whisky from a legitimate supplier (who knew of their intentions), added herbs to it, and marketed it as 'Welsh Whisky'. The plaintiff as a producer of one type of Scotch whisky alleged that this was passing off, an extension of product misrepresentation and inverse passing off. Though clearly the facts revealed neither a typical *Advocaat* claim[166] nor a typical inverse passing off claim (there was no stealing of credit or commendation from the 'legitimate' article as there were not two distinct products), Laddie J refused to strike out the action and thereby arguably supported an action based on an 'appropriation' of the product itself.[167]

(ii) Product equivalence misrepresentation

Product misrepresentation may be involved where the defendant (incorrectly) alleges that his goods are 'equivalent to' or 'the same as' the claimant's. This is product misrepresentation, with similarities to the extension accepted in *Advocaat* (see (iii) below) but linked to the claimant alone. An injunction was granted in *Masson Seeley & Co v Embossotype Mfg Co*[168] because of the defendants' 'conduct calculated and intended to induce people to believe that the goods offered by them were, contrary to fact, the same as the goods supplied by the plaintiff company'. In *Combe International Ltd v Scholl (UK) Ltd*,[169] the plaintiffs marketed a shoe insole with 'activated charcoal', to reduce foot odour. The presence of charcoal in their product was emphasized by the plaintiffs in their advertising. The

---

[164] Interestingly, of course, the *INS* case has not led to any clear development towards a misappropriation action in America itself.

[165] [1998] FSR 718, p. 724.

[166] Discussed in detail later in the text. The plaintiffs conceded that the defendant could have called their product e.g. 'Buckingham Palace whisky': would 'Owen Glendower' whisky have been permissible and if so, how would this have been different from the name 'Welsh Whisky'?

[167] Discussed in detail, below.

[168] (1924) 41 RPC 160, p. 165, Tomlin J.

[169] [1980] RPC 1, Fox J.

defendants produced a rival product, strikingly similar in appearance[170] but with ordinary charcoal, a product without odour-reducing qualities. Yet the defendants had drawn attention to the use of charcoal, though the function of this ingredient was not explained. The plaintiffs claimed that their product was 16 per cent more effective than the defendants' and that this difference in performance would be perceived by the customer in use. Overall, the effect of the advertising, product description, and packaging was to suggest that the product was the same as the plaintiffs, and Fox J found this to be passing off. Rather than a connection misrepresentation, the defendants were liable for an equivalence misrepresentation.

However, a *caveat* must be entered against this variety of product misrepresentation also. There are few reported cases where equivalence misrepresentation has been successfully alleged.[171] No doubt this is due to the courts' reluctance to be drawn into assessing the validity or otherwise of advertising or promotional data. In line with malicious falsehood,[172] 'mere puffs' or comparisons lacking specific content would not be sufficient for establishing the tort, as was accepted by Michael Wheeler QC in *Coopervision Inc v Aspect Contact Lenses Ltd*.[173] Of course another reason for the lack of case law in this area is that plaintiffs may feel that they stand more chance alleging a connection misrepresentation as in *Kimberley-Clark Ltd v Fort Sterling Ltd*.[174]

(iii) Misdescription concerning a distinctive product: 'extended passing off'[175]

The protection against wrongful assertion of equivalence was extended in *Advocaat* to misdescription concerning a distinctive product (rather than a distinctive claimant).[176] Product misrepresentation (where that is a distinctive product) was seen as an evil in its own right. This extended form of passing off was first recognized and applied by Danckwerts J in *Bollinger v Costa Brava Wine Co*[177] and subsequently by other judges in the other so-called 'drinks'[178] cases, where the plaintiffs were the producers

---

[170] White on one side, black on the other with dotted white lines for various shoe sizes (a Combe innovation); packed in a rectangular cardboard box, rather than flat in an envelope.

[171] It was unsuccessfully raised in *Schulke & Mayr Ltd v Alkapharm* [1999] FSR 161.

[172] *Hubbuck v Wilkinson* [1899] 1 QB 86, CA.

[173] (1987) Lexis transcript, Michael Wheeler QC.

[174] [1997] FSR 877.

[175] 'Extended passing off' was the name given to this type of misrepresentation by Laddie J in *Chocosuisse Union des Fabricants de Chocolat v Cadbury Ltd* [1998] RPC 117.

[176] Jacob J in *Hodgkinson & Corby Ltd v Wards Mobility* [1995] FSR 169, p. 175 notes that in *Combe* the deception is that the defendant's goods are the same as those of the plaintiff; whereas in *Advocaat* the deception is that the defendant's goods are the same as the goods sold by a class of persons of which the plaintiff is a member.

[177] [1960] RPC 16.

[178] The various cases involved sherry, Scotch whisky, and champagne producers attempting to prevent others using the term 'sherry', 'Scotch whisky' or 'champagne' to misdescribe

or blenders of particular alcoholic drinks from particular geographical areas. In none of these cases were the defendants claiming to sell the particular plaintiffs' goods. In none of these cases did the particular plaintiffs have the exclusive reputation in the goods as described: the name 'champagne', e.g., was not distinctive of the particular plaintiffs. The issue was whether a trader who together with other traders uses a recognized description for his goods can allege passing off against another who misuses that description to describe his goods. In essence, the plaintiffs were complaining that the defendants were misdescribing their product.

In *Bollinger v Costa Brava Wine Co Ltd*[179] (where the plaintiffs successfully alleged passing off against the producers of 'Spanish champagne') Danckwerts J was prepared on the slimmest of previous authority[180] to extend passing off to such a case. He stated: 'there seems to be no reason why such licence should be given to a person, competing in trade, who seeks to attach to his product a name or description with which it has no natural association so as to make use of the reputation and goodwill which has been gained by a product genuinely indicated by the name or description.'[181]

The net effect of these cases[182] was to extend the tort and indicate a wider role for passing off, but the scope and logic of that extension was unclear. In particular, it was contended that the geographical link of the cases was important.[183] In *Advocaat* the House of Lords had to review the drinks cases to determine their significance. Though these earlier cases had a common geographical link, *Advocaat* revealed that this was not an important feature of the extended tort.

In *Advocaat*, the plaintiffs, amongst other Dutch traders, had for many years manufactured a liquor called 'advocaat', the essential ingredients of which were a spirit, Brandewijn, and egg yolks. The product had acquired a substantial reputation in Britain. The defendants marketed a drink, 'Keeling's Old English Advocaat' from dried egg powder and Cyprus

their product. *Vine Products v Mackenzie* [1969] RPC 1, small number of sherry producers and shippers; *John Walker v Henry Ost* [1970] RPC 489, some of the blenders/exporters of Scotch; *Bulmer v Bollinger* [1978] RPC 79. See also *Siegert v Findlater* (1878) 7 Ch D 801, Fry J misuse of generic term, 'Angoustura Bitters'.

[179] The subsequent claim for an injunction is at [1961] 1 All ER 561.

[180] In particular *Dent v Turpin* (1861) 2 J&H 139; *Southern v Reynolds* (1865) 12 LT 75. In both cases, a business had been bequeathed to two sons who subsequently used the same trade name but carried on independent businesses. In both cases one son sued a defendant who used that name, although having no connection with the family.

[181] [1960] 1 Ch 262, pp. 283–4 (held an action for passing off maintainable); [1961] 1 All ER 561 (injunction granted).

[182] Though it has to be noted that the 'genuine' producers were not successful in all the cases.

[183] Given the product must have a 'recognizable and distinctive quality' it may be easiest to use this form of allegation where a geographical limitation or designation is involved.

sherry. Given the ingredients, the defendants were able to market their product at a lower price and had captured a substantial part of the plaintiffs' English market. As Lord Diplock noted, this was not a 'classic' case of passing off.[184] As the question whether to extend or not was 'essentially one of legal policy'[185] and as Parliament had striven in recent years to protect consumers against misdescriptions, the extension was called for. Here, there was no source misrepresentation—it was obvious that the defendants' product did not emanate from the plaintiffs. However, the name 'advocaat' was understood by the public in England to denote a distinct and recognizable species of beverage. Advocaat was a 'product endowed with recognizable qualities'. The defendants' product, on the other hand, was really egg flip, not advocaat. They had deliberately induced the public into the belief that they were buying advocaat when in fact they were not. The plaintiffs' goodwill in the product (which they shared with the other 'genuine' producers) was damaged both by reduced sales and by the reputation of the product being debased.

It is 'product goodwill' that is here being protected. But that does not mean that the product itself is being protected by the tort. In line with the classic trinity, it is the claimant's own goodwill in the product (as producer/supplier of the product) that is at stake. This was stressed by Lord Diplock: 'Warninks with 75 per cent of the trade have a very substantial stake in the goodwill of the name "advocaat" and their business has been shown to have suffered serious injury as a result of [the defendants'] competition.'[186] Indeed, the court did acknowledge that with shared goodwill it would generally be true that the larger the class the more difficult it must be for an individual member of it to show that the goodwill of his business has sustained more than minimal damage.[187] 'Mere entry into the market would not be sufficient as the plaintiff must have used the descriptive term long enough in the market in connection with his own goods and have traded successfully enough to have built up a goodwill for his business.'[188]

There are clear distinctions between a classic source misrepresentation action and one involving a product misdescription, as noted by Laddie J in *Chocosuisse Union des Fabricants Suisses de Chocolat v Cadbury Ltd*.[189] In particular the 'extended' form of the action can protect descriptive words (as in 'Swiss Chocolate').[190] However, it is clear that provided the ingredients of

---

[184] *Advocaat* [1979] AC 731, p. 741.　　　　　　　　　　　　　　[185] Ibid. 739.
[186] [1979] AC 731, p. 748. Lord Fraser (p. 756) the trader 'who owns goodwill in relation to that class of goods'.
[187] Ibid. 744.
[188] Hence it would be misleading to see this as a right equivalent to an appellation contrôlée cf. Laddie J in *Chocosuisse Union des Fabricants Suisses de Chocolat v Cadbury Ltd* [1998] RPC 117.
[189] [1998] RPC 117, pp 125–6.　　　　　　　　　　　　　　[190] [1998] RPC 117, p. 125.

the classic trinity are adhered to, this form of misrepresentation fits into the tort neatly.[191] As Walton noted:[192] 'it is clear that the offence [in *Advocaat*] is no more than a generalization of the more individual case of the *Combe v Scholl* type and the gist of the offence consists in misrepresenting that the defendant is selling goods which are the plaintiff's goods in the sense only that they are an equivalent.' In any allegation of passing off the misrepresentation must be a relevant one; it must be material and it must be relied upon.

Of course, to keep the tort within bounds it is important that the courts demand that the claimant show he is protecting a separate and clearly defined class of goods (in line with misdescriptions of the claimant's products). This was acknowledged by Lord Diplock in *Advocaat* who commented that 'if one can define with reasonable precision the type of product that has acquired the reputation, one can identify the members of the class entitled to share in the goodwill'.[193] More recently, Laddie J in *Chocosuisse Union des Fabricants Suisses de Chocolat v Cadbury Ltd*[194] noted that there must be a 'defined class of goods with a distinctive reputation'. Significantly, however, he was willing to accept that it is the public perception of special qualities that is important, even though there is no real qualitative difference in fact between the plaintiffs' and defendants' products. In this case he accepted that the 'designation' Swiss Chocolate had a bearing on consumer choice.

As with product equivalence, the courts will not be drawn into quality assessment. In the *Parma Ham* case[195] the Court of Appeal noted that the plaintiff must show a difference in kind, not merely one of degree. The court would not entertain disputes about a subjective quality such as flavour,[196] Leggatt LJ noting that the courts cannot be invited 'to provide what would in effect be a form of quality control when determining disputes between rival traders'.[197]

---

[191] Naresh, above, n. 32, p. 98 is unhappy with the extension in *Advocaat* as it 'involves a sharp break with traditional conceptions of the interests protected by passing off and of the appropriate limits to competitors' actions against each other'.

[192] Walton, A., above, n. 91, p. 162.

[193] [1979] AC 731, p. 747.

[194] [1998] RPC 117.

[195] [1991] RPC 351.

[196] According to Balcome LJ [1991] RPC 351, p. 375: disputes as to quality and no more. Nourse LJ, p. 372: 'it must be shown that [the defendant's] ham has suffered such a deterioration in quality through its pre-slicing and packaging that it no longer answers the description of Parma Ham.'

[197] [1991] RPC 351, p. 379.

(B) GOODWILL AND DESERVING CLAIMANTS

Definition

The central importance of the House of Lords' decision in *Spalding v Gamage*[198] is that it identified the interest that the tort protects. There is no right of property in the name, mark, or get-up that the claimant uses. Rather, the property right[199] is in the customer connection[200] or 'goodwill' emanating from the reputation of the claimant's products. '[The plaintiff] can only show that a right to goodwill has become attached to the name by showing that this has occurred by reason of the reputation of the class of goods or services to which the name relates.'[201] The tort protects the trading activity that has created a reputation for the claimant's goods. Indeed, it may be the goods, the services or the business as a whole that gains this reputation.[202] The classic definition of goodwill is contained in Lord Macnaghten's speech in *CIR v Muller & Co's Margarine Ltd*:[203] '[Goodwill] is the benefit and advantage of the good name, reputation and connection of a business. It is the attractive force that brings in business . . . goodwill has no independent existence. It cannot subsist by itself. It must be attached to a business.'[204] It is this that justifies common law protection. The relevant date for determining whether a claimant has established the necessary goodwill is the date of the commencement of the conduct complained of.[205]

Thus the damage that must be shown (as actual or prospective) is damage to the integrity of the claimant's goodwill. Classic goodwill is

---

[198] (1915) 32 RPC 273.

[199] That goodwill is a property right is consistently acknowledged in leading case law see, e.g., Lord Diplock in *Advocaat* [1980] RPC 31, p. 92; Lord Parker in *Spalding v Gamage* [1915] 32 RPC 273, p. 284; Buckley LJ in *Bulmer v Bollinger* [1978] RPC 79, p. 94: 'the law regards such a reputation as an incorporeal piece of property, the integrity of which the owner is entitled to protect'; Goddard LJ in *Draper v Trist* [1939] 3 All ER 513, p. 526. In *Jif Lemon* [1990] RPC 340 Lord Jauncey noted (p. 418): 'the fact that the proprietary right which is protected by the action is in the goodwill rather than in the get-up, distinguishes the protection afforded by the common law to a trader from that afforded by statute to the registered holder of a trade mark who enjoys a permanent monopoly therein.'

[200] Normally, goodwill is concerned with the relationship of trader and public as consumers of his goods; however, goodwill is wide enough to cover a trader's connection with suppliers, business customers, and others.

[201] Slade J in *My Kinda Bones Ltd v Dr Pepper's Stove Co Ltd* [1984] FSR 289, p. 296. See also Lord Diplock in *Star Industrial v Yap Kwee Kor* [1976] FSR 256.

[202] *Bulmer v Bollinger* [1977] 2 CMLR 625, p. 629 Buckley LJ.

[203] [1901] AC 217, p. 223, HL.

[204] A claimant generates goodwill by the use of a distinctive name, mark, or get-up in relation to his goods, services, or business.

[205] Lord Scarman in *Cadbury Schweppes Pty Ltd v Pub Squash Co Pty Ltd* [1981] RPC 429, p. 494 (not the date of commencement of proceedings as the judge had decided in *Pub Squash*).

source related: it is the claimant alone who is attacked. After *Advocaat*, product goodwill is also protected by the tort, i.e. the goodwill generated for the business *by a product* even though the claimant does not have an exclusive right to produce that product. However, it is important to stress that the claimant must still show he has gained his own goodwill in the product.

Goodwill and traders

Goodwill is acquired through trading and for the classic trinity there must be the possibility of damage to some business or trading activity.[206] Hence only traders can rely on passing off.[207] Case law, however, reveals that the concept of trader extends some way beyond normal commercial trading activities. Professional organizations can sue[208] as can authors[209] and others involved in a professional, artistic, or literary occupation.[210] It is also clear from *British Legion v British Legion Club (Street)*[211] that a voluntary association can sue a commercial organization. Indeed, Walker J in *British Diabetic Association v The Diabetic Society*[212] accepted that a passing off action could be brought by one charity against another, at least where the charities are involved in trading type activities by fund-raising.[213]

---

[206] Note, however, the rule in *Routh v Webster* (1847) 50 ER 698 protecting even non-traders against an unauthorized use of their name, whereby they might be exposed to liability. Wadlow, above, n. 1, pp 143–5.

[207] It would appear that the defendant must also be involved in trade: *Rolls-Royce v Zanelli* [1979] RPC 148. Here the defendant had plans to convert Rolls-Royce cars to make them look like more expensive models and sell the end results. He was restrained from doing this but it was held that he could use his own converted Rolls-Royce for domestic purposes. The Court of Appeal in *Chocosuisse Union des Fabricants de Chocolat v Cadbury Ltd* [1999] RPC 866 held that a trade association that did not itself trade lacked *locus standi* to sue in passing off.

[208] See e.g. *BMA v Marsh* [1931] 48 RPC 565; *Law Society of England & Wales v Society of Lawyers* [1996] FSR 739. In *Society of Accountants and Auditors v Goodway and London Association of Accountants Ltd*, [1907] 1 Ch 489 Warrington J held that the designation 'incorporated accountant' had come to mean to the public a member of the plaintiffs' society. Given such a description meant that a certain professional standard had been achieved, the defendant association was prevented from recommending to its members to adopt the designation, misleading the public into believing that the defendants' members were the plaintiffs' members.

[209] *Byron v Johnson* (1816) 35 ER 851; in *Clark v Associated Newspapers* [1998] RPC 261 Lightman J accepted that there would be damage to the plaintiff (a politician and author) through false attribution of authorship. However, this protection would seem to apply only to authors in their trade as authors: *Kaye v Robertson* [1991] FSR 62, p. 69 the plaintiff actor was not a trader in relation to his interest in his story about his accident and recovery.

[210] The claimant does not have to aim to trade at a profit and may be a public body e.g. *BBC v Talbot Motor Co Ltd* [1981] FSR 228.

[211] (1931) 48 RPC 565.

[212] [1996] FSR 1.

[213] The goodwill is the attractive force that brings in financial support from the public. He relied on Australian, American, and South African authorities. He distinguished between 'self-help' and 'non-self-help' charities. In the former category of charity the donations of the

Thus Wadlow concludes that the action for passing off is open 'to almost anyone who can be said to derive an income from the provision of goods or services'.[214] However, there must be some commercial activity. Thus in *Kean v McGiven*, where the name 'Social Democratic Party' was claimed by two political parties, an action for passing off would not lie.[215]

Ownership

The owner of the goodwill will be the person with whom the public identifies the character or quality of the goods. Buckley LJ accepted this in *Dental Manufacturing Co v C de Trey & Co*:[216] 'the plaintiff's goods need not be goods manufactured by the plaintiff. They may be goods which he purchases, or which he imports or otherwise acquires and which he sells under some "get-up" which conveys that they are goods which whether made, imported or sold by him, carry with them the advantage of a reputation that the plaintiff's well known firm are responsible for their quality or their character.' Goodwill, therefore, can include marketing activities, an important point for those involved in the character merchandising industry—an industry that involves marketing products by reference to real or fictional characters.[217] The character (real or fictional) may be associated with the product by name alone, or by the application of its likeness or other distinguishing elements of its characterization or personality.[218] In *Mirage Studios v Counter Feat Clothing*[219] (*Teenage Mutant Ninja Turtles*), the court awarded an injunction for the first time in a character merchandising case on the basis of an arguable connection misrepresentation. It should be stressed, however, that the goodwill in such

---

membership are related to the services provided by the charity—this constitutes goodwill (the subscriptions are in view of benefits); in the latter where services are provided to other than the donors (e.g. RNLI; NSPCC) there may not be goodwill and therefore no action in passing off. See Wadlow, above, n. 1, pp 102–19.

[214] Wadlow, above, n. 1, p. 3.

[215] Cf. *Price v Pioneer Press* (1925) 42 TLR 29. Here there were rival election advertisements, with the plaintiff and defendant printers employed by two rival political parties. The defendant printers used the plaintiff printers' name on their poster. This was held to be libellous and in the alternative, an improper use of the plaintiff's name.

[216] [1912] 3 KB 76, p. 88. It is essentially a question of fact: the relative merits of the parties may decide the issue: *Nishika Corp v Goodchild* [1990] FSR 371.

[217] The character need not be an independent fictional character, subsequently applied to merchandise. In *Fido Dido Inc v. Venture Stores (Retailers) Pty Ltd* (1988) 16 IPR 365, Fed Court of Australia, protection was afforded to a character, devised simply as a merchandising tool. Compare such activity to where a character is appropriated in order to develop it or to develop goods about it, e.g. *Grundy Television Pty Ltd v Startrain Ltd* [1988] FSR 581, Millett J (unofficial fanzine, held no representation that it was authorized).

[218] e.g. the voice of a well-known actor assumed for a television advertisement as in *Sim v Heinz* [1959] RPC 75 (where, however, no injunction was granted).

[219] [1991] FSR 145, Sir Nicholas Browne-Wilkinson V-C.

merchandising cases exists in the trading activity, and it is that which is protected, not the character itself.[220] Of course, reliance must also be shown—arguably a difficult task in such cases.

Relevant business activity

Goodwill must exist at the time of the passing off and must be within the jurisdiction.[221]

(i) Temporal goodwill

Where a trader ceases trading he may still be able to persuade the court that he intends to resume trading in the future and that his goodwill survives. However, goodwill cannot survive indefinitely in such circumstances.[222] Where a business ceases, 'elements' of the original goodwill may remain which may perhaps be gathered up and revived again.[223] So in *Ad-Lib Club Ltd v Granville*[224] residual goodwill was found, though the club in question had been closed for five years. However, as cases such as *Norman Kark Publications Ltd v Odhams Press Ltd*[225] reveal it is a question of fact and degree, Wilberforce J noting 'proof that the name continues to be distinctive of the plaintiff's goods is the essence of the action . . . a mere intention not to abandon the name is, in my view, not enough; the vital question is one of reputation'.

As for the claimant who has yet to commence trading, logically it

---

[220] However, at times the Vice-Chancellor in the *Turtles* case appeared to suggest that goodwill could only apply to trading in pre-existing intellectual property rights. However, there is no additional requirement that the claimant show pre-existing intellectual property rights that he has been licensing. This is obviously so where a personality's name is used without authority, but can also apply to fictional character names. An analogy might be drawn with such cases as *Group Newspapers Ltd v Rocket Record Co Ltd* [1981] FSR 89. Here the plaintiffs were publishers of the *Sun* newspaper famous for its Page Three girls. The newspaper was advertised by reference to this feature and a range of merchandise was marketed, using the words as a selling device. The defendants were restrained from using the phrase 'Page Three' as the title on their single record as the court held a connection misrepresentation was arguable, given the plaintiffs were already merchandising. The connection that would be presumed by the public was held to be an injurious one and an injunction was granted.

[221] Note the anomaly where the passing off occurs abroad, harming an English business. Wadlow, above, n. 1, pp. 49–50: 'it is well-established that there may be passing off actionable under English law even though both parties compete solely in the export trade. Although such a plaintiff may have no goodwill in England, it would appear that damage to the plaintiff's business in England is the basis of the action.' See *Johnston v Orr-Ewing* (1882) 7 App Cas 219 (HL).

[222] See *Star Industrial v Yap* [1976] FSR 256 PC and cf. the facts of *Ad-Lib Club v Glanville* [1972] RPC 673 with those of *Norman Kark v Odhams* [1962] RPC 163

[223] Lord Macnaghten in *CIR v Muller & Co's Margarine Ltd* [1901] AC 217, p 223.

[224] [1972] RPC 673, Pennycuick V-C.

[225] [1962] RPC 163, p. 169 Wilberforce J.

would be assumed that no action in passing off could succeed. However, the argument of such claimants that they should be deemed to have good-will based on the demand for their product or service (created by pre-launch publicity) and on their expensive marketing activities, has been accepted by some judges, for the purposes of awarding an interlocutory injunction.[226] Of course, it may be that extensive pre-launch publicity means a rapid acquiring of goodwill, once the product is launched. In *Allen (WH) & Co v Brown Watson Ltd*[227] extensive pre-launch publicity appeared to justify the protection by Pennycuick J of a recently launched product.[228] However, some plaintiffs have obtained the protection of an injunction *prior* to any customers having been attracted.[229] So in *BBC v Talbot*,[230] an interlocutory injunction was awarded even though the BBC's new traffic information service, CARFAX, had yet to be launched. The defendants planned to use the same name for their car spare-parts service. The extensive pre-launch publicity undertaken by the BBC, including a television broadcast with an estimated audience of 3 million, appeared to justify the injunction. Subsequently, in *Elida Gibbs v Colgate-Palmolive*[231] the plaintiff, a toothpaste manufacturer, obtained an injunction to stop what was in effect a blocking tactic[232] by its trade rival. The plaintiff had decided on a marketing campaign for a new toothpaste, based upon a tree theme. There had been a trade campaign and the marketing idea had been launched to the press and professional bodies. However, the day before the plaintiff's public campaign was to begin, the defendant placed a tree-themed advert for its own product in the national press. Again, in *My Kinda Bones Ltd v Dr Pepper's Stove Co Ltd*[233] the plaintiffs intended shortly to open restaurants, to be known as the Chicago Rib Shack, with spare ribs as the main feature on the menu. They objected to the defendants'

---

[226] Mervyn Davies J in *The Chamberlain Group Inc v Access Garage Doors and Gates* (15.11.89, Lexis transcript) asserts that the *Budweiser* case [1984] FSR 413 does not rule out the argument for pre-launch goodwill. There might be an initial objection that in *Budweiser* there was a demand for the plaintiffs' unavailable product: but in that case, of course, there was as yet no intention to obtain customers within the jurisdiction.

[227] [1965] RPC 191.

[228] And see Slade J in *My Kinda Bones v Dr Pepper's Stove Co Ltd* [1984] FSR 289, p. 299: 'It may well be that if the goods or services are placed on the market after extensive preparatory publicity a very short time thereafter will suffice for the public to assess their merits and for the relevant reputation to be acquired.'

[229] Cf. *Windmere Corp v Charlescraft Corp Ltd* (1988) 23 CPR (3rd) 60, Rouleau J, Fed Court of Canada. As well as extensive promotion of the product yet to be launched, the plaintiff had taken advance orders.

[230] Megarry VC [1981] FSR 228.

[231] [1983] FSR 95 Goulding J.

[232] The defendant marketed a toothpaste in France/Belgium using a tooth/tree analogy. They placed the advert here to assert their entitlement to this theme.

[233] [1984] FSR 289 Slade J.

proposal to use the phrase 'Rib Shack' in their restaurant.[234] Slade J rejected the defendants' application to strike out the passing off action.

Yet if goodwill emanates from customer connection then it is more than arguable that some customers must have experienced the product. This was certainly the view of Slade J in *My Kinda Bones Ltd v Dr Pepper's Stove Co Ltd*.[235] He refused to strike out the plaintiffs' claim but was unhappy with the conclusion: 'prima facie, it seems to me, a substantial number of customers or potential customers must at least have had the opportunity to assess the merits of those goods or services for themselves. *Prima facie* it seems to me, they will not have sufficient opportunity to do this until the goods or services are actually on the market.' He found 'considerable force'[236] in the defendants' submission that as a matter of principle a projected restaurant could not yet have attracted goodwill. Thus, apart from authority of *Allen v Brown Watson Ltd* he would have inclined to the view that at least some entry onto the market by the particular goods or services under the particular relevant name was ordinarily necessary. His doubts were echoed by Mervyn Davies J in *The Chamberlain Group Inc v Access Garage Doors and Gates*.[237]

Cases on pre-launch publicity could be dismissed as incorrect, based on a misreading of the decision in *Allen v Brown Watson Ltd* (relied on in *BBC v Talbot* and in *My Kinda Bones v Dr Pepper's Stove Ltd*). Treated as authority for actions concerning pre-launched products, the case actually concerned a product already on the market. However, in fact these decisions reveal the tensions in the tort itself and the quest to extend it into a misappropriation or unfair trading tort (discussed in detail below). So though the majority of the Court of Appeal in *Marcus Publishing plc v Hutton-Wild Communications Ltd*[238] refused an injunction on the basis that the product was not yet on the market, Staughton LJ commented: 'it may be ... that it is now possible to create goodwill for a future product by lavish hospitality or advertising of some other kind and that a competitor ought not to be allowed to appropriate to himself the goodwill so engendered.'[239]

(ii) Territorial goodwill[240]

Some plaintiffs—those with international reputations but no trading

---

[234] In the case itself, the plaintiffs had acquired a lease, created a special recipe for the spare ribs, produced a special menu, and devised a special decor for the new restaurants. In addition they had obtained editorial publicity and had served the spare ribs, made to the new recipe, at their other restaurants (accompanied by publicity).

[235] [1984] FSR 289.   [236] [1984] FSR 289, p. 299.

[237] 15.11.89, Lexis transcript.   [238] [1990] RPC 576, p. 585.

[239] And see *Electro Cad Australia pty Ltd v Mejali RCS* [1999] FSR 291, p. 309.

[240] To do acts abroad which may damage the claimant's UK goodwill is passing off. In

activity within the jurisdiction—have attempted to equate goodwill with mere reputation in order to gain the protection of passing off. They have achieved some judicial support for their attempt to prevent 'pirates' using their famous and commercially attractive name in England.[241] However, the present position[242] is that goodwill within the jurisdiction is not to be equated with reputation. In *Anheuser-Busch Inc v Budejovicky Budvar PN*[243] the plaintiff, an American company who supplied US bases in England, had a product—Budweiser—known to a substantial number of people in England as a result of visits to America and 'spill over' advertising.[244] Yet they were unable to prevent the defendant using the same name for their beer, given the plaintiff's product was not available to the English public as such. It should be noted that foreign traders under section 56(2) of the Trade Marks Act 1994 may now gain injunctive relief against confusion, based on reputation alone, provided they are proprietors of 'well-known' trade marks.[245]

There must, therefore, be goodwill within the jurisdiction to sue in passing off. But it is unclear from case law involving foreign traders whether that activity must emanate from a trading base within the jurisdiction or whether it simply demands that the claimant show they have customers within the jurisdiction. One line of cases appears to demand trading activity within the jurisdiction. Lord Diplock stressed in *Star Industrial Co Ltd v Yap Kwee Kor* that goodwill: 'is local in character and divisible; if the business is carried on in several countries, separate goodwill attaches to it in each.'[246] This view appeared reaffirmed by Lord Fraser in *Advocaat*.[247] For him, the plaintiff's business should consist of, or

---

Mecklermedia Corp v DC Congress Gesellschaft mbH [1997] FSR 627, the plaintiff had goodwill in the UK and was concerned over the use of a similar name by the defendant in trade fairs held outside England (but promoted in the UK). There was a connection misrepresentation and it was irrelevant that none of the defendants' activities took place within the territorial jurisdiction of the court. Of course, whether the court had jurisdiction over the defendant abroad was a separate issue, under the Brussels Convention.

[241] See Graham J in *Baskin-Robbins Ice Cream Co v Gutman* [1976] FSR 545: note however, no injunction was in fact awarded and *Maxim's v Dye* [1977] FSR 364. In the former, Graham J refused to set out 'artificial' limits to geographical areas over which reputation and goodwill can extend: 'some businesses are . . . truly international in character and reputation and the reputation and goodwill attaching to them cannot in fact help being international also.'

[242] Following *Athlete's Foot Marketing Associates Inc v Cobra Sports Ltd* [1980] RPC 343 and *Anheuser-Busch Inc v Budejovicky Budvar PN* [1984] FSR 413. *Alain Bernadin et Cie v Pavilion Properties Ltd* [1967] RPC 581, though it also rejects reputation as sufficient, is probably no longer useful, given the hard line on customer connection that it takes. See Browne-Wilkinson V-C in *Pete Waterman v CBS* [1993] EMLR 27.

[243] [1984] FSR 413.

[244] i.e. advertising in films and American magazines available here.

[245] They can prevent the use of an identical or similar trade mark on similar goods/services where confusion is likely. [246] [1976] FSR 256, p. 269, PC.

[247] Lord Diplock's speech did not lay stress on this, but rather provided a more general test.

include, *selling in England* a class of goods to which the particular trade name applies.

However, a more relaxed and modern approach is that goodwill does not demand a trading base here. Indeed, it does not even demand that customers must purchase the claimant's goods or contract with the claimant from within the jurisdiction. Rather the issue becomes whether the claimant has generated goodwill in the jurisdiction: a question of fact and degree. The question is simply 'does the plaintiff have customers here'.[248] This was stressed by Walton J in *Athletes Foot Marketing Associates Inc v Cobra Sports Ltd*. Indeed, these customers need not have direct contractual relations with the claimant. It may be sufficient to have the goods imported and sold here. In *SA des Anciens Etablissements Panhard et Levassor v Panhard Levassor Motor Co Ltd*[249] the plaintiffs' cars were imported and sold in England by a third party and were purchased abroad and imported by English residents.[250] Again, the plaintiff may have licensed the use of his name or mark on products which are sold here. In *Globelegance v Sarkissian*[251] the plaintiff fashion designer had exhibited in England, had sold patterns here, made up into dresses sold under his trade name, and supplied a limited number of ties for resale here. This was held sufficient to constitute goodwill, at least for interlocutory purposes. Conversely, in *Nishika Corp v Goodchild*[252] the plaintiffs had yet to launch their new camera in the United Kingdom and were preempted by the defendants, who falsely represented that they were connected with them. It was held that the defendants' activities had created sufficient goodwill for the plaintiffs within the jurisdiction. The selling of the cameras in the jurisdiction was *per se* lawful and had created a sufficient goodwill for the court to protect. It is also established that to advertise here, in order to solicit mail order purchases,[253] will suffice.

Following this formula, there may be customers in the jurisdiction, though they travel abroad to obtain the claimant's goods or his services. The most important case on this point is the decision of the Supreme Court of Ireland in *C&A Modes Ltd v C Waterford Ltd*.[254] Here, customers travelled from the Irish Republic to Northern Ireland to trade with the

---

[248] Walton J in *Athletes Foot Associates v Cobra Sports Ltd* [1980] ROC 343, p. 357. However, later he states: 'the plaintiffs disclose not one single solitary transaction by way of trade with anyone in this country at all' (p. 357).

[249] (1901)18 RPC 405.

[250] And see *Poiret v Jules Poiret Ltd* (1920) 37 RPC 177.

[251] [1974] RPC 603.   [252] [1990] FSR 371.

[253] *Grant v Levitt* (1901) 18 RPC 361. In *Jian Tools Inc v Roderick Manhattan Group Ltd* [1995] FSR 924, Knox J sales from the American plaintiff to a small number of English customers 'transatlantically inspired' by magazines and recommendations by foreign residents were sufficient to create goodwill.

[254] [1978] FSR 126, SC of Ireland.

plaintiff. This was held to create sufficient goodwill for the plaintiff *in the Republic*. The decision was commented upon favourably by Walton J in his review of relevant case law in *Athletes Foot Marketing Associates Inc v Cobra Sports*. He asserted that this decision was 'fully in line ... with general principles'. If goodwill is in essence the 'attractive force that brings in custom', then it is the customers *qua customers* who decide the case. This was strongly the view of Browne-Wilkinson V-C in *Pete Waterman v CBS*: 'what is necessary is for the plaintiffs to show that they have a trade connection here which will normally consist of customers forming part of their goodwill, wherever that goodwill is situate.'[255] By concentrating on customers rather than the site of the trading activity, it becomes clear that goodwill can reach beyond national boundaries. To be goodwill within the jurisdiction, however, the attractive force must exist as a reason for travel. If they travel as tourists and happen to experience the claimant's goods or services, that should not be sufficient to create goodwill within the jurisdiction. On this analysis, goodwill beyond territorial boundaries would be difficult to establish.[256]

(C) DAMAGE TO GOODWILL: COMPLETING THE TRINITY

The third central element of the tort is that of damage.[257] Mere confusion is not sufficient. The misrepresentation must be 'calculated to injure' the claimant's business or goodwill and must cause or be probable to cause such damage.[258] Proving financial loss (to the claimant) or gain (to the defendant) is not sufficient. The link between damage and goodwill is an important limitation on the tort, especially after *Advocaat* added product misdescription to the list of relevant misrepresentations. If simply any damage—in the sense of damage to the claimant's competitive edge—was sufficient, then the tort could expand into something closer to an action for unfair competition.

For many years it was unclear whether anything more than nominal damages could be awarded against an innocent defendant. In *Draper v*

---

[255] [1993] EMLR 27.

[256] See Cooke P in *Dominion Rent-A-Car Ltd v Budget Rent-A Car Systems* [1987] 2 NZLR 395, NZ Court of Appeal. For him the reason that trade within the jurisdiction tends to be the norm stems in part 'from a sense that unless a trader has already entered or at least is clearly about to enter the local market and thus contribute to the local economy ... the local law should not allow him to stifle local enterprise' (p. 405).

[257] A necessary consequence of passing off being an action on the case under the old forms of action.

[258] See Lord Diplock in *Advocaat* [1980] RPC 31 and Lord Oliver in *Reckitt & Colman Products v Borden Inc* [1990] RPC 340 (the *Jif Lemon* case).

Trist,[259] two of the members of the Court of Appeal expressed doubts over whether damages were recoverable in the absence of fraud or dishonesty on the defendant's part, while the question was left open by the House of Lords in *Marengo v Daily Sketch & Sunday Graphic Ltd*.[260] However, in *Gillette UK Ltd v Edenwest Ltd*[261] Blackburne J asserted that the tort should follow the registered trade mark practice and allow recovery in damages against an innocent defender. He rejected the historical debate as to the availability of damages as 'unreal', given the tort did not achieve its modern form until the early part of the twentieth century.[262]

Proving damage: the spectrum

What would appear to be the case is that there has developed a spectrum along which proving damage or the probability of damage becomes more important. The classic case of passing off involves a trade rival passing off his goods as the claimant's. In such a case, there is an intrinsic likelihood of damage. Thus in *Spalding v Gamage*, Lord Parker noted 'it is sufficient to say that the misrepresentation being established, *and being in its nature calculated to produce damage*, the plaintiffs are prima facie entitled both to an injunction and to an inquiry as to damage' [emphasis added]. Indeed, where fraud is involved: 'no court would be astute when they discovered an intention to deceive, in coming to the conclusion that a dishonest defendant had been unsuccessful in his fraudulent design.'[263] This is one end of the 'proof of damage spectrum' in passing off.

Where less typical cases of passing off are involved they do not present the same automatic consequential diversion of trade. Indeed, in *Advocaat*, Lord Diplock accepted that the tort of passing off does not require the plaintiff and defendant to be competing traders in the same line of business. At the other end of the spectrum, therefore, are cases where, though there may be confusion, the parties are not in competition and no diversion of trade is alleged. The lack of a common field of activity is of course

---

[259] [1939] 3 All ER 513.   [260] [1948] 1 All ER 406.

[261] [1994] RPC 279, Blackburne J.

[262] As far as other remedies are concerned, it is not uncommon for plaintiffs to seek a *quia timet* injunction. In *Advocaat*, Lord Diplock stated that where damage is probable rather than actual a *quia timet* action would be involved. Although deciding whether the action is *quia timet* or otherwise may not always be easy: see e.g. the disagreement between the first instance judge (Jeffries J) and Court of Appeal in the New Zealand case, *CIVC v Wineworths Group Ltd* [1992] 2 NZLR 327. The issue was also debated by the Court of Appeal in *British Telecommunications plc v One In A Million*, [1999] FSR 1. An account of profits may be sought.

[263] Lord Loreburn *Claudius Ash, Son & Co Ltd v Invicta Manufacturing Co Ltd* (1912) 29 RPC 465, 475. See also *C&A Modes v C&A (Waterford) Ltd*. The lower court had found an intention to deceive and the parties were in similar lines of trade. The plaintiffs were not required to prove damage: 'in those circumstances the law assumes a resulting damage' per Henchy J, citing Greene MR (p. 518) and Goddard LJ (526) in *Draper v Trist* [1939] 3 All ER 513.

not fatal to a claim in passing off, but such a case is an unusual action in passing off. Thus, in *Stringfellow v McCain*[264] the plaintiff objected to the defendant using the same name as his prestige night club for their oven-ready chips. Although there was an argument that public confusion might result from the use of the same name, the Court of Appeal refused to infer a likelihood of consequential damage to the plaintiff's business, especially where the defendant was innocent and in a completely different line of business.[265] Rather in such a case the Court required: 'clear and cogent proof' of actual damage or proof that the real likelihood of damage was 'substantial'.

Heads of damage

It is clear that the classic trinity demands that a head of damage should relate back to the claimant's goodwill—the interest protected by the tort.[266] The type of injury to the goodwill is obviously related to the nature of the misrepresentation alleged. Certain types of harm are commonly pleaded and they all contain varieties within them. Measuring the damage caused can be difficult whether the allegation be loss of sales or a more general damage to goodwill.

(i) Diversion of trade

The classic case of the defendant passing off his goods as the claimant's involves an obvious allegation of diversion of trade. Loss of sales[267] is thus the basic head of damage for passing off. There is no further require-ment in such a case to allege that the defendant's goods are inferior for the defendant should not be allowed 'to cheat the plaintiffs of some of their legitimate trade'.[268] Such loss may also be involved, of course, in less typi-cal cases of passing off—especially those involving harm through product misrepresentations. In *Advocaat*, where the misrepresentation involved product misdescription, the damage, *inter alia*, was lost sales to the owners of goodwill in the genuine article.[269]

---

[264] [1984] RPC 501, CA.

[265] See especially Stephenson LJ [1984] RPC 501, pp. 546–7: 'the case is very far removed from the case of a small and perhaps disreputable trader deliberately seeking to attract to his business the goodwill attaching to the well-established business of a well-known trader in the same field.'

[266] This was underlined by Millett LJ in *Harrods v The Harrodian School* [1996] RPC 697, p. 716 (rejecting the plaintiffs' claim for dilution): 'I have an intellectual difficulty in accepting the concept that the law insists upon the presence of both confusion and damage and yet recognizes as sufficient a head of damage which does not depend on confusion.'

[267] For an example of indirect loss see *Hoffman La-Roche & Co AG v DDSA Pharmaceuticals Ltd* [1969] FSR 410, CA.

[268] Lord Herschell, *Reddaway v Banham* [1896] AC 199, p. 209.

[269] There was also a potential debasement of the genuine article if the name Advocaat were

(ii) Devaluation of Reputation

There is obviously a need to protect the claimant's reputation as goodwill is in part based on this. This second head of damage has two distinct areas.

The first involves the *Spalding v Gamage* situation. The claimant's inferior goods are passed off as his superior. In fact, the ability to complain of substitution goes wider than inferior alternatives. Lord Parker makes this clear in *Spalding v Gamage* itself : 'A cannot without infringing the rights of B, represent goods which are not B's goods of a particular class or quality to be B's goods of that particular class or quality.' Wadlow gives a fact situation based on *Revlon Inc v Cripps & Lee Ltd*[270] as a possible example of substituting different but not inferior goods of the claimant. Thus he examples the defendant selling the claimant's medicated shampoo as non-medicated. This would be passing off, even though both shampoos were of a high quality.[271]

The second head of damage in this area is that of 'injurious association'.[272] There are variations on the theme of injurious association. The most obvious variety occurs when the defendant's misrepresentation is likely to lead to a depreciation of the claimant's reputation. If such an allegation is well founded, obviously the 'attractive force that brings in custom' is in jeopardy. Should the defendant, who has misrepresented himself or his goods as in some way connected to the claimant, have a bad[273] or even indifferent reputation, then damage is likely. Thus in *Annabel's v Schock*[274] a high-class London nightclub, Annabel's, successfully restrained the defendant from carrying on the business of an escort agency under the name Annabel's Escort Agency. The public's indifferent estimation of escort agencies in general led to a legitimate concern that the plaintiff's reputation might be 'tarred with the same brush', should the public confuse the two. However, there should be some evidence of public perception[275] being less than positive towards the defendant: in

permitted for use in egg drinks generally and not confined to those that are spirit-based. See also *Bristol Conservatories* case [1989] RPC 455, CA.

[270] [1980] FSR 85.

[271] Wadlow, above, n. 1, p. 270.

[272] The phrase is used by Megarry J in *Unitex Ltd v Union Texturing Co Ltd* [1973] RPC 119, p. 122 (the case went to CA). The alternative title would be 'devaluing of reputation'. As such, the *Spalding v Gamage* situation—selling the plaintiffs' inferior stock as his superior line—would fall under this head of damage.

[273] See *Sony v Saray* [1983] FSR 302, CA. It is the public's perception that is important: see *Nationwide Estate Agents v Nationwide Building Society* [1987] FSR 579, the plaintiff showed the risk of injurious association from newspaper reports alleging mortgage fraud against someone alleged to be associated with the defendant.

[274] [1972] FSR 261, CA.

[275] The fact that it was the public's perception that was important was noted in *Nationwide Estate Agents v Nationwide Building Society* [1987] FSR 579.

Unitex Ltd v Union Texturing Co the Court of Appeal stressed the need for a 'real, tangible risk' of damage.[276] *Combe v Scholl*[277] involved harm from both diversion and injurious association. There the defendant's inferior product was in effect represented to be the same as the plaintiff's. As such the quality of the plaintiff's product was impugned.

Probably the most extreme version of 'injurious association' is the allegation that the defendant's misrepresentation may lead to legal liability for the claimant or more generally the risk of litigation.[278] This was an item of damage successfully pleaded in *Illustrated Newspapers v Publicity Services* where the defendant had added advertising material to the plaintiffs' illustrated newspaper.[279] Should objectionable matter have been included in these advertisements, the plaintiffs ran 'a reasonable risk of being exposed to litigation—not successful litigation, but litigation which may nonetheless be very annoying and possibly cause them considerable expense'.[280]

Obviously the facts may reveal further variations on the theme of injurious association. Thus the claimant may allege that an apparent connection with the particular defendant may lead to a loss of goodwill with existing trade connections. This was raised in *Spalding v Gamage*:[281] the fact that the defendant might appear to have been given a discount by the plaintiff might well cause ill will with legitimate outlets. Again, the harm caused where confusion causes post to be diverted may be damage for the purposes of the tort: see *Lloyds v Lloyds (Southampton) Ltd*.[282]

(iii) Restriction on expansion potential

This is commonly pleaded by claimants and on the facts it may be a legitimate item of damage. Thus the claimant may be able to show that he intended to diversify into goods similar to the defendant's, as was shown in *Alfred Dunhill Ltd v Sunoptic SA*.[283] There, the plaintiffs, originally the producers of tobacco goods had diversified into luxury items for men and

---

[276] *Unitex Ltd v Union Texturing Co* [1973] RPC 119. The Court of Appeal stressed the need for a 'real, tangible risk' of damage.

[277] [1980] RPC 1.

[278] Note the related rule of *Routh v Webster* (1847) 50 ER 698 which extends such protection to non-traders.

[279] 55 RPC 172.

[280] 55 RPC 172, p. 182. See also *Sony KK v Saray Electronics (London) Ltd* [1983] FSR 302, CA: the misrepresentation of dealership would include the misrepresentation that the defendants were empowered to give guarantees on behalf of the plaintiff.

[281] And see *Unitex Ltd v Union Texturing Co* [1973] RPC 119 where the plaintiffs alleged that if there was perceived to be a connection between them and the defendants, their customers would believe that they had entered into competition with them. However, there was no risk of this on the facts.

[282] (1912) 29 RPC 433.

[283] [1979] FSR 337, CA.

were able to prevent the defendants using their name for sunglasses (there was indeed some evidence that the plaintiffs were planning to add to their diversification by producing sunglasses under their mark). Or a claimant may be able to show that he is already licensing his name.[284] However, there should be clear evidence of this probable harm, to avoid this head of damage simply being an argument in favour of monopoly or a method of creating licensing rights in a name.

Thus merely to allege the loss of a licensing or expansion opportunity should not be sufficient where there is no licensing or merchandising goodwill. Unless the court links this head of damage clearly to the claimant's actual goodwill, it verges on an allegation of misappropriation, rather than passing off. Without establishing existing goodwill to justify protecting future activities, the allegation becomes an attempt to close off markets to others, even before the claimant has entered them. This David and Goliath scenario was accepted by Russell LJ in *Dunhill v Sunoptic SA*:[285] 'a court must always be careful to see that a large, powerful and wealthy corporation does not use its overwhelming financial muscle to the detriment of what would or may ultimately prove to be genuine commercial competition.' Again, Whitford J in *LRC v Lilla Edets*[286] stressed 'the defendants are entitled to raise the question as to how far beyond their own specific field of activities the plaintiffs are entitled to extend the area within which they ought to be given protection'. It may, of course, be useful, should a legitimate allegation of damage to goodwill be possible, to use this argument to tilt the balance of convenience in favour of the claimant. But as a head of damage it has to be squared with the rationale of the tort.

Indeed, this head of damage has often been rejected. In *Newsweek Inc v BBC*,[287] the Court of Appeal refused to restrain the BBC from using the plaintiff's magazine title, *Newsweek*, for a current affairs programme, though the plaintiff proposed to move into the English television market. For Lord Denning, the possibility of confusion was too speculative. In *Stringfellow v McCain*[288] the owner of a famous and up-market nightclub objected to the defendants' using the name 'Stringfellows' for their oven-ready chips[289] and alleged that future licensing potential was thereby prejudiced (he had yet to merchandise the name or image). The Court of Appeal refused to indulge in 'pure speculation': there was no evidence that the plaintiff would have been in a position profitably to exploit merchandising the club's image or name nor was it likely that up-market

---

[284] e.g. a character merchandiser: though there are still problems in proving reliance.
[285] [1979] FSR 337, 368, CA.   [286] [1973] RPC 560, p. 564.
[287] [1979] RPC 441.   [288] [1984] RPC 501.
[289] The misrepresentation was made out because of the accompanying advertisement that had a nightclub theme and appeared modelled on Stringfellows.

goods would seek to be associated with the name. In *Pentagon Stationers Ltd v Pentagon Business Systems Ltd*[290] an interlocutory injunction was refused because the plaintiffs' claim was 'simply that the defendants are trading in an area into which the plaintiffs hope to expand'.[291]

However, that is not to say that this head of damage is not frequently alleged, though more often than not as part of a package of similar allegations involving loss of control and dilution (discussed below). This was the case most famously in *Lego v Lego M Lemelstritch*,[292] where the plaintiffs successfully argued expansion restriction even when not licensing their own name (and having given no evidence of intention to diversify or license). The plaintiffs complained that they were deprived of a licensing fee, lost opportunities to license others or develop into those new areas and loss of control of their own reputation. It is surely relevant that Falconer J cited with approval the High Court of Australia's decision in *Henderson v Radio Corporation*.[293] There it was held that an appropriation of the plaintiffs' business reputation damages goodwill by depriving the plaintiffs of the right to use it or exploit it for their own benefit. Thus merely because there were opportunities for licensing/franchising the Lego mark, there was damage under this head. What is revealed, therefore, is that this allegation (like loss of control and dilution) attempts to gain much wider protection from the tort than it has traditionally given. In effect protection is sought for the name itself.

(iv) Confusion and loss of control

Mere confusion based on a false connection is not sufficient in itself to give rise to the likelihood of damage. In *Unitex Ltd v Union Texturising Co Ltd*[294] there was confusion but no real tangible risk of damage arising from such confusion. Though there are *dicta* to the effect that mere confusion can be sufficient, such cases can sometimes be explained by the 'proof of damage spectrum'. Slade LJ, e.g., in *Chelsea Man Menswear Ltd v Chelsea Girl Ltd*[295] noted the 'injury which is inherently likely to be suffered by any business' when on frequent occasions it is confused by customers or potential customers with the defendants' business or there is a misapprehension that they are connected. Where there is direct

---

[290] (1985) Lexis transcript, Judge Baker QC.

[291] To an extent this was appreciated in *Lyngstad v Annabas Products Ltd* [1977] FSR 62 (the Abba case). Here the famous pop group had yet to merchandise themselves but sought to prevent others using their glamorous image to market their products. They were attempting to close off markets even before they had decided to trade in them. The real concern in such cases is not to protect goodwill—there is none—but to allege that the defendants are 'cashing-in' on the plaintiff's success. As such that is an insufficient allegation for passing off.

[292] [1983] FSR 155.　　　　　　[293] [1969] RPC 218.　　　　　　[294] [1973] FSR 181.

[295] [1987] RPC 161, CA. And see Jenkins LJ in *Brestian v Try* [1958] RPC 161, CA.

competition such confusion seems 'calculated to cause harm' through diversion of trade or injurious association.[296]

Again, there may be cases where the misconnection could have disastrous results for the claimant in question and for this reason the court is not prepared to allow the claimant's goodwill to be at risk. Here 'loss of control' may be argued as a head of damage, provided the particular facts of such cases reveal at least the potential of a 'real, tangible risk' of harm to the claimant. This might be because the claimant's business (or the defendant's business) is particularly vulnerable to catastrophe[297] or public concern.[298]

However, at times claimants allege 'loss of control' simply as a means of preventing a false connection *per se*. Falconer J in *Lego v Lego M Lemelstritch*[299] accepted the lack of control over the quality of the defendants' products as a reason for the injunction he granted, even though the parties were in vastly different trades (toy bricks/gardening equipment) and even though the plaintiffs made it clear that they were not making any allegation as to the quality of the defendants' products at that point in time. There was no allegation that the defendants' products were of inferior quality: they were indeed a reputable foreign company that had been legitimately using the name 'Lego' (derived from the owners' names) for many years in Israel. Here the court appeared to concentrate on the fact that the Lego mark was a 'household name'. The Court of Appeal in *Harrods Ltd v Harrodian School Ltd* appeared to accept 'loss of control' as a legitimate head of damage[300] as did Jacob J in *Mecklermedia*

---

[296] In *British Legion v British Legion (Street) Ltd* 48 RPC 555, there was nothing in the evidence to suggest that the defendant's club was carried on in anything other than a perfectly proper manner. However, it was held that damage was a real possibility 'if evil befalls the defendant and it finds itself . . . in trouble either under the licensing laws or in financial trouble or in some other way of discredit'—Farwell J. However, it should be noted that here there was a common pool of 'customers'. Diversion of trade appears to be inherent in such a case.

[297] In *Hulton Press Ltd v White Eagle Youth Holiday Camp Ltd* (1951) 68 RPC 126 the publishers of the boy's comic, the *Eagle* restrained the defendants from using the name 'White Eagle Youth Holiday Camp' for a children's holiday camp. As the plaintiff was associated with a club to provide holiday camps for children, there was evidence of confusion. Though there was no evidence of the defendants being perceived as disreputable, for Wynn-Parry J the key factor was that 'it would require but one such disaster as an epidemic at a holiday camp like this, or a bad accident' to harm the plaintiff.

[298] In *Associated Press v Insert Media* [1991] 1 WLR 571 the defendants inserting advertising material into the plaintiff's publications without consent posed 'an obvious, appreciable risk of loss of goodwill and reputation by the plaintiff', particularly as the plaintiff enforced high advertising standards for legitimate advertisers. Note also, however, that the CA found there to be a risk of diversion of trade, given advertisers might choose the cheaper option of the defendant rather than the direct advertising with the plaintiff.

[299] [1983] FSR 155.

[300] [1996] RPC 697. Millett LJ accepted the reasoning of the *Lego* case that 'the danger in such a case is that the plaintiff loses control over his own reputation' (p. 715). Sir Michael

Corp v DC Congress Gesellschaft mbH.[301] On the basis of these cases it might be difficult to see when a connection misrepresentation would ever require an additional proof of damage: the false connection would always be sufficient. Again, the head of damage has the potential for taking the tort beyond its traditional field, into that of misappropriation.

(v) Dilution . . . and the need for a rationale

Dilution as a head of damage is increasingly found in passing off claims (though often as a supplement to other more orthodox heads of damage).[302] The theory behind the concept of dilution harm is that 'the more widely a symbol is used, the less effective it will be for any one user'.[303] It was proposed by the American academic Schechter in 1927, in an article[304] that influenced the majority of the American states to introduce anti-dilution legislation. Indeed, there is now a Federal Dilution Trademark Act which defines dilution as 'the lessening of the capacity of a famous mark to identify and distinguish goods or services'.[305]

Schechter in fact proposed a theory of protection against what might be termed 'pure dilution'—an allegation of a 'lessening of the capacity to distinguish',[306] 'an erosion of the mark', or 'blurring of the product identification' *without any confusion.* However, in recent years it would appear that English claimants[307] are relying on a modified version of the theory: what might be termed 'confusion dilution'. Here, though there is customer confusion connecting the claimant to the defendant, no damage to goodwill is clearly identified. The concept is commonly alleged where

Kerr (dissenting in the case itself) equated a connection misrepresentation with the loss of distinctiveness and loss of control (p. 724).

[301] [1997] FSR 627, p. 633.

[302] See e.g. Knox J in *All Weather Sports Activities Ltd v All Weather Sports (UK) Ltd* 1987, Lexis; Blackburne J in *Dalgetty Spillers Foods Ltd v Food Brokers Ltd* [1994] FSR 504; Jacob J in *Mecklermedia v DC Congress* [1997] FSR 627; Laddie J in *Matthew Gloag v Welsh Distilleries* [1998] FSR 718. McGechan J in *Taylor Brothers Ltd v Taylors Group Ltd* [1988] 2 NZLR 1, p. 15 considered the three types of damage which may be incurred in passing off to be diversion, damage to reputation, and dilution.

[303] Brown, R., 'Advertising and the Public Interest' 57 Yale LJ (1940) 1165, p. 1191.

[304] Above, n. 2.

[305] Federal Dilution Trademark Act 1995.

[306] Wadlow, above, n. 1, p. 173 notes that loss of exclusivity might be a legitimate head of damage where, in an extreme case, the plaintiff's name or mark is swamped or submerged by the subsequent use of that name or mark by a larger defendant. For an example of this see *Falcon Travel Ltd v Owners Abroad Travel plc*, [1991] 1 EIPR D–11, HC of Ireland. Rather than involving dilution, this involves obliteration of goodwill and as such is clearly within the tort.

[307] Welkowitz, D., 'Re-examining Trademark Dilution', 44 Vand LR (1991) 531 notes that American case law appears to acknowledge three different categories of dilution: confusion dilution; pure dilution (including dilution by tarnishment); and dilution through generification (where the mark becomes descriptive of the product itself: here it is arguable that in English law, classic passing off could provide a remedy provided the plaintiff acts quickly).

there is a connection misrepresentation or a product misdescription: the argument being that such misrepresentations may dilute the distinctiveness of the name or product involved. The apparent acceptance of dilution as a head of damage by the Court of Appeal in *Taittinger SA v Allbev Ltd*[308] requires a reassessment of the scope of the tort (see below)

Once vague and speculative allegations of loss of control, loss of expansion potential, or loss of distinctiveness are raised, the net result is that the courts are being asked to change the nature of the tort. What lies behind all of these claims (where evidence of likely harm is lacking) are attempts to complain about misappropriation.[309] These heads of damage—but particularly the allegation of dilution—pose one of the most important issues for the development of the tort in the twenty-first century. The twentieth century saw an expansion of the tort in line with an origin and quality information protection function. The proposed protection against dilution (whether the courts realize it or not) calls into question the classic trinity and requires a sea-change in the rationale of the tort. It demands protection for commercial magnetism alone and would take the tort into the wider allegations of misappropriation or unfair competition. The rationale for such an expansion would appear to be the protection of already successful traders.

To understand the tensions within the tort and debate its proper scope, it is important to articulate the rationale of the tort, as is evidenced by the classic trinity. It is against this rationale that the many ways in which claimants seek to further enlarge the tort can be assessed.

THE RATIONALE OF PASSING OFF AND THE CLASSIC TRINITY

As a misrepresentation tort that helps to control trading practices, it is clear that passing off is in line with the public interest in encouraging correct information to be presented to consumers.[310] But of course customers cannot sue under this tort. The prime concern of the action is to protect the claimant 'rather than champion the consumer'.[311] And the

---

[308] [1993] FSR 641. In *Marks & Spencer plc v One in a Million plc* [1999] FSR 1, p. 23 Aldous LJ commented: 'the registration of the domain name . . . is an erosion of the exclusive goodwill in the name.'

[309] For a more detailed analysis see Carty, H., 'Dilution and Passing Off: Cause for Concern' 112 LQR (1996) 632.

[310] For a more detailed discussion of this see Naresh, above, n. 32, pp. 119–25.

[311] Fleming, J., *The Law of Tort*, 9th edn. (Sydney: LBC Information Services, 1998), p. 784. Aldous LJ in *Marks & Spencer plc v One in a Million plc* [1999] FSR 1, p. 11 commented that just as Parliament intervened in the interests of consumers and traders to ensure commercial honesty 'it is therefore not surprising that the courts have recognized that the common law, in that particular field, should proceed upon a parallel course'.

mere allegation of trade misrepresentation is not sufficient. The claimant trader must be harmed in a specific way—namely his customer connection must be threatened. The tort focuses on the success of the claimant, rather than the 'free-ride' achieved by the defendant. Thus the tort allows the courts to intervene and prevent 'excessive' competition or misinformation only where there are clear boundaries to that jurisdiction. The tort is, then, of limited scope, leaving the main attack on trade misrepresentations to the State.[312]

However, the need to show a misrepresentation that has been relied upon and the need to show that customer connection has been harmed, ties in with the information role of the tort and indicates that the public interest is part of its rationale. What emerges from judicial discussion of the tort[313] is that the public interest is an important but *indirect* justification for the tort. The rationale of the tort is to protect the trader who is particularly damaged by the defendant's misrepresentation *where the effect is to encourage efficient market choices*. As Cane notes: 'one of the fundamental requirements for the operation of a free market is that the participants in the market have enough information to enable them to choose the commodity which represents the best value for money.'[314]

This then is the function of the classic trinity: to protect 'deserving' claimants where it is in the public interest so to do. As Fisher J noted in the New Zealand case of *Tots Toys v Mitchell*:[315] 'there is a legitimate private interest in protecting business goodwill against the deceptive conduct of competitors. Even more importantly, there is a strong public interest in preserving the means of identifying the source of the products.' The tort harnesses 'the self-protective energy of competitors to the protection of consumers'.[316]

Thus the forms of misrepresentation that are actionable are shaped by the fact that they must be representations affecting customer base (and they must be relied on in some way in order to be material). The net effect of this is that the tort still focuses on misrepresentations as to origin or quality, in line with the traditionally recognized function of trade marks generally. The tort, therefore, meets the demands of the public interest by policing the information on which consumer choices are made, mirroring (but only in a limited way) Parliament's 'progressive intervention in the interests of consumers'.[317]

---

[312] Traders have no right to sue under the Trade Descriptions Act 1968.

[313] Lord Parker in *Spalding v Gamage* (1915) 32 RPC 273 emphasized the basis of the tort in misrepresentation and its role in the protection of the plaintiff's goodwill; Lord Diplock in *Warnink (Erven) BV v Townend & Sons Ltd* [1979] AC 731, pp. 742–3 extended the misrepresentations applicable to the tort, given that was what 'the public interest demands'.

[314] Cane, P., *Tort Law and Economic Interests*, 2nd edn. (Oxford: Clarendon Press, 1996), p. 120.   [315] [1993] 1 NZLR 325.

[316] Cornish, above, n. 1, p. 53.   [317] Lord Diplock in *Advocaat* [1979] AC 731, pp. 742–3.

The need for goodwill both determines the misrepresentations that are actionable and demands that the claimant be 'deserving' of protection. Goodwill requires not just effort but success (in achieving a customer base). This part of the trinity limits protection, consistent with the reluctance of the common law to allow claimants wide scope to police competitive or trading practice. This was acknowledged by Lord Scarman in *Pub Squash* when he commented that 'competition is safeguarded by the necessity for the plaintiff to prove that he has built up an intangible property right'.[318] Moreover, given goodwill is about customers, and the tort seeks to prevent customer connection being threatened, this second element of the trinity also reflects the aim of protecting the public interest. For this reason, the tort does not as such protect a product or name, however famous: as Millett LJ commented in *Harrods*: 'to date the law has not sought to protect the value of the brand name as such, but the value of the goodwill which it generates; and it insists on proof of confusion to justify its intervention.'[319] As we will see, this proposition is subject to attack by claimants, dissatisfied with the tort's level of protection.

The third element of the trinity is damage and, logically, that requires damage (actual or potential) to the claimant's goodwill. Deserving claimants are protected against harm to their success. As damage is joined to misrepresentation and goodwill by the need to show reliance, the public interest is served by protecting against reliance on misinformation.[320]

It is clear that the classic trinity provides 'valuable fence posts'.[321] As all three elements of the trinity are interlinked, so they help to define and limit each other. At the start of the twenty-first century the tort is still limited by the same factors as applied at the start of the twentieth century: there must be customer reliance, based on the defendant's misrepresentation which harms the goodwill of the claimant.

PASSING OFF AT THE CROSSROADS

Yet case law reveals the tort to be at a crossroads in its development. Although in the twentieth century the tort expanded enormously, the major advances were in line with the classic trinity and the perceived

[318] [1981] RPC 429, p. 490.

[319] [1996] RPC 697.

[320] The importance of reliance was stressed by Jacob J in *Hodge Clemco Ltd v Airblast Ltd* [1995] FSR 806 citing Judge Learned Hand in *Crescent Tool v Kilborn & Bishop* (1917) 247 F299 'the critical question of fact . . . is whether the public is moved in any degree to buy the article because of its source and what are the features by which it distinguishes that source'.

[321] Burley, S., 'Passing off and character merchandising: should England lean towards Australia?' 137 EIPR (1991) 277, p. 229.

rationale described above. Thus misdescription of the claimant's products, connection misrepresentations, and even the three forms of actionable misrepresentations that can be termed 'product misdescription' are all within the above rationale, *provided* they are applied within the overall structure of the classic trinity. Again, the emergence of product goodwill is compatible with the rationale above, *provided* the claimants can demonstrate their individual customer base, emanating from the product in question. Furthermore, atypical heads of damage can be accommodated, *provided* there is evidence of at least potential rather than speculative harm to the claimant's goodwill.

However, it is inevitable that claimants should seek wider coverage of a tort which offers a competitive advantage (or at least the possibility of demanding a licence fee), where the borders of that tort have yet to be fully explored.[322] The implicit aspiration in some of the more unusual allegations of passing off is that the tort should develop into an action for unfair competition and/or misappropriation. Indeed, some predicted at the time of the decision of *Advocaat* that the tort was the subject of just such a development.[323] Though in the past judges have been careful 'to ensure that [the tort] is not applied indiscriminately to analogies which fall outside the classic case'[324] this caution is less evident today.[325] This may be because of the relentless drive by powerful claimants such as those with international reputations, merchandising potential or prestige products to gain even more market power and control. As most passing off actions are dealt with at interlocutory level only and at such a level some judges are clearly influenced in their decision by what they perceive to be sharp practice by a defendant, it is not surprising that at times (as we shall see) such claimants persuade the courts to consider such wider protection.[326]

---

[322] Noted by Wadlow, above, n. 1, p. 2.

[323] See e.g. Dworkin, G., 'Unfair Competition: Is the Common Law Developing a New Tort?' [1979] EIPR 241. Of course the possibility of such an action has been raised by judges and plaintiffs alike: Cross J in *Vine Products Ltd v Mackenzie & Co Ltd* [1969] RPC 1, p. 23 re *Spanish Champagne*: 'in truth the decision went beyond the well-trodden paths of passing off into the unmapped area of "unfair trading" or "unfair competition".' Unfair trading was alleged in *Pub Squash* and Lord Scarman refrained from deciding whether any cause of action could lie in the absence of confusion. Is it significant that Laddie J remarked (in *Chocosuisse Union des Fabricants Suisses de Chocolat v Cadbury Ltd* [1997] RPC 117, p. 127 'although *in the current state of development* the common law does not recognize a general right in one trader to complain of damaging dishonest trading practices committed by his competitors, nevertheless in this area the law has advanced in effect to give rise to a civilly enforceable right similar to an *appellation contrôlée*' [emphasis added].

[324] Presumably because it provided wider protection compared to the other economic torts involving misrepresentations.

[325] A prime indication of this is contained in the judgment of Laddie J in *Matthew Gloag & Son Ltd v Welsh Distilleries Ltd* [1998] FSR 718 (discussed, later in the text).

[326] See in particular *Baskin-Robbins Ice Cream Co v Gutman* [1976] FSR 545, Graham J; *Allen*

Moreover, this push for greater protection is also likely to be fed by the modern debate[327] as to the 'proper' scope of trade mark law generally. This debate identifies trade marks as having not only an origin and quality function but also an advertising and investment function. Clearly trade marks do serve as advertising and marketing tools and where brands are well known 'their valuation as assets will run into billions of pounds'.[328] The major controversy is whether trade mark protection (and the related protection provided by the tort of passing off) should extend beyond the protection of origin/quality (with its public interest) into the protection of commercial magnetism (with its emphasis on commercial interest alone). The move is from protecting trading information to protecting persuasive marketing *per se*. As the registered trade mark system now protects against dilution (at least where dissimilar goods are concerned)[329] the need for such a debate is clear. Indeed, the debate has been brought into prominence by the ECJ decision in *Parfums Christian Dior SA v Evora BV*.[330] Though the ECJ has in the past not sought to define the purpose of trade mark protection exhaustively,[331] it has emphasized the origin function (in the sense of guaranteeing both source and quality) as worthy of protection. In *Dior*[332] the ECJ revealed that the protection of trade marks might go further, under EC law, to include the protection of the mark and its prestige in its own right. So in *Dior* where the famous perfume producer objected to the style of advertisements for their product by an unauthorized distributor (a cut-price chemists group) the ECJ

& Co v Brown Watson Ltd [1965] RPC Pennycuick J, p. 194: 'one need have no sympathy for the defendants . . . because it is abundantly clear [that they did what they did] . . . simply in order to cash in on the advertisement and reputation of the plaintiffs' book'; and *Elida Gibbs v Colgate-Palmolive Ltd* [1983] FSR 9 Goulding J. Conversely, where the defendants' activities are seen as legitimate, the court is reluctant to grant an interlocutory injunction see *Nationwide BS v Nationwide Estate Agents* [1987] FSR 579, pp. 592–3. Browne-Wilkinson V-C found there to be a connection misrepresentation and the possibility of harm through lack of control. However, no interlocutory injunction was granted as such a remedy would give the plaintiff 'a new and exclusive goodwill . . . by unfair commercial competition'.

[327] This debate referred to by AG Jacobs in *Parfums Christian Dior Sa v Evora BV* [1998] RPC 166, pp 180–1 as the origin/quality function versus the commercial/investment/advertising function.

[328] Cornish, above, n. 1, p. 597.

[329] Trade Marks Act 1994, s.10(3): infringement by use of a similar or identical sign in relation to dissimilar goods or services where the mark has a reputation in the UK and the use of the sign takes unfair advantage of or is detrimental to the distinctive character or repute of the plaintiffs' trade mark.

[330] [1998] RPC 166. For a useful discussion of this area see Norman, H., 'Perfume, Whisky and Leaping Cats of Prey' 20 8 EIPR (1998) 306.

[331] Advocate General Jacobs in *Sabel BV v Puma AG* [1998] RPC 199, p. 209.

[332] And see *Frits Loendersloot v George Ballantine & Son Ltd* [1998] RPC 199 which also, according to Norman, above, n. 330, p. 312 poses the possibility that 'those who deal in trade marked goods by way of resale may be liable for harming the image of the mark itself without having changed the condition of the goods'.

noted that a reseller must not under Article 7(2) of the First Trade Marks Directive act unfairly in relation to the legitimate interests of the trade mark owner. Those legitimate interests could include maintaining the luxurious image of the product by relying on their trade mark rights.[333]

The search for greater protection: passing off as unfair competition or misappropriation

Claimants increasingly seek to push the tort towards a more general protection against unfair competition or misappropriation. The rationale for such attempts centres on protecting the claimant against 'theft' of a market or a commercial asset (though at times the public interest may also be invoked). Where claimants are seeking to expand the tort significantly beyond the classic trinity, it is usually the concept of goodwill that is under attack, with the damage alleged being vague[334] or speculative. The success rate to date has been patchy (the further from the classic trinity the allegation, the less chance of success they have so far encountered). But seeds of uncertainty have clearly been sown. Moreover, claimants will be heartened by the comments of Aldous LJ in *British Telecommunications plc v One In A Million*[335] that Lord Diplock's test in *Advocaat* did not confine the cause of action forever 'as to do so would prevent the common law evolving to meet changes in methods of trade and communication as it had in the past'.

There are various ways in which claimants have been attempting to extend the tort. Some attempts arise from claimants' concerns over imitation (of product or promotional technique) and trade misdescriptions. Here, the nub of the allegation against the defendants is that they have gained an 'unfair competitive advantage' by their misrepresentation. At other times, claimants seek to use the tort to prevent the defendant from 'cashing in' on their success, whether that be due to the commercial magnetism of their name, image, or prestigious product. Here dilution is often the heart of the damage alleged, not surprisingly given Schechter, the 'father' of the dilution theory, believed that 'the advertising power of the trademark was the primary—perhaps the only—real value of a trade mark worth protecting'.[336] It is useful to categorise these attempts under

---

[333] On the facts Evora had not acted unfairly. Indeed, the decision of the ECJ in *Silhouette International Schmied GmbH & Co KG v Hartlauer Handelsgesellschaft mbH* [1998] FSR 729 protects the 'investment' function of trade marks. The ECJ decided that different national rules on international exhaustion of rights were contrary to the EC Trade Mark Directive 89/104 (Art. 7(1)). Parallel imports from non-EC countries could be prevented.

[334] The word 'insidious' is often used in such cases see e.g. Sir Thomas Bingham MR in *Taittinger v Allbev* [1993] FSR 641 and Laddie J in *Matthew Gloag v Welsh Distilleries* [1998] FSR 718.

[335] [1999] FSR 1.   [336] Welkowitz, above, n. 307, p. 533.

key headings, in order to assess their success and implications for the future. In all these cases, the claims fail to fit clearly into the classic trinity.

Product misdescriptions as unfair competition or misappropriation

A trade misdescription *per se* cannot be passing off. This was underlined in *Schulke & Mayr UK Ltd v Alkapharm UK Ltd*[337] where the plaintiffs took exception to the claims made by the defendants, their trade rival, in their advertisement. It was alleged that the defendants' claims for their product were false. Jacob J refused the injunction sought, applying the classic view that 'passing off involves . . . a false representation related to the plaintiffs' product or goodwill, not any free-standing false representation'.

However, claimants may seek to dress up an action based on trade misdescriptions as an action for *classic* passing off by alleging indirect (and unlikely) attacks on their goodwill. In both *SDS Biotech UK v Power Agrichemicals*[338] and *Hodge Clemco Ltd v Airblast Ltd*,[339] the real complaint was that the plaintiffs had complied with government regulations, while the defendant trade rival wrongly indicated that they had too.[340] It was the unfair competitive advantage that rankled,[341] though the plaintiffs in both cases attempted to argue that there was a misrepresentation that the defendants' products were within the relevant regulations. They further argued that as 'authorized' producers of the products in question their goodwill would somehow be affected. The judges concerned, Aldous J

---

[337] [1999] FSR 161, Jacob J. The plaintiffs attempted to claim that this was a *Combe v Scholl* [1980] RPC 1 type of case but the judge found the false allegation (if it was false) to be 'free-standing'. Malicious falsehood was also unsuccessfully claimed. See also *BBC v Talksport Ltd*, *The Times*, 29 June 2000, Blackburne J. Though the defendants misdescribed their service as 'live broadcasting', the BBC had no goodwill in 'live broadcasting', given that those words were merely descriptive of the service they provided.

[338] [1995] FSR 797, Aldous J—in fact decided in 1989.

[339] [1995] FSR 806, Jacob J.

[340] In *Hodge Clemco*, the defendants produced cheaper spare lenses, advertised as 'to suit' the plaintiffs' safety helmet. Their lenses did not have the approval of the Health and Safety Executive, which meant that it would be unlawful to use the equipment. The plaintiffs argued that there was a misrepresentation that the product, when fitted with the defendants' spares, would comply with safety regulations and that was passing off. In *SDS*, the plaintiffs marketed a fungicide, having obtained MAFF approval which entitled them to use a MAFF number in relation to their product. The defendants marketed a fungicide with the same chemical base but wrongly applied a MAFF number to their product to which they were not entitled. As 'authorized' traders, the plaintiffs argued that the misrepresentation harmed their shared goodwill—but in what did the goodwill reside?

[341] Thus in *Hodge Clemco* Jacob J commented that the gist of the plaintiffs' case was that the defendants were 'unfairly' gaining a market advantage by supplying rival goods which, unlike the plaintiffs' product, did not comply with statutory safety regulations [1995] FSR 806, p. 809.

and Jacob J, queried whether simply complying with a certain standard could bestow goodwill, but accepted that there was a 'real argument' whether passing off could be so extended. Neither would deny that the tort might be invoked, Jacob J acknowledging that he was dealing with 'the outer limits of the tort'.[342] Ultimately neither judge awarded the injunction sought—Aldous J because the claim was not strong enough for summary judgement and Jacob J because on the facts the balance of convenience was against an interlocutory remedy—but they left the debate over such claims open. This was so even though it was difficult to see how the plaintiffs' goodwill was harmed in either case. There is an obvious danger of overprotecting claimants if complying with a standard *per se* grants goodwill.[343] Counsel for the defendants in *Hodge Clemco* warned that the plaintiffs' argument might allow a passing off action against a car manufacturer who wrongly claimed that his car was capable of 110 mph, in a case where he was sued by a manufacturer whose cars could do that speed. Interestingly, Jacob J thought this would be argued one day. These trade misdescription claims are attempts to gain the wider protection of an unfair competition action, without the need to show harm to goodwill.

Perhaps one of the most unlikely allegations of passing off based on a trade misdescription is that contained in *Matthew Gloag & Son Ltd v Welsh Distilleries Ltd*.[344] Laddie J refused to strike out an action where the *Advocaat* extended form of the tort was alleged, combined with an inverse passing off allegation (though even the plaintiff conceded that the claim was typical of neither form of passing off!). In the case, Scotch whisky (with the consent of the producer in question) was flavoured with herbs and sold by the defendants as 'Welsh Whisky'. The plaintiffs, as Scotch whisky producers, alleged that this was some sort of actionable product misdescription and the harm alleged was that the defendants were 'diluting' the reputation of Scotch whisky by using its quality to sell their own product. Even if there was a misdescription,[345] the terminology used throughout the judgment reveals this to be a misappropriation claim. Laddie J asserted that the defendants would not be allowed to build up the reputation of their goods by using a product 'of predictable and

---

[342] [1995] FSR 806, p. 809.

[343] And note *BBC v Talksport Ltd*, *The Times*, 29 June 2000, Blackburne J. There the defendants falsely represented that they were providing live coverage of Euro 2000 when in fact they were providing unofficial 'off tube' coverage of the matches concerned. Despite the misrepresentation (and likely confusion, owing to the dubbing of ambient sound on the commentary) the BBC had no goodwill in the descriptive phrase 'live sports broadcasting' and therefore the tort was not made out.

[344] [1998] FSR 718, p. 724.

[345] Laddie, J noted that the defendants were 'misleading the public for the purpose of advancing their business', [1998] FSR 718, p. 724.

renowned quality', thereby pulling themselves up the reputation ladder. Nor did he feel that the defendants should be allowed to achieve a reputation for quality 'which truly belongs to Scotch Whisky'. Dilution was accepted as possible harm, given 'the defendants are wrongly generating a goodwill in Welsh Whisky on the back of what is, in fact, Scotch whisky'.[346]

The discussion of the tort in *Matthew Gloag* extends the protection beyond the classic trinity analysis. Here there was no inverse passing off as the defendants were not alleging that the plaintiffs' goods were their goods nor was there any false attribution of commendation or indeed any misrepresentation as to quality. Rather, Laddie J reworked the notion of inverse passing off to include a misappropriation focus. Nor was this a clear example of the extended tort. Though there was some discussion of *Advocaat* and product misrepresentation, there was no reference on the facts to the product actually used to produce the new spirit. Rather, the plaintiffs successfully mixed together the concepts of inverse passing off and extended passing off to allege that there was a misdescription that could damage the (uncredited) plaintiffs' product goodwill. Once we are two stages removed from a classic case of passing off, it is probably wise for any court to demand clear evidence of harm to goodwill. Yet here the only head of damage was dilution and an unsubstantiated guess that the defendant, having used the Scotch quality to promote their product, might then seek to promote the sales of any spirit which they chose to sell under the name 'Welsh Whisky'.

Still in the area of product misdescription, the push for extended protection by the owners of prestige names or marks has led to a number of judicial indications that the nature of goodwill may be the subject of a startling extension. *Dicta*[347] lend some credence to the view (obviously useful for the owners of prestige names) that in a product misrepresentation action, the tort of passing off protects the product name itself, rather than the goodwill that has developed from the plaintiffs' trade using that name. Such a proposition was rejected for classic passing off by Lord Herschell one hundred years ago, in *Reddaway v Banham*.[348] It was also rejected for extended passing off—involving product misrepresentations—by Lord Diplock in *Advocaat*.[349] Yet Laddie J in *Chocosuisse Union*

---

[346] [1998] FSR 718, p. 723. It was dilution of the reputation of Scotch whisky that was being referred to.

[347] Even Lord Scarman falls into the error of misleading terminology in *Pub Squash* [1980] RPC 31.

[348] And see Millett LJ in *Harrods v Harrodian School* [1996] RPC 697.

[349] For Lord Diplock 'as respects subsequent additions to the class [of traders who produce the distinctive product], mere entry into the market would not give any right of action for passing off; the new entrant must have himself used the descriptive term long enough on

des Fabricants Suisses de Chocolat v Cadbury Ltd[350] indicated that, provided the product had attracted goodwill, the trader might not need to have built up his own reputation in the product, given that 'protection is given to a name or word which has come to mean a particular product'.[351] This argument would mean that goodwill (and the need for 'deserving claimants') was replaced in such cases by a 'designation' right, with the defendant penalized for misappropriating a designation rather than harming the claimants' goodwill. Indeed, Laddie J asserted that *Advocaat* was the start of a process that has created a civilly enforceable right, similar to an *appellation contrôlée*.[352]

This development is part of the wider campaign to divert the tort from the protection of goodwill to the protection against 'dilution'. Indeed, in *Chocosuisse* Laddie J noted that in the *Advocaat* extended form of the tort, 'it is mainly reduction of the distinctiveness of the descriptive term which is relied on as relevant damage'[353] for '[if confusion is present] it must follow that the exclusivity of the designation[354] . . . must suffer and that will damage the plaintiffs'. Such an analysis involves a shift from protecting the claimant's customer connection to protecting his name or success in its own right—a development that may well be boosted by the decision of the Court of Appeal in *Taittinger SA v Allbev Ltd*[355] (discussed below).

Connection misrepresentations as unfair competition or misappropriation

An allegation of connection misrepresentation is obviously particularly useful where the claimant seeks to protect the promotional or advertising magnetism of a product or its image against free-riders.[356] Given the exact nature of the connection relevant for this type of misrepresentation is unclear and vague, it is not too difficult for claimants, in interlocutory proceedings, to allege such a misrepresentation against a trade rival and claim possible harm to sales as a result.

---

the market in connection with his own goods and have traded successfully enough to have built up a goodwill for his business' *Advocaat* [1979] AC 731, p. 747.

[350] [1998] RPC 117, p. 125.

[351] He further noted that 'once a trader becomes a legitimate member of the trade using a protected descriptive term . . . if he joins in a passing off action to protect that term, the courts have not inquired too deeply into how extensive his own trade has been' [1998] RPC 117, p. 124.

[352] [1998] RPC 117, p. 127. There has been a progressive extension of EC provisions to protect specific geographical designations: see discussion in Cornish, above, n. 1, pp. 782–3.

[353] [1998] RPC 117, p. 127.

[354] i.e. 'Swiss Chocolate'. [355] [1993] FSR 641.

[356] Particularly as this form of misrepresentation is most likely to protect well-known or household names, against a background of judicial acceptance of the public awareness of licensing and diversification.

In some cases where a connection misrepresentation is alleged, the real issue is the defendant's 'unfair' promotion of his rival product. Brand leaders have waged a campaign to try to prevent 'own-brand lookalikes', arguing that the use by major retailers of packaging similar to the brand leaders' products (to enable consumers to readily identify the type of product involved) gives the rival product a free ride into the market.[357] Indeed, during the passage of what became the Trade Marks Act 1994 they unsuccessfully sought statutory protection against this phenomenon. Case law reveals that they seek to achieve common law protection by using an action in passing off to attack the defendants' 'unfair' promotional activities. Where the amount of copying has been great, claimants have been successful in claims of passing off, using the elastic allegation of connection misrepresentation.[358] So in both *United Biscuits v Asda*[359] and *Kimberley-Clark Ltd v Fort Sterling Ltd*[360] the plaintiffs' main concern was that the market entry of the defendants' new product was aided by reference to the plaintiffs' competing product. In *United Biscuits* the reference to the plaintiffs' successful product, the Penguin biscuit, was by means of similar get-up and similar cute seabird (a puffin). Customers would thereby immediately know the type of chocolate biscuit they were dealing with (indeed, the plaintiffs themselves had produced a Penguin-type bar for Marks & Spencers, called the Pelican, for exactly the same reason). In *Kimberley-Clark*, the defendants' promotional offer (that should a customer be dissatisfied with their product, they would replace it with the plaintiffs' product) identified the defendants' new product as (unusual for recycled paper) a soft toilet paper. In both instances the court held that the defendant had gone too far[361] in creating a lookalike[362] or comparison but neither was a clear-cut case of passing off. In *Kimberley-Clark* Laddie J found that the claim was not an easy issue to resolve,[363] while the fact that the defendants in *United Biscuits* had decided to live dangerously appeared to tip the balance against them. The complaint is not of passing off but of easier market entry.

The most extreme version of connection misrepresentation that fails the classic trinity test but succeeds at times in the courts, involves allega-

---

[357] Mills, B., 'Own Label Products and the "Lookalike" Phenomenon: a Lack of Trade Dress and Unfair Competition Protection', vol. 20, EIPR (1995) 116.

[358] Spence, M., 'Passing Off and Misappropriation of Valuable Intangibles' 112 LQR (1996) 472, p. 474: in some cases 'the courts have been prepared to find passing off on the basis of only very improbable misrepresentations to the eventual customer'.

[359] [1997] RPC 513 Walker J.   [360] [1997] FSR 877 Laddie J.

[361] Cf. *Bostick Ltd v Sellotape GB* [1994] RPC 556 where the claim, again based on easier market entry, failed.

[362] The defendant had aimed to take cues from the plaintiff's packaging in *United Biscuits* but had miscalculated the degree of 'match' or 'parody' which was tolerable.

[363] [1997] FSR 877, p. 889.

tions of what might be termed 'confusion dilution', part of a wider campaign to introduce the concept of dilution into the tort. Though pure dilution has yet to be pleaded in the tort, it is apparent from case law that claimants are seeking protection against connection misrepresentations where there is no probable harm to their customer connection. They are attempting to protect themselves against the 'harm' of association in its own right (or prevent the defendants' free use of that association). These claims of 'confusion dilution' replace source goodwill with the concept of dilution of the success or magnetism of the claimant's product or image. The aim is to submerge the concept of goodwill under the nebulous concept of misappropriation. This has happened by the backdoor method of including dilution as a relevant head of damage for the tort. And as has already been seen, vague allegation of loss of expansion potential or loss of control are in fact also claims of dilution.[364]

This shift in the tort appeared to be confirmed by the decision of the Court of Appeal in *Taittinger SA v Allbev Ltd*.[365] Here the producers of a sparkling non-alcoholic cordial labelled it 'Elderflower Champagne'. Having found a connection misrepresentation, all three members of the Court of Appeal, in granting the injunction[366] to restrain the use of the word 'Champagne', saw the real injury as the potential debasement of the exclusive reputation of champagne. Echoing Schechter, Mann LJ spoke of the possible loss of distinctiveness and exclusivity of the name 'Champagne', while Peter Gibson LJ feared for its 'erosion' or 'blurring'. Indeed, Sir Thomas Bingham MR found there to be no real threat of diversion of sales but concentrated on the goodwill in the description Champagne deriving 'from the very singularity and exclusiveness of the description Champagne'. The defendants' action threatened to erode the 'singularity and exclusiveness of the description Champagne and so cause the first plaintiffs damage of an insidious but serious kind'. Nor did he concentrate on the damage caused specifically by the defendants' product: once the erosion has started, the term 'champagne' could be highjacked by all and sundry. The plaintiffs had a product goodwill that included 'a sense of something special and privileged' and that merited protection. It is hardly surprising, therefore, that dilution has become a standard head of damage in the tort. This is despite the subsequent view of Millett LJ in

---

[364] Jacob J in *Mecklermedia Corp v DC Congress* [1997] FSR 627, p. 633: 'in other cases the court is entitled to infer damage including particularly damage by way of dilution of the plaintiff's goodwill'; 'to a significant extent the plaintiff's reputation is in the hands of the defendant'.

[365] [1993] FSR 641.

[366] The other reason for the injunction was the possible breach of Article 15(5) of Council Regulation 823/87 (which seeks to prevent confusion by the use of established wine designations).

Harrods v Harrodian School[367] who sought to put the tort back on the straight and narrow, stressing that it protects only the trading activity behind a name and not the name itself. Yet in a dissenting judgment in the same case, Sir Michael Kerr specifically exampled dilution of reputation (as a result of the defendant's action) as a relevant head of damage in the tort and noted that a mistaken connection means that the plaintiff has to that extent 'lost control of his reputation'. Indeed, he went on to conclude that this danger could be only the first step in which the use of the name would have to be abandoned by the plaintiff as the continued use of the name 'Harrodian' by the defendant would mean that it was highly likely that it would proliferate and that the free use of the name might even spawn 'Harrodian garages, newsagents and other businesses'.[368]

Interestingly, the language of the plaintiffs and sympathetic judges in 'dilution' cases indicates a shift in emphasis. When potential harm is discussed in these cases, there is a subtle change in focus: from the traditional analysis of harm, based on loss or damage to the plaintiff's goodwill to an analysis that focuses on the unfair gain to the defendant. So in *Taittinger SA v Allbev* Sir Thomas Bingham asserted that the use of the prestige name by the defendants meant that the defendants were 'cashing in' on the reputation of champagne. Again, in *Harrods*, Sir Michael Kerr expressly referred to the misappropriation basis of the plaintiff's claim[369] and noted that the defendant was not entitled to 'ride on the back of' the reputation of the name Harrods. Laddie J in *Kimberley-Clark Ltd v Fort Sterling Ltd*[370] felt that the courts should protect against a competitor 'strengthening his position' by taking the benefit of the plaintiffs' mark and reputation.

A further stream of cases where plaintiffs have attempted to replace the classic trinity with 'confusion dilution' are those brought by foreign traders who lack goodwill here but rely on their international reputation. Their real complaint is that the defendants are obtaining a free ride in the market by stealing the plaintiff's trade value or the commercial magnetism surrounding his product. Though, as has been shown, the view of key cases in this area is that mere reputation is not sufficient, the attack on goodwill will continue, given it has been replaced by the concept of reputation in other common law jurisdictions such as in Australia,[371] Hong

---

[367] [1996] RPC 697.   [368] [1996] RPC 697, p. 726.
[369] [1996] RPC 697, p. 722.   [370] [1997] FSR 877, p. 890.
[371] *Conagra Inc v McCain Foods (Aust) Pty* 23 IPR 193: Lockhart J held that where a defendant attempted to pre-empt the launch of the plaintiffs' product on the Australian market the plaintiffs' reputation was sufficient for relief. In *Hogan v Koala Dundee Pty Ltd* (1988) 83 ALR 187, Pincus J Fed Court of Australia and *Pacific Dunlop Ltd v Hogan* (1989) 87 ALR 14, Beaumont J, Fed Court of Australia, it was held that the creator of the successful fictional character 'Crocodile Dundee' could prevent the wrongful misappropriation of that character by manufacturers. The confusion caused by the misrepresentation (that there was a commercial

Kong,[372] New Zealand,[373] India,[374] and Canada.[375] Moreover, such plaintiffs are doubtless encouraged by the injunctions granted on the basis of pre-launch publicity, where goodwill appears to have been replaced by protection of expenditure and advertising pull.[376]

Product simulation as unfair competition or misappropriation

Product simulation involves the defendants copying a successful product. Though plaintiffs in such cases have sought the protection of the tort of passing off here, they have encountered judicial reluctance to assist them. In such cases, given the allegation is far removed from the classic trinity, judges are most receptive to the argument that imitation is the lifeblood of successful competition. So, such claimants may fail to show confusion and thereby fail the most basic requirement of the tort, misrepresentation.

Perhaps the clearest recent judicial view of this sort of case is that contained in the judgment of Jacob J in *Hodgkinson & Corby Ltd v Wards Mobility Ltd*.[377] The defendants intended to sell rival prophylactic cushions made by the former French distributors of the plaintiffs' product, using a different trade name. They had clearly copied the plaintiffs' product for the 'perfectly honest' reason that the plaintiffs' product (unprotected by patent) worked well and health-care professionals were happy to consider equivalents and lookalikes. An allegation of product simulation in the absence of confusion was not sufficient; nor was the plaintiffs' argument that the defendants were 'riding on the back' of the plaintiffs' product success. As Jacob J noted:[378] 'there is no tort of copying. There is no tort of taking a man's market or customers. Neither the market nor the customers are the plaintiffs to own. There is no tort of making use of another's goodwill as such. There is no tort of competition.' There might have been lost

---

arrangement between the plaintiff and defendant) was sufficient: there was no need to show that the plaintiff was trading in the character. Although both cases followed *Taco Bell (pty) Ltd v Taco Co of Australia Inc* (1981) 40 ALR 153 in other aspects of the tort, as such they implicitly reject that case's insistence on goodwill.

[372] *Ten-Ichi Co Ltd v Jancar Ltd* [1990] FSR 151, Sears J, Hong Kong. For the judge the plaintiff's high international reputation constituted goodwill.

[373] *Esanda Ltd v Esanda Finance Ltd* [1984] 2 NZLR 748.

[374] *re Whirlpool Trade Mark* [1997] FSR 906 (High Court of India) Anil Dev Singh J, p. 917: 'knowledge and awareness of the goods of a foreign trader and of its mark can be available in a place where goods are not being marketed and consequently not being used. The manner in which or the source from which the knowledge has been acquired is immaterial.' His interlocutory injunction was upheld by the Supreme Court of India.

[375] *Orkin Exterminating Co Inc v Pestco of Canada Ltd* (1985) 19 DLR (4th) 90, Ontario Court of Appeal.

[376] So in *BBC v Talbot* [1981] FSR 228, p. 237 Megarry V-C asserted that the defendants should not reap what the plaintiffs had sown.

[377] [1995] FSR 169.   [378] [1995] FSR 169, pp. 174–5.

sales but there was no diversion of sales through misrepresentation. Nor has the related argument that post-sale confusion might be present in such cases yet to gain the approval of the English courts on the facts of any case.[379] Indeed, even where confusion is present, courts appear hesitant to assume the necessary reliance by the public. In *Politechnika Ipari Szovertkezet v Dallas Print Transfers*,[380] where the defendant produced a rival copy of the plaintiffs' successful puzzle, the Rubik Cube, Dillon J refused relief (though there was a danger of confusion) as 'people were interested in the cube itself as a puzzle rather than in its source'. Thus unless the appearance of the goods is itself a misrepresentation of quality or origin (as in *Jif Lemon*) and that misrepresentation is relied upon, there is no action for passing off, despite the 'free ride'.

Of course a similar analysis—and a similar lack of success—could apply to those cases where claimants seek to protect their character merchandising 'rights'. Plaintiffs involved in the character merchandising industry have sought to prevent others free-riding on their successful character by using the tort of passing off.[381] Even if confusion can be shown, the courts have on the whole[382] been reluctant to accept reliance as self-evident in such cases. Laddie J noted in *Elvis Presley Trade Marks*:[383] 'when people buy a toy of a well-known character because it depicts that character, I have no reason to believe that they care one way or the other who made, sold or licensed it. When a fan buys a poster or a cup bearing an image of his star, he is buying a likeness, not a product from a particular source.' Indeed, as Walton J recognized in *Taverner Rutledge v Trexapalm Ltd*[384] a trader can use another name established in some other field and make it distinctive of his own goods and thereby acquire goodwill. Such

---

[379] See above, n. 52.

[380] [1982] FSR 529. And see also *British American Glass Co Ltd v Winton Products (Blackpool) Ltd* [1962] RPC 230, Pennycuick J the plaintiffs complained when the defendants copied the shape of their novelty ornamental glass dogs. Pennycuick J denied redress: 'a member of the public buying an ornamental trinket of this nature is concerned only with what it looks like and is unlikely to care by whom it is made.'

[381] They may be able to show harm to goodwill where they complain of competition from the appropriator of their character: *Samuelson v Producers' Distributing* [1932] 1 Ch 201, where passing off was used to prevent the defendants implying that their film was based on the plaintiff's successful revue sketch; see also *Shaw Bros v Golden Harvest* [1972] RPC 559 SC (HC).

[382] Sir Nicholas Browne-Wilkinson V-C in *Mirage Studios v Counter Feat Clothing Co Ltd* [1991] FSR 145 appeared to query the need to show reliance in such cases (p. 159) but Laddie J in *Elvis Presley Trade Marks* [1997] RPC 543, p. 553 noted the *ex tempore* status of the judgment (appeal dismissed, [1999] RPC 567, CA).

[383] [1997] RPC 543, p. 554. The appeal was dismissed: [1999] RPC 567, CA. Similarly, Laddie J refused to assume deception in *BBC Worldwide Ltd v Pally Screen Printing Ltd* [1998] FSR 665, p. 674.

[384] [1977] RPC 275, followed by Robert Walker J in *Nice and Safe Attitude Ltd v Piers Flook* [1997] FSR 14.

goodwill could be protected even against the originator or his licensee, a point underlined most recently by Robert Walker J in *Nice and Safe Attitude Ltd v Piers Flook*.[385] Here, the plaintiff, a clothing manufacturer, had used NASA's[386] well-known logo without permission. The defendant sought to argue that the plaintiff could not succeed in the tort as NASA had given the defendant permission to use the logo on clothing. Robert Walker J rejected this argument on the basis that a mere licence in a name was irrelevant—underlining the fact that the character merchandising industry is still not clearly protected by the tort of passing off. Interestingly in an Australian decision[387] that protected merchandising rights without harm to goodwill, Pincus J accepted that there was a degree of artificiality in claiming passing off in such cases, given the real concern was the lost licensing fee.

CONCLUSION: THE FUTURE OF PASSING OFF

Some might argue that a general tort of misappropriation/unfair competition should take the place of the tort of passing off. Logically this would eliminate the claimant's need to establish either a misrepresentation or goodwill. However, for the foreseeable future such a development is unlikely. The fear is that the balance must not be tilted too far away from encouraging competition. This was noted by Jacob J in *Hodgkinson & Corby Ltd v Wards Mobility Ltd*:[388] 'at the heart of passing off lies deception or its likelihood ... never has the tort shown even a slight tendency to stray beyond cases of deception. Were it to do so it would enter the field of honest competition, declared unlawful for some reason other than deceptiveness. Why there should be any such reason I cannot imagine. It would serve only to stifle competition.' This echoes, of course, the sentiments of Lord Scarman, expressed in *Cadbury Schweppes v Pub Squash Co*.[389]

However, this reluctance to embrace a tort as general as misappropriation/unfair competition does not rule out the possibility that the tort of passing off could be expanded in the direction of unfair trading. The more unusual allegations of passing off, discussed above, reveal that there is such a campaign and that it targets (both by direct and indirect attack) the concept of goodwill. Apart from spurious claims of harm to goodwill, some of which succeed at interlocutory level, claimants who seek an

---

[385] [1997] FSR 14.
[386] National Aeronautics and Space Administration.
[387] *Hogan v Koala Dundee Pty Ltd* (1988) 83 ALR 187, pp. 198–9.
[388] [1995] FSR 175.   [389] [1981] RPC 429, PC.

unfair trading action need to persuade the court to redefine goodwill or cause it to be jettisoned altogether.[390]

The direct attacks on goodwill take various forms. Some claimants seek to replace it by the concept of 'reputation', others wish to replace it by the concept of 'name goodwill' (by using the concept of 'dilution') or 'potential goodwill' (where expensive pre-launch advertising or promotion has taken place). Interestingly, the leading American commentary on unfair competition subdivides goodwill zones into selling zones, advertising zones and reputation zones, potential goodwill zones and expansion zones.[391]

The concept of goodwill is under similar direct attack elsewhere in the common law world. Indeed, there is Australian authority replacing goodwill with 'wrongful appropriation of business reputation'. In *Henderson v Radio Corp Pty Ltd*[392] the plaintiffs were well-known professional ballroom dancers who objected to the use of their photograph (as dancers) on the cover of the defendants' dance record. The court found there to be a misrepresentation (a false representation that they recommended the record). However, they also found that there was no need to prove that there was likely injury to their professional reputation as such nor that their earning capacity had been impaired. Rather, sufficient damage resulted from the 'wrongful appropriation' of their business or professional reputation. Their professional recommendation had a monetary value and its appropriation was 'as much an injury as if the appellant had paid the respondents for their recommendation and then robbed them of the money'. Thus a connection misrepresentation was sufficient for liability, given the commercial value of their personalities.[393] The court was prepared to protect their 'saleable commodity in a capacity for sponsorship'.[394] As the merchandising business is anxious to create a merchandising right, to cover both fictional and real personalities[395] (and indeed famous brands and trade marks, given their status as valuable commer-

---

[390] Of course, this is what has happened in s.52 of the Australian Trade Practices Act 1974 which allows traders and consumers alike (though it is mostly used by trade rivals) to gain relief against misleading and deceptive conduct. Jacob J in *Schulke v Alkapharm* [1999] FSR 161 noted that 'the experience in Australia . . . has indicated that such an extension of the law leads to much litigation. Members of the Australian Bar have much to say by way of thanks to the short s.52.'

[391] Noted by the Ontario Court of Appeal in *Orkin Exterminating Co Inc v Pestco of Canada Ltd* (1985) 19 DLR (4th) 90.   [392] [1969] RPC 218, HCNSW.

[393] Henderson was applied in *Twentieth Century Fox Corp v South Australian Brewing Co* (1996) 66 FCR 451 where the defendants were prevented from producing a beer with the same name as that featured on the popular 'Simpsons' television series. The court found that a connection would be assumed and that there would be lost licensing fees. But would anyone rely on the connection made?

[394] Gummow, W., 'Carrying on Passing Off', Syd Law Rev (1974) 224, p 226.

[395] See Frazer, T., 'Appropriation of Personality: a New Tort' 99 LQR 280 (1983).

cial commodities) it is likely that the tort will be subjected to continued and ever wider pressure to redefine or even abandon goodwill altogether.

At the same time, the indirect attack on goodwill has gained significant success in establishing dilution as a head of damage. Together with the similar concepts of loss of control and loss of expansion potential, protection against dilution replaces the need to show potential harm to customer connection with a nebulous and imprecise claim of misappropriation, with the public interest no longer central to the analysis.[396]

For the courts, the choice is between a tort of limited application, bounded by the certainty of the classic trinity and a wide tort, based on trade misrepresentation,[397] without a clear public interest being served. With an extended unfair trading action the judicial role would be greater, the court having to decide whether to protect on the basis of policy considerations. The obvious danger with the latter choice is that the tort could then constitute an undue constraint on the competitive process. The future of the tort will be addressed in the final chapter.

---

[396] This could explain why anti-dilution statutes have not proved popular with American courts. See Welkowitz, above, n. 307.

[397] Holyoak, J., 'United Kingdom Character Rights and Merchandising Rights Today' [1993] JBL 444, p. 456: a tort that would revel in its own uncertainty and continue its slow but 'inexorable' expansion in every direction.

9

Negligence and Pure Economic Loss

INTRODUCTION

The main concern of the economic torts is to protect the claimant's economic interests in the sense of his existing wealth or financial expectations. From case law (reviewed below) it is clear that the tort of negligence can be used successfully to gain such protection. Negligent interference with economic interests as such can be actionable. But to label the tort as an economic tort is rather misleading. Rather, in exceptional circumstances, it performs the functions of an economic tort. It is obviously important to consider when those circumstances arise and how the tort of negligence relates to the established economic torts.

HISTORY

Actions on the case for negligence became common from the early nineteenth century onwards[1] 'no doubt spurred on at first by the increase in negligently inflicted injuries through the use of the new mechanical inventions such as the railways and later by the abolition of the forms of action'.[2] The importance of *Donoghue v Stevenson*,[3] was the recognition that the categories of negligence are never closed. Lord Atkin's neighbour principle meant—though this was not immediately acknowledged—that the tort was not limited to special categories of duties of care but rather became 'a fluid principle of civil liability'.[4] Once this principle emerged as

---

[1] Fleming, J., *The Law of Torts*, 9th edn. (Sydney: LBC Information Services, 1998), p. 149: 'the action on the case for negligence emerged during the formative era of the common law in a limited number of situations where a defendant could be held responsible for loss caused by negligence which would not have been actionable by the writs of trespass or nuisance.'

[2] Brazier, M., and Murphy, J., *Street on Torts*, 10th edn. (London: Butterworths, 1999), p. 171.

[3] [1932] AC 562, HL.

[4] Hepple, B., 'Negligence: the Search for Coherence' [1997] CLP 69, p. 69. Burrows, A., 'Restitution: Where Do We Go From Here?' [1997] CLP 95, p. 108: 'at the turn of the century the tort of negligence was not identified as such. One rather had a range of individual instances of liability for negligence. It took Lord Atkin to draw them together into a tort of negligence based on the neighbourhood principle—the duty to use reasonable care not to harm one's neighbour.'

a general approach to liability for negligently inflicted physical harm,[5] it of course became inevitable that as the twentieth century progressed the boundaries of the tort would be tested beyond the protection against physical damage.

As part of this process, the traditional resistance to recovery for pure economic loss began to be questioned. Though a policy 'never . . . clearly enunciated in those terms',[6] its existence was clear in cases such as *Cattle v Stockton Waterworks Co*,[7] Blackburn J accepting that the courts, in an attempt to do 'complete justice', should not 'transgress the bounds which our law . . . has imposed on itself, of redressing only the proximate and direct consequences of wrongful acts'.[8] (Indeed, it was in this era that the courts established a clear distinction between intentional and negligently caused economic loss).[9] However, for a while—between 1970 and 1984— the categories of negligence looked 'infinitely expandable'[10] with foresight of harm being the key to liability generally, in the absence of policy reasons to deny the claim.[11] *Junior Books Ltd v Veitchi Ltd*[12] was the prime example of this where, according to Hepple and Matthews[13] 'a majority in the House of Lords broke down the barrier between physical harm and economic loss'. Yet, subsequently the courts have resiled from this expansive approach to duty,[14] accepting that 'Lord Atkin's ambitious generalization about duty relations—bounded only by the horizon of foreseeability of injury—could hardly have envisaged risks other than personal injury or damage to tangible property'.[15] There has been approval for the warning of Brennan J in the Australian case, *Sutherland Shire Council v Heyman*[16] that 'the law should develop hard categories of

---

[5] Weir, T., *A Casebook on Torts*, 9th edn. (London: Sweet & Maxwell, 2000), p. 567 the 'paradigmatic case of tortious negligence is when dangerous conduct has caused physical harm'.

[6] Atiyah, P., 'Negligence and Economic Loss', 83 LQR (1967) 248, p. 248.

[7] (1875) LR 10 QB 453. Note, however, that this case was treated by the court as principally a *Rylands v Fletcher* action.

[8] Ibid. 457. He was in fact quoting Coleridge J in *Lumley v Gye* (1853) 2 E&B 216, p. 252.

[9] Hepple, B., above, n. 4, p. 75.　　　　　　　　[10] *Street on Torts*, above, n. 2, p. 175.

[11] The 'Anns 2-stage approach' (*Anns v Merton LBC* [1978] AC 728).

[12] [1983] 1 AC 520.

[13] Hepple, B., and Matthews, P., *Tort: Cases and Materials*, 4th edn. (London: Butterworths, 1991), p. 151.

[14] Burrows, A., *Understanding the Law of Obligations* (Oxford: Hart Publishing, 1998), states (p. 213): 'Over the last 25 years, no area of civil liability has proved more troublesome than pure economic loss in the tort of negligence. It is in respect of this area of negligence, above all, that the courts dramatically pushed forward the boundaries of negligence and then, equally dramatically, backtracked with the overruling of *Anns v Merton LBC* . . . in *Murphy v Brentwood DC*.'

[15] Fleming, above, n. 1, p. 193. In *Murphy v Brentwood DC* [1991] 1 AC 398, Lord Oliver said 'the infliction of physical injury to the person or property of another universally requires to be justified'.

[16] (1985) 60 ALR 1, pp. 43–4; cited by Lord Bridge in *Caparo Industries v Dickman* [1990] 2 AC 605.

negligence incrementally and by analogy with established categories', And it was principally in economic loss cases such as *Murphy v Brentwood DC*[17] that this occurred. What has become clear is that the duty of care is affected by the nature of the damage caused[18] and that the rule excluding recovery for pure economic loss remains the general rule. Lord Fraser asserted in *The Mineral Transporter* that 'some limit or control mechanism has to be imposed on the liability of a wrongdoer towards those who have suffered economic damage as a consequence of negligence', a position which is 'a pragmatic one dictated by necessity'.[19] While Lord Oliver in *Caparo Industries v Dickman*[20] noted the need for 'some intelligible limits to keeping the law of negligence within the borders of common sense and practicality'.[21]

NEGLIGENCE AND PURE ECONOMIC LOSS: THE POLICY FACTORS

The courts have not allowed the tort of negligence to become a mainstream economic tort. There appear to be two main policy reasons for this.[22]

Most evident is the fear of disproportionate and limitless liability, mirroring the fear raised by Cardozo J in *Ultramares Corp v Touche*[23] of 'liability in an indeterminate amount for an indeterminate time to an indeterminate class'.[24] Thus Lord Pearce[25] noted in *Hedley Byrne & Co Ltd v Heller & Partners* that: 'economic protection has lagged behind protec-

---

[17] [1991] AC 398, HL. This overruled *Anns v Merton LBC* [1978] AC 728. Lord Steyn noted in *McFarlane v Tayside Health Board* [1999] 4 All ER 961, p. 975 that since *Anns* was overturned, 'a judicial scepticism has prevailed about an overarching principle for the recovery of new categories of economic loss'.

[18] This was expressly acknowledged by Lord Bridge in *Caparo v Dickman Industries* [1990] 2 AC 605, p. 618. However, the House of Lords in *Marc Rich v Bishop Rock Marine Co* [1996] 1 AC 211 applied the same test to physical and economic loss (though it would presumably be rare to impose liability for pure economic loss).

[19] *Candlewood Navigation Corp Ltd v Mitsui OSK Lines Ltd* [1986] AC 1, p. 17.

[20] [1990] 2 AC 605, p. 633.

[21] In *Spartan Steel v Martin* [1973] 1 QB 27, Lord Denning said (p. 36) 'the question of recovery of economic loss is one of policy'.

[22] Usefully discussed and criticized by Jane Stapleton in 'Duty of Care and Economic Loss: a Wider Agenda' 107 LQR (1991) 249. She notes that some arguments in the cases cannot have been intended as of more than ancillary weight, instancing *inter alia* the argument that there is no precedent for the claim.

[23] (1931) 255 NY 170, p. 179.

[24] Cited, e.g., by Lord Pearce in *Hedley Byrne v Heller* [1964] AC 465, p. 537; by Lord Bridge in *Caparo Industries v Dickman* [1990] 2 AC 605, p. 621; by Lord Griffiths in *Smith v Bush* [1990] 1 AC 831, p. 865. Stapleton, above, n. 22, p. 254 notes that the concern is twofold: the unfairness in holding the defendant liable to an indeterminate number of claimants (especially due to the 'ripple effect' of the original negligence) and the claims being of indeterminate size.

[25] [1964] AC 465, pp. 536–7.

tion in physical matters where there is injury to person and property. It may be that the size and the width of the range of possible claims has acted as a deterrent to extension of economic protection.' This view was echoed by Lord Oliver in *Caparo Industries v Dickman*, who noted that 'the opportunities for the infliction of pecuniary loss from the imperfect performance of everyday tasks upon the proper performance of which people rely for regulating their affairs are illimitable and the effects are far-reaching'.[26] This policy is particularly stressed where the economic loss the claimant has suffered is consequential economic loss as a result of harm to another or to that other's property.[27] So in *Cattle v Stockton Waterworks Co*,[28] the classic case where pure economic loss was held irrecoverable, the plaintiffs, whose contracts were rendered more onerous because of the negligent flooding of another's land, were left remediless. There was a similar lack of recovery in *Weller v Foot and Mouth Institute*[29] (a case of pure economic loss to auctioneers, affected by the defendants' negligent harm to farmers' cattle). However, this policy does not prevent the recovery of economic loss, consequential on physical damage to the claimant's property.[30] In *Spartan Steel & Alloys Ltd v Martin & Co Ltd*[31] where the negligently caused power failure resulted in physical harm to the plaintiff's molten metal and resultant loss of profits on that melt, both were recoverable. No recovery was allowed, however, on the expected profits from the melts that could not take place because of the lack of power.

The other major policy that is cited to justify the non-imposition of a duty[32] in the area of pure economic loss is the perceived need not to

---

[26] [1990] 2 AC 605, pp. 632–3. See also Millett LJ in *Kapfunde v Abbey National plc* [1999] ICR 1, p. 13 where misrepresentations cause pure economic loss, 'there is a potential for foreseeable but indeterminate and possibly ruinous loss by a large and indeterminate number of plaintiffs'.

[27] Fleming, above, n. 1, p. 196 'the most ingrained opposition is against recovery for injury to relational interests'.

[28] Above, n. 7.

[29] [1966] 1 QB 569.

[30] However, the rule that the claimant must have a proprietary or possessory interest in the chattel damaged does extend beyond claims caught by the policy against indeterminacy. This was demonstrated by the decision of the House of Lords in *Leigh & Sillavan Ltd v Aliakmon Shipping Co Ltd* [1986] AC 785. There the risk of damage but not the ownership of the goods damaged by the defendants' negligence had passed to the plaintiff. Lord Brandon was content to base the non-recovery on the need for certainty. In so doing, he rejected Goff LJ's 'transferred loss' theory at Court of Appeal level in this case. This 'serious lacuna in the law' (Lord Goff, *White v Jones* [1995] 2 AC 207, p. 265) was remedied by the Carriage of Goods by Sea Act 1992.

[31] [1973] 1 QB 27.

[32] Note also that the courts may decide to reject a duty on the basis of countervailing laws. Stapleton, above, n. 22.

override the 'contractual matrix'[33] that links the parties.[34] Thus the courts may refuse to apply the tort of negligence where the contract framework behind the economic loss is deemed to provide the answer—and a balanced answer that the tort would disrupt.[35] Here the policy that prevents the tort applying is that its application would be 'incompatible with the transactional set up or background'.[36] So liability is usually denied[37] where the parties are bound together by a series of contracts, typically in shipping[38] or construction cases.[39] There is a similar reluctance to allow recovery in the tort where the complaint concerns quality defects in goods or property,[40] where the parties are in a contract chain but not themselves bound by privity. Here the real basis of the claim is for a *de facto* transferrable warranty of quality.

However, the tort may protect pure economic interests—no policy has the effect of completely excluding it from this area. As the House of Lords' decision in *Hedley Byrne v Heller*[41] revealed, should the facts involve no floodgates concern, then, rather than undermine the contractual structure to which the parties have agreed,[42] the tort may be pleaded to fill a gap in contract law and liability may be imposed. So a bank carelessly giving favourable references concerning its client to the plaintiff's bank (on his behalf) owed a duty of care to that plaintiff.[43]

---

[33] Fleming, 'Tort Law in a Contractual Matrix', 33 Os Hall LJ (1995) 661.

[34] A related issue identified by Stapleton (above, n. 22) is an appreciation that the claimant could have been adequately protected by alternative means.

[35] In *Henderson v Merrett Syndicates Ltd* [1995] 2 AC 145, HL, Lord Goff noted that the assumption of responsibility may be inconsistent with the contract structure, 'the parties having so structured their relationship that it is inconsistent with any such assumption of responsibility' (p. 196), citing Bingham LJ in *Simaan General Construction Co v Pilkington Glass Ltd (no. 2)* [1988] QB 758, p. 781. *Henderson* itself was deemed to be an unusual case and the decision itself not necessarily leading to other sub-agents being held directly liable to the agent's principal in tort.

[36] Weir, above, n. 5, p. 70.

[37] *Junior Books v Veitchi Co* [1983] AC 520 being the main exception. Lord Goff found it unnecessary to reconsider *Junior Books* in *Henderson*.

[38] e.g. *The Mineral Transporter* [1986] AC 1.

[39] e.g. *Simaan General Construction Co v Pilkington Glass Ltd (no. 2)* [1988] 1 QB 758, p. 782 (infact, a defect of quality case). However, cf. other commercial settings: in *Bailey v HSS Alarms Ltd, The Times,* 20 June 2000, CA, the defendants had assumed responsibility for monitoring a burglar alarm, though they had subcontracted that responsibility from the installers who had gone out of business and with whom the claimants had the contract. They were liable for the loss caused by a burglary at the claimants' premises when they negligently failed to monitor the signal from the alarm. Here there was 'proximity'and the imposition of a duty of care was 'fair and reasonable'.

[40] Though Lord Bridge, *obiter* in *Murphy v Brentwood DC* [1991] 1 AC 398, suggested that a defect that is a potential source of injury to persons or property may lead to liability on the part of the builder.

[41] [1964] AC 465.

[42] Whittaker, S., 'Privity of Contract and the Tort of Negligence: Future Directions', 16 OJLS (1996) 191.

[43] The House of Lords reviewed the authorities to conclude that liability for misstate-

THE HEDLEY BYRNE PRINCIPLE

The true width of the *Hedley Byrne* principle was obscured until recently by the facts and background to the case. A case on pure economic loss, it also involved careless advice. As such, liability had to be reconciled with the decision in *Derry v Peek*.[44] At the end of the nineteenth century, *Derry v Peek* put the brake on developments in equity that might have led to liability for careless misrepresentations. In the nineteenth century the common law courts required self-reliance from plaintiffs and apart from the extreme case of deceit, looked to contract for the imposition of guarantees, consequent on representations. The decision in *Derry v Peek*, according to Lord Bramwell, represented the victory of general principle over 'the desire to effect what is or what is thought to be, justice in a particular instance'.[45] Though some twenty-five years later an equity-minded House of Lords in *Nocton v Ashburton*[46] created an exception to *Derry v Peek* where there was a 'special relationship' between the parties, until *Hedley Byrne & Co Ltd v Heller & Partners Ltd* in 1963,[47] this was thought to be 'a narrow, uncertain category'.[48] Thus in this litigation the question of liability in negligence for economic loss became entangled with liability for misstatements. The focus of the claim and of the decisions in the House of Lords was on the question of liability for negligent misstatements,[49] only Lords Hodson and Devlin addressing the separate issue of liability for pure economic loss.[50] As Stapleton notes, 'whatever problems economic loss presented they were assimilated to those presented by negligent words'.[51]

What then does the *Hedley Byrne* principle involve? In the decision itself the court stressed the need for a 'voluntary assumed responsibility'

ments was not limited to fraud, contract or fiduciary relationship. Stevens, R., 'Hedley Byrne v Heller: Judicial Creativity and Doctrinal Possibility', 27 MLR (1964) 121, p. 122 suggests that the reasons for this extension lie in 'the development of a complex commercial system and [in the twentieth century] a more general participation in that system by the population at large'. Although, of course, the disclaimer actually led to no liability on the facts.

[44] (1889) 14 App Cas 337.

[45] (1889) 14 App Cas 352.

[46] [1914] 2 AC 932.

[47] [1964] AC 465.

[48] Cornish, W., and Clark, G. de N., *Law and Society in England 1750–1950* (London: Sweet & Maxwell, 1989), p. 221. Devlin J in *Heskell v Continental Express Ltd* [1950] 1 All ER 1033, p. 1042 'negligent misstatement can never give rise to a cause of action'.

[49] Thus Stapleton, above, n. 22, underlines its flaw (p. 278): 'the root of the problem is that in *Hedley Byrne*, instead of considering other ways in which economic loss can be caused, the House of Lords spoke of negligent words and spoke of this as if they were special and in need of special treatment.'

[50] [1964] AC 465, Lord Hodson (p. 509: 'it is difficult to see why liability as such should depend on the nature of the damage'); Lord Devlin (pp. 502–3).

[51] Above, n. 22, p. 261.

as between the defendant and plaintiff—in what was *de facto* a two-party scenario[52]—and a foreseeable and reasonable reliance by the plaintiff on the advice or information that resulted. However, it is clear from the judgments of Lords Devlin and Morris that the assumption of responsibility and reliance could also apply to negligent acts or services. This is hardly surprising, given there may be a fine line between words and acts, as is evidenced by the American case of *Glanzer v Shepard*.[53] There, a negligent public weigher overestimated the quantity of beans and gave an inaccurate certificate to the purchaser, who in reliance overpaid the seller of the beans. He was held liable by Judge Cardozo 'not merely for careless words but for the careless performance of a service—the act of weighing—which happens to have found in the words of the certificate its culmination and summary'. However, surprisingly, it was not until the late twentieth century that it was expressly accepted that the *Hedley Byrne* principle for recovering pure economic loss in negligence can apply beyond advice. Lord Goff in *Henderson v Merrett Syndicates Ltd*[54] accepted that 'the principle extends beyond the provision of information or advice to include the performance of other services'[55] and that omissions may be included,[56] noting that this had already been recognized by Oliver J in *Midland Bank v Hett, Stubbs & Kemp* (a case of negligent omission by the plaintiff's solicitor).[57] Of course, the main difference between careless advice and careless services is that in the former case, the added requirement is that the claimant must have decided to act on that advice.[58]

---

[52] Though a third party, the plaintiff's bank, actually made the request for the information, it was clear that they were acting for a client (the plaintiff). In effect, therefore, the plaintiff made the request for information from the defendant bank, via their own bank. The House of Lords treated it as a two-party case.

[53] (1922) 233 NY 236, p. 241.

[54] [1995] 2 AC 145. And see Lord Goff in *Spring v Guardian Assurance* [1995] 2 AC 296, p. 318.

[55] In *Caparo Industries v Dickman* [1990] 2 AC 605, Lord Bridge stressed, however, that he was only concerned with liability for negligent misstatements. In *Welton v North Cornwall DC* [1997] 1 WLR 570 threats by the environmental health officer—perhaps an extreme form of advice or service—were held to be within *Hedley Byrne*. His requirement that the plaintiff owners of a guest house undertake expensive alterations, unnecessary under the relevant legislation, was held by the Court of Appeal to fall within the principle of an assumption of responsibility. However, subsequently in *Harris v Evans* [1998] 3 All ER 522, CA, Scott V-C made it clear that he was unhappy with this result, questioning whether such a duty would be consistent with the relevant statutory framework.

[56] Lord Goff in *Henderson v Merrett Syndicates* [1995] 2 AC 145, p. 181: he examples 'when a solicitor assumes responsibility for business on behalf of his client and omits to take a certain step, such as a service of a document which falls within the responsibility so assumed by him'. Omissions are most likely to lead to liability where there is a contract framework, requiring a positive duty to act as in *Midland Bank v Hett, Stubbs & Kemp* [1979] Ch 384.

[57] [1979] Ch 384, p. 416. There was a failure to register an option.

[58] Hart, H. A. L., and Honoré, T., *Causation in the Law*, 2nd edn. (Oxford: Clarendon Press, 1985), p. 51 'in cases of careless words, the victim's own decision to act upon them is typically interposed'. So the reason for the claimant's action becomes important. Words may also

So *Hedley Byrne* accepted that there may be a duty to take care to avoid pure economic loss but in so doing made it clear that such liability would not be founded on the same basis as the duty to avoid physical harm. The key factor in the principle was the presence of a 'voluntary assumption of responsibility'. It has subsequently become clear that the *Hedley Byrne* principle applies to the provision of information, advice, or the performance of other services as between the parties and rests upon a relationship between the parties which may be general or specific to a particular transaction. It is also clear, following *Henderson v Merritt Syndicates Ltd*, that it applies to a contractual relationship as well as to mere undertakings.

In the search for guidance in this area, the importance of the principle in *Hedley Byrne* and in particular whether it forms a universal test for the imposition of liability in negligence for pure economic loss cases needs to be assessed.

NEGLIGENCE AND PURE ECONOMIC LOSS: THE BASIS OF LIABILITY

Ever since *Hedley Byrne*, the perceived need to set limits to liability for negligent misstatements (and now services) that cause pure economic loss, on a narrower basis than the principle of *Donoghue v Stevenson*,[59] has dominated this area of tort law. Something more than 'mere foreseeability' was required.[60] In *Hedley Byrne* itself the court stressed the need for an assumption of responsibility by the defendant to the plaintiff and also, as the claim involved advice, reasonable reliance by the plaintiff. The resulting special relationship led to a duty situation.[61] Thus the negligent performance of a voluntary undertaking to another could make the other party liable for economic loss.

This concept of an 'assumption of responsibility' as the basic test for liability has proved attractive in subsequent leading case law on the issue of pure economic loss. It was relied on by some of the members of the House of Lords in each of the most important recent cases on pure

---

present a higher risk of indeterminate liability as 'words are more volatile than deeds, they travel fast and far afield, they are used without being expended' (Lord Pearson in *Hedley Byrne v Heller* [1964] AC 465, p. 532).

[59] [1932] AC 562. Lord Slynn in *McFarlane v Tayside Health Board* [1999] 4 All ER 961, p. 971 noted: 'in respect of economic loss, in order to create liability there may have to be a closer link between the act and the damage than foreseeability provides.'

[60] Millett LJ in *Kapfunde v Abbey National plc* [1999] ICR 1, p. 13 'foreseeability of loss is not an adequate limiting factor in these cases'.

[61] See [1964] AC 465, pp. 483 and 580 (Lord Reid); pp. 537 and 616 (Lord Pearce).

economic loss: *Henderson v Merrett Syndicates Ltd*,[62] *White v Jones*,[63] *Spring v Guardian Insurance*,[64] and *Williams v Natural Life Health Foods Ltd*.[65] In *Williams*, Lord Steyn asserted that 'there is no better rationalization for the relevant head of tort liability than assumption of responsibility' and that 'the extended *Hedley Byrne* principle is the rationalization or technique adopted by English law for the recovery of damages in respect of economic loss caused by the negligent performance of services'.[66] Indeed, reference has been made recently to the 'emerging tort of assumption of responsibility'.[67]

However, it is clear from cases such as *Smith v Bush*[68] and *Spring v Guardian Assurance*[69] that, in determining the imposition of liability, it is not a test of universal application. So in *Smith v Bush* there was no voluntary assumption of liability, given the presence of an express disclaimer and in *Spring v Guardian Assurance* the court was faced not with the two-party *Hedley Byrne* scenario[70] but rather with advice about the plaintiff to a third party. Yet in both cases the plaintiff succeeded in negligence.

What such cases reveal is that once the facts do not fit the *Hedley Byrne* model, then the courts, though reluctant to impose liability, may yet be persuaded so to do. But they will need to be convinced that the economic harm was foreseeable, there was 'proximity' between the parties and— probably most importantly of all—the imposition of such liability would be 'fair, just, and reasonable'.[71] Above all, the courts appear keen that

---

[62] See in particular Lord Goff [1995] 2 AC 145, p. 182; Lord Browne-Wilkinson (p. 266) found that in assessing the relationship between contract and the duty of care arising under *Hedley Byrne*, the traditional approach of equity to fiduciary duties was 'instructive'.

[63] [1995] 2 AC 207, esp. Lord Goff (p. 268).

[64] [1995] 2 AC 296. Lord Goff and Lord Lowry based their decision on the *Hedley Byrne* principle. Though note Lord Woolf (p. 342) 'before there can be a duty owed in respect of economic loss, it is now clearly established that it is important to be able to show foreseeability of that loss, coupled with the necessary degree of proximity between the parties. It is also necessary to establish in all the circumstances it is fair, just and reasonable for a duty to be imposed in respect of the economic loss'. Lord Slynn felt that the principle did not decide the case before them (p. 335). Lord Keith dissented.

[65] [1999] 1 WLR 831.

[66] Ibid. 837. Though he did agree that coherence must sometimes yield to practical justice, with *Smith v Bush* [1990] 1 AC 831 and *White v Jones* [1993] 3 WLR 756 being decided 'on special facts'.

[67] Grantham, R., and Rickett, C., 'Directors "Tortious" Liability: Contract, Tort or Company Law?' 62 MLR (1999) 133.

[68] [1990] 1 AC 831.

[69] [1995] 2 AC 296.

[70] In *Hedley Byrne*, the bank acted as middleman, the plaintiff instigated the request, and the defendants acted on that request. This was acknowledged by Lord Mustill (dissenting) in *White v Jones* [1995] 2 AC 207, p. 283.

[71] This approach was suggested for the tort generally by Lord Keith in *Peabody v Parkinson* [1985] AC 210, p. 240. Lord Keith of course dissented in *White v Jones* and *Spring v Guardian Assurance*. Lord Oliver in *Caparo* noted ([1990] 2 AC 628) that what are treated as three sep-arate requirements are, in most cases, 'in fact merely facets of the same thing . . . a

developments in the tort should be incremental only, so that presumably the further from the *Hedley Byrne* factual frame, the less likely that liability will result. So in *Caparo v Dickman*[72]—where there was a lack of direct communication between the parties—the tripartite test of foreseeability, proximity, and 'fairness'[73] was stressed. For Lord Bridge it was necessary that: 'the defendant in giving the advice or information was fully aware of the nature of the transaction which the plaintiff had in contemplation, knew that the advice or information would be communicated to him directly or indirectly and knew that it was very likely that the plaintiff would rely on that advice or information in deciding whether or not to engage in the transaction in contemplation.'[74] In *Caparo*—which concerned the statutory audit of the accounts of a public company—the auditors did not owe a duty of care to potential investors in the company for whom the report had not been prepared (though it might be foreseeable that they would rely on that report). Their statutory duty was to report to members of the company. The investors were not the intended recipients and advising them was not the intended purpose.

What then are the necessary ingredients for pure economic loss liability to arise in the tort of negligence? It would appear that the most important feature is the presence of a special relationship between the parties, with mutuality in the transaction in question. In addition, the concept of reliance is a necessary ingredient in all cases of two-party misrepresentations.[75] Here there is a need for the claimant to act, to positively rely on the defendant's misrepresentation.[76] With words, reliance plays a causal role.[77] Where the issue concerns negligent services,[78] however, the

---

description of circumstances from which, pragmatically, the courts conclude that a duty of care exists'. Lord Slynn applied the tripartite approach in *Phelps v Hillingdon* [2000] 3 WLR 776 asserting that the 'assumption of responsibility' test may amount to no more than the fact that the law regognizes that there is a duty of care (p. 791). In *Henderson v Merritt* Lord Goff rejected the 'fair, just and reasonable' approach, but only in the context of a two-party case, clearly within the *Hedley Byrne* principle.

[72] [1990] 2 AC 605.

[73] As noted by Millett LJ in *Kapfunde v Abbey National plc* [1999] ICR 1, pp. 13–14.

[74] [1990] 2 AC 605, pp. 620–1 (reviewing *Hedley Byrne*; *Smith v Bush* and the dissenting judgment of Lord Denning in *Candler v Crane Christmas* [1951] 2 KB 164).

[75] In *Marc Rich & Co AG v Bishop Rock Marine Co* [1996] 1 AC 211 Lord Steyn stressed that there was no assumption of responsibility because the cargo owners had not even been aware of the classification society's examination of the ship (p. 242).

[76] Lord Oliver, *Caparo Industries v Dickman* [1990] 2 AC 605, p. 635: 'the damage which may be occasioned by the spoken or written word is not inherent. It lies always in the reliance by someone upon the accuracy of that which the word communicates.'

[77] Lord Goff in *Henderson v Merrett Syndicates Ltd* [1995] 2 AC 145, p. 193: reliance is necessary re information/advice because 'otherwise the negligence will have no causative effect'. Lord Steyn in *Williams v Natural Life Health Foods Ltd* [1998] 1 WLR 830 also stressed the 'causative' role of reliance.

[78] Lord Browne-Wilkinson in *White v Jones* [1995] 2 AC 207, p. 272: though reliance is necessary where misstatements are concerned, 'it does not follow that in all cases based on

requirement of 'reliance' may add little to the notion that the defendant has assumed responsibility.[79] So 'reliance' may simply mean that the defendant knows he is being relied on[80] in the sense that he knows that the claimant's economic well-being is dependent on his careful conduct of the claimant's affairs.[81] Reliance, of course, is not sufficient for liability.[82]

These ingredients offer a limited role for the tort and a result that does not conflict with the two policy reasons against general liability for pure economic loss.

The need for a special relationship: assumption of responsibility or proximity[83]

The need for a special relationship or assumption of responsibility (or the related notion of an 'undertaking') are phrases used by the judges in *Hedley Byrne* and other leading cases on pure economic loss.[84] Lord Devlin in *Hedley* noted that 'the essence of the matter in the present case and in others of the same type is the acceptance of responsibility',[85] while Lords Morris and Reid stressed that liability emanated from the defendant's 'undertaking'.[86] Later Lord Devlin concentrated on the

---

negligent action or inaction by the defendant it is necessary in order to demonstrate a special relationship that the plaintiff has in fact relied on the defendant or the defendant has foreseen such reliance'.

[79] Though in *Glanzer v Shepard* (1922) 233 NY 236 there was a direct reliance on the negligent service when the purchaser decided to pay the seller.

[80] Thus though Lord Goff in *Henderson v Merrett Syndicates Ltd* [1995] 2 AC 145, p. 193 commented on the 'assumption of responsibility, together with its concomitant reliance', in *Spring v Guardian Assurance* [1995] 2 AC 296, p. 318 he defined reliance in a wide sense: 'where the plaintiff entrusts the defendant with the conduct of his affairs in general or in particular, the defendant may be held to have assumed responsibility to the plaintiff and *the plaintiff to have relied on the defendant to exercise due skill and care in respect of such conduct*' [emphasis added]. And, indeed, as Goff LJ in *Muirhead v Industrial Tank Specialities* [1986] QB 507, p. 527 he noted that there is 'a sense in which it can be said that *every* successful plaintiff in an action of negligence has relied on the defendant not to be negligent'.

[81] Paraphrasing Lord Browne-Wilkinson in *White v Jones* [1995] 2 AC 207, p. 272.

[82] Millett LJ in *Kapfunde v Abbey National plc* [1999] ICR 1, p. 13 'it is not sufficient for the plaintiff to prove that he had relied upon the statement of which he complained. Such reliance by itself did not establish the necessary relationship between the party who made the statement and the person who relied upon it.'

[83] Lord Slynn in *McFarlane v Tayside Health Board* [1999] 4 All ER 961, p. 971 noted that the relationship depended on whether it is 'fair, just and reasonable' for the law to impose the duty.

[84] In *Hedley Byrne*, Lord Morris noted that the defendant should possess a 'special skill': Lord Goff in *Henderson* [1995] 2 AC 145, p. 180 held that the concept was to be understood in a broad sense, 'to include special knowledge'.

[85] [1964] AC 465, p. 531.

[86] Ibid., Lord Morris 'undertaking to apply that skill' (p. 502); Lord Reid 'undertaking a responsibility' (p. 483); 'undertaking to assume a duty of care' (p. 492).

'special relationship', 'equivalent to contract',[87] involved. It is apparent that all these phrases are meant to convey the same test: so a special relationship is established[88] by showing that the defendant assumed responsibility for the advice/services.[89] Thus the tort of negligence could be used to fill a gap, to remedy economic loss caused by promises which the law of contract cannot enforce.[90] Such an assumption of responsibility can be implied—Lord Devlin in *Hedley Byrne* thought it would be useful, in assessing this, to check whether the defendant derived any indirect benefit and whether the advice/service was given as part of a professional relationship.[91] Indeed, the fact that the claimant is of limited resources clearly is in favour of an assumption being inferred.[92]

Of course, the House of Lords in *Henderson v Merrett Syndicates Ltd*[93] held it to be the 'logical conclusion' of the *Hedley Byrne* principle that it should apply even where a contract existed between the parties.[94] A contract for services is perhaps the ultimate 'assumption of responsibility'. Here, rather than overcome the problem of lack of consideration (which was in issue in *Hedley Byrne*), the court was willing to accept that the tort had a separate 'gap-filling' role: to overcome the disadvantages of a claim framed in contract. In *Henderson*, the plaintiffs sought successfully to take advantage of the more favourable date for the accrual of a cause of action in tort, as opposed to that in contract.[95]

But even in the absence of a 'voluntary assumption of responsibility' (at least in the sense that phrase was used by Lord Devlin in *Hedley*

---

[87] *Al Saudi Banque v Clark Pixley* [1989] 3 All ER 361, 367 Millet J: there should be either an assumption of responsibility or a relationship 'equivalent to contract'.

[88] Lord Reid [1964] AC 465, p. 486 'to have accepted a relationship with the inquirer which requires him to exercise such care as the circumstances require'.

[89] Cf. *Fairline Shipping Corp v Adamson* [1975] QB 180, on this basis with *Williams v Natural Life Health Foods Ltd* [1999] 1 WLR 831. In the former the company director was personally liable in negligence because on the facts he had created the 'clear impression' he was personally answerable for the services, per Lord Steyn in *Williams*, p. 836.

[90] As was, of course, expressly accepted by Lord Steyn in *Williams v Natural Life Health Foods Ltd* [1998] 1 WLR 830.

[91] In *Spring v Guardian Assurance* [1995] 2 AC 296, p. 319 it was accepted that references may not lead to liability where they are given in circumstances 'so informal as to negate an assumption of responsibility by the employer'.

[92] In *White v Jones* [1995] 2 AC 207 Lord Goff noted that mistakes of the kind that arose in the case were most likely to occur in small firms 'with the result that it tends to be people of modest means who need the money so badly who suffer'. Contrast this with *Peach Publishing Ltd v Slater & Co* [1998] PNLR 364, where the plaintiff, the recipient of the advice, was an experienced business operator. The court cited Neill LJ in *James McNaughton Paper Group Ltd v Hicks Anderson & Co* [1991] 2 QB 113, p. 125 on this point.

[93] [1995] 2 AC 145.

[94] Ibid. Lord Goff, p. 193.

[95] Lord Goff noted that some would argue that a radical reform was necessary, so that incidental rules (such as limitation) would follow the nature of the harm suffered, rather than the nature of the liability asserted, but felt that this 'is perhaps crying for the moon' (ibid. 186).

Byrne)[96]—the courts may be willing to impose liability. So in *Smith v Bush*, the plaintiffs were able to claim for the negligent overvaluation of the property they bought, relying on the defendant surveyors' report. Here there was no assumption of responsibility—the defendants had rather 'manifested every intention to the contrary',[97] with an express disclaimer—and the advice was given not to the plaintiff mortgagors but to the building society who financed the purchase. It is hard not to agree with the approach of Lord Griffiths[98] in that case, rejecting the *Hedley Byrne* test as not 'helpful or realistic', preferring proximity and a general approach of whether it was 'fair and reasonable' to impose liability. A close proximity resulted from the payment by the plaintiff to the defendant surveyor, in effect 'engaged' to perform a service on behalf of the plaintiff.

Therefore, it would appear that for pure economic loss to be recoverable there must be a special relationship between the parties and that can be evidenced by an assumption of responsibility or a similar close proximity between the parties, with a 'particular transaction in mind'.[99] Indeed, in *Kapfunde v Abbey National plc*, Kennedy LJ asserted that the notion of 'special relationship' and 'proximity' amount to the same thing.[100]

The need for a special relationship means that the claimant and defendant will be parties to the transaction in issue.[101] This factor was indeed asserted to be a requirement of the principle by Lord Mustill in his dissenting judgment in *White v Jones*. For him, the principle can only

---

[96] As Kit Barker's analysis has shown ('Unreliable Assumptions in the Modern Law of Negligence', 109 LQR (1993) 461), the notion of an assumption of responsibility contains within it at least three different models of liability. He identified these as promise (which would appear to be the meaning used in *Hedley Byrne* itself, particularly by Lord Devlin), choice (see *MHLG v Sharp* [1970] 2 QB 223, Salmon LJ, p. 279; *Caparo* [1990] 2 AC 605 Lord Jauncey, p. 871) or (at its widest) mere voluntary action (*Reid v Rush & Tomkins plc* [1990] 1 WLR 212, p. 229, Ralph Gibson LJ).

[97] *Street on Torts*, above, n. 2, p. 220.

[98] [1990] 1 AC 831, pp. 864–5.

[99] Denning LJ (in the dissenting judgment) in *Candler v Crane Christmas & Co* [1951] 2QB 164, p. 173 noted that the court must assess 'the very purpose of a particular transaction'. In *Phelps v Hillingdon* [2000] 3 WLR 776 it was held that a duty of care to the child can arise 'where an educational psychologist is specifically called in to advise in relation to the assessment and future provision of a specific child and it is clear that the parents . . . and the teachers will follow that advice' (Lord Slynn, p. 791). And see *Law Society v KPMG Peat Marwick*, CA [2000] 1 WLR 1921. The Law Society, as trustee of the compensation fund, was owed a duty by the defendant accountants who prepared reports on solicitors' accounts, given that it was clear to the defendants that these reports were needed to indicate whether any intervention by the Law Society might be required.

[100] [1999] ICR 1, p. 12.

[101] Where liability ensues from an ongoing service such as that provided by a solicitor to his client, the 'transaction' to which they are parties seems to cover the whole range of services provided (or that should be provided) by the solicitor.

apply where there is 'mutuality', i.e. 'both the plaintiff and defendant played an active part in the transaction from which the liability arose'.[102] In essence liability under the *Hedley Byrne* principle arises 'internally from the relationship in which the parties had together chosen to place themselves'.[103] Even beyond the *Hedley Byrne* principle, however, the need for 'proximity' and a 'fair' result may well demand that there be mutuality. This echoes the *Caparo* requirement that the defendant must have a particular transaction and a particular claimant (or class of claimants) in mind. This means that normally no liability will arise for pure economic loss caused to the claimant as a result of negligent advice or services provided to a third party.[104] This requirement—of mutuality, a close proximity in the transaction—has been particularly important in relation to professional advice[105] about the claimant to a third party, where it is the third party that has sought that advice (and no contract exists between the adviser and the claimant).[106] So in *Kapfunde v Abbey National plc*,[107] the employer's occupational health adviser, retained to assess applicants' medical suitability for employment, owed no duty of care to the applicant in making her assessment.[108]

---

[102] *White v Jones* [1995] 2 AC 207, p. 283. So in *Hedley Byrne*, the relationship between the parties was 'bilateral, being created on the one hand by the acts of the plaintiffs in first asking for a reference in circumstances which showed that the bankers' skill and care would be relied upon and then subsequently relying on it; and on the other hand by the bankers' compliance with that request' (p. 287).This means that such claims are the antithesis of the standard negligence claim for physical harm or loss: Stapleton, above, n. 22, p. 249: 'the tort of negligence emerged in its clearest modern form in the late nineteenth and early twentieth centuries as a cause of action for a stranger who had been physically injured by the negligent act of the defendant-stranger.'

[103] *White v Jones* [1995] 2 AC 207, p. 287, Lord Mustill.

[104] This is evidenced by the decision of the Court of Appeal in *Kapfunde v Abbey National plc* [1999] ICR 1.

[105] And for services: note *Goodwin v BPAS* [1996] 1 WLR 1397 (allegation of negligent failure to advise on consequences of vasectomy; no duty to subsequent pregnant sexual partner).

[106] Cf. *Spring v Guardian Assurance* [1995] 2 AC 296. This ties in with the notion of reliance, crucial in the area of negligent misstatement, see later.

[107] The Court of Appeal overruled *Baker v Kaye* (1997) 39 BMLR 12 .

[108] Note in *Spring v Guardian Assurance* [1995] 2 AC 296, Lords Goff and Woolf approved of the decision of the NZCA in *South Pacific Manufacturing Co Ltd v New Zealand Security Consultants and Investigators Ltd* [1992] 2 NZLR 282. An investigator, reporting on the cause of a fire to an insurance company, owed no duty of care to the insured whose claim was rejected because of the defendant's alleged negligent report. The defendant was not giving the advice or rendering a service to the plaintiff, though it was predictable that the report would affect the plaintiff. Lord Browne-Wilkinson in *X v Bedfordshire CC* [1995] 2 AC 633 noted that in such cases no duty of care to the applicant is owed: unlike the client who seeks the report, the subjects of such reports will not regulate their conduct in reliance on the report. However, in *Phelps v Hillingdon* [2000] 3 WLR 776, HL, it was held that an educational psychologist reporting on a child to a school, prima facie owed a duty of care to the child where it was clear that the parents and the teachers would follow their advice. Here the court was not prepared (in effect) to find that the advice was merely 'about' the child. Rather it was 'for the benefit of the child'.

Yet mutuality (and therefore liability) can in fact arise even where the actual advice or services are provided by the defendant to a third party.[109] So in *Smith v Bush*,[110] though the advice was given under a contract between the defendants and the building society, the plaintiffs were not 'strangers to the transaction', given they had actually paid the defendants for the advice/service. In *Spring v Guardian Assurance*,[111] an existing relationship[112]—that of employer/employee (where onerous terms are implied into the contract because of the relationship at the heart of the deal)[113]—gave rise to a duty of care in relation to the issuing of references.[114] The facts were not within the framework of *Hedley Byrne*—the advice in *Spring* was sought by a third party about the plaintiff—but the majority of the House of Lords were willing to impose liability. Though Lord Goff based his judgment on the *Hedley Byrne* principle, both Lord Slynn and Lord Woolf expressly rejected the application of this principle to the facts. Rather, Lord Woolf favoured the tripartite test and a 'measured extension to the ambit of the law of negligence'. Here there was a special relationship already existing between the parties[115] and there was mutuality—as Millett LJ noted in *Kapfunde v Abbey National plc*[116] 'it was the existence of the relationship which made it possible for their Lordships to treat the reference as provided, not (or not solely) at the request of the prospective employer, but rather at the request of the former employee and as an incident of his former employment'.[117]

---

[109] The third party could of course be acting as agent or middleman for the claimant—as was the case of the bank in *Hedley Byrne* or the claimant could be part of a wider class of intended recipients. In such cases there is no problem, obviously, with 'mutuality'. In *Farah v British Airways, The Times*, 26 January 2000, the CA noted that though *Caparo Industries v Dickman* [1990] 2 AC 605 was the starting point for a consideration of the duty of care, where sufficiency of proximity was in issue, the later decisions such as *White v Jones* [1995] 2 AC 207 and *Spring v Guardian Assurance* [1995] 2 AC 296 could be applied.

[110] [1990] 1 AC 831. And note *Barex Brokers Ltd v Morris Dean & Co* [1999] PNLR 344, CA. A negligent overvaluation by the defendants to the original lender; however no duty owed to the subsequent mortgagee.

[111] *Spring v Guardian Assurance* [1995] 2 AC 296.

[112] The fact of an existing relationship—contractual or fiduciary—may enable the courts to extend the *Spring* principle beyond employer–employee. Lord Goff noted [1995] 2 AC 296, at 319 that he could see no reason why a solicitor should not be under a duty to his client to exercise due care and skill when making statements to third parties.

[113] Note, as an alternative to liability in tort, Lords Woolf, Goff, and Slynn were prepared to imply a term into the contract of employment.

[114] Lord Woolf, [1995] 2 AC 296, p. 345, stressed that there had been a contract relationship and noted the indirect benefit to the employer of giving references, making his own recruitment of staff easier.

[115] As Millett LJ noted in *Kapfunde v Abbey National plc* 'their Lordships did not derive the duty of care from the relationship between the maker of the statement and the subject of the statement . . . they found it in the pre-existing relationship between an employer and his former employee'.

[116] [1999] ICR 1, CA.

[117] [1999] ICR 1, p. 15. Lord Goff described the provision of references as 'a service regu-

Overall, the cautious approach of the courts and the focus on a special relationship has kept the recovery of pure economic loss strictly controlled. Moreover, this approach is most likely to lead to a 'fair, just, and reasonable' imposition of a duty. The only important exceptions to this approach in recent years have been *White v Jones* and the earlier Court of Appeal decision in *Ministry of Housing and Local Government v Sharp*.[118]

In *White*, the solicitor was negligent in delaying carrying out the testator's instructions to prepare a will in favour of the plaintiffs. The will had not been prepared by the time of the testator's death, so the plaintiffs sued for their expectation loss. Here the *Hedley Byrne* principle would not seem readily applicable, despite the views of Lord Goff and Lord Browne-Wilkinson[119] otherwise. There was no special relationship or mutuality between the parties; there had been no reliance by the plaintiffs. The deemed extension of the assumption of responsibility (from the testator to the beneficiaries) is clearly not a satisfactory basis for the decision. Rather, the special characteristics of the case appear to have dictated the outcome—with indeterminacy not in issue, the whole point of the transaction was undermined by the careless advice/service[120] and there was no obvious other method of redress.[121] For Lord Goff: 'the real reason for concern in cases such as the present lies in the extraordinary fact that, if a duty owed by the testator's solicitor to the disappointed beneficiary is not recognized . . . the only person who may have a valid claim has suffered no loss and the only person who has suffered a loss has no claim.' In effect, Lord Goff fell back on the need to do justice as the principle here for liability,[122] creating a 'specialist pocket of tort law'.[123] And, indeed, that explains the strong dissenting judgments from Lords Keith and Mustill. Rather than create a new principle of general use in this area, the case appears to be limited to wills.[124]

---

larly provided by employers to their employees'. Millett LJ in *Kapfunde v Abbey National plc* [1999] ICR 1, p. 15: 'a reference by an employer . . . is likely to be regarded as provided to the former employee who is the subject of the reference for his use as a passport to future employment rather than as a service to any particular prospective new employer.'

[118] [1970] 2 QB 223.

[119] An 'extension of the principle' in *Hedley Byrne* [1995] 2 AC 207, p. 270.

[120] Cardozo stressed liability was based on negligence in the 'end and the aim of the transaction', *Glanzer v Shepherd* (1931) 255 NY 170.

[121] [1995] 2 AC 207, p. 262. *White* was applied to an insurance company employing professional will-drafters in *Esterhuizen v Allied Dunbar* [1998] Fam Law 527.

[122] Note Lord Goff reviews similar cases in other jurisdictions and concludes that other courts are 'overwhelmingly in favour of liability' [1995] 2 AC 207, pp. 254–5.

[123] Which Lord Mustill believed the court should avoid, preferring 'principled reasoning' in his dissenting judgment: [1995] 2 AC 296, p. 291.

[124] Stephen Smith, 'Rights, Remedies and Normal Expectancies in Tort and Contract' 113 LQR (1997) 426, p. 430: '*White v Jones* should be understood . . . as exactly what it appears to be: a pragmatic attempt to get round either the privity rules or the rules on wills and estates.'

What then of *Ministry of Housing and Local Government v Sharp?*[125] Here, the Ministry had registered a land charge, having compensated the owner of the land in question for refusal to allow development. The effect of the land charge was that, should permission to develop subsequently be granted, the compensation would have to be repaid to the Ministry by the then owner of the land. A subsequent purchaser of this land, which by now could be developed, was not advised of the Ministry's charge and hence took free of this obligation to compensate. The Ministry success-fully claimed damages for this third-party misrepresentation from the Local Authority (who employed the clerk who made the mistake). There is little analysis of the basis of liability and it has been dismissed by Weir as a 'really odd case'.[126] As Mesher notes the rules laid down in *Sharp* 'are stated in remarkably vague and curt terms and without any reasoned discussion as to their value in the law of negligence'.[127] Certainly there is no special relationship, reliance, or mutuality involved. It is likely that it will not prove to be a starting point for a bold extension of liability for pure economic loss for misrepresentations made to a third party that harm the claimant.

RATIONALE AND RELATIONSHIP TO THE ECONOMIC TORTS

The *general* rule is that the tort of negligence is not an economic tort. In this area the courts are concerned over indeterminate liability and the effect on the contractual structures to which the parties have agreed. They are also concerned that negligence should not be overstretched in the attempt to find the deepest pockets. Lord Hoffmann in *Stovin v Wise*[128] warned that 'the trend of authorities has been to discourage the assump-tion that anyone who suffers loss is *prima facie* entitled to compensation from a person (preferably insured or a public authority) whose act or omission can be said to have caused it. The default position is that he is not.'[129]

However, the courts have rejected the certainty that would result from

---

[125] [1970] 2 QB 223.

[126] Weir, above, n. 5, p. 71, though he points out 'there, of course, the Registrar had the very name of the incumbrancer before his eyes, just as the solicitor in *White v Jones* had the names of intended legatees'.

[127] Mesher, J., 'How to get sued without really trying', 34 MLR (1971) 317, p. 322.

[128] [1996] AC 923, p. 949.

[129] And note the comments of Stapleton, J., 'Tort, Insurance and Ideology' 58 MLR (1995) 820, p. 845 'any distaste for the dependency culture should be brought to bear with greater stringency on commercial plaintiffs complaining about economic disappointment in their risk-taking'. Conversely it should not be of much weight 'in cases of personal injury caused by the defendants' affirmative act'.

accepting a 'bright line' rule of non-recovery in tort for pure economic loss.[130] In particular they are prepared to accept a relationship-based liability. Burrows[131] identifies the two main areas where pure economic loss may be recoverable as negligent misstatement (on which the claimant has relied) and negligent performance of a beneficial service (usually[132] under contract). In both cases a gap-filling function is involved, based on a concern to do 'practical justice'.[133] This gap-filling can take two forms: giving effect to an undertaking, not supported by contract or evading 'unwarranted disadvantages' in contract law (especially the different rules on limitation and remoteness) by allowing the use of the tort.[134] Of course, the effect of this is surprising where beneficial services are concerned, given the effect of tort liability here is not to protect against harmful interference or detrimental reliance (tort's main function)[135] but rather to protect expectations,[136] the failure to benefit (usually the role of contract law).

The question remains why the courts are happy to accept liability for pure economic loss in such circumstances, especially where positive obligations and expectation interests may be involved.

Unlike standard negligence claims (where the claimant is a random victim of the defendant) the principle of *Hedley Byrne* involves a relationship between the parties that has given rise to an undertaking which

---

[130] Stapleton, above, n. 22, pp. 256–7.

[131] Above, n. 14, p. 214.

[132] Though not necessarily so: in *Port v NZDB* [1982] 2 NZLR 282 liability arose for the negligent supply (not under contract) of the 'wrong' cattle semen to the farmer—as a result of which fewer calves were conceived than had been anticipated and those that were born were less valuable than should have been the case.

[133] Of course, *Hedley Byrne* also applies where a contract results from the misrepresentation: *Esso Petroleum Co Ltd v Marsden* [1976] QB 801. Parliament was moved to act in the same period as *Hedley Byrne* creating in the Misrepresentation Act 1967 a statutory misrepresentation tort where the defendant has, through a false representation, induced the claimant into a contract with him.

[134] As was accepted by the House of Lords in *Henderson v Merrett Syndicates Ltd* [1995] 2 AC 145. Lord Goff, p. 185 'if concurrent liability in tort is not recognized, a claimant may find his claim barred at a time when he is unaware of its existence', a real possibility he felt where professional men were concerned. He identifies the advantages of a tort action over a contract action (apart from the limitation rules) as: the rules of remoteness less restricted; the existence of a right to contribution between the negligent contract breakers; the availability of leave to serve proceedings outside the jurisdiction.

[135] Cf. Stapleton, 'The Normal Expectancies Measure in Tort Damages', 113 LQR (1997) 257 who argues that liability for negligent failure to benefit is commonly imposed in the tort of negligence. However, Burrows, above, n. 14, p. 40 disagrees with Stapleton as does Whittaker, S., 'The Application of the "Broad Principle of Hedley Byrne" as between Parties to a Contract', 17 LS (1997) 169.

[136] Burrows, A., *Remedies for Tort and Breach of Contract*, 2nd edn. (London: Butterworths, 1994), p. 172: once we move from statements to the performance of beneficial services, 'a complaint of negligently causing pure economic loss naturally embraces a complaint of failure to benefit'.

should be economically beneficial to the claimant. Thus deliberate under-takings form a grey area between the realm of contract and tort. It is hardly surprising, therefore, that the net result of the *Hedley Byrne* prin-ciple is that the closer to a contract relationship between the parties, the greater the chance of success in negligence. This was noted by Lord Devlin in the case itself[137] and more recently in *Spring* Lord Goff remarked 'the *Hedley Byrne* duty arises where there is a relationship which is, broadly speaking, either contract or equivalent to contract'.[138] The notion of 'proximity' also helps to limit liability to such narrow relation-ships.

But that is not the only reason for the courts' interest in this area. The imposition of a duty for advice and services means that the most likely setting for such liability is the provision of professional or quasi-profes-sional services (including advice).[139] In *Caparo* Lord Bridge notes that the typical litigation arises 'in relation to statements made by a person in the exercise of his calling or profession';[140] Lord Goff in *Henderson*, stressed the plaintiffs' reliance on the defendants' special expertise and in *White v Jones* noted that 'an expectation interest may well occur in cases where a professional man such as a solicitor, has assumed responsibility for the affairs of another'.[141] In that same case, Lord Browne-Wilkinson commented on the professional status of the solicitor and what society expected of such professionals.[142] Professional services are increasingly important in everyday life and 'while the matter may be one of degree, there does remain a difference in most people's perception between the sort of level of both expertise and ethical standards to which profession-als such as doctors, lawyers, accountants and, possibly, bankers should be

---

[137] Lord Devlin in *Hedley Byrne* [1964] AC 465 said: 'as a problem it is a by-product of the doctrine of consideration'—with the courts in the past willing to construct artificial consid-eration as in *De La Bere v Pearson Ltd* [1908] 1 KB 280.

[138] [1995] 2 AC 296, p. 324. And see Lord Goff in *White v Jones* [1995] 2 AC 207, p. 263: the problems caused by the doctrines of consideration and of privity of contract 'encourage us to seek a solution to problems of this kind within our law of tortious negligence'. Of course, Parliament has now entered this arena: by the Contracts (Rights of Third Parties) Act 1999 third parties may be able to enforce contracts if the contract expressly so provides or contains a term that purports to confer a benefit on them. As such the beneficiaries in a claim like *White* would not be protected, however.

[139] *Chaudhry v Prabhakar* [1989] 1 WLR 29 is wrong: a case where the duty was (wrongly) conceded. Despite the decision of the Privy Council in *MLC v Evatt* [1971] AC 793 it is likely that the principle is not, of course, limited to defendants whose business or profession is to provide information or advice: the decision in *Evatt* was called into question in *Spring v Guardian Assurance* [1995] 2 AC 296, p. 320.

[140] [1990] 2 AC 605, p. 619.

[141] [1995] 2 AC 207, p. 269.

[142] This also justifies the imposition of liability under *Hedley Byrne* for omissions: because of the professional duty to act on behalf of the client.

and are kept'.[143] For Allen[144] 'the power inherent in the possession of a special skill or responsibility almost invites the courts to impose responsibility for its use'.[145] Thus after *Hedley Byrne* 'the information professions ... who play so important a role in today's economy became accountable in tort', though the principle encourages greater care without imposing overpowering liability.[146] Lord Bridge stressed in *Caparo* that any such liability should not be extended 'to the world at large' allowing third parties to 'appropriate for their own purposes the benefit of the expert knowledge or professional expertise attributed to the maker of the statement'.

The rationale of liability in negligence is thus different from that in the main economic torts. Its development has not been guided expressly by the issue of free competition and the need to map out the limits of permissible behaviour in the market place. Rather its main development has been in an area where as between two parties it has been deemed compelling that the defendant should be required to answer for his undertaking to the claimant. Negligence liability looks to dependency; the economic torts look to unlawful acts.[147] Where tort's protection is concerned, neighbours are clearly a different species to competitors: 'while the rules of negligence just give people "out", as it were, like an umpire in a cricket match, these decisions [in economic tort litigation] lay down the rules of the game, rules as a basis for action, determining what is permitted and what is not.'[148]

At the same time the courts are aware that the tort of negligence could undermine the limited role of the economic torts and impinge on competitive practice. Thus far no liability for negligent interference with contract

---

[143] Whittaker, S., 'Privity of Contract and the Tort of Negligence: Fresh Directions', 16 OJLS (1966) 191, p. 218 n. 132. He appears now to doubt this, however, see above, n. 135, p. 177, contending that *Hedley Byrne* is not limited to professionals or semi-professionals.

[144] Allen, T., 'Liability for References: the House of Lords and Spring v Guardian Assurance', 58 MLR (1995) 553, p. 558.

[145] Lord Goff, *Henderson v Merrett Syndicates Ltd* [1995] 2 AC 145, p. 181: 'the concept [assumption] provides its own explanation why there is no problem in cases of this kind about liability for pure economic loss; for if a person assumes responsibility to another in respect of certain services, there is no reason why he should not be liable in damages for that other in respect of economic loss which flows from the negligent performance of those services.'

[146] Fleming, above, n. 1, p. 189: [For 200 years between *Pasley v Freeman* (1789) 3 Term Rep 51 and *Hedley Byrne*] 'the courts were daunted by the prospect of a vast liability that was feared to descend on the frail shoulders of such as accountants, surveyors, bankers and lawyers whose daily job is to offer guidance in financial transactions of frequently considerable dimensions'.

[147] Or in the case of the tort of passing off, the protection of the property right in 'goodwill'.

[148] Weir, above, n. 5, p. 569.

or for negligently interfering with trade has been imposed.[149] As Cane notes, though liability for the negligent performance of services is now included in the tort, 'we should not deduce from [that] any general principle of liability for negligently depriving a person of some contractual expectancy for such a principle would be unduly subversive of free markets'.[150] If negligently inflicted economic loss were recoverable simply on the basis of foreseeability, the tort would undermine the main economic torts.

That is not to say that there may not be overlaps between the economic torts and the tort of negligence causing pure economic loss. Thus the tort of passing off could arise, consequent on a negligent misrepresentation (concerning the source or product) and negligence may prove a more successful basis for an action than torts requiring intended falsehoods such as deceit[151] or malicious falsehood.

But such overlaps do not reveal a rationale close to the other economic torts or a willingness to create a general principle of liability for negligently inflicted economic harm.

For passing off, the essence of the claim is a misrepresentation that is detrimental to trader and consumer alike. The tort has a clear information role and can arise even from innocent misinformation. But the *Hedley Byrne* principle does not focus on the truth or otherwise of the advice etc. but rather on the undertaking to provide careful advice or services. Moreover, the width of the tort of passing off (dubbed a 'protean tort' by Lord Diplock in *Advocaat*) in the context of third-party misstatements, means that the emergence of liability for negligent misrepresentation has had little effect on that tort. Though Mesher predicted[152] that negligence might provide a way of imposing liability for misrepresentations on the borderline of the tort of passing off, by and large the borderline he identified back in 1971 (including inverse passing off, equivalence passing off, and product passing off) has now been incorporated into mainstream passing off liability.

Again, as far as malicious falsehood is concerned, the decision of the House of Lords in *Spring v Guardian Assurance* 'bypassed the limitations of the tort of malicious falsehood where proof of mere negligence is

---

[149] Note the decision of the Californian Supreme Court in *J'Aire Corp v Gregory* 24 Cal 3d 799 where the café owner/tenant's business was affected by the defendant's delays in work undertaken for the landlord. The claim for negligent economic harm succeeded.

[150] Cane, P., *Tort Law and Economic Interests*, 2nd edn. (Oxford: Clarendon Press, 1996).

[151] The tort of negligence clearly overshadows the tort of deceit. For both torts liability is most likely to arise where the parties are close to a contract relationship. For both detrimental reliance by the claimant is the norm and both torts will render the defendant liable where, though the statement is initially made to another party, the defendant knew that the statement would be conveyed to the claimant.

[152] Mesher, above, n. 127, p. 322.

insufficient'.[153] However, the decision does not indicate a general extension of the principle of *Hedley Byrne* to cover statements *about* the claimant rather than *to* the claimant. The tort of negligence protects where there is mutuality. The malicious falsehood tort, unlike negligence, always protects in a three-party setting[154] and can apply to denigration or disparagement published generally, without the need for a specific transaction to be contemplated by the parties. The typical malicious falsehood is published 'to the public at large'.[155] One of the leading cases on malicious falsehood, *Radcliffe v Evans*,[156] involved the defendant falsely claiming that the plaintiff had ceased business. There would be no liability in negligence for a careless assertion to the same effect.[157]

CONCLUSION

It may be that the *Hedley Byrne* principle and the related tripartite test in *Caparo* will not prove to be enduring, all-embracing rules in the area of negligently inflicted pure economic loss.[158] For Stapleton, in her seminal article on the tort of negligence and economic loss, the courts need to address openly the policy issues that are raised by claims in negligence that fall outside the paradigm case of physical harm.[159] What is clear, however, is that the courts have, within narrow limits, been prepared to expand professional liability, to accept 'a quasi-disciplinary function'.[160] By *Hedley Byrne* 'the information professions, from auditors to architects and designers, who play so important a role in today's economy, became accountable in tort, alongside those whose activities spell physical danger to others'.[161]

---

[153] Hepple, above, n. 4, p. 69.

[154] Millett LJ in *Kapfunde v Abbey National plc* [1999] ICR 1, p. 15: 'a duty of care will generally be owed to the person to whom [the misstatement] is made and who relies upon it.'

[155] Mesher, above, n. 127, p. 156.   [156] [1892] 2 QB 524.

[157] Rogers, W. V. H., *Gatley on Libel and Slander*, 9th edn. (London: Sweet & Maxwell, 1998), para. 21.5 'if in *Radcliffe v Evans* the newspaper had carelessly reported that the plaintiff's firm had gone out of business, it is thought that there would still be no liability'.

[158] Though note the caution expressed by Lord Steyn in *McFarlane v Tayside Health Board* [1999] 4 All ER 961, p. 975: 'the common law has a great capacity for growth but the development of a new ground of liability, or a new head of such liability, for the recovery of economic loss must be justified by cogent reasons.'

[159] And note the leading Australian case, *Caltex Oil v The Willemstad* (1976) 136 CLR 529 where according to Fleming (above, n. 1, p. 199): 'the High Court distanced itself from any broad exclusionary rule, stressing instead that liability was controlled both as regards claim and loss.' For a review of recent decisions in this area in the High Court of Australia and the Supreme Court of Canada see Feldthusen, B., 'Liability for Pure Economic Loss: Yes, But Why?', 28 UWALR (1999) 84.

[160] Rogers, W. V. H., *The Law of Torts*, 15th edn. (London: Sweet & Maxwell, 1998), p. 107.

[161] Fleming, above, n. 1, p. 190.

The tort has only a minor part to play in terms of trade competition, therefore, seeking as it does to create liability out of a relationship—out of an 'impulse to do practical justice'. In the three-party scenario,[162] it is the economic torts that play the more important part in maintaining commercial links and profitability between the claimant and (potential) customers or consumers.

[162] i.e. where the claimant and defendant are not 'parties to the same transaction'.

10

Conclusion: A Framework Suggested

THE NEED TO CLARIFY THE ECONOMIC TORTS

As the discussion in the preceding chapters has revealed, the economic torts are indeed a 'difficult if not to say obscure branch of the law of tort'.[1] The scope of the torts of inducing breach of contract, unlawful interference with trade, and passing off are all unclear, while the relationship between deceit, malicious falsehood, and the unlawful interference tort is uncertain. That the economic torts are in a mess is due to the lack of coherent framework for their development.

Given this weak conceptual basis, there is constant pressure from claimants to increase protection against the infliction of economic loss.[2] This is most apparent in the tort of passing off, where product misrepresentation is now accepted as an 'extended' form of passing off and 'inverse' passing off[3] seems established. It has even been held arguable that a defendant's commercial success resulting from modifying another's product is tortious, as this 'wrongly generated a goodwill', though no obvious source or product misrepresentation arose (*Matthew Gloag & Son Ltd v Welsh Distilleries Ltd*).[4]

However, this expansion pressure is evident throughout the economic torts.[5] So with the tort of inducing breach of contract, the need for inducement[6] and breach,[7] and the meaning of intention (still a matter for judicial debate some 150 years after *Lumley v Gye*)[8] have all been questioned by claimants.[9] With the tort of unlawful interference with trade—described

---

[1] Butler-Sloss LJ *Associated British Ports v TGWU* [1989] 1 WLR 939, p. 961. The decision was reversed by the House of Lords on other grounds.

[2] As in, e.g., *Joyce v Sengupta* [1993] 1 All ER 897; *Millar v Bassey* [1994] EMLR 44.

[3] Factually the reverse of classic passing off. See discussion in Ch. 8.

[4] [1998] FSR 718, Laddie J.

[5] Bar simple conspiracy.

[6] Beldam LJ in *Millar v Bassey* [1994] EMLR 44 questioned whether inducement was necessary, provided the defendant's act caused the breach.

[7] The 'tort' of interference with a contract, where no breach results was referred to most recently by Beldam LJ in *Law Debenture Trust Corp v Ural Caspian Oil Corp Ltd* [1995] Ch 152, p. 167.

[8] Most recently in *Millar v Bassey* [1994] EMLR 44. Of course, there was also uncertainty for some time over the scope of the tort of unlawful conspiracy, following *Lonrho v Shell (no. 2)* [1982] AC 211: see Ch. 2.

[9] *Middlebrook Mushrooms Ltd v TGWU* [1993] IRLR 232. The fact that there was a risk that contracts might exist that might be breached by the defendants' activities was accepted as sufficient to grant an injunction by the High Court, but this view was rejected by the Court

in the Court of Appeal as of 'uncertain ambit'[10]—there has been pressure for the courts to accept a wide concept of 'unlawful means' as sufficient for liability. This pressure was successful in *Acrow (Automation) Ltd v Rex Chainbelt Inc*,[11] where procuring the breach of an injunction was held to be unlawful means[12] and in *Department of Transport v Williams*,[13] where the fact that the defendant had intentionally interfered with the plaintiffs' exercise of their statutory powers provided the necessary unlawful acts. Moreover, it has been suggested (and accepted by at least one member of the Court of Appeal) that for this tort foresight of 'probable' consequences could suffice to prove intended harm.[14]

Where harmful lies are the issue, recognition of a three-party version of the tort of deceit is sought, linked to unlawful interference with trade,[15] while the limits of the tort of malicious falsehood have been expanded to include prospective financial loss by non-traders (*Joyce v Sengupta*[16] and *Kaye v Robertson*).[17] Indeed, though there has been no attempt to 'modernize' this tort, it has recently been accepted that it can compensate for injury to feelings.[18]

If, as Weir suggests, the economic torts are about 'defining the rules of the game'—signalling what is permitted rather than excessive economic activity—then a delay in providing such a framework is to be regretted.[19] The role of tort law in this area, though primarily corrective, is to act as a deterrent.[20] Cane notes 'as a generalization it is probably true to say that

---

of Appeal. Indeed, the uncertainty surrounding the scope of the tort even led to the plaintiffs in *Lubenham Fidelities Co Ltd v S. Pembrokshire DC* (1986) 33 BLR 39, CA alleging *inter alia* (without success) that the defendant was liable for *negligently* causing interference with his contract.

[10] *Lonrho v Fayed* [1990] 2 QB 479 (the House of Lords only dealt with the tort of unlawful conspiracy [1992] 1 AC 448). [11] [1971] 1 WLR 1676, CA.

[12] A decision supported by Beldam LJ in *Law Debenture Trust v Ural Caspian Oil Corp Ltd* [1995] 1 All ER 157.

[13] (1993) 138 Sol LJ LB5 1993, CA. And, of course, see the views of the Court of Appeal in *Associated British Ports v TGWU* [1989] 3 All ER 796, discussed in Ch. 5.

[14] See Woolf LJ in *Lonrho v Fayed* [1990] 2 QB 479, p. 494.

[15] Accepted in *Lonrho v Fayed* [1990] 2 QB 479: and see Ch. 6.

[16] [1993] 1 WLR 337, CA. Morison, W., 'The New Law of Verbal Injury' 3 Syd LR (1959–1961) 4 contends that *Sheperd v Wakeman* (1662) 1 Sid 79, where liability arose from depriving the plaintiff of her opportunity of marriage, was a case in defamation and should not be seen as the origin of the tort of malicious falsehood.

[17] [1991] FSR 62, CA. [18] *Khodaparast v Shad* [2000] 1 All ER 545, CA.

[19] Some of the economic torts have been used successfully where other than economic interests have been in issue: so the plaintiff in *Godwin v Uzoigwe* [1993] Fam Law 65 successfully used the tort of intimidation where she had been kept in the defendants' home as a virtual slave and physically beaten.

[20] Though Cane, P., *Tort Law and Economic Interests*, 2nd edn. (Oxford: Clarendon Press, 1996) also notes that prevention is most likely to emanate from regulatory law rather than tort law given regulation is more systematic and proactive than tort law. Also of course regulatory law is often well publicized and has enforcement procedures and penalties that cannot be bargained around (p. 391). .

the deterrent theory of tort liability is most likely to be relevant to torts involving liability for calculated conduct and to businesses as defendants'.[21] That being so, it is vital that the rules of liability be as clear and predictable as possible, while seeking to prevent distortions in competition.

However, in order to offer such a framework it is first necessary to address certain preliminary issues. In particular, a framework must be based on a clear role for the common law in the competitive/economic process. At the same time, no coherent framework can emerge without distinguishing the economic torts from overlapping doctrines that may also provide relief against excessive economic behaviour.

The role of the common law in the economic process

What is the proper role for the common law in this area? For Heydon, *Allen v Flood* denied the economic torts theoretical consistency and the courts a practical weapon against intolerable conduct.[22] He argues that the law would be placed on a much sounder theoretical basis if defendants were liable on the basis of 'damage caused intentionally and without justification'.[23] Such a principle would make the law 'much more capable of handling bad behaviour and abuse of rights and of power; much more flexible; and much more based on factors of substance rather than technicality'.[24] Such a view finds echoes in the analyses of Fleming,[25] Salmond,[26] and Finnis.[27] It also reflects the development of the *Lumley v Gye* principle in America. There, the need for actual breach was abandoned. The tort refocused on interference with contractual performance which rendered the contract more onerous. Indeed, interference with economic relations became tortious, even in the absence of contract. The key limit on liability thus became whether the act could be justified.

A principle that it is tortious to injure another intentionally without

---

[21] Cane, ibid. 470.

[22] Heydon, J. D., *Economic Torts*, 2nd edn. (London: Sweet & Maxwell, 1978), p. 28.

[23] Heydon, 'The Future of the Economic Torts' 12 UWALRev (1975–6) 1, p. 13.

[24] Ibid. 14.

[25] Fleming, J., *The Law of Torts* (LBC Information Services: Sydney 9th edn. 1998) 'modern law has come to attach crucial significance to the use of unlawful means ... yet in the complex factual context especially of industrial relations, this can produce capricious results in which the distinction between permissible and impermissible tactics comes to turn on fictitious and ... even irrelevant factors' (p. 761).

[26] Buckley, R. A., *Salmond and Heuston on the Law of Torts*, 21st edn (London: Sweet & Maxwell, 1996).

[27] Finnis, J, 'Intention in Tort Law', in *Philosophical Foundations of Tort Law*, ed. Owen, D. G. (Oxford: Clarendon Press, 1995), p. 241.

justification may be appropriate where the physical torts are involved.[28] However, in an economic order committed to competition[29] such a 'moral message'[30] appears inappropriate where liability for pure economic loss is concerned. Though 'social life must not be a jungle . . . economic life is bound to be a race'.[31] Competition is based on profiting from a competitor's loss; commercial/economic behaviour is often most successful when deliberately harming another. Thus it is hardly surprising that the extension of economic tort liability in America has given rise to wide academic debate and criticism there.[32] Perlman is highly critical of the definition of liability for intentional interference with contractual relations[33] in the Restatement (Second) of Torts, where 'improper' motive is important. The list of seven factors to assess the propriety or otherwise of the interference—including the interest advanced by the defendant and society's interest[34]—is 'hardly limiting or edifying'.[35]

The common law is better seen as a safety net to catch clear excessive economic behaviour. This policy demands that limits to liability should be provided either by a requirement of unlawful means or (in the tort of

[28] For Cane, above, n. 20, p. 194, 'this is an argument of some substance' but he adds a proviso: rather than distinguish between personal injury and physical damage to property on the one hand and pure economic loss on the other ' the relevant distinction is between economic interests and non-economic interests: there is no good reason why tangible property should receive better protection than other economic interests in cases where the owner's interest in it is purely economic'.

[29] And a common law historically committed to competition: Wyman, B., 'Competition and the Law' 15 Har L Rev (1902) 427.

[30] Bagshaw, R., 'Can the Economic Torts be Unified?' 18 OJLS (1998) 729, p. 731.

[31] Weir,T., 'The Economic Torts: Chaos or Cosmos' [1964] CLJ 225 'matters less grave' (p. 226). Weir, T., *Economic Torts* (Oxford: Clarendon Press, 1997): 'The fact that the economic torts are restricted in this way illustrates the lower priority which the law of tort accords to the protection of pure economic or financial interests as opposed to the protection of physical integrity and of property rights.'

[32] See 'Cause for Concern in Competitive Torts' 77 Har LR (1964) 888, p. 968 (anonymous); Perlman, H., 'Interference with Contract and Other Economic Expectancies: A Clash of Tort and Contract Doctrine' 49 Univ Ch LR (1982) 298.

[33] Perlman, above, n. 32, p. 61. He in fact also rejects the orthodox tort of inducing breach of contract, arguing that liability should be based on the use of unlawful means alone.

[34] Liability is defined in s.766; the factors to be considered are contained in s.767. Thus the court must assess 'the social interests in protecting the freedom of action of the actor and the contractual interests of the other' (the commentary notes the 'appraisal of the private interests of the persons involved may lead to a stalemate unless the appraisal is enlightened by a consideration of the social utility of these interests'). The list also includes: the nature of the actor's conduct, the actor's motive, the interests of the other with whom the actor's conduct interferes, the proximity or remoteness of the actor's conduct to the interference, and the relations between the parties.

[35] Perlman, above, n. 32, p. 298, 'it is startling that doctrine of this type is superimposed on an economic order committed to competition'. He notes the 'repeated call for a scaled-back reformulation of the tort'. And see the negative comments by Danforth, J., 'Tortious Interference with Contract: A Reassertion of Society's Interest in Commercial Stability and Contractual Integrity' 81 Columbia Law Review (1981) 1491: 'more than one commentator has expressed alarm at the progressive expansion of this form of tort liability.'

passing off) by the fence posts of goodwill and misrepresentation. The requirement of 'unlawful means' may involve an unlawful act of the defendant himself, as in unlawful interference with trade ('primary' unlawfulness) or the unlawful act of a third party, with the defendant participating in that unlawfulness, as in inducing breach of contract ('secondary' unlawfulness). Protection will be afforded to a claimant where the economic harm done to him is clearly 'wrong' on this basis. Formalism is therefore preferred to a specific investigation of the substantive merits of each party's position.[36] Beyond this, the role of fostering a healthy competitive order—whether that be by the regulation of monopolies, anti-competitive agreements, or policing trade descriptions—is essentially a matter for state regulation, in the interests of the public at large, not particular traders.[37]

The standard judicial response in England to the scope and application of the economic torts has been in line with this view. The judges have eschewed the job of 'business management'[38] and rejected a significant role as regulators in the competitive/economic process.[39] This was clear in decisions taken at the end of the nineteenth century which gave shape to the main economic torts.[40] As Fry LJ remarked in *Mogul Steamship v McGregor* (at Court of Appeal level): 'to draw a line between fair and

---

[36] Cane, above, n. 20, p. 194, notes that if the courts have discretion to decide what constitutes unlawful means 'some of the force of this argument is removed'. The thesis of this book, of course, is that there is no such discretion: unlawfulness is determined by the existing common law and must amount to a tort or breach of contract.

[37] For Cane, above, n. 20, p. 194, 'the obvious weakness of this objection is that taken to its logical conclusion there would be no common law tort liability for passing off, breach of confidence . . . to the extent that these heads of liability can be used effectively to protect intellectual property rights in ways in which the relevant legislation does not protect them'. The courts on the whole are, however, wary of transforming the tort of passing off into a misappropriation tort. With passing off, goodwill—which requires not just effort but success (at least in establishing a customer connection)—is protected only against excessive competition that involves certain misrepresentations damaging customer connection. With breach of confidence it is clear that the courts could take a more adventurous role but as yet they have not. Of course, where anti-trust allegations are involved, the Competition Act 1998 will call into question the role of the courts: see Ch. 2.

[38] Chafee, Z., 'Unfair Competition' 53 Harvard LR (1940) 1289, p. 1301. Although the notion of unfair competition is wider in the USA than here, it is interesting that on the whole American courts tend to follow the lines of the tort of passing off: see Carter, S., 'Trade Mark Trouble' 99 Yale LJ (1990) 759, p. 764.

[39] We may be out of line with our European partners in not having an action for unfair competition whether through judge-made law as in France (based on CC Arts. 1382 and 1383, inflicting damage through fault) or by statute, as in Germany. In both of these countries, the focus is on the concept of dishonest commercial practice, reflecting the thrust of Art. 10 *bis* of the Paris Convention on Industrial Property. But as Adams, J., 'Unfair Competition: Why a Need is Unmet' 14 8 EIPR (1992) 259 points out (p. 260) we are also out of line in having an adversarial procedure which requires clearly defined torts and strict rules of evidence.

[40] See discussion of these cases in Ch. 1. The courts were also, of course, wary of the role of juries in this area: hence in particular the dislike in *Allen v Flood* of the concept of 'malice'.

unfair competition . . . passes the power of the courts.'[41] *Allen v Flood*
'demonstrated this understandable reluctance to become involved in
adjudication on the merits of the form or purposes of economic pressure',
in the absence of unlawfulness.[42] And this reluctance and the concern for
the competitive process was still apparent in the twentieth century. In
1981 Lord Scarman delivered the judgment of the Privy Council in
Cadbury Schweppes Pty v Pub Squash Co. Pty Ltd[43] and rejected a wider role
for passing off as a misappropriation tort, commenting: 'competition
must remain free' (a principle re-emphasized more recently by Jacob J in
Hodgkinson and Corby Ltd v Wards Mobility Services Ltd).[44] Indeed, though
Lord Diplock in the *Advocaat* decision widened the scope of the tort of
passing off, he noted in his speech that the common law should be wary
of running the risk of hampering competition: 'in an economic system
which has relied on competition to keep down prices and to improve
products.'[45] As for the torts of inducing breach and unlawful interference
with trade, Peter Gibson LJ stressed in *Millar v Bassey*[46] that 'it would not
be right for the law to discourage competition by encouraging actions by
unsuccessful competitors or to allow tort actions by those who suffer only
incidentally from another person's activities'.

Thus the courts have been unwilling to create liability based on what
some would see as simply 'hard-nosed competitive business behaviour'.[47]
The tort of passing off aside, where economic interests are harmed by a
deliberate act, the added ingredient to establish liability is either primary
or secondary unlawfulness. The exception to this approach—and a major
cause of the uncertainties in this area—has arisen in pockets of judicial
hostility to the growth and power of the trade unions,[48] though *Allen v
Flood* itself was 'plainly influenced by a desire to reduce judicial intervention in labour disputes'[49] as well as in the marketplace. Though the tort of

---

[41] (1898) 28 QBD 598, pp. 625–6.

[42] Fleming, above, n. 25, p. 751 'no general theory of intentional tort has emerged. The
principal reason for this failure is that it would have to be balanced by a calculus of justifications, which judges in the British tradition would have rather left to the legislative role.'

[43] [1981] RPC 429, PC.

[44] [1995] FSR 169. Thus though Cane, above, n. 20, p. 195, is right to point out that the tort
of passing off is related to the concept of unfair competition, the notion of protecting trade
values as such has not been accepted by the courts.

[45] [1979] AC 731. Though it is true that worrying alternative views are sometimes raised
as *dicta* in case law. So Hoffmann J in *Associated Newspapers plc v Insert Media Ltd* [1988] 1
WLR 509, commented (p. 514) 'new forms of tort may emerge'.

[46] [1994] EMLR 44, CA.

[47] Whish, R., *Competition Law*, 3rd edn. (London: Butterworths, 1993), p. 59.

[48] So while malice was rejected as a basis of liability in *Allen v Flood*, it was used to outlaw
union activities in *Quinn v Leathem*: see discussion in Ch. 1.

[49] Fleming, above, n. 25, p. 766.

passing off has developed differently, it too has a limited application, so that the public interest in imposing liability is clearly involved.

Overlapping doctrines distinguished

The structure of the economic torts can only be made coherent if similar doctrines—often overlapping doctrines—are identified and separated from the torts themselves. This process ensures that such doctrines are not allowed to impinge upon the definition and development of the economic torts.

This is particularly important in relation to the protection of contract rights. Separate from any tort liability, equity has been prepared to step in to extend the protection of contract rights against inconsistent acts by third parties.[50] The principle in *De Mattos v Gibson*[51] enables the court to grant an injunction, upholding a restrictive stipulation in a contract as to the use of a chattel against a subsequent acquirer[52] (with notice). Though Browne-Wilkinson J contended[53] that this principle is the 'equitable counterpart' of the economic tort protecting against interference with contract rights, it predates that tort and is not based on inducement but on knowledge.[54] This principle appears to have been associated with the parallel principle in land law, the doctrine relating to restrictive covenants in land law.[55] Another obscure principle of equity—the *Springhead Spinning*[56] principle—appears to entitle the court to award an injunction to protect 'property' against criminal acts. Property has been ascribed a very wide meaning in some cases, including the 'economic advantages of an exclusive contract'[57] and even 'business interests'.[58] This principle needs to be kept separate to avoid an overwide definition of 'unlawful means' in the tort of unlawful interference with trade. Similar caution needs to be

---

[50] Bagshaw, R., 'Inducing Breach of Contract' in Horder, J. (ed.), *Oxford Essays in Jurisprudence*, 4th series (Oxford: OUP, 2000), p. 144 'the difficulty is to coordinate the tort with rules that exist to facilitate secure dealings with property'.

[51] (1858) 4 De G&J 276; cited with approval by the Privy Council in *Strathcona SS Co v Dominion Coal Co* [1926] AC 108.

[52] By contract or gift according to Knight Bruce LJ (1858) 4 De G & J 276.

[53] In *Swiss Bank Corpn v Lloyds Bank Ltd* [1979] Ch 548; the case was reversed in the House of Lords on other grounds, [1982] AC 584.

[54] See Ch. 3 for fuller discussion.

[55] See Gardner, S., 'The Proprietary Effect of Contractual Obligations under *Tulk v Moxhay* and *De Mattos v Gibson*' 98 LQR (1982) 279, p. 279. Thus the principle is associated with that in *Tulk v Moxhay* (1848) 2 Ph 774, though that subsequently acquired special requirements of negativity and appurtenance (which usually involved benefiting adjacent land). For Gardner (p. 323), 'the general doctrine articulated by Knight Bruce LJ remains essentially sustainable, not being undermined by the special rules under *Tulk v Moxhay*'.

[56] *Springhead Spinning Co v Riley* (1868) LR Eq 551, see discussion in Ch. 5.

[57] Waller LJ in *Ex parte Island Records* [1978] 1 Ch 122, p. 144.

[58] In the *Springhead Spinning* case itself.

applied to the doctrine of economic duress—a means of vitiating consent in the law of contract where the courts may be able to intervene even in the absence of unlawful pressure. This must be distinguished clearly from the tort of intimidation and not equated with 'unlawful means' in the general tort, otherwise the doctrine becomes a tort by the backdoor.[59]

Another separate category of legal principle that bears a superficial likeness to the economic torts concerns abuse of a public office/misfeasance in a public office. Tort liability may attach to such behaviour and to inducing such behaviour and the claimant may well be concerned with economic loss (lack of a licence, etc.).[60] But the real interest being protected is the public interest in fair administration. It is better seen as a different principle, the development of which has no influence on the development of the economic torts. It extends beyond targeted harm because it focuses on a deliberate and dishonest abuse of power.[61] Also, case law on the refusal of a tradesman—such as a carrier or innkeeper— to exercise a common calling—inducing which may lead to liability[62]— should probably also be kept apart from the economic torts.[63] Such liability results from the notion of public duty.

The following framework, therefore, is based on the need for a clear and consistent divide between acceptable and unacceptable competitive/economic behaviour which does not undermine the logic of *Allen v Flood* and tort law generally.[64] It ascribes a limited role to the judiciary, with the state providing any more complex regulation deemed necessary. The framework is also consistent with the rationales of the torts, identified earlier.

---

[59] See Chs. 4 and 5.

[60] Hirst LJ in *Three Rivers District Council v Bank of England (no 3)* [2000] 2 WLR 15, p. 66, notes that though originally a tort virtually confined to disputes over voting rights, the tort came to life in the second half of the twentieth century in connection with official powers especially in areas of official regulation of private economic activity through systems of licensing and other controls. On appeal, Lord Steyn stressed the important part played by motive in this tort ([2000] 2 WLR 1220, p. 1230).

[61] 'The essence of the tort is the abuse of public office', Steyn LJ, *Elguzouli-Daf v Commissioner of Police of the Metropolis* [1995] QB 335, p. 347; *Three Rivers District Council v Bank of England (no 3)* [2000] 2 WLR 15 (in his dissenting judgment, Auld LJ noted that the tort was not to be equated with the torts of conspiracy and deceit). On appeal, [2000] 2 WLR 1220, HL: 'reckless indifference' sufficient for liability.

[62] *James v Commonwealth* 1938 62 CLR 399.

[63] Cf. Fleming, above, n. 25, p. 757. For him this is part of a wider view that the violation of a legal right committed knowingly will give rise to a cause of action. However, there is a need for caution in applying such a principle, see Ch. 3.

[64] Bagshaw, above, n. 30, rightly objects that 'clarity is . . . not in itself a sufficient reason for accepting a particular factor as a determinant of tort liability' (p. 732). However, by placing the economic torts squarely within existing common law liability it is submitted that they do approximate to 'behaviour that is unacceptable between competitors and should give rise to liability in tort'.

A FRAMEWORK FOR THE ECONOMIC TORTS

Though contradictions and uncertainties abound in the judicial (and academic) discussion of these torts, what is certain is that there is no 'genus' tort that provides a base for all the economic torts. Despite the use of that term by Lord Diplock when introducing us to the tort of unlawful interference with trade,[65] no one tort can cover the different rationales of the established economic torts. Weir[66] suggests that there is a single principle of order in these torts, namely that it is 'tortious intentionally to damage another by means of an act which the actor was not at liberty to commit'. Though this principle underlines the philosophy of the courts in this area,[67] it is insufficiently complex to guide the development of these torts.[68] The notion of acts the defendant is 'not at liberty to commit' is too vague[69] and fails to pinpoint the significant differences between liability for inducing breach of contract and liability for unlawful interference with trade. It also, of course, fails to include liability for simple conspiracy and for passing off.

What is revealed in the discussion of the separate torts in this book is that there are a number of different focal points[70] in economic tort liability that need to be identified in order to provide a useful framework and parameters for their development. This analysis also needs to explain why the economic torts spread beyond intentional harm in the single instance of the tort of passing off.

Again, the traditional division of the economic torts into two groups— the general economic torts and the misrepresentation economic torts— does not help to solve the 'mess' of these torts.[71] Such a division, though neat, fails to highlight the differences between torts grouped within the same category and masks the interconnections between torts separated by the two categories.

As we have seen, the tort of inducing breach of contract (in its 'pure',

[65] *Merkur Island Shipping v Laughton* [1983] 2 WLR 778.

[66] 'Chaos or Cosmos?', above, n. 31, p. 226. Weir argues in *Economic Torts*, above, n. 31, that the *Lumley v Gye* tort is as much part of the general principle of liability for economic harm deliberately caused (through the seduction of the plaintiff's contract partner) as where independently unlawful means are used (p. 28): 'I believe that the tort of inducing breach of contract has now been absorbed into the general tort of causing harm by unlawful means.'

[67] And rightly draws attention to the need for wrongs rather than the protection of 'rights'.

[68] Oliphant, K., Book Review on Weir, *Economic Torts*, 62 MLR (1999) 320 notes that it is 'excessively reductive' (p. 322).

[69] See further discussion below and in Ch. 5.

[70] Hence it is not surprising that these torts have 'lacked their Atkin', Wedderburn, K. W., 'Rocking the Torts' 46 MLR (1983) 223, p. 229.

[71] Such a categorization is followed by Heydon, above, n. 23, but he admits this is a 'crude' separation.

Lumley v Gye form) has a different rationale to that of unlawful interference with trade, while the tort of simple conspiracy is based on a different principle to the tort of unlawful conspiracy. Again, the tort of passing off is based on an entirely different approach to liability than the other 'misrepresentation' economic torts. The joy of the tort of passing off for claimants is that it shifts the focus from intentional harm to the misrepresentation itself. Provided the misrepresentation is likely to affect informed consumer choice as to source or product type, there is no need to prove fault. In this respect, it is revealed to be a tort, unique within the economic torts generally.

As for interconnections, given the wide remit of the tort of unlawful interference with trade, it is also clear that there will be links between it and the misrepresentation economic torts based on intentional harm. The classic form of the tort of deceit , being two-party, means that it is not an important economic tort (on a par with negligence) but in a three-party setting deceit may provide the necessary unlawful means for the tort of unlawful interference, while most instances of malicious falsehood amount to the general tort also.

Thus the divide into general and misrepresentation economic torts does not aid the process of rationalization.[72]

A more complex framework is revealed by the survey of the economic torts undertaken in this book. It is suggested that there are four categories of economic tort, based on different liability justifications. In the first three categories, intended harm to the claimant is necessary—that is the bond or nexus[73] between the claimant and defendant (and a nexus that needs to be established, given most commonly these torts are three-party torts). However, with these intentional torts there is a 'nexus-plus' requirement—that is the legacy of *Allen v Flood*. The nature of the 'plus' varies between the torts and it is this factor which demands separate categorization, as revealed below. With the fourth category—liability for passing off—its background in trade mark protection, the influence of equity and

---

[72] Heydon appears to favour the division between general and misrepresentation economic torts as he contends it reveals the two different types of harm that the torts protect against. Thus he argues that in the 'general' economic torts the claimant is principally complaining that the defendant has deliberately caused him loss, while in the 'misrepresentation' economic torts the essence of the complaint is that the defendant has made a gain which 'properly' belongs to the claimant. However, such a description does not reveal a framework for liability: misrepresentation cases can be just as much about attack as theft e.g. *Joyce v Motor Surveys Ltd* [1948] Ch 252; general economic torts can be just as much about commercial competition as can e.g. passing off e.g. *Lumley v Gye*.

[73] Sales P., and Stilitz, D., 'Intentional Infliction of Harm by Unlawful Means' 115 LQR (1999) 411, p. 412 stress that it should be clear why the claimant has established a sufficient nexus between the loss he has suffered and the unlawful conduct of the defendant, despite the remoteness of the defendant's conduct from the plaintiff's loss: 'it is [the defendant's] intention to cause harm to [the claimant] that establishes this nexus.'

recent emphasis on the protection of the consumer have led to a different approach. However, in all categories, caution is the key consideration.

Category A. The secondary liability economic torts: nexus plus participation

Here liability is based on inducing a third party to commit an actionable wrong[74] or conspiring with him to commit an actionable wrong. There is a primary civil wrong—tort, breach of contract, breach of statutory duty—which in itself is actionable in damages by the claimant.[75] As Erle J asserted in *Lumley v Gye*[76] 'he who maliciously procures the damage to another . . . ought to be made to indemnify and that whether he procures an actionable wrong or a breach of contract'. In order to trap the defendant within the circle of liability he must have induced that wrong or been part of a conspiracy to commit that wrong. The role of these torts, as forms of secondary liability,[77] is to extend the circle of liability, to include further potential defendants for the claimant to sue.[78]

Within this category come the torts of inducing breach of contract,[79] inducing breach of statutory duty and unlawful conspiracy.

With inducing breach of statutory duty and unlawful conspiracy the wrong induced or the subject of the conspiracy will be a tort in its own right.[80] Whether the defendant or the third party realize that a tort is involved is, of course, irrelevant. Rather they must be aware of the circumstances that in fact render the act tortious. With inducing breach of contract, however, the defendant must know of the contract in sufficient detail and intend its breach (just as the claimant's contracting partner must so intend).

---

[74] In *Allen v Flood* Lord Watson remarked 'there are . . . two grounds upon which a person who procures the act of another can be made legally responsible for its consequences. In the first place, he will incur liability if he knowingly and for his own ends induces that other person to commit an actionable wrong. In the second place . . . the inducer may be liable if he can be shown to have procured his object by the use of illegal means directed against [the claimant].' The first ground is category A liability; the second ground describes category B liability (discussed below).

[75] Which term is used to distinguish these wrongs from 'equitable' wrongs.

[76] (1853) 2 E&B 216, p. 233.

[77] See the impressive article by Sales, P., 'The Tort of Conspiracy and Civil Secondary Liability', 49 CLJ (1990) 491. In *Credit Lyonnais v ECGD* [1999] 2 WLR 540, Lord Woolf commented on *Lumley v Gye* liability that 'the responsibility for the actionable wrong is a form of secondary liability'.

[78] Cooper, D., 'Secondary Liability for Civil Wrongs', unpublished Ph.D thesis (Cambridge, 1995) contends that part of the reason why the economic torts are in a mess is because the courts have failed to recognize the secondary nature of much of the liability in issue.

[79] Sales and Stilitz, above, n. 73, p. 433: 'this is an example of civil secondary liability.'

[80] Though it may be that there is liability for conspiracy to breach contract: see later.

These torts follow the same pattern for imposing secondary liability as the doctrine of joint tortfeasance.[81] This doctrine holds parties liable for the same harm where they are linked to the primary tort complained of by the claimant.[82] Though liability under the doctrine of joint tortfeasance can arise from a relevant 'relationship' link[83]—most importantly that of employer and employee—it can also arise from a relevant 'participation' link between the defendants—a link based on fault. The extent of this participation must be significant enough to justify the imposition of responsibility and the courts have been rightly cautious about defining such links. Case law reveals that to be jointly liable, the defendant must have a causal link based on procuring or authorizing the primary tort or a complicity link, based on membership of a combination to commit the tort. Once these participation links are revealed, it becomes obvious that the torts of inducing breach and unlawful conspiracy are modelled on the same participation links. Indeed, inducing a breach of statutory duty or conspiring to commit a tort will give rise to liability as torts in their own right *and* under the doctrine of joint tortfeasance.

Again, the tort of inducing breach of contract follows the same pattern as the doctrine of joint tortfeasance, focusing as it does on the procuring/inducing of the civil wrong.[84] Seen as a form of secondary liability, it becomes clear that liability in *Lumley v Gye* is not based simply on intentional interference with legal rights:[85] the notion of procurement is an important limiting factor.[86] Procuring is different to causing:[87] corruption

---

[81] For a more detailed discussion of this area see Carty, H., 'Joint tortfeasance and assistance liability' 19 LS (1999) 489.

[82] Cf. several concurrent tortfeasors (to use the terminology suggested by Williams, G., *Joint Torts and Contributory Negligence* (London: Stevens, 1951). Here separate, independent torts combine to produce the damage complained of by the claimant. For Williams, 'several concurrent tortfeasors are independent tortfeasors whose acts concur to produce a single damage. The *damnum* is single, but each commits a single *injuria*' (p. 16).

[83] There is also a need to prove the relevant setting for the tort e.g. 'course of employment'.

[84] In *CBS Songs Ltd v Amstrad* [1988] AC 1013 Lord Templeman asserted that the opera singer and the defendant were 'joint wrongdoers participating in an unlawful common design' (p. 1058). Joint liability in tort can also arise from 'authorisation'—a concept which is clearly related to procurement, though it focuses on permission or command rather than persuasion.

[85] Sir Leonard Hoffmann in Birks, P. (ed.), *The Frontiers of Liability* (Oxford: Oxford University Press, 1994) commented 'the general principle on which *Lumley v Gye* is based is that intentional interference with legal rights is actionable' (p. 28). However, this appears to be substituting the true principle in *Lumley v Gye* for the overwide reformulation of it by Lord Macnaghten in *Quinn v Leathem* [1901] AC 495, p. 510, viz. 'the violation of a legal right committed knowingly is a cause of action'. See for more detailed discussion in Ch. 3.

[86] Lord Woolf in *Credit Lyonnais v ECGD* [1999] 2 WLR 540. 'The statement of Erle J is capable of being treated as saying no more than if you procure the commission of an actionable wrong by another then you are liable for that actionable wrong. The responsibility for the actionable wrong is a form of secondary liability.'

[87] Though it is obvious as Bagshaw comments that 'the distinction between procuring

rather than mere prevention is necessary.[88] *Lumley v Gye* finds the defendant liable because he procured the breach of the contract (for whatever motive). As the doctrine of joint tortfeasance, as such, cannot make the procurer jointly liable for the breach of contract, the common law instead makes him liable for the derivative tort of inducement. By accepting the secondary nature of this tort and its parallels to the doctrine of joint tortfeasance, it is clear that mere assistance and inconsistent transactions are not part of the tort.[89]

Category A therefore, imposes liability for the participation by the defendant in another's tort or breach of contract,[90] where intentional harm to the particular claimant on the part of the defendant can be proved. The unlawful act is someone else's unlawful act to which the defendant is tightly bound by his complicity or which has been prompted (to whatever degree) by the defendant. It is clear that the need to show procurement in particular avoids the 'slippery slope' whereby seduction into contract breach is watered down into liability for knowingly disappointing expectations of economic gain.[91] To prevent performance and cause a breach is not within category A liability (though it may be within category B liability, if the defendant has used wrongful means to achieve that breach). Nor is mere assistance sufficient (just as it is not sufficient in the doctrine of joint tortfeasance). Active participation in the wrong, on a par with the doctrine of joint tortfeasance, renders the defendant's economic activity 'excessive'.

and preventing will raise difficult boundary disputes' (above, n. 30, p. 734). A lawful threat issued in order to procure the breach would also render the defendant liable—as an ultimate form of procurement (answering Bagshaw's question, posed at p. 734).

[88] See Weir, above, n. 31, pp. 27–43. Cf. Bagshaw, above, n. 50, who by claiming that the tort of inducing breach protects against both interference with the contractor's willingness to perform *and* his capacity to perform would see this tort as based on a wider principle: procuring or preventing performance by positive acts.

[89] For a more detailed discussion see Carty, H., 'Joint tortfeasance and assistance liability' 19 LS (1999) 489; cf. Bagshaw, above, n. 50, who believes inconsistent dealings should come within the tort otherwise 'difficult questions about implied inducements would arise' as 'there is a thin line between an inducer communicating that he or she is willing to deal if the party becomes free of prior engagements and encouraging the breaking of such engagements' (p. 144).

[90] As far as category A liability is concerned therefore, procuring a breach of trust is not a tort. See *Metall v DLJ* [1990] 1 QB 391 where Slade LJ stressed that he could see no sufficient justification for a new tort of procuring a breach of trust as liability for such behaviour already existed in equity (though *Prudential v Lorenz* (1971) 11 KLR 78 was not cited). Should the courts be tempted to extend the notion of unlawful means to cover all civil wrongs, this should be part of a wider debate about the dividing lines in the law of obligations. The rigid distinction between tortious and equitable liability is under fire from commentators such as Cane, above, n. 20, p. 75, n. 310 who comments that '[the] distinction between tortious and equitable liability makes no sense except in historical terms'.

[91] Weir's concern over this 'slippery slope' was noted by Bagshaw, above, n. 30, p 735. So dicta in *Thomas v Pearce* [2000] FSR 718 that appear to equate liability for assistance in a breach of trust, confidence or contract should be read with caution.

Category B. Unlawful act economic torts: nexus plus unlawful means

Here the use by the defendant himself of unlawful means[92] to intention-ally harm the claimant justifies the imposition of liability. Unlike secondary liability economic torts, this category of liability creates primary liability. These torts constitute 'free-standing, independent species of primary liability, founded on the central concept of the inten-tional infliction of harm upon another by unlawful means'. The claimant has a cause of action, parasitic on the unlawful means used by the defend-ant against another party.[93] However, the necessary nexus between the defendant and claimant must be proved and that nexus is intended harm. To comply with the need for clarity and certainty it is necessary that wrongs, capable of being actionable as torts or breaches of contract, should be involved.[94] The 'magic' of category B economic torts is simply to expand liability that is already acknowledged. This category does not allow the creation of liability out of allegations of 'impropriety' nor does it enable claimants to 'tortify' pure crimes, breaches of statutory provi-sions and breaches of fiduciary duties or equitable obligations.[95]

This rationalization of liability is embodied in the tort of unlawful interference with trade, involving as it does intentional harm, unlawful means, and actual harm to trade/economic interests. However, once the focus of this category is identified, it is also clear that this general tort includes liability for direct[96] and indirect interference with contract rights and performance. The chaos of the economic torts is in part due to the fail-ure to separate category A from category B liability. Direct and indirect interference are not in fact part of the tort of inducing breach: they do not

---

[92] *Allen v Flood*, having rejected the 'right to trade' argument, the focus inevitably shifted to the defendant's unlawful acts.

[93] Sales and Stilitz, above, n. 73, p. 412. Bagshaw, above, n. 30, p. 730: 'the general economic tort provides an additional scope of tort protection for plaintiffs because it is para-sitic on means that are defined as unlawful otherwise than because they amount to torts to the plaintiff.'

[94] See more detailed discussion in Ch. 5.

[95] In *Economic Torts*, above, n. 31, Weir does not debate the concept of unlawful means: 'I leave aside the complaint that it is difficult to know what is illegal and what is not, for while that may not be easy it is certainly easier than saying what is immoral or improper and what is not' (p. 74).

[96] Cf. Heydon, above, n. 22, and Bagshaw, above, n. 50, p. 146. Bagshaw argues that directly preventing performance should receive the same level of protection as inducing breach, given he asserts that the protectable interest involves both an interest in the willing-ness *and* the capacity to perform on the part of the claimant's contractual partner (see more detailed discussion in Ch. 3). Sales and Stilitz, above, n. 73, p. 433 believe that direct inter-ference with contract may lie between categories A and B. However, they appear to favour it being placed in category B in order to avoid 'excessively wide liability', which would be difficult to reconcile with *Allen v Flood*.

rely on contract rights being breached; rather they focus liability on the use of unlawful means. Weir argues that by locating these other varieties within the tort of inducing breach, subsequent courts have at times focused on protecting the plaintiff's contract, rather than on the wrong-doing of the defendant. In particular there has been a tendency to extend the tort of inducing breach so as to embrace prevention of performance, creating the half-way tort of unlawful interference with contract performance.[97] This tort should be rejected as only adding to the obscurity of this area of tort.

The tort of intimidation also falls within this category, given the threat must be of unlawful action. However, it is important to note that the tort of intimidation adds an important gloss to liability to this category: it extends liability from unlawful acts to unlawful threats.[98] It equates threatened unlawful acts to the unlawful acts themselves.[99]

And finally, this category also includes the tort of three-party deceit.[100] The classic tort of deceit creates liability out of a lie on which the defendant intends the claimant to rely. However, *National Phonograph v Edison-Bell* and *Lonrho v Fayed*[101] indicate that there is a three-party version of the tort, where the third party was intended to rely on the lie and there was the necessary nexus between the defendant's lies and the claimant. That nexus is intended harm. Oliver LJ noted in *RCA v Pollard* that in *National Phonograph* the fraudulent conduct had been 'aimed specifically at the plaintiffs'.[102] The claimant must be the target of the lie: his trading interests are in particular being attacked.[103] Though both varieties of the tort

---

[97] This development was prompted by Lord Denning in *Torquay Hotel v Cousins* [1969] 1 All ER 522, and was arguably supported by Lord Diplock in *Merkur Island Shipping Corp v Laughton* [1983] 2 WLR 778, with the fruit of this 'wretched development' being *Millar v Bassey* [1994] EMLR 44, a striking out action but rightly noted by Weir as having alarming implications (see below).

[98] In the pre-*Rookes* cases, of course, the unlawful threat was in fact unlawful acts in their own right. It was *Rookes* that accepted the threats in themselves could create liability—and threats of breach of contract at that.

[99] For Sales and Stilitz, above, n. 73, p. 417 the tort of intimidation underlines the liberal concept of unlawful means that they advocate for the tort (p. 417) as 'the very fact that [the third party] accedes to the threat in order to avoid suffering loss entails that no cause of action will exist between [the defendant and the third party]'. However, given the threat has to be of an actionable civil wrong this is merely adding a new dimension to the concept of an actionable legal wrong rather than undermining that requirement.

[100] Weir, 'Chaos or Cosmos', above, n. 31, p. 228 'malicious falsehood and intimidation are the same tort of intentionally hurting another by impermissible means. We do not need two names and especially not those two names. A threat has nothing a lie does not have.'

[101] For Cane, above, n. 20, p. 152, unlawful interference with trade includes the torts of deceit and malicious falsehood.

[102] [1983] Ch 135, p. 151.

[103] Dillon LJ in *Lonrho v Fayed* could see no valid reason why the tort should need to have been complete 'to the extent that the third party had himself suffered damage' [1990] 2 QB 479, p. 481.

of deceit are based on fraudulent misrepresentation,[104] the two-party version depends on lying at your peril (having intended to cause reliance on the part of the claimant); the three-party version focuses on intended harm, the lie being the necessary limiting unlawful means. Three-party deceit is part of liability for unlawful interference with the claimant's economic interests. Category B as a result includes lies intended to cause harm[105] and acts intended to cause harm.[106]

Category B, therefore, involves primary liability, within the logic of existing common law liability. There is a need for an identifiable unlawful act (either in tort or contract) and intended harm between the defendant and the claimant. It is liability based not on participation but on causation. Though Beldam LJ in *Millar v Bassey* commented that he failed to see the distinction between causing and procuring, the difference is at the heart of understanding these torts.[107] To procure a breach is the tort of inducing breach; to cause a breach (or any other interference) is the tort of unlawful interference, but only if unlawful means are used.

Category C. Simple conspiracy liability: nexus plus malice

This economic tort demands its own category. It requires neither unlawful acts nor an attack on the rights of the claimant by participation in another's wrong. Rather, there must be concerted action in furtherance of an agreement, causing intended harm to the claimant. Due to the reluctance to become involved in the competitive process[108] and (eventually) in the management of industrial relations[109] a wide concept of justification applies.[110]

In effect this is a tort of malice and of limited application.[111] It is an

---

[104] So if there had been deliberate deceit by the solicitor in *Ross v Caunters* [1980] Ch 297 surely the beneficiaries could have sued in deceit?

[105] As for malicious falsehood, see below.

[106] Liability thus is not for lies *per se*. It would appear from the decision in *National Phonograph Co v Edison-Bell* [1908] 1 Ch 335 that the potential for an expansion in liability based on deceit has been dormant in the common law for a number of years.

[107] See Weir, *Economic Torts*, above, n. 31.

[108] *Mogul Steamship Co Ltd v McGregor, Gow & Co* [1892] AC 25.

[109] *Crofter Hand Woven Harris Tweed Co Ltd v Veitch* [1942] AC 435.

[110] Fleming, above, n. 25, p. 772 'the action fell into steep disfavour in revulsion against the ugly manner in which the conspiracy doctrine was once wielded by civil and criminal courts alike to stem the tide of organized labour'.

[111] Epstein, R., 'A Common Law for Labor Relations: A Critique of the New Deal Labor Legislation' 92 Yale LJ (1983) 1357, p. 1369: 'malice in its pure form means more than an intention to inflict some temporal injury . . . instead it refers to actions done out of spite or ill-will . . . any prohibition against malicious conduct, therefore, at most reaches only the fringes of individual and union behaviour.'

aberration, at odds with the common law policy of abstentionism where economic interests are concerned. As such, it provides no clues as to the 'proper' development of the other economic torts. Born out of the courts' desire to curb 'abusive' economic power,[112] it will be overshadowed by the civil liability for abuse of a dominant position and cartels, contained in the Competition Act 1998.[113] Liability for simple conspiracy will continue to be anomalous, focusing not on the public interest but on self-interest.

Category D. Passing off liability: misrepresentations damaging goodwill

Though clearly an economic tort protecting pure economic interests, the tort of passing off, unlike the other economic torts, is not based on fault.[114] It protects 'goodwill', a property right based on the success of the claimant trader, against consumer misinformation as to the source or quality of the defendant's goods or trade. As advertising and commercial activity generally has become more sophisticated, so the potential for such misinformation has expanded. This is reflected in the growth of the tort, encompassing connection and product misinformation as well as the more traditional source misinformation.

Cane[115] questions why exploiting another's goodwill, as opposed to damaging it should be actionable without proof of fault.[116] The answer to that lies in the history and focus of the tort of passing off.

The torts of three-party deceit and malicious falsehood also involve misrepresentations, but they focus on unlawful acts—lies,[117] either about the defendant or about the claimant.[118] However, though the tort of passing off was initially based on the tort of deceit, equity eventually re-focused its protection on the misrepresentation itself. Rather than simply

---

[112] Though at the time it was the growing power of the trade unions that was the stimulus to that development. As criminal conspiracy was withdrawn from peaceful industrial pressure, so the common law developed a parallel control in tort. Of course the tort of malicious falsehood also involves liability based on 'malice' but its basis is not abusive economic power but rather 'perilous falsehoods': see later in this chapter.

[113] See discussion in Ch. 2.

[114] Though obviously lies might be involved—indeed this tort developed from deceit.

[115] Above, n. 20, p. 99, reflecting Heydon's comment, above, n. 23, p. 17 'it is odd that there is such a difference between lying about the goods of others and lying about one's own; between the destruction of reputation and its theft'.

[116] And it might be asked why goodwill should be better protected than contract rights.

[117] Malicious falsehood does in fact cover more than lies: see later in text.

[118] They can been seen as part of the tort of unlawful interference with trade but with the *caveat* that the tort of malicious falsehood can apply beyond the area covered by unlawful interference. See later in text.

see the misrepresentation as an unlawful act and develop liability on that basis, the misrepresentation is central to liability *because it is a misrepresentation*. So even innocent misrepresentations are sufficient. But it is not all misrepresentations that give rise to liability, even though inevitable harm to the claimant may be involved. Misrepresentations about the defendant's trade will not as such amount to passing off. The nature of the misrepresentations relevant to the tort of passing off mirrors the traditional protection afforded to trade marks and their equivalent. The claimant is protected, therefore, only against source/quality consumer misinformation about the defendant's trade that is likely directly to harm the claimant's goodwill.[119]

However, though clearly wider than the other economic torts (and hence the subject of most pressure for expansion) it is still a tort that has been shaped by caution. Adherence to the classic trinity (with customer reliance as its cement) means that the tort is capable of providing protection within a clear framework, without undue market restraint. By basing the tort on the classic trinity the common law has avoided being involved in disputes about competitive practice *per se*. So allegations of 'reaping what you have not sown',[120] 'product misdescription *per se*',[121] and 'product simulation'[122] have been denied redress. This caution mirrors the caution of the economic torts generally and for the same reason—the courts do not see their role as market regulators. The tort only protects a particular form of economic interest, against a particular form of harm, due to a particular type of misinformation by the defendant about his own trade. It is a tort of misinformation, not misappropriation *per se*.

THE FRAMEWORK: IMPLICATIONS

1. The economic torts are essentially three-party torts

The above framework underlines the fact that the true importance of the economic torts is their imposition of liability in a three-party scenario. They enable claimants to attack the real cause of their economic harm, even though that has resulted indirectly through an intermediary. As Weir notes, such use of an intermediary is hardly surprising given 'one can bloody one's neighbour's nose unaided but to ruin him usually requires

---

[119] Thus the tort has an identification function (to indicate origin), with a secondary and derivative guarantee function (to indicate quality).

[120] *Cadbury Schweppes v Pub Squash Co* [1981] RPC 429, PC.

[121] *Schulke v Alkapharm* [1999] FSR 1.

[122] *Hodgkinson & Corby Ltd v Wards Mobility Ltd* [1995] FSR 175.

assistance'.[123] The economic torts that are clearly two-party based, classic deceit and negligence, are relationship-based and add little to the understanding of the economic torts as such.[124]

2. Intention and the economic torts

The fact that the economic torts are in essence three-party torts necessitates a strong nexus between the defendant's act and the harm to the claimant (the tort of passing off apart).

Unlawful interference with trade (and its varieties)[125] is almost universally accepted to require a strong version of intention. This involves deliberate harm in the sense that the claimant is targeted or aimed at by the defendant (for whatever reason).[126] It is the claimant's trade/economic interests that are in issue—the fact that he is the inevitable victim of the action is insufficient.[127]

But there is no consensus as to the definition of intended harm in the tort of inducing breach of contract. Rather judges and commentators divide into two camps. There are those who believe intention in this category is the same as that in the category B torts.[128] However, Sales and Stilitz, Bagshaw and Oliphant[129] see the intention required for category A torts as 'based on altogether different underlying principles'.[130] For them the fact of pre-existing rights in the category A torts means that it is inappropriate to demand the stronger intention of category B torts. So Bagshaw asserts 'the required mental state for the tort of procuring breach of contract is a sufficient degree of knowledge of the likelihood that conduct may bring about a breach of contract and a choice to persist with that conduct despite the knowledge'.[131] As we have seen this dilute form

---

[123] And that use of a third party to hurt the claimant can only be successful by 'promising something good if [the third party] does hurt the plaintiff, by promising something bad if he does not and by misleading him', above, n. 31 ('Chaos or Cosmos'), p. 227. Perhaps for the sake of completeness he should add 'or doing something bad'.

[124] Though there are examples where category B torts have been used in a two-party situation, it is preferable in such situations to base liability on the specific unlawful act alleged.

[125] The same means must amount to unlawful acts within the torts covered by category B despite suggestions otherwise (see Lord Devlin in *Rookes v Barnard* [1964] AC 1129, p. 1210 and Henry J in *Barretts and Baird (Wholesale) Ltd v IPCS* [1987] IRLR 3, p. 9).

[126] With deceit the lie (though it may be reckless) must be aimed at the claimant.

[127] The specific economic target must be established in more complex cases (particularly those arising from industrial action).

[128] See in particular, Weir, *Economic Torts*, above, n. 31, and Peter Gibson LJ in *Millar v Bassey* [1994] EMLR 44 and discussion in Ch. 3. And see Lord Wedderburn, *Clerk and Lindsell on Torts*, 18th edn. (London: Sweet & Maxwell, 2000), para. 24–11 'the better view may be . . . that the levels of knowledge and intention required are not in principle different in the torts of procuring breach of contract and unlawful interference'.

[129] Above, n. 68.   [130] Sales and Stilitz, above, n. 73, p. 412.

[131] Bagshaw, above, n. 50, p. 142.

of intention was accepted by the Court of Appeal in *Associated British Ports v TGWU*.[132]

However, once the above framework of liability has been identified it becomes clear that the intention in category A torts must be as strong as that required for category B torts. There are two grounds for this view.

First, inducing breach of contract and unlawful interference with trade are both based on a tight nexus (as is the category C tort, simple conspiracy). Of course, inducing breach focuses on contract rights rather than economic harm *per se*.[133] Bagshaw[134] notes that 'part of the uncertainty over the mental element has flowed from a failure to distinguish between the defendant's state of mind towards the contract, the breach, the claimant and the damage'. But there is no reason to dilute the nexus required for one category, given the rationale for such a tight nexus is the same throughout the intentional economic torts.[135] Hence Peter Gibson LJ in *Millar v Bassey*[136] notes the 'insistence' by Jenkins LJ in *Thomson v Deakin*[137] that the interference had to be 'not only with knowledge of the contract but with a view to bringing about its breach'.

Secondly, inducing breach of contract focuses on participation in the intended breach of another. Category A torts are not concerned with mere causation or interference. The defendant must be shown to have participated in the wrong, to have contributed to that wrong by being part of the decision to breach. For secondary liability to arise consequent on participation in a breach of contract, there must be knowledge of the contract on the part of the defendant and an intended breach by the contract partner. And that *intended* breach must have been *intentionally* induced by the defendant.[138] Knowing interference is not sufficient; rather the defendant must be shown to have deliberately procured an intentional breach. The intended breach may be an end in its own right or (more likely) a means to an end (as in *Lumley v Gye*: the opera singer had to break her contract in order to sing for the defendant). Thus the contract must be deliberately aimed at, rather than consequentially harmed.

---

[132] [1989] 1 WLR 939.

[133] Peter Gibson LJ in *Millar v Bassey* [1994] EMLR 44 'it is necessary that [the tortfeasor's] conduct must have been directed against the plaintiff in the sense that the breach of his contract or the interference with his interests was intended'. So the defendant cannot avoid liability by proving that he did not believe that the breach would cause any consequential harm: *South Wales Miners' Federation v Glamorgan Coal Co* [1905] AC 239, p. 246.

[134] Above, n. 30.

[135] The secondary liability economic tort of unlawful conspiracy involves intended harm, as Cane, above, n. 20, notes (p. 156) intention to harm 'was assumed by the House of Lords to be an element of unlawful means conspiracy, in *Lonrho v Fayed* [1992] 1 AC 448.

[136] [1994] EMLR 44.

[137] [1952] Ch 646.

[138] There was no liability in *BP v Ferguson* (1940) 1 All ER 479 where the defendants did not believe they would cause a breach.

The more dilute version of intention favoured in *Associated British Ports v TGWU* and by the majority in *Millar v Bassey* is the result of a confusion between procurement and mere causation of contract breach. The link between the defendant and the contract breach is itself diluted once the court reshapes the principle in *Lumley v Gye* to allow for liability on the basis of knowing interference with contract relations. Such an error appears to have resulted from the wider formula suggested by Lord Macnaghten in *Quinn v Leathem*.[139] He asserted that *Lumley v Gye* was based on the ground 'that a violation of legal right committed knowingly is a cause of action and that it is a violation of legal right to interfere with contractual relations recognized by law if there be no sufficient justification for the interference'. So in *Associated British Ports v TGWU*,[140] Neill LJ referred to inducing breach as a tort which involves 'the interference with a person's legal rights';[141] Stuart-Smith LJ saw the tort as the commonest example of Lord Macnaghten's general tort of interference with rights.[142] Again, Beldam LJ in *Millar v Bassey*[143] referred to the tort in *Lumley v Gye* as 'the tort of interference by a third party with contractual relations', which may well explain his inability to distinguish between liability for procurement and mere causation. But the tort of inducing breach is a form of secondary liability resulting from participation in an unlawful act—it does not arise from an interference with a right *per se*.

For this reason *Millar v Bassey* is wrong.[144] It is an example of causing breach of the claimant's contracts, not the tort of procuring such breaches. The approach of the majority is perilously close to an acknowledgement that the inevitable consequences of any breach of contract may lead to liability in this tort. In the case itself, the target of the action (in the sense of the intended victim of the defendant's alleged breach of contract) was the defendant's own contractual partner, though the claimants were inevitable consequential victims. Neither procurement nor intended harm were present.

The category A torts require the same strong intention link as do the torts in categories B and C, therefore. In order to deliberately procure an intentional breach, the defendant must target that contract. Intention in the economic torts is different from the 'broad way' in which it is usually treated in tort law:[145] inevitable consequences are not sufficient.

---

[139] [1901] AC 495, p. 510.
[140] [1989] 1 WLR 939.
[141] Ibid. 952. Butler-Sloss LJ classed inducing breach as part of the tort of 'direct invasion of legal rights' (p. 959).
[142] Ibid. 963.
[143] [1994] EMLR 44.
[144] As is *Falconer v ASLEF* [1986] IRLR 331. The target there was British Rail, the employer whose workers were called out on strike, causing inevitable loss to passengers such as the plaintiff. The plaintiff was no more the target of the action than were the abattoir owners in *Barretts & Baird v IPCS* [1987] IRLR 3.
[145] Bagshaw, above, n. 30, p. 731 notes that the Restatement (Second) of Torts s.88A, deter-

3. Unlawful means and breach of confidence

The intentional economic torts require more than intention: they follow a pattern of 'nexus-plus'. With category B torts, it is submitted that the plus factor involves torts or breaches of contract only. Certainty and a framework based on existing common law liability results from categorizing category B torts as parasitic torts.[146] They follow the parameters of liability already accepted.

An issue that urgently needs to be resolved, given this, is whether breach of confidence is a tort.[147] The jurisprudential basis of this action has long been debated (though more by commentators than the courts). As yet the most readily accepted basis for this action is that of an equitable duty of good faith. However, there are indications that the action may be developing into a tort.[148] It is highly unsatisfactory, however (and leads to continued uncertainty in the economic torts), that no clear judicial categorization of the action is forthcoming. It is preferable that if the courts seek to create tort liability they should expressly acknowledge that the action is an action in tort. That done, inducing breach (or conspiring to break faith) would fall within category A economic tort liability while intentionally inflicting harm on the claimant by breach of confidence would amount to category B economic tort liability.

Of course the question would then still remain whether the action for breach of confidence, as a tort, should be classified as an economic tort. Though clearly also encompassing e.g. the protection of privacy and state security, the action plays an important part in the protection of commercially useful information. In this area it does form part of the common law protection against excessive competition. However, it should be developed in line with the caution applied to the other economic torts—to protect information simply on the grounds that it had been 'improperly' divulged or acquired would be out of step with the approach to the economic torts generally.

---

mines that 'the word "intent" is used throughout the Restatement of this subject to denote that the actor desires to cause consequences of his act, or that he believes that the consequences are substantially certain to result from it'.

[146] With deceit the courts are happy to accept that the unlawful act is capable of being actionable.

[147] An action, of course, that also raises issues of unfair competition and is capable of expansion into a wider protection against misappropriation. For Heydon, above, n. 23, p. 1, it is a 'related cause of action'.

[148] See discussion in Ch. 5. The CA in *Douglas v Hello! Ltd*, The Times, 16 Jan 2000, seemed to assume it is a tort.

4. Secondary civil liability

Once the principle of secondary civil liability has been identified in category A torts, two matters arise for resolution.

First, having identified category A torts as mirroring the doctrine of joint tortfeasance, it is important to see whether this category of torts has a separate validity from that doctrine.

Where the primary liability results from a tort, those liable through their 'secondary' involvement become principals in the commission of the tortious act. There is, of course, no need for the parties to be aware that they are committing a tort, provided they are aware of the relevant facts that render the action tortious. However, those jointly liable require the same fault and/or knowledge requirements of the main tort.[149] Tort law is not modified by the doctrine of joint tortfeasance. The courts have refused to create a tort of procuring or authorizing another's tort.[150] This means that the doctrine of joint tortfeasance covers the same area as that covered by the tort of inducing breach of statutory duty (given that breach must in itself be actionable) and that covered by the tort of unlawful conspiracy. In both cases the independent tort is unnecessary.[151] (Of course the doctrine goes wider than these economic torts, given any tort might be sufficient and the state of mind necessary for joint liability will vary according to the state of mind required for the primary tort.)

With inducing breach of contract, however, the doctrine of joint tortfeasance, though providing the pattern of liability, cannot apply. There is a need for a separate tort.

Secondly, it may be asked whether the framework of secondary liability that applies to the economic torts—a framework mirroring the doctrine of joint tortfeasance—might not also be applied more generally

---

[149] This was noted by Slade LJ in *C. Evans Ltd v Spritebrand Ltd* [1985] 1 WLR 317, p. 329 when he asserted: 'I would accept that if the plaintiff has to prove a particular state of mind or knowledge on the part of the defendant as a necessary element of the particular tort alleged, the state of mind or knowledge of the director who authorized or directed it must be relevant if it is sought to impose personal liability on the director merely on account of such authorization or procurement; the personal liability of the director in such cases cannot be more extensive than that of the individual who personally did the tortious act.'

[150] The attempt in *Credit Lyonnais v ECGD* [1999] 2 WLR 540, HL to create a tort of assisting another's tort was unlikely to succeed, therefore.

[151] As for the tort of unlawful conspiracy, it would only be necessary if the courts were willing to accept tortious liability for a conspiracy to break a contract. As the tort of inducing breach bases liability on the procured breach of contract, it would appear logical that the tort of conspiracy could create tort liability for a conspiracy to breach another's contract, though Lord Devlin in *Rookes v Barnard* [1964] AC 1129, pp. 1210–11 refused to state whether there would be liability for such a conspiracy; criticized by Wedderburn, K. W., 'Intimidation and the Right to Strike' 24 MLR (1965) 257, p. 267. Nourse LJ appears to accept that unlawful conspiracy includes a conspiracy to break a contract in *Kuwait Oil Tanker Co SAK v Al Bader (no. 3)* [2000] 2 All ER (Comm) 291.

in the civil law. Certainly the terminology of 'secondary liability' and 'secondary parties' is creeping into the civil law.[152] It would appear that the doctrine of joint tortfeasance could provide a framework for a consideration of the normal limits of secondary liability in the civil law—demanding clear participation links based on causation or complicity between the primary and secondary parties. Thus secondary liability[153] would seem to follow where there has been the procuring or authorizing of a tort, or of a breach of trust[154] or breach of equitable obligation—or a conspiracy to do any of these things (with conspiracy being clearly distinguished from facilitation). However, it should be stressed that such secondary liability would mirror the primary liability. Procuring a breach of trust would not be a tort: liability would remain in equity. Thus in *Metall und Rohstoff AG v Donaldson Lufkin & Jenrette Inc* Slade LJ[155] stressed that he could see no sufficient justification for a new tort of procuring a breach of trust as liability for such behaviour already existed in equity, while in *Royal Brunei* Lord Nicholls noted that the accessory's liability was 'a liability in equity to make good resulting loss'.[156] Similarly with liability for those who induce a breach of fiduciary or equitable obligation.[157]

However, this would be a general framework only. Despite the views of Sales[158] and Cooper[159] there does not exist a latent standardized approach to 'secondary' liability in the civil law,[160] applying the same test for secondary liability to tort, contract breach[161] and breach of fiduciary/equitable obligation. So though there may be 'assistance' liability in actions for breach of trust/fiduciary duty,[162] such rules are special to

---

[152] So Lord Woolf in *Credit Lyonnais v ECGD* [1999] 2 WLR 540 commented on *Lumley v Gye* liability that 'the responsibility for the actionable wrong is a form of secondary liability'.

[153] Mirroring the primary liability, whether that be in tort or equity.

[154] In *Midgley v Midgley* [1893] 3 Ch 282 the solicitor was held liable as the instigator of the breach of trust in issue.

[155] [1990] 1 QB 391, p. 481.

[156] [1995] 2 AC 378, p. 392.

[157] That there is liability is clear from *Prudential Assurance Co Ltd v Lorenz* (1971) 11 KIR 78, Plowman J. There, insurance agents withheld payment of their premiums to their employer, as part of an industrial dispute. This was held to be a breach of their fiduciary duty to account and the inducers were liable for procuring this breach of trust. Liability followed the pattern of joint tortfeasors but logically such procurers could not be liable in *tort*. Rather, they should be made jointly liable in equity. However, it has to be said that Plowman J in that case seemed to assume that the action was tortious. This case was not referred to by the Court of Appeal in *Metall und Rohstoff v Donaldson, Lufkin & Jenrette Inc* [1990] 1 QB 391.

[158] Sales, P., 'The Tort of Conspiracy and Civil Secondary Liability' [1990] 49 CLJ 491.

[159] Cooper, above, n. 78.

[160] Parallel to secondary criminal liability.

[161] So for Cooper, above, n. 78, it is wrong that we should use the tort label for inducing breach of contract, rather it should be categorized as a mode of secondary participation in the breach of contract.

[162] As now clarified by the Privy Council decision in *Royal Brunei Airlines v Tan* [1995] 3 WLR 64. There the controlling director of a company dishonestly assisted in a breach of trust

equity and do not extend to common law actions. The *Credit Lyonnais v ECGD*[163] litigation supports the view that any framework of secondary civil liability would not include facilitation liability.

5. Malicious falsehood: beyond unlawful interference with trade

The leading cases on malicious falsehood often fall within the pattern of unlawful interference with trade, involving lies intended to harm the claimant.[164] Indeed, difficult cases where malicious falsehood was deemed to be applicable such as *Customglass Boats v Salthouse*[165] and *Serville v Constance*[166] are probably better explained as examples of unlawful interference with trade liability.[167] These cases do not involve lies 'about' the claimant, but rather lies about the defendant, which clearly will affect the claimant's economic interests. So in *Serville*, potential liability arose where the defendant falsely claimed to be the welterweight champion boxer of Trinidad—a title belonging to the plaintiff. And in *Customglass* the defendant[168] falsely claimed to be the designer of a boat, when in fact the designer was the plaintiff. In such cases the issue is lies intended to harm the claimant, rather than lies specifically 'about' the claimant's trade . The frame of 'nexus' plus unlawful act is the approach of the courts here: so in *Serville*, the judge found there to be slander of title but no intention to injure,[169] while in *Customglass*, the court stressed the defendant's intention to injure.[170]

However, the tort of malicious falsehood can provide protection beyond the deliberate use of lies to harm the claimant. This results from the origins of the tort—providing as it did protection against denigrations

by the company and was held liable to the beneficiary for the resulting loss. It was held that dishonest assisters could be liable, though themselves not bound by the fiduciary duty and not in receipt of the trust property. Harpum, C., 'Accessory Liability for Procuring or Assisting a Breach of Trust' 111 LQR (1995) 545, p. 548 contends that the true nature of this assistance liability in trust is 'as the equitable analogue of the economic torts'. It is clear that this writer disagrees with this view. Why dishonest assisters might be liable in equity is discussed in Carty, above, n. 89, pp. 511–13. The CA in *Thomas v Pearce* [2000] FSR 718 applied the *Brunei* test to hold a third party who honestly (though negligently) used information disclosed to them in breach of confidence not liable.

[163] [1998] 1 Lloyd's Rep 19, CA; [1999] 2 WLR 540, HL.
[164] *Western Counties Manure Co v Laws Chemical Manure Co* (1874) LR 9 Ex 218; *Ratcliffe v Evans* [1892] 2 QB 524; *Joyce v Motor Services Ltd* [1948] Ch 252.
[165] [1976] RPC 589.   [166] (1954) 71 RPC 146.
[167] Indeed, falsely claiming the claimant's title or commendations may well amount to inverse passing off, where of course fault does not have to be shown (*Serville*, however, did not involve passing off because the plaintiff had no goodwill within the jurisdiction).
[168] In fact the issue of malicious falsehood arose in a counterclaim by the second defendants—so it was the plaintiff who was liable to the defendants on this matter.
[169] Similarly, in *Lonrho v Fayed* [1990] 2QB 479, the Court of Appeal accepted that lies told about the defendant must be directed at the claimant in some way, to give rise to liability (under the tort of unlawful interference with trade).   [170] [1976] RPC 589, p. 603.

concerning the plaintiff's title to land. The true basis of liability for malicious falsehood is that the defendant utters falsehoods about the claimant at his peril. This 'peril factor' overrides the approach of the general economic tort[171] in two ways.[172] First, lies which are inherently likely to harm the claimant ('calculated to harm') are spoken at the defendant's peril. If they harm the economic interests of the claimant, they will render the defendant liable without proof of intention to harm him (a form of imputed intention).[173] Second, spiteful or *mala fides* intentional economic harm resulting from the defendant's falsehoods ('calculated to harm') will render him liable, though no deceit be involved. The intentional harm with such motivation requires no lie to render the defendant liable.[174] He speaks 'spitefully' at his peril in such circumstances.

Having developed through a patchwork of related actions, the tort of malicious falsehood needs to be clarified for the twenty-first century. This need is particularly acute now that it is acknowledged to be capable of growth by both the Court of Appeal and the House of Lords.[175] What the above analysis reveals is that though leading case law on malicious falsehood may fall within the pattern of the general tort of unlawful interference, the tort of malicious falsehood has its own pattern, based on 'perilous falsehoods'. However, the concept of 'perilous falsehoods' is best left within the area of utterances 'about' the claimant.[176] In the wider context of lies that harm the economic interests of the claimant, the general tort of unlawful interference alone should apply—requiring the proof of intended harm and fraudulent misrepresentation.[177]

---

[171] Sales and Stilitz, above, n. 73, acknowledge the similar feel of this tort to unlawful interference with trade (p. 432). However, they conclude that a number of its features 'reveal a strong influence from the law of defamation' as a result of which it has developed 'somewhat different principles of liability'.

[172] Note in the Restatement of Torts, s.624, the tort was defined as injurious false statements made without privilege. However, in the Restatement (Second) of Torts s.623A lies are required and an intention to cause pecuniary harm (though there is a *caveat* that *mala fides* could constitute an alternative ground).

[173] Glidewell LJ in *Kaye v Robertson* [1991] FSR 62. Hence this is wider in scope than liability under the tort of unlawful interference with trade.

[174] The lack of 'unlawful means' again means that the tort of malicious falsehood is wider in scope than liability under the tort of unlawful interference with trade.

[175] In *Khodaparast v Shad* [2000] 1 All ER 545, CA and *Gregory v Portsmouth CC* [2000] 1 All ER 560, HL.

[176] Indeed, Glidewell LJ in *Kaye v Robertson* [1991] FSR 62 asserted that included within the essentials of the tort of malicious falsehood was the fact that the words must be 'about the plaintiff'.

[177] Hence in *Bristol Conservatories Ltd v Conservatories Custom Built Ltd* [1989] RPC 455, CA, an allegation of malicious falsehood on similar facts to *Customglass Boats v Salthouse* [1976] RPC 589 (an allegation by the defendant that they had designed and built conservatories, in fact designed and built by the plaintiffs) was rejected by the trial judge (Judge Fallon) on the basis that there was no link in the misrepresentation between the product shown and the plaintiffs' product. Ralph Gibson LJ cited with approval the view of the trial judge that 'there was no false statement made about the plaintiffs' goods at all' (p. 459).

What is still clear, however, is that the tort of malicious falsehood does not protect the claimant's reputation as such. So, 'the remedy provided by the law for words which injure a person's reputation is defamation'.[178]

6. The future of the tort of passing off

The need to show fraud and intentional harm having been expressly abandoned,[179] the tort of passing off had immense potential. However, the courts, in line with the caution elsewhere in the economic torts, developed two mechanisms for protecting the competitive process from undue judicial control. So *Spalding v Gamage* stressed the need for misrepresentation and justified the court's intervention on the basis of protecting the plaintiff's property right in the goodwill of his business.[180] These mechanisms—embodied in the classic trinity—limit the tort and deny the imposition of liability for 'unfair trading'.[181] Rather efficient consumer choices are protected,[182] with the focus of the tort on the success of the claimant ('goodwill') rather than the 'free ride' achieved by the defendant. The rationale of the tort is not the protection of trade values or advertising tools *per se*.[183] Any movement away from protecting deserving claimants where consumer misinformation is in issue would '[place] in the hands of traders an instrument that they are more likely to use to bar new entry into their industries than to advance the cause of accurate information for consumers'.[184] By placing the tort within the same framework and policy as the other economic torts, that underlying caution of the courts is justified. To allow it to develop into a misappropriation action would be out of step with the caution of the economic torts generally. Such a view rejects the validity of the concept of 'dilution' in the tort as simply an obscure way of claiming unfair competition or misappropriation.[185]

---

[178] Sir Donald Nicholls V-C, *Joyce v Sengupta* [1993] 1 WLR 337, p. 341. And see Otton LJ in *Khodaparast v Shad* [2000] 1 All ER 545, pp. 557–8.

[179] This was clearly accepted by *Spalding v Gamage* (1915) 32 RPC 273.

[180] Lord Parker rejected the notion that the property right protected by the tort was a property right in the mark or name improperly used by the defendant.

[181] For more detailed discussion see Carty, H., 'Dilution and Passing Off' 112 LQR (1996) 632, esp. pp. 650–5.

[182] Naresh, S., 'Passing off, Goodwill and False Advertising' [1986] CLJ 97, p. 120: the tort harnesses: 'the self-protective energy of competitors to the protection of consumers.'

[183] It is a small step from an objection based on harm to commercial magnetism to an objection based on preventing 'free-riders' from reaping commercial success based on the seeds sown by the claimant.

[184] Naresh, above, n. 182, p. 125.

[185] That said, the tort will be under pressure to mirror the extension of statutory trade mark law protection to cover dilution, Trade Marks Act 1994, s.10(3). Although s.2(2) states that it does not affect the law relating to passing off, it is typical in a trade mark case to plead both statutory and common law protection: the expansion of statutory protection may well, therefore, affect the development of the tort.

CONCLUSION

The thesis of this book is that a framework for the economic torts can be constructed. It should be based on the policy that economic behaviour should only be controlled by the common law on a narrow basis. The greater the flexibility of the economic torts, the greater the incentive to litigate rather than compete, an outcome not in the public interest.[186] Such a policy is also consistent with the wider principle of freedom of speech[187] which may be relevant where these torts take place within peaceful protest or commercial debate. As Weir comments: 'economic torts have something to do with liberty.' Though there has been statutory intervention to allow peaceful protest where industrial action is involved,[188] these torts may arise in other protest situations—such as the consumer picket[189] or within rigorous debate over the claimant's commercial or professional activities.[190] The above framework provides a clear basis for liability while allowing both freedom to compete effectively and freedom of expression.

[186] The Australian Trade Practices Act 1974 (with analogous state Fair Trading legislation) prohibits commercial conduct that is misleading or deceptive (or likely so to be) and specifically prohibits false representations in connection with the supply or promotion of goods (s.52). As Fleming, above, n. 25, notes this protection goes much wider than that provided by the common law: the statements do not need to be false statements of fact, fault is not necessary: its potential for consumer protection is therefore remarkable (p. 651), especially as the protection extends to 'any person who suffers loss or damage by [prohibited] conduct'. Some argue that competitors will have the incentive (and resources) to police misleading and deceptive promotional material and thereby act on behalf of the consumer. However, Ramsey, I., *Consumer Protection* (London: Weidenfeld & Nicolson, 1989) notes the limitations to this form of enforcement: (p. 167) traders will only act where there is a significant threat to their market share and indeed could be tempted to use such legislation to 'dampen competition . . . or entrench a dominant market position at the expense of aggressive new entrants as a method of trade protection, at the expense of consumers'. Jacob J in *Schulke v Alkapharm* [1999] FSR 1 commented on the Trade Practices Act 1974 'such an extension of the law leads to much litigation. Members of the Australian Bar have much to say by way of thanks to the short s.52.'
[187] Given that freedom—as defined in Article 10 ECHR—is subject to 'the protection of the reputation or rights of others'.
[188] See Ch. 1.
[189] Weir, *Economic Torts*, above, n. 31 rightly condemns the first instance judgment in *Middlebrook Mushrooms v TGWU* [1993] IRLR 232 in which an interlocutory injunction was issued to restrain a peaceful protest outside a supermarket supplied by the protesters' employer, with whom they were in dispute, on the basis there might be contracts that might, in consequence, be breached.
[190] *Drummond-Jackson v BMA* [1970] 1 All ER 1094, CA.

Index